The Middle East
and
the United States

Perceptions and
Policies

The Shiloah Center for Middle Eastern and African Studies
Tel Aviv University

The Shiloah Center is, with the Department of Middle Eastern and African History, a part of the School of History at Tel Aviv University. Its main purpose is to contribute, by research and documentation, to the dissemination of knowledge and understanding of the modern history and current affairs of the Middle East and Africa. Emphasis is laid on fields where Israeli scholarship is in a position to make a special contribution and on subjects relevant to the needs of society and the teaching requirements of the University.

Collected Papers Series

The books published in this series consist of collections of selected papers presented mostly in seminars and conferences of the Shiloah Center. The views expressed in these papers are entirely those of the authors.

M. Confino and S. Shamir (eds.) / *The U.S.S.R. and the Middle East*
I. Rabinovich and H. Shaked (eds.) / *From June to October; The Middle East between 1967 and 1973*
S. Shamir (ed.) / *The Decline of Nasserism, 1965-1970: The Waning of a Messianic Movement* (Hebrew)

Editorial Board

This volume is based on the proceedings of an international Colloquium held jointly in March 1978 by the Shiloah Center and the Center for Strategic Studies at Tel Aviv University.

The Middle East and the United States

Perceptions and Policies

Edited by

Haim Shaked
Itamar Rabinovich

Transaction Books
New Brunswick (U.S.A.) and London (U.K.)

Library of Congress Cataloging in Publication Data
Main entry under title:

The Middle East and the United States.

(Collected papers series – The Shiloah Center for Middle Eastern and African Studies)
"Based on the proceedings of an international colloquium held jointly in March 1978 by the Shiloah Center and the Center for Strategic Studies at Tel Aviv University."
Includes index.
1. Near East—Foreign relations—United States—Congresses.
2. United States—Foreign relations—Near East—Congresses.
3. Jewish-Arab relations—1973-　　—Congresses.
I. Shaked, Haim.　II. Rabinovich, Itamar, 1942-　　III. Series:

Mekhon Shiloah le-heker ha-Mizrah ha-tikhon ve-Afrikan. Collected papers series – The Shiloah Center for Middle Eastern and African Studies.
DS63.2.U5M45　　327.73056　　80-14290
ISBN 0-87855-329-0
ISBN 0-87855-752-0 (pbk.)

Contents

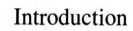

Introduction

Introduction

Like its two predecessors in this series, the present volume originated in an international colloquium organized by the Shiloah Center and, in this case, cosponsored by the University's newly-established Center for Strategic Studies.

The choice in the summer of 1977 of this topic for the 1978 Shiloah Center Annual Seminar and the colloquium was based on two assumptions: firstly, that despite the growing body of published work on American relations with the Middle East, more probing was still called for, particularly insofar as Middle Eastern perceptions of and policies towards the U.S. were concerned; and secondly, that a convergence of developments—the coming of a new American administration, the change of government in Israel, the fresh efforts to settle the Arab-Israeli conflict—was likely to launch a particularly interesting chapter in the story of Middle Eastern-American interaction.

Indeed, by March 1978 when the colloquium met, its topic had become a subject of major importance with which domestic, regional, and international political systems were preoccupied. The deliberations of the colloquium were therefore marked by some of the advantages and subject to some of the difficulties that are inherent in a public discussion of topical issues by an academic gathering. Such a discussion could clearly benefit from the sense of closeness to—even, to some extent, participation in—an unfolding process; from the intense public interest; and from the participants' feeling that they could contribute to a better understanding of the course of events. Concomitantly, though, the same set of considerations tended to magnify the difficulties involved in any study of contemporary politics and policies: the particular acuteness of the problems of objectivity and detachment; the paucity of reliable source material; and the likelihood that oral and written analyses might become outdated due to the accelerated pace of events.

It was in order to minimize the impact of such factors that the bulk of the papers, though not the discussion, focused on processes and basic interests and outlooks, perceptions and images, underlying issues and structural elements. Much has happened in the Middle East and to the relations between various countries in the region and the United States since March 1978: the Camp David accords were reached; the Shah's regime was toppled by a revolution in Iran; Egypt and Israel concluded a peace treaty which was signed on the White House lawn; and the American posture in the area and its immediate vicinity (such as the Horn of Africa) changed more than once. Nonetheless, most papers printed in this volume required only slight revision. Only one paper, dealing with the American-Egyptian-Saudi arms deal of 1978 and focusing on the very topical issues of that day, has been outdated by events and is therefore not included in the published proceedings.

Since each of the papers presented at the colloquium dealt with more than one important issue, none can or should be neatly fitted into one of the subdivisions listed in the contents of this volume. By the same token, the issues which came up during the lively discussions which many of the papers generated crossed the formal session limits set out in the colloquium program. The full text of the papers forms the bulk of this book. The introduction aims to provide a brief summary of the major points raised during the discussion (the full text of the proceedings of the colloquium is on file at the Shiloah Center archives). Six broad issues could be discerned in the deliberations: the evolution of the American position in the Middle East; the images and perceptions that Middle Easterners and Americans have had of each other; American interests in the region; the international context within which American policy has been conducted; the formulation of American policy; and the bilateral relationship between a number of Middle Eastern countries and the U.S.

The historical evolution of American policy in the Middle East after 1945 was the topic to which Elie Kedourie and Wilfrid Knapp addressed themselves specifically, but other aspects of the same subject came up in the discussion of other papers, most notably those of Bernard Reich and Shimon Shamir. It was during this discussion that Professor Kedourie was prompted to compare the current Soviet-American rivalry in the Middle East to Britain's rivalry with France and Germany in the same region in earlier times. The threats presented to Britain's position in the Middle East by France, Russia and Germany, he explained, were all eliminated due to military defeats they sustained elsewhere. In comparison to Britain the U.S., he argued, had an additional disadvantage to contend with, namely:

> "that the Soviets, like their Czarist predecessors, are there. They are very near and their propinquity has become a more important issue to take into account simply because the propinquity of the Russians to the Ottoman Empire and Persia was balanced by the presence of British power in India and in the Eastern Mediterranean. This has now disappeared and there is a lack of parallelism, which from an American point of view ought to be very disquieting."

Another issue which arose in the same discussion concerned the personnel which carried out and, to a large extent, formulated American policy in the Middle East after the United States assumed a position of leadership in that area. In his comments, Wilfrid Knapp emphasized the professional orientation of the foreign service officers who conducted American policy in the Middle East. He thought that they were motivated by their conception of American interests rather than by ideological imperatives. It should also be remembered, he said,

> "that some of the important operatives in the early years were C.I.A. men. Kermit Roosevelt and Miles Copeland in particular, and Kermit Roosevelt had a commitment to the Arabs. It wasn't of a particularly ideological kind and insofar as the C.I.A. had an attitude towards the Nasserist officers, I think it was much more [a hope] that these were people who in the long run would be on their side, rather than an ideological view of what the future would be."

The same point was analysed by Elie Kedourie in rather different terms. He thought that the State Department's view of Egypt's Free Officers and other forces and events in the Middle East had been influenced primarily by an ideological outlook. In the Middle East as elsewhere, he contended, a Presbyterian missionary zeal was

transformed into a belief in the "religion of progress." But the
thrust of his comments focused on another process: the way in
which a group of foreign service officers who had dealt with a
remote and unimportant area in the interwar period came to possess
a great measure of influence in and over that area, the importance of
which had grown in American eyes. It was as a part of that process
that their predilections and views acquired the force of orthodoxy:

> "And that orthodoxy one finds, by looking at papers . . .
> certainly in the Foreign Office, certainly in the State
> Department. It assumes the character of an apostolic suc-
> cession and that is perhaps to be explained simply by the
> fact that there is a hierarchical organization where the
> junior looks up to the senior and imbibes his outlook."

Ideology was also an element in the discussion of the actual
record of American policy in the Middle East during the first decade
of the post-war period. Thus John Waterbury wondered whether a
conflict between the United States and Egypt was inevitable.
"Which came first," he asked, "Nasser's Arabism or the U.S. and
Britain's efforts to put together the Baghdad Pact?" His own feeling
was that Nasser had picked up Arabism as a matter of convenience,
in order to combat the Baghdad Pact. Shimon Shamir's view was
different: "If Nasser and his officers were dedicated, as I believe
they were, to the notion of building up a regional power, then Arabism was really the only choice." Daniel Dishon, too, thought that
Nasser's commitment to Arabism preceded the Baghdad Pact. In his
opinion, it was a different aspect of American policy which irritated
Nasser:

> "The main burden of Nasser's attack against the Baghdad
> Pact was that it was going to make Baghdad the center of
> the Arab world. It was not quite the same as an attack
> against Western influence as such, although, this, of
> course, went along with it."

While several papers dealt with American perceptions of Middle
Eastern countries and issues, two papers, by Bernard Lewis and
Haim Shaked, dealt specifically with the manner in which Middle
Easterners—Turks, Iranians, Egyptians—have viewed and depicted
the United States and its role in the area. The discussion which followed these presentations centered on the impact that domestic politics had, or failed to have, on the international orientation of such

countries as Egypt and Turkey. President Sādāt's American orientation was, as Professor Waterbury demonstrated, intimately linked to his domestic policy of economic *infitāh*. But Turkey's case was different, since, as Professor Lewis put it:

"The thing that is striking in the whole history of the Turkish Republic is the very limited extent to which party politics or parliamentary maneuvering have affected foreign policy."

In response to a question on the impact that radical and Leftist groups may have had on Turkey's attitude towards the United States, he added:

"I would rather put it the other way round and say that the emergence of these groups and the considerable measure of tolerance which has been accorded to them is part of the larger change resulting from Turkish reassessment of the situation. . . . Until roughly 1960 there was a very strong . . . or almost complete Turkish commitment to the Western alliance. From 1960 onwards . . . this begins to change. One can see in a number of ways a . . . growing feeling that the Western alliance is not very reliable, that it is not safe to enter into commitments or to run risks in the assumption that Western help will be forthcoming when required and as promised, and therefore, that some mending of fences is necessary: and this meant in the first place a mending of fences in the north. The first sign was the cessation or, let's say, toning down of anti-Russian cartoons in the daily press."

Discussions and debates on the foreign policies of the United States and other countries often tend to focus on the notion of "objective national interests." The discussion which followed the presentations by Bernard Reich, Richard Rosecrance, Uzi Arad and Gad Gilbar brought out some of the theoretical and practical difficulties inherent in this concept when applied to U.S. policy in the Middle East. How does one discern and establish the nature of Washington's "objective" interests in the Middle East beyond a variety of personal, sectional and bureaucratic interests? Is it at all possible to set up a hierarchy of interests, structured according to their relative importance, so that a policy choice can be made when two or more interests are, or seem to be, in conflict? David Vital referred to "the different ways in which the U.S. looks at the Middle East and the different interests that it has identified in the Middle East," suggesting that:

"There are various ways of dealing with this. One is to try and live with them and then there is some sort of an ambiguity which we are pretty familiar with. Another is to try to combine them together in a package along the line of Professor Spiegel's outline. And a third is to look for some overarching, overriding interest, such that can resolve the contradiction by some process of elimination."

"Professor Spiegel's outline" alluded to by Professor Vital suggested that the Carter administration chose to emphasize the overriding importance of oil and consequently of Saudi Arabia in the configuration of American interests in the Middle East. This interpretation and the factual basis on which it rested was at the center of Uzi Arad's and Gad Gilbar's papers and of the discussion they generated. Professor Kanovsky, even more than Uzi Arad, tended in his comments to minimize the actual power of Arab oil producers and of Saudi Arabia in particular. The financial resources which became available to the oil-producing states by 1977, he argued, failed to live up to the predictions made in 1973 and 1974. Saudi Arabia's own development needs seriously curtailed its ability to use its economic power elsewhere. On the other hand, Western economies adapted themselves to new conditions and the option of switching to alternative energy sources had became available. This was not how Wilfrid Knapp and Gad Gilbar viewed the same issues. Saudi Arabia, Mr. Knapp argued, did indeed play a cardinal role in American eyes, but this began with Henry Kissinger and was not a novel element introduced by the Carter administration. Energy and Saudi Arabia, he continued, were indeed of major importance. To be sure, Saudi Arabia's actual capability of imposing an oil embargo was not as important as the anticipated impact of a Saudi threat to do so. In a similar vein Dr. Gilbar suggested that the Saudis could also introduce a "hidden embargo" by failing to increase production from 8.5 to 20 million barrels a day. Taking issue with Professor Kanovsky on another matter as well, he argued that consumer dependence on the oil producers was growing and that Saudi Arabia and Kuwait possessed funds that were sufficient

for both development needs at home and their investment requirements abroad. The past, too, was not neglected as a guide for the
future. Several participants wanted to know how genuine and effective the 1973 oil embargo had been. Uzi Arad conceded that in the
final analysis, in the minds of Arab oil producers, economic considerations had prevailed over the political ones, but he maintained that
the embargo had been real and effective. Finally, it was Bernard
Reich who suggested that whatever the actual importance of the
"oil weapon" it was certainly the "petro-dollar" weapon which
became the essential issue—"increasingly that is the one issue
which American interests view as being more crucial and affecting
the situation."

The international environment within which American policy in
the Middle East was being conducted was examined by Richard
Rosecrance, Yaacov Ro'i and Udo Steinbach. Dr. Ro'i's paper dealt
with the image of American Middle East policy in the then recent
Soviet writings and statements. Following this presentation, Oded
Eran made a comment on the conceptual problems apparently besetting Soviet foreign policy analysts trying to develop a comprehensive explanation of Washington's conduct in the Middle East. The
accent of the ensuing discussion shifted to the American assessment
of Soviet policy aims and capabilities as well as the role assigned
by the U.S. to the Soviet Union in a future settlement of the Middle
East conflict. It was by and large agreed that the Carter administration was less preoccupied than its predecessor with the threat posed
to its interests in the Middle East by the Soviets and that it was
determined to provide the Soviet Union with some role in the
framework of a comprehensive Middle Eastern settlement. The
nature of that role was defined in vivid terms by Steven Spiegel as
"side-kick to Lone Ranger":

> "That is the role that those in the Brookings group and, I
> think, those in the administration who saw the Russians
> as playing a major role did see for the Russians. The
> Russians were going to come along with the help-out.
> Remember, Brzezinski was the man who actually spoke
> about a Soviet-American force at one point and Soviet-
> American guarantees are in the Soviet-American com-
> muniqué [of October 1, 1977]."

As depicted by Udo Steinbach, Washington's relationship in the

Middle East with west European allies was friendlier but hardly less complicated. It was with a view to reducing these complications that Dr. Joffe suggested that it might be better for the U.S. and the Common Market countries to try not to coordinate or even consult on their policies in the Middle East. His reasoning was clearly influenced by the events of October 1973:

"Consultation is a burden that both sides would gladly not have assumed. The reason resides in the fundamental asymmetry in power, responsibility and interests between Europe and the U.S. Europe is much more vulnerable to Arab pressure. Hence it is much more interested in keeping the Arabs happy. And hence . . . it cannot assume the responsibility required as a factor of military stability . . . or as an even-handed broker in the process of resolving the political conflict."

Consequently, he argued that "studied ambiguity" and lack of consultation rather than attempted coordination were called for. The basic assumptions underlying this argumentation were not disputed by Dr. Steinbach, who advocated a loose and informal consultation. While agreeing that Europe possessed limited leverage with regard to the Arab-Israeli conflict, it was in his opinion well placed to play an important role in other Middle Eastern issues such as Greek-Turkish relations and the Cyprus problem. Here the European Economic Community (E.E.C.) could use the affiliation with the Common Market that Greece and Turkey desired in order to impose restraint. Or, on a bilateral level, west European countries could supply the Turkish army during the time of the American embargo.

How were the various interests, images, perceptions and constraints affecting the American outlook on the Middle East transformed through the prism of a given administration into a particular policy line? An explanation of this process as exemplified by the Carter administration was offered by Steven Spiegel's paper. His approach and thesis elicited an animated discussion. While several participants endorsed his conclusions, others voiced a measure of criticism. Thus Wilfrid Knapp thought that the analysis was focused too narrowly on Washington and that the transition from the Ford-Kissinger policy to that of the Carter administration was presented in too stark a fashion. He also felt that too much emphasis was placed on Carter's moral fervor—after all, oil and Saudi Arabia's importance had little to do with moral issues. Yair Evron, in turn, did not think that a shift of emphasis from an East-West dichotomy to a North-South one and the position occupied within such a spectrum were necessarily related to a particular approach to the Arab-Israeli conflict. Yoram Dinstein felt that, like other intellectual endeavors, Professor Spiegel's was an attempt to impose a grand design on a state of chaos. David Vital agreed with most of Spiegel's analysis but thought that when viewed from a thirty years' perspective, the Carter administration's policy "was not anomalous but [on the contrary] perhaps characteristic." This, to his mind, was true of its general style as well as its attitude towards Israel and the Arab-Israeli conflict.

In his response Professor Spiegel pinpointed and underlined some of the themes which had appeared in his paper. He reasserted that the Carter administration was different from its predecessors

"in the unanimity of its decision-making approach, especially for a Democratic administration and secondly, in the unanimity of its views and, thirdly, on the question of oil. It is the first administration to see oil as more important than the Russians."

This shift in emphasis, he then argued, explained the essential differences—despite the apparent similarities—between Kissinger's Middle Eastern policy and that of his successors: with oil becoming a more important issue than the Soviet Union, Saudi Arabia assumed an importance far greater than that of Egypt.

Washington's relationship with Cairo and Riyād was also discussed as part of a broader examination of American relations with the Arab world in general and her bilateral relations with several Middle Eastern countries. The papers presented by Itamar Rabinovich, Shimon Shamir, John Waterbury, Steven Rosen, Bernard Lewis, Gideon Gera, Yoram Dinstein and Yair Evron analysed Washington's relations with, respectively, the Arab world in general, Egypt, Saudi Arabia, Turkey and Iran, Libya and Israel. It was probably due to the tense circumstances which obtained in late March 1978 that various aspects of the American-Israeli relationship generated the most animated, often agitated discussion and debate. Several questions were raised concerning the nature and direction of American-Israeli relations, particularly as they developed under the Carter administration. Was the American-Israeli relationship losing its special character, and what, in fact did a term such as "special" mean in the context of international relations? Was American policy toward Israel based on sentiment, on a perception of interests or on a combination of both? Did the Carter administration feel that American interests, as it defined them, required a shift in favor of the Arab states? If so, what could Israel do about it by way of viable policy options?

One attempt at providing a comprehensive answer was made by Professor Moshe Arens, Chairman of the Israeli Knesset's Foreign and Security Affairs Committee. In his opinion there was a fundamental compatibility of interests between the U.S. and Israel, but a difference of opinion with regard to tactics. This difference resulted from divergent approaches to the question of risks that Israel ought to take in order to achieve a settlement of the Arab-Israeli conflict. The differences, he explained, were aggravated by the fact that Washington's ability to obtain Israeli concessions had become a major policy instrument in its dealings with the Arab states. He saw the operative question in the following terms:

> "Here are two countries with the same objectives, different views regarding the risks that should be taken in pursuing some of these objectives and with tactics that are not completely consistent with one another. How is this question going to be solved?"

One obvious way of seeking to reduce the risks undertaken by Israel in the process of reaching a settlement of the Arab-Israeli conflict seemed to be for the U.S. to guarantee Israel's security. This notion and the possible modalities for its implementation had been the subject of public and academic debate in previous years. During the colloquium three interrelated issues were discussed in this context: American guarantees to Israel, an American-Israel treaty and the stationing of American troops in Israel or the administered territories.

Two radically different perspectives on these issues were presented by two Israeli participants: Yair Evron, who saw important advantages to Israel in a formalized American commitment and Yoram Dinstein, in whose eyes the disadvantages of such an arrangement clearly outweighed its potential benefits. Evron's view was endorsed by a number of discussants, particularly Professor Rosecrance and Colonel Trevor N. Dupuy. Professor Rosecrance argued that the diminished military capabilities of the U.S. which developed in the wake of the October 1973 crisis did not, in fact, reduce the effect of an American commitment or guarantee:

"It's the effect of the commitment of American forces in however small a number. There is only one function served by American forces in Berlin, and that would be served by a thousand men as well as five thousand. And that is: to die. It means that when an attack occurs it is American forces that are killed before anybody else, even before, in some cases, German forces. That involves the U.S. in a way that is just incapable of disentanglement."

But is it? Several Israeli participants did not think so. Thus Professor Arens expressed skepticism with regard to the value of guarantees in general and American guarantees to Israel in particular. General (res.) Aharon Yariv felt that the American-Egyptian-Saudi arms deal had repercussions on this issue:

"So far as the Israeli public is concerned I think the linkage [between the supply of arms to Arab countries and to Israel] ... has dealt a certain blow to the credibility of such understanding on the part of the U.S. vis-à-vis Israel."

By early 1979 the term "linkage" had become pregnant with meaning in an entirely different context of Middle Eastern politics, but the underlying issues shaping Washington's relations with both Israel and the Arab countries underwent little change. To a large extent, this was illustrative of the general pattern of Middle Eastern-American mutual perceptions and policies. Over a generation or more of growing American involvement in the Middle East much had changed, particularly in so far as details and tactics were concerned. Yet, there was also a significant continuity of attitude, strategy and undercurrents. While some of the first will again have changed by the time this volume is published, much of the latter will proibably still remain with us for a long time.

★ ★ ★

The preparation of an International Colloquium and the publication of the papers read by its participants entails the work of numerous individuals who belong to a number of institutions. It is a pleasure to extend our thanks to all of these and particularly to Yardena Bar-

Uryan, Lydia Gareh, Naomi Handelman, Edna Liftman and Amira Margalit. Special thanks are also due to the Cultural Attaché of the U.S. Embassy and to the Representative of the British Council in Israel as well as to the Barclay Jewish Trust for their generous support and encouragement.

Tel Aviv, March 1979   I.R. and H.S.

Background
and
Evolution

The Transition from a British to an American Era in the Middle East

Elie Kedourie

British interest in the Middle East, understood in a political rather than an economic sense, dates roughly speaking from the French Revolutionary and Napoleonic wars. If we take either the Suez fiasco in 1956, or the abandonment of the Persian Gulf in 1971, as constituting the terminus of any substantial British connection with the area, British power (and sometimes predominant power) would then have lasted, give or take a few decades, something like a century and a half. The interest of the United States in the Middle East has, to date, been of much shorter duration. We can affirm, in fact, that it does not date, in any substantial sense, from much before the Second World War.

British interest in the Middle East, both in its beginnings and subsequently, stemmed from two distinct preoccupations. It was, in the first place, an outcome of European balance-of-power considerations. The French, the Russians and the Germans were successively seen by British statesmen to pose, by their overweening ambitions, a threat to this balance. The preservation of the balance required at times the adoption of policies which entailed intervention in the Eastern Mediterranean, and the formulation of a policy towards the Ottoman Empire and its neighbors.

In the second place, British interest in the Middle East derived from what may be called Imperial preoccupations. These preoccupations centered predominantly round India, and may in turn be divided into two categories: first, those which had to do with securing the route to India, or at any rate making sure that no Great Power was in a position to threaten it, and second, those connected with what might be called the regional interests of the Government of India. Taken as a regional power, the Government of India had

3

considerable weight. It controlled large, disciplined armed forces, and through a great part of the nineteenth century—before and after the abolition of the East India Company—it was engaged in territorial expansion and consolidation. Again, in the latter half of that century, fear of Islamic militancy in India, which might be encouraged from the outside, became yet another consideration in the foreign policy of the Government of India. Added to all this there was, as may be expected, a miscellany of issues of which a powerful regional state had to take notice. A good example was the suppression of piracy and of the arms trade in the Persian Gulf—activities which, unintentionally and indirectly, laid the foundations of British preponderance in this area.

As may be easily seen, the European and the Imperial considerations were not identical. They could in fact at times pull in different directions. At any time, on any Middle Eastern issue, up to the end of the Second World War there could be three different views emanating from three different centers within the British Government all of which had some influence on the formulation and execution of Middle Eastern policy. There were the Foreign and India offices in London, and the Government of India in Calcutta (and later New Delhi). To these three centers we have to add for the period between 1920 and 1948 the Colonial Office, in respect principally of its responsibility for Palestine.

The contrast between Great Britain and the United States in the Middle East is therefore very great. The United States is a Great Power—more, it is a superpower, but it is not an Imperial Power. It has no possession like India, it does not maintain an army of occupation as Great Britain maintained one in Egypt, it does not have a *place d'armes* fully under its control as Cyprus was after 1878. It has a Sixth Fleet dependent in many important respects on North Atlantic Treaty Organization (NATO) allies—allies who are now shaky, unreliable or disaffected. The concomitant of this contrast in the situation of the two powers is a contrast in outlook just as great, if not greater and more decisive. For the outlook which goes with an Imperial position, which is bound up with the continuous need to safeguard tangible and substantial territorial interests—an outlook made up of caution, scepticism and a sense of political realities which such responsibilities perforce inculcate—is infinitely more difficult to instill and maintain among United States political figures, superpower though the United States is.

And what we see at the beginning of the period of United States preponderance in the Middle East is not only the absence of an Imperial position and the preoccupations which go with it, but also the presence of an anti-imperialist preoccupation. As William Roger Louis has recently shown in *Imperialism at Bay*, Franklin D. Roosevelt and many other influential political figures, as well as high officials in the State Department and foreign service officers, believed that the British (and French) Imperial positions had, somehow or another, sooner or later, to be liquidated, and the people ruled by Imperial Powers helped to independence. So far as one can tell from the available evidence, neither Roosevelt nor other prominent U.S. political figures gave any thought to the consequences in international politics of weakening or crippling friendly Imperial Powers or, more specifically, to what bearing the policy they favored would have on the formidable problem of dealing with the Soviet Union (but this was probably not seen as a problem, let alone a formidable one).

Again, there seems to have been little consideration given to the character of the international society which would emerge when the existing empires were dismantled. For what would replace these empires would be a multitude of weak, unstable, frequently irredentist and litigious governments most of whom had never formed part of a society of states functioning according to political assumptions and attitudes worked out and articulated in Western Europe, governments, moreover, whose international behavior would, of necessity, be profoundly influenced by the absence, in their internal politics, of constitutional traditions and practices. The problem of dealing with such an eventuality was not seriously faced, that the problem would exist at all was not even envisaged.

These remarks apply to South East Asia, as they were later to apply to Africa, and they also as fully apply to the Middle East. But so far as this particular area is concerned, two points need to be added. In the first place, the notion that a stable and friendly Middle East would result from the encouragement of aspirations to political independence—a notion so congenial to U.S. policy-makers—received a great deal of support and reinforcement from the British policy of the period. As Philip J. Baram has shown in his recently published work, *The Department of State and the Middle East*

1919-1945, many U.S. foreign service officers looked up to the British in the Middle East and were predisposed to adopt their categories and assumptions about Middle Eastern politics. Now, since the mid-1930s the predominant British view on the Middle East had been the Foreign Office view.

This view was that British interests in the area could be preserved precisely by working with what was believed to be the emerging dominant force of nationalism. Hence reliance on a deal with the Wafd for the preservation of British interests in Egypt, hence the stance adopted towards the French in the Levant, and the encouragement of Pan-Arabism. This was a very recent line of policy, but it happened to be the dominant one in the 1935-1945 decade. It was this line of policy which was adopted in the State Department and by most foreign service officers—with the natural difference, of course, that in their minds the United States and not the United Kingdom would be the one to benefit from the new order.

The second point is somewhat different. If the encouragement of a new regional order was ideological in its character and somewhat hazardous in its consequences, another feature of United States policy in this period of transition was strictly practical and non-problematic. This was simply to ensure free and equal access for U.S. oil companies in the Middle East. This was only to uphold a long-standing policy of insisting on the open door in international economic enterprise. If the successful pursuit of that policy meant that the British would be overshadowed and supplanted, it was, in effect, indirectly to undermine Great Britain's Imperial position. And however legitimate and straightforward the desire to protect and advance the interests of U.S. oil companies (which were purely business enterprises), it was to have increasingly political sequels and consequences in the decades following 1945.

The ideological stance adopted by U.S. policy makers during World War II remained more or less the same in the period which followed. Two examples among many are especially striking. The first is the encouragement of the Egyptian revolutionary officers and of Nasser who emerged as their leader in the 1952-1955 period. This encouragement was justified by the view that these officers were a force for reform, that Egyptian society badly needed reform, that a new society had to be built up in Egypt, that if it was not there would be no stability in the country, and that only a government that was composed of young, modern, progressive, forward-looking men could effect the necessary transformation. The policy was grandiose, but deeply misconceived in itself, and in the benefits for the United States which it was anticipated would accrue from its application. But even confining oneself strictly to U.S. interests, the policy must be adjudged a failure since Nasser and the revolutionary officers in the end followed a policy of friendship with the Soviet Union, what the United States aimed to prevent. As for the reform of Egyptian society, it would be hazardous in the extreme to claim that the military regime has fulfilled the hopes which its advent widely aroused.

The second example relates to the Suez affair of 1956. The policy which the United States adopted led to the ruin of the British and French influence in the Eastern Mediterranean, and ultimately elsewhere. It was accompanied by a great outpouring of principles and professions about the impermissibility of aggression, and the like. The advantages anticipated from this heavily ideological policy remain mysterious. But there is nothing mysterious about the disadvantages which Nasser's triumph, procured chiefly by the United States, shortly afterwards produced for the United States. In so far as anything can be said to be a consequence of anything else, it may safely be said that the coup d'état of 14 July 1958 in Iraq and the civil war suffered by the Lebanon at the same time were both consequences of United States policies in 1956.

Apart from the fact that it had not been an Imperial Power, and that its policies as a Great Power and as a superpower had been to a considerable extent infected by ideological predilections, the United States was different from the United Kingdom in another very important respect. In the United Kingdom the conduct of foreign affairs has traditionally been part of the Crown prerogative, which in modern times means that it is in the hands of ministers, over whom parliamentary control in this area has been very difficult to enforce, even when the House of Commons was more powerful than it is now. The government of the United Kingdom, again, rests on the assumption that the Queen-in-Parliament is sovereign. But given the supremacy attained by the House of Commons over the House of Lords, and given Cabinet control of Commons through the operation of party discipline, ministerial discretion in conducting foreign policy becomes practically unlimited.

Conditions in the United States, as is well-known, are very different. Through its treaty power and control over appointments, the Senate is practically the president's partner in foreign affairs. The government of the United States is a government of checks and balances in which the executive arm is by no means able to control the legislative. This makes for greater responsiveness, ultimately, to the wishes of the electorate. And this electorate consists, to an appreciable extent, of descendants of immigrants with all their varied sympathies and connections abroad. In the circumstances, these are sometimes successful, in a manner unknown in the United Kingdom, in bringing to bear pressures which both the legislative and the executive have to take acount of. All this is to say that in the United States policy and its execution are subject in a wholly legitimate way to influences and constraints from which other Great Powers have been immune. It is very difficult to say, *prima facie* and as a general rule, whether this makes for the successful or unsuccessful conduct of foreign affairs. It is at any rate certain that a foreign policy conducted under such conditions becomes an extraordinarily complex thing to observe and study, and that the pitfalls standing in the way of the historian are more numerous than usual.

As has been said, the Rooseveltian stress on the liquidation of empires neglected the issue of whether such a policy would make the Soviet threat more or less dangerous. But it became clear, fairly soon after the end of the war, that the threat could not be denied or gainsaid. This threat in fact has forced on United States policy a discipline of the kind which the possession of overseas territories imposed on the defunct empires. The threat in due course evoked a counterthreat, the display of force the creation of a counterforce. The need for a counterforce has, willy-nilly, been one of the two poles between which the United States has oscillated since 1945. The other is, of course, the ideological one best exemplified by support for Nasser after 1952, by pressure on the British to give up their bases on the Suez Canal and, most strikingly, by the policy adopted at the time of the Suez expedition. But this ideological stance has more than once been justified by power-political considerations. It is the threat from the Soviet Union which enforced discipline on the United States. But since its inception the Soviet Union has itself been highly adept at using ideology as a weapon. Hence it has tempted its opponents to spread a counterideology, which has been justified by the argument that showing sympathy for "third-world" aspirations and a forthcoming eagerness in the "North-South dialogue," as well as other similar gambits would themselves be a potent weapon against the Soviets. Potent an ideological weapon may be, but it is not clear who will be hurt or deterred by it, nor whether to counter ideology with ideology will not itself be something of a victory for the Soviet Union. In any case, if in using ideology a leaf is being taken out of the Soviet book, it is salutary to remember that for the Soviets ideology has never been a substitute for military power.

The United States and the Middle East: How Many Special Relationships?

Wilfrid Knapp

The theme of this paper, a historical survey anchored to the present rather than the past, is that the United States is a superpower which is engaged throughout the world in rivalry with the Soviet Union, and which has sought to identify or create pillars of stability in the Middle East. In the development of United States global policy the Middle East was initially of secondary importance, except for the special relationship with Israel, both because of more urgent crises with the Soviet Union and because of the relationship of the Middle East and the U.S. to the countries of Western Europe.

However, decade by decade (1956, 1967) the concern of the United States has increased. The most important stimulus to its involvement was the activity of the Soviet Union. To that extent the relationship with the Middle East remained secondary. The direct relationship with the Soviet Union or the Vietnam War took precedence at various times. Moreover the local conflict in the Middle East had to be managed with reference to the Soviet Union, by working out rules of the game, partly in reaction to Soviet initiatives (whether autonomous or prompted by the actions of the local powers), partly in exercising choice between the limitation of Soviet influence and the involvement of the Soviet Union on the assumption of shared interest.

There are three aspects of the "indirectness" of the American relationship which are worth noting. The first is that in spite of the experience of four Arab-Israeli wars and in spite of the deployment of Soviet forces the U.S. has been chary of involving its armed forces. The single occasion when United States troops have been deployed (in Lebanon in 1958) was uncharacteristic and may have proved a seductive example to be followed, with disastrous results,

11

in other parts of the world. The same may be true of the intelligence operation in Iran in 1953, outstandingly successful on its own premises. (The non-involvement of support or operational forces does not of course minimize the importance of military missions, especially in Iran and Saudi Arabia, or the activities of the Central Intelligence Agency [C.I.A.], again in Saudi Arabia, or the participation of technicians in the Sinai disengagement.)

By its political and military involvement the Soviet Union has helped to define some rules of the game as they are observed by both Israel and the United States. But the Soviet view of the whole game has not become clear, and may not be clear in Soviet eyes. Of course the Soviet Union has sought and has gained access to the Middle East, and has sought to counter U.S. naval forces in the Mediterranean. But it is difficult to delineate convincingly a consistent policy either of stabilizing a Russian presence in the area or using it disruptively or even using the Middle East to turn the southern flank of the North-Atlantic Treaty Organization (NATO). This may be because the Soviets have found it as difficult as anyone else to operate in the Arab world, or even more difficult since Marxist analysis is a poor guide to Arab behavior.

However this gives added importance to the second aspect of the indirectness of the United States relationship, namely that United States perceptions both of the Arab world and of Israel have inevitably been shaped by the fact that in all Middle East crises the Soviet Union has been a present and immediate danger—least perhaps in the Palestine question, certainly in the Iranian crises of 1946 and 1953, in the Suez affair and its aftermath as well as the third and fourth Arab-Israeli wars. As far as the Arab world is concerned, one can make a comparison with the European imperialists of the nineteenth century who, for all their curiosity about the territories they ruled, looked dimly at the Middle East through the cataract of their presuppositions about race and empire. Similarly the United States in the twentieth century trained a sensitive and knowledgeable corps of foreign service officers in the State Department (and in the C.I.A.), but over the past thirty years the distortions and limitations of the Soviet-oriented prism have repeatedly intruded. Not only have perceptions been faulty but they have played their own part in forming Arab misperceptions of the United States. At the same time the view of Israel as an ally against the

Soviet Union has sometimes simplified élite perceptions to the point of distortion and has contributed to a popular image of Middle Eastern politics which is highly favorable to Israel and ill-informed about the Arab world.

The third characteristic of the indirectness of American interests in the Middle East is the importance of the region to Europe. Initially this meant a recognition of the predominant role of the United Kingdom. Before that role finally dwindled almost to zero (with the withdrawal from the Gulf in 1970) Europe had become strategically dependent on Middle Eastern oil to a greater extent even than the United States, because of the weakness of the European economies and the paucity of energy resources south of the English Channel and the North Sea.

During the early years the relationship with Britain in the Middle East fell mid-way between the "special relationship" which characterized their European policies and the conflict of ambitions which caused such bitterness in the Far East. Iran and Palestine were the two entry points for the United States to the Middle East, during or immediately after the Second World War. In neither case was there close cooperation; the British cannot be said to have played their weak hand with any great skill, perhaps because in Iran their assets in diplomacy and intelligence seemed so considerable, while in Palestine their switch from one policy to another resembled ever more closely the desperate efforts of a pilot to pull his plane out of a spin. Nor were there other European powers present in the Middle East to establish a European counterweight to the United States.

If the cooperative relationship of West-European affairs was absent, so during the war and post war years was the intensive rivalry which dominated wartime relations between America and Britain in the Far East where (as Christopher Thorne has shown) the Americans suspected the British of old imperialism and the British suspected the Americans of new imperialism, and both were right. But in the Middle East differences were muted. The flurry of anxiety in the United States about future supplies of oil died away; differences over Palestine lost their sharpness as the State of Israel established itself; in Iran American tactics in resistance to Russia differed from British but did not threaten the British position at Abadan, and as the vulnerability of Iran to Russian expansion intensified American anxiety, the oil companies were held in check lest they exercise an uncontrollable influence on the delicate political balance.

This muted opposition of views was no doubt deceptive. The sense of shared interest and the agreement to differ even when perceptions varied or ambitions clashed was enhanced by the easy communication between State Department and Foreign Office. But in 1947-48 it was not the State Department which made Palestine policy; in 1956 communication from London to Washington was deliberately cut and was not easily restored while the president refused to speak to the prime minister, and the United States ambassador to London could not stand his secretary of state, who in any case went into the hospital. In 1973 a sharp divergence of interests appeared not only between the U.S. and Britain but also the Europeans, and it was not smoothed by Kissinger's diplomacy.

Given that the United States in the period immediately following World War II sought no direct involvement in the affairs of the Middle East, it was inevitable that it should try to ensure stability and deny access, as far as possible, to the Soviet Union. The two things were for the most part connected: political instability and economic weakness, it was thought, increased the attractiveness of Communism, and the interest of the Soviet Union would be to destabilize the area in the pursuit of its own advantage. In chronological order there were two states which first attracted American attention and then became integral parts of the American system in the Middle East, Iran and Israel. They could scarcely be more different.

Iran, like Turkey, stands out in Middle Eastern politics for the way in which it came to behave like a nation-state. In September 1947 George Allen made an historic speech to the Iran-American Society which went no further, textually, than to assure the Persians "that the American people will support fully their freedom to make their own choice" regarding a Russian demand for oil concessions. For all the restraint of its language it signaled a major commitment to the independence of Iran. The country was a descendant of ancient empires and most of its people had retained a national identity through centuries of weakness and foreign intrusion. But it could scarcely be regarded as a successful nation-state. Its ruler had been forced to abdicate in the face of British and Russian pressure. His reputation was thereby saved and his country perhaps liberated from the harsh rule of a declining despot, but the Iranian people were deeply affected by their humiliation. Reza Shah's young successor had not yet acquired a sure control over the army; he was challenged by a landed class which had suffered under his father; the northern part of the country had been under Russian occupation and the British ran their own mini-state at Abadan. Only half the population spoke the national language; the tribes retained a large degree of autonomy, safeguarded by poor communications and the venality of the army, while their khans exercised a powerful influence over government in the capital.

It was scarcely surprising that the stability of Iran, and therefore its security from subversion and invasion by the Soviet Union, should take precedence in the American mind over questions of oil. The Persians for their part were strong enough (or at least their prime minister, Qavam as-Sultaneh, was wily enough) to escape from the Russian grip, but not to attract the same treatment, in supplies and commitment, as Turkey. Iranian nationalism found its populist expression in Mohammad Mossadegh, who showed himself to be a precursor in the nationalization of Iranian oil until the United States, in uneasy alliance with the British, maneuvered his downfall to the advantage of Mohammed Reza Shah Pahlavi.

It would be wrong to exaggerate the importance of Iran in the global policies of the United States. Nonetheless it has had a distinctive role. The Azerbaijan crisis was of major importance both in raising the temperature of the cold war and in encouraging those who believed that firmness would induce Soviet withdrawal (even where American power, on the ground, was very weak). The continuation of that policy was an important factor in the renewal of the air base at Dharhan in 1950; the intervention of 1953 was decisive in determining the future of Iran at least for a generation, until the present day. Initially the relationship was one of the dependence of Iran on the United States as Iran was a subordinate member of the American alliance system receiving American financial and military support. But the product of such support was the growth of a strongly organized nation-state still dependent (but not financially) on the United States for sophisticated weapons, with defined borders and the resources to pursue an independent foreign policy and bring some pressure on the United States. The tipping from dependence to independence came a decade after the oil crisis, as the Shah flirted with the Russians so that he should not be taken for granted by the

Americans, far less be persuaded to import a pale version of Kennedy's new frontier into Iran, even though the bazaar sold carpet portraits of the young President.

The Shah's Iran thus emerged, it might be thought, as the perfect if not the only candidate for Nixon's "Guam doctrine" ("we shall furnish military and economic assistance when requested in accordance with our treaty commitments. But we shall look to the nation directly threatened to assume the primary responsibility of providing the manpower for its defense"). In fact Iran on the one hand remains virtually defenseless against the Soviet Union and on the other has gone well beyond the limited role of the Guam doctrine, so that it can justly claim to have realized in part its aspiration to be a regional great power. In that role it pursued a foreign policy difficult to fault on the assumptions of American desiderata in the area: the relinquishment of a claim to sovereignty over Baḥrayn opened the way for the quiet withdrawal of Britain from the Gulf; the assertion of sovereignty over the Tumbs and Abu Mūsa was accomplished with a fine sense of timing; assistance to the Zufār rebels was accompanied by the cultivation of a relationship with China which itself, perhaps paradoxically, contributed to stability.

The importance for beleaguered Israel is clear. In its attempt to encircle the Arab world Israel laboriously constructed a relationship with black African states on the basis of a shared interest in development—an insecure foundation against the onrush of oil. Even in Ethiopia the alliance against radical Arabism proved insubstantial as Ethiopia was itself radicalized. But with Iran there grew up a common interest against proximate enemies—Nasser's Egypt and Iraq; and an exchange of scarce resources—an outstanding Israeli intelligence service against Iranian supplies of oil even in times of embargo.

Iran failed to become, as no doubt the Shah would have wished, a "pole" in regional politics. Since power attracts (especially intellectuals), it is reasonable to expect that any country which exercises power, even to the extent that Iran does, should become a "pole" of attraction in a multipolar world. Clearly this was not the case with Iran. Neither amongst the successors to its empire to the southeast, nor amongst the Arab states across the Gulf and certainly not in Iraq, did the Shah's Iran serve as an example or a model. The Ayatollah Khomeini and Islamic fundamentalism brought to power by popular revolution exercised an attractive power which the Shah never achieved.

The contrast with Israel as an American partner is striking, and it has been argued that the United States relationship with Israel has nothing to do with stability. Can one not transpose to the 1940s a recent statement of Kissinger's about a possible Palestinian state and say that "whatever the declaration, whatever the intention, the creation of a Jewish state in Palestine will bring instability to the area"? That Zionist pressure disgusted Truman we know; the evidence concerning the influence of the Jewish vote remains inconclusive; it is certain that Truman was deeply affected by the plight of the Jews in Europe and impressed by the force of Weizmann's personality. He committed himself to the immigration of 100,000 Jews into Palestine and then, drawn along by events, discounted the State Department's view regarding the creation of the state, either refusing to believe that in this instance stability in the long term was the single overriding objective, or reaching the conclusion (as the cold war in Europe intensified) that no other solution offered a better chance of short term stability than the creation of the state.

Whatever its importance in the decisions of 1948 the Jewish community assumed a powerful role in the making of American foreign policy. Its link with Israel moreover adds to the many peculiarities of that country as a quasi-nation-state. Created by the force of Zionism, Israel remains an unfinished state. It has no historic borders as European states have and the appeal to history is not to a pre-existing legal order of decades or even centuries ago but to the archaeological past. Its borders are therefore justified by claims based on the need for security and the right of conquest following defensive wars. The state has always included amongst its citizens those with an ideological commitment to expansion, and the national community as a whole has had as its single overriding consideration in foreign policy the maintenance of national security. It is in the normal behavior of nation-states that these three components—the absence of agreed borders, ideological commitment and the pursuit of security—make for expansion "whatever the declaration, whatever the intent." The Arab states, in their refusal to recognize the state, connived at such expansion and guaranteed the fulfillment of their own prophecies.

The fact remains that the single most enduring commitment of the

United States in the Middle East is the commitment to Israel. But it is the quality of the commitment which is important. George Kennan, who was never counted as a gentile Zionist, has made the revealing comment that the United States should continue its commitment to Israel (which is thus placed in a privileged category with Japan) because it has already had such a commitment for so long, but should not commit troops. At two crucial moments therefore in the history of the state the American wish to support Israel has been matched by an almost equal desire not to commit its own forces: this was the case with Truman in 1948 and with Johnson in 1967. In both cases there was, from the American point of view, danger from the Soviet Union; on both occasions the Middle East was secondary in importance to other areas of conflict, whether in Europe or in Vietnam. Israel therefore appeared as a pillar of stability in the defense of American interests. As long as the level of armaments in the Middle East was low and kept low by the Tripartite Declaration, all was more or less well. As soon as the Tripartite Declaration was levered open by the French and then burst apart by the Russians, the way was open for the introduction of sophisticated weaponry into the area. Once this competition was engaged the United States took the lead, identifying, in various ways, its own security with that of Israel.

The Israelis see the reverse side of the same relationship. It is very different, as any European must readily understand. For West Europeans, who do not normally think that their survival is at stake, see the irreducible minimum of NATO as being the presence of United States troops in Europe, a target or trip-wire to guarantee an American response if NATO is challenged. Israelis, for whom survival is at stake, have as their single dependable ally a superpower which almost above all else wants to avoid the commitment of its armed forces to the area. The importance to Israel of the ability to manipulate the United States stems from this asymmetry in their relationship. Fortunately for Israel the means for such manipulation exist: the committed and well-organized Jewish community operating in a political environment predisposed towards Israel; a resourceful diplomatic service which can exploit divisions within the American administration; an intelligence community with distinctive resources deployed against the K.G.B. which can trade with the superior technological equipment of the Americans.

The outcome is American military support for Israel on such a scale that it has been argued in the United States that Israel has or will have the resources to wage offensive war without anxiety in the short run about problems of resupply. The argument is not accepted in the National Security Council. But it is difficult to discount the calculation that, short of direct Soviet involvement or a radical and unlikely change in American policy, in the immediate future, Israel can remain decisively ahead in the Middle East arms balance because of the advantage it enjoys in technological skill. The supply of arms by the United States to Saudi Arabia can contribute to the balance in the Gulf and, together with the supply of F-5Es to Egypt it indicates a diplomatic shift, and possibly a shift in the political attitude to Israel. But it does not at present alter the fundamental military balance vis-à-vis Israel. Meanwhile the sophistication of the equipment supplied to Israel maintains a dependence on the United States for spare parts in normal times apart from the needs of actual war and thus provides the possibility of pressure which does not suffer from the Congressional furor evoked by the sale of planes. But it would be wrong to exaggerate the ease with which such a lever can be used effectively.

More important is the fact that, while Israel lacks defined borders, the United States has committed itself to a "strong Israel" but not to a territorially defined Israel. Truman supported the claim to the Negev; but with that exception the United States has been resistant to Israeli claims to territorial expansion, though not to security—a policy which is consistent both with American legalism and American relations with the Arab world. This was true during the abortive negotiations with 'Abdallah; it was the basis of Dulles's policy before Suez and of the pressure exerted after Suez and it has been continued in acceptance of the ambiguities of Resolution 242.

The Israeli demand for security will therefore always be heard sympathetically in the United States, given Washington's desire not to commit American forces and the Jewish community's sensitivity to Israeli needs. But territorial expansion in the guise of the "liberation" of the West Bank is another matter.

The crises over Iran and Palestine first brought the United States into the Middle East. Then it entered the hazardous world of the Arab states, hazardous in that no major extra-regional power can enter Arab diplomacy without having to adapt to the peculiar rules which govern the behavior of Arab states amongst themselves. Arab states are not, clearly, nation-states, whatever else they are. They belong to the Arab world, which has some of the components of nationalism—a sense of past grandeur and a common language (sanctified by being the language of the Qoran). There is no other region of the world where national borders have been drawn by imperial rulers between people with a shared sense of an earlier golden age—though not, it hardly needs saying, an age of political unity.

The peculiar characteristics of inter-Arab behavior remain to be explained. The weakness of institutions in the conduct of foreign policy, the absence of a body of treaties and agreements kept furbished by a foreign service no doubt contributes to the volatility of the behavior of Arab states, but does not explain the intensity of political rivalry. A sociological explanation (supposing it to be possible at all) should perhaps start from the persistence of primary loyalties in Arab politics.

However that may be, the United States was unable to enter the diplomacy of the Arab world without making its own impact on Arab rivalries. Its task was made the more difficult as a result of its commitment to Israel. For while it can be argued that it is in the long-run interest of Israel to seek Arab unity, its short run policies naturally seek to divide the Arab states, which in any case are only too able to present divisions amongst themselves ready to be exploited. The United States search for pillars of stability in the Arab world starts therefore from the handicap that its participation in Arab politics (like that of other outside powers) has added to inter-Arab rivalry.

The Sādāt initiative had the potential to alter the stakes of inter-Arab rivalry. Nasser, we know, sponsored the Palestine Liberation Organization (P.L.O.) as a substitute for an attack on Israel following the Arab summit conference of 1964 and engineered the war of 1967, we assume, to regain leadership in the Arab world. Ten years later Arab confrontation states accepted the existence of Israel. Sādāt was ready, by going to Jerusalem, to gamble with what the Arabs regarded as their only ace—a full recognition of Israel. If he succeeded he would gain, not only directly from Egypt's peace with Israel, but in addition by winning an advantage over his rivals in the Arab world in an initiative to peace. The contrast with 1966, when

Ḥusayn could provoke Nasser by doubting his bellicosity, is striking. The gamble to reverse the board game carried risks commensurate with the potential gain. But it was never a bid to contract out of the game of Arab politics; it was under certain conditions *almost* a separate peace, but never quite.

Whatever the nature of Arab rivalry it is scarcely surprising that the United States has found it easiest to establish relations with the two states which are commonly classified together as "traditional monarchies," Jordan and Saudi Arabia. In fact they are as different from one another as chalk from cheese: the one poor, modernizing, open to the world, with a westernized royal family vulnerable to assassination; the other rich, closed, governed by a royal family which so far has acted like a self-sealing tyre when punctured but which in the long run may prove too heavy a weight for society to bear. Their relationship to each other is marked by one of the oldest rivalries of the modern Middle East. The United States, especially ARAMCO, has always been the principal western partner of Saudi Arabia (and excited the animosity of Anthony Eden for its complicity in the flow of Saudi money into Hashemite Iraq). Finally Saudi Arabia has become powerful (within limits) while Jordan has not.

The United States relationship with Jordan is often seen as one of the key points of its stability system in the Middle East. In fact the relationship has been catastrophic; and nowhere are the mood swings of American policy towards the Middle East more apparent than in relationships with Israel and Jordan in the 1966-73 period. The first part of the period was characterized by neglect, of the whole Middle East, and especially of the central area as distinct from Egypt. The dangerous significance of the Samū' raid was not grasped. Had it been, King Ḥusayn's fateful decision to enter the war against Israel *might* have been prevented (of course it might not; he is an independent person). Ḥusayn's decision, and the military success of Israel in the Six Day War created the problem of the West Bank, and the problem of refugees turned into the Palestine problem. The immediate crisis was resolved, from the American point of view, by Resolution 242. But the next crisis, in September 1970, was centered in Jordan. In contrast to Johnson's neglect of the Middle East prior to the 1967 war, Nixon and Kissinger went into top gear to manage a crisis which they saw primarily as a crisis in their relations with the Soviet Union. They enjoyed the sense of power which crisis management produced and were pleased with the result. But, like Johnson, they missed the significance of local events. They underestimated the importance in Arab politics of using the Israelis as proxies (even the British had squirmed in their alliance with Israel in 1956). They paid too little attention to Syrian internal politics. They saw the contribution which Israel had made to the balance against Russia and missed the significance of Ḥusayn's action against the P.L.O. This, coupled with the death of Nasser (who in any case had accepted the Rogers plan before he died), presented the United States with an opportunity to do more easily what it is trying to do now. But global politics took precedence, the opportunity to stabilize the central area was underexploited and the Palestinians moved to Lebanon where they tipped the fragile balance of Lebanese politics into armed anarchy.

The American relationship with Saudi Arabia is longer-standing, though initially less active than that with Iran; and the United States, particularly ARAMCO, built up an unrivaled knowledge of Saudi Arabia which remained exclusive to a small élite. The reluctant readiness of the Saudis to impose an oil embargo in 1973 had a decisive effect on the politics of the October war. As the swing producer in the Organization of Petroleum Exporting Countries (OPEC), Saudi Arabia decides the price of oil (although it responds to U.S. pressure in doing so) and its reserves and production alone can meet the commonly assumed increase in energy demand over the next few years. Some 20-25% of U.S. oil imports (accounting for 40-50% of consumption) come from Saudi Arabia and a major part of the Saudi surplus is invested in the United States. Meanwhile the American public remain uninformed and uninterested in Saudi Arabia, seeing the country through a widespread antipathy to rich Arabs and to oil companies. It does not follow that they would like Saudi Arabia any more if they were better informed.

Never before has there existed such great economic power associated with so little political or military power, or any of the components of population, education, industrial strength which enter into normal calculations of power. This partly explains the extremely blunt and Samson-like quality of Saudi power, except in Arab politics. (The exception is important.)

Saudi Arabia is closely associated with the United States in the pursuit of a stable world order. But the commitment to that world

order and the closeness of ties to the United States limit maneuverability. Even in the next five to ten years, as the United States
becomes increasingly dependent on Saudi oil, the generally destructive effect of any renewed oil embargo will inhibit though not prevent its use. Saudi holdings of dollars do not provide any safeguard
against a fall in the value of the dollar (even though it is possible to
imagine a scenario in which OPEC, with sufficient skill, could
stabilize all the world's major currencies) and they are too large to
permit speculation against the dollar (even though private holdings
of dollars are at present so immense that they can be moved
speculatively).

It is fortunate, for the world economy, that the United States
deficit represents so large a part of the OPEC surplus, since the
United States economy is strong enough to carry the burden. At the
same time the bonds which join the United States and Saudi Arabia
are conservative in some particularly unconstructive ways. The
Saudis have shown little imagination with regard to their surpluses
and sometimes appear to believe that their responsibility ends when
they place their funds at the disposal of the international banking
community; the United States, at the best of times cool towards any
North-South dialogue, is rendered yet more cautious by the world
recession.

However what is more important from our point of view is to
discover how the United States-Saudi relationship operates in Middle Eastern politics. Historically the answer is not too difficult to
give. Both the great 'Abd al-'Azīz ibn Sa'ūd and King Faysal were
clear and explicit in their hostility to Zionism, although Faysal
muted his hostility to the Jews. Roosevelt made conflicting promises
to 'Abd al-'Azīz and to the American Zionists; from Truman on, the
Saudis were disregarded in American support for Israel. This was
one instance where American policy not only succeeded in squaring
the circle but derived some benefit (and consequently incurred some
cost) in doing so. The United States counted on Israel as an ally
against the Soviet Union while Faysal nurtured his enmity towards
Zionism and Communism, scarcely called on to choose between
them since they were twin branches of the same evil. But this was
in the period when Israel and Saudi Arabia shared a common enemy
in Nasser and when Faysal's pursuit of the Islamic Union was the
first venture of Saudi Arabia into international politics outside the

Arab world. Distance and Saudi insularity separated Jerusalem from Riyād so that the United States could operate more easily with its two (unofficial) allies. The cost was twofold: in this period of "Arab cold war" the United States appeared as a supporter of Israel *and* conservative Arab states; and the United States may have underestimated the ideological hostility of Saudi Arabia to Israel, given that such hostility not only jumps geographical distance but gets stronger in the jumping.

But history is an uncertain guide to the new period we have now entered. The collapse of Iran and the Egypt-Israel Treaty have thrust Saudi Arabia into an exposed position in regional politics and have tipped the balance in favor of Arab rather than American pressures on the royal family. Geopolitics have also changed.

At the beginning of the present decade, as the British withdrew, the Shah of Iran safeguarded American as well as his own interests in the Gulf; Iran is distant from Israel, and its unofficial ally. Saudi Arabia as well as being a Gulf power has an airbase a few minutes flying time from Israel and at the same time almost touches the Horn of Africa. These simple facts of political geography underlay the debate on the sale of F-15s to the country with which the United States has, apart from Israel, had the most special relationship in the Middle East.

There remains the case of Egypt, for so long the key point of the Arab world in consideration of its prestigious history, its population, standard of education, nascent industrialization and strategic position. Was there an opportunity missed for the United States to pursue a successful Egyptian policy and, is a second opportunity now being lost? The first part of the question may be phrased in this way: given that Nasser's policies were full of contradictions, was it possible to tip the balance towards stability in the western interest? From this point of view the most important contradiction or at least duality in Nasser's policies was the attempt to stimulate a self-reliant policy or economic development coupled with leadership of the Arab world. If it had been possible to assist Nasser in a quasi-autarchic economic development policy, would it have been possible to prevent Egypt from turning east? In spite of the Baghdad pact?

Counterfactuals in history necessarily leave an unpleasant aftertaste, however attractive the bouquet may have been. However the historical record is without doubt one of misperceptions and miscalculations. In Washington a key decision was taken not to finance the Aswān dam. Having decided, Dulles said "I sure hope we've done the right thing." But his anxieties and the calculations of those around him seem to have turned on whether an opening would be offered to the Soviet Union, not to an ensuing scenario which included the nationalization of the Suez Canal, far less the Anglo-French-Israeli invasion of Egypt. It was these events which tipped Egyptian economic development towards socialism at the same time as Nasser became the hero of an Arab world made more turbulent by the eruption of Suez. In American calculations the Soviet danger quickly eclipsed all else, while the Arabs saw the Eisenhower doctrine as a justification for Americans to "fill the vacuum" in the Middle East, a vacuum which (since it meant the expulsion of the British) most Arabs welcomed.

From the Egyptian side the misperceptions continued. Whatever the limitations of American policy, a serious attempt was made to establish a satisfactory relationship with Egypt. It was initiated by Dulles and given a new look by Kennedy. By now the American foreign service was reaping the reward of investment in Arabists; the United States Embassy, the Agency for International Development (AID) next door, the United States Information Service (U.S.I.S.) and the availability of counterpart funds to the American University provided the personal and institutional base for a successful relationship. It was not matched by any corresponding development on the Egyptian side. While in the United States the Jewish community gained added strength, Nasser drove every American diplomat to despair by speeches "for domestic consumption."

Perhaps in the end it made no difference. The few Egyptians who will now justify Nasser's policies see an irreconcilable conflict between Nasser's aspiration to change in the Arab world and American conservatism and misguided anti-Communism. The objective observer interprets Nasser's destabilizing influence differently: it was less his leadership than his ability to incite but not control. However it is interpreted, it led to the war in Yemen, the break with America (Nasser's Vietnam), the turning of U.S.-Saudi relations against Egypt and finally the break with America.

Today all is different. Sādāt has expelled the Russians, conducted a political-military war whose success depended on American diplomatic intervention in its support, opened the economy and established a regime which one would think is as far to the right as can be were it not for the extremist opposition on the right as well as the left. At last, it might be thought, Egypt has become a pillar of stability suitable to the American order in the Middle East. But the price of stability may be two things, neither of which the United States can provide: some success from the Sādāt initiative, and major success in economic development. At present the second may appear easier than the first; but in fact it may well be that the late twentieth century is following the pattern of the late nineteenth, when Mehemet Ali's attempt to pull Egypt up by its own bootstraps was followed by the distortion of the Egyptian economy by the destructive impact of international predators. The Sādāt initiative *might* have opened the way to a block of stability reaching to the borders of Ethiopia with Israeli technique, the Egyptian need for peace and progress, Sudanese land, and American and Saudi money combined.

There is thus an inherent tragedy in the United States relationship with Egypt. It is the more important since, in Middle Eastern terms, Egypt cannot be seen without Israel. Anti-imperialism and moral indignation, together with the independence of the Eisenhower administration from the constraint of the Jewish community, produced the pressure which brought Israeli withdrawal from Sinai, coupled with an American commitment regarding the straits of Tiran. Just as the British agreement to withdraw from Egypt in 1954 ought to have been accompanied by contingency plans based on Cyprus so the American guarantee of Tiran ought to have been followed by a readiness to manage crises in the Middle East. But a decade later the United States was overcommitted around the world and the absence of an ambassador appointed to Cairo symbolized the loss of leverage which stemmed from American anti-Communism and Nasser's involvement in Yemen.

This brief survey omits a great deal not only because it is a summary but also because of the limitations of the United States relationship with the Middle East. Syria has a minimal part in the foregoing narrative, in spite of its importance. The Palestinians have even less part and this may seem even more anomalous. Nation and state in the Middle East are full of ambiguities and create problems for analysts nurtured in a discipline of international relations which has grown up within a nation-state system. At least until the Carter administration, the United States resolved these ambiguities in the simplest manner: the government gave no recognition to the P.L.O.; the Jewish community, with the exception of its more adventurous fringe, shunned the Palestinians and the educated public remained content in a happy state of ignorance.

Formulation
of American
Policies

Objectives of U.S. Middle East Policy

Richard Rosecrance

Introduction

There have been four basic objectives of American policy toward the Middle East: 1) to reduce Russian influence in the region or to keep it to manageable proportions; 2) to maintain political and economic access to Arab oil in increasing amounts; 3) to protect the territorial integrity of Israel (though the definition of Israel's proper limits has remained unclear); and 4) to bring about either a *de jure* or *de facto* settlement of the Arab-Israeli conflict.

The thesis of this paper is that it has been increasingly difficult for Washington to pursue all of its aims simultaneously with equal success. This inability has reflected itself in growing discontent with the policy of the Israeli government. In addition, as U.S. policy objectives have come into greater conflict with one another, there has been some change in their relative degree of urgency and priority. At certain periods in the past the two paramount objectives were to keep Russian influence to the minimum and to protect Israel. The need to have access to oil supplies of the Persian Gulf was less critical, and, for a time at least, the necessity of an overall political settlement of the conflict was also undemonstrated. It now appears that objectives 2 and 4 have achieved a higher priority, though it remains uncertain whether they now rank above objectives 1 and 3.

The conflict of objectives, of course, need not continue indefinitely. If a satisfactory settlement of the conflict were reached, it would serve to help Israel, assure the supply of oil, and also limit Soviet influence. It is not surprising, therefore, that the United States has placed great stress upon a negotiated accord, both before and after the Camp David summit. If there is no resolution of current differences between Cairo and Tel Aviv, growing attenuation of the link between Jerusalem and Washington is possible.

Periods in the Development of U.S. Middle Eastern Policy

(What follows is a general characterization of American policy in five distinct periods. The changes from period to period that are recorded help to explain the present situation, even though the short sketch below does not do full justice to the intricacy and variety of Middle Eastern politics.)

1. Up to 1967

The period from 1947-48 to the June War in 1967 offered the least complication to U.S. Middle Eastern policy. Over the twenty-year period U.S. goals were quite compatible. After 1954 Nasser rejected all previous attempt to form a pro-Western defense alignment in the region. The Baghdad Pact divided countries into apparently pro- and anti-Western factions: Turkey, Iran and Iraq (temporarily) were in one camp; Egypt and Syria in another. John Foster Dulles made an abortive attempt to woo Nasser in 1955, but the next year witnessed the take-over of the Suez Canal and the ensuing Anglo-French and Israeli occupations of Egyptian territory. This completed and solidified the basic bifurcation of orientation (though Arab rivalries continued to divide even those who were most anti-Western). After 1958 and the turmoil in Iraq and Lebanon, Nasser appeared as the strongest Arab leader, and his links with the Soviet Union deepened.

For most of this period there was no real conflict between the first and third objectives of American policy. To oppose the Soviet Union (once it became clear that Nasser could not be weaned from his dependence on Moscow) was also to oppose Russia's Middle Eastern friends, Egypt and Syria. To help Israel gain arms and defensible frontiers was to repel a combined Soviet and Arab challenge. In this early period the United States maintained its link with Persian Gulf states, particularly Saudi Arabia and Iran. The tension between Saudi Arabia and Egypt over Yemen lessened possible disagreement between Riyād and Washington over Israel. True, there was no prospect of a negotiated settlement of competing claims between the Arabs and Israel, but neither did it appear that the failure to win an agreement would be disastrous. As long as intra-Arab rivalries dominated political life, Egypt, Syria, and Jordan would not be able to make common cause against Israel.

2. 1967-70

The June 1967 War proved that the Arabs could allow themselves to be drawn *ensemble* into a war with Israel. But the overwhelming Israeli triumph seemed to convey a deterrent lesson of striking, perhaps even decisive, proportions. Even though the Arabs were now slightly more united politically, the strongest Arab armies must still hesitate to attack Jerusalem. Some U.S. policy makers believed that the tide of economic and military events increasingly favored Israel, rendering a new Arab challenge less and less likely. Thus, while a *de jure* settlement between Israel and her enemies was still desirable, it seemed less necessary. The *de facto* might in time transform itself into the *de jure*.

This belief, of course, was unfounded. But one must remember that in 1967-70 the United States was tempted to overstate Israeli strength. Washington was in process of losing the war in Vietnam; the U.S. position in Europe had suffered, politically, economically, and militarily. Some officials saw two strong cohesive nations in world politics still capable of drastic and effective action: one was North Vietnam, the other Israel. America's inability to master Hanoi helped nurture the belief in Jerusalem's invincibility.

In this period there was no need to worry about access to oil. Oil prices hovered around $1.50 a barrel and there was an abundant supply. Saudi Arabia was not yet tempted to take a strong political role in the Arab-Israeli conflict. Even if the Organization of Petroleum Exporting Countries (OPEC) had tried to force prices up, the members of the cartel could not have maintained the increase without a restriction in supply. To this OPEC states had been unable to agree. Thus it briefly appeared that Washington might eat its petroleum cake while still partaking of *matza*. The conservative oil producers remained concerned about Soviet influence in the region; on the whole they accepted U.S. policy.

Once again, therefore, there was a coincidence of separate policy goals. The United States could back Israel because Israeli deterrence might succeed. Only in retrospect was it clear that the new territory Israel had acquired would present two difficulties: 1) it would permit an invader to launch an attack with very little warning; 2) it would present the problem of a large and increasingly rebellious subject population.

3. 1970-73

By 1970 Israeli "deterrence" no longer sufficed. The "war of attrition" made clear that Egypt, with Russian help, was quite prepared to continue the fighting, exacting costs in Israeli manpower. The greater Soviet assistance to Egypt in 1970 strengthened Washington's belief in the linkage between radical Arab regimes and the U.S.S.R. To support Jerusalem thus seemed to perform a double service. At the same time Saudi friends of the United States maintained a low posture on Israel. But change was in the wind. Oil prices began to rise and by the summer of 1973 had reached $2.70 a barrel. The Western world had begun to gorge itself on cheap Middle Eastern oil as the most efficient source of power. Demand was beginning to increase to the point where high prices could be maintained without restrictions in supply.

The next turning point occurred in 1972. When Egypt expelled Soviet advisers, technicians, and military personnel, the longstanding premise of U.S. policy that Israeli enemies were also friends of Russia was discredited. For the first time since 1955 Washington could think about better relations with independent Arab nations, even though they remained antagonistic to Israel. Outwardly, however, there was no immediate change in U.S. policy. After the early failure of the Rogers Plan, Washington was not ready to start a new peace effort or to move to a more equidistant position between Israel and the Arabs. Meanwhile Israeli deterrence had failed, and the Arabs saw that they might force the world as well as the Israelis to consider their claims more seriously.

4. 1973-76

The October War of 1973 and the "oil weapon" were the means of bringing about a reorientation in American policy and solidifying the already pro-Arab stance of Europe and Japan. The partial Arab victories and the proclamation of the oil embargo (even though a failure) brought U.S. officials up short. Previously it had begun to be recognized that objectives 1 and 3 were not fully consistent: to support Israel unwaveringly might jeopardize new U.S. ties with Russia's erstwhile Arab clients. But 1973 brought a new element: to work for a peace settlement required a much more even-handed American approach to Middle East politics. Thus objective 4 also partly conflicted with unswerving support for Jerusalem.

out _missing_ _bad sering A-1-anprint_

The "oil embargo" and its potential future implications also made it clear that a peace settlement was essential. This in turn could not be obtained without Israeli withdrawal from most of the occupied territories. Thus U.S. support for Israel (objective 3) was partly set against the need to maintain oil supplies (objective 2), to keep down Soviet influence (objective 1), and to reach a peace settlement (objective 4). In April 1976 elections on the Israeli-controlled West Bank demonstrated the hold of Arab nationalism on local sympathies. This made it even more transparent that a *de facto* settlement with Israeli soldiers in occupation could work only for a limited period.

The Present Situation

The basic impetus behind U.S. sponsorship of the Camp David accords was the fear that U.S. policy objectives might come into increasing conflict with one another. To seek to realize one goal might be to imperil another. Broadly, in August 1978 the U.S. faced three choices: 1) to seek a further and higher level reconciliation of the goals, accepting that they all remain important; 2) to reemphasize U.S. commitments to Israel, hoping that this would not have a decisive impact on Soviet gains in the region, the availability of Arab oil, and the longer term possibility of peace; 3) to reemphasize U.S. ties with independent Arab nations and the states of the Gulf, seeking to limit Soviet influence, while hoping that this will not greatly disadvantage Israel or worsen U.S.-Israel relations.

The first tack, which was of course the Camp David agreement, involved a real peace settlement between the Arabs and Israel. If it is finally carried out the other objectives of U.S. policy would attain a new compatibility and consistency. If real peace is achieved, it would have great advantages for the United States as well as the states of the region (including Israel).

First, it would limit Soviet influence in the Middle East. Though there is some debate on the ultimate goals of Soviet policy, there can be little doubt that the Soviet role has prospered as a result of continuing tension in the region. Moscow has fed on antipathies: Iraq vs. Iran; Syria vs. Israel; Egypt vs. Israel and Syria vs. Egypt. It is now benefiting from the violence and tension in Iran. A settlement of territorial and political differences would make Soviet help less necessary, for war would no longer be a likely prospect. The cycle of war, depletion of stocks, and rearmament would be broken. The Arabs would need to depend less on Moscow and would be able further to diversify their sources of support. Israel would need fewer arms and would be able to reduce the crushing burden of defense expenditure. Trade between Middle Eastern countries would begin and increase, and Israeli exports would appear in Egyptian, Lebanese and other markets. Egypt could turn her energies to internal development and economic stabilization.

A peace settlement would greatly simplify U.S. and also European and Japanese energy problems. If the Organization of Economic Cooperation and Development (O.E.C.D.) countries continue to use oil at current rates they will import 36 million barrels a day in 1985. On present reckoning only 26 million barrels will probably be available to meet this need, and Iranian uncertainties could reduce this total still further. The original intent of Carter's energy proposals was to reduce projected U.S. import demand in 1985 from 11.5 million barrels a day to 5 million (compared with current imports of 8.4-8.5 million barrels a day). However, Congressional treatment of Carter's energy plan means that this target cannot be hit. At best one can hope for a cut of 3 million or less to 8.5 to 9.0 million barrels a day in 1985.* Even if Western Europe and Japan shave four million barrels a day from their projected figure seven years hence (an unlikely prospect), daily import demand would total 27-29 million barrels. This amount cannot be attained without additional increases in production from the Persian Gulf, and continued high production from Iranian fields. Thus, the Carter administration's failure to devise and implement a satisfactory conservation plan pushes U.S. policy in a pro-Arab direction.

Whether Riyād will be willing or able to attain the required production will depend greatly on political as well as economic factors. If there is no Middle East peace, economic considerations could further dominate political ones, and the Saudis could decide to operate at less than full capacity, leaving oil in the ground to be pumped at a later time for higher prices. (Indeed, even if a settle-

---

* Even the most recent optimistic estimates of U.S. imported oil consumption range from 9.6 to 10.4 million barrels a day in 1985. The government's worst case forecast is for 12 million barrels a day.

ment is reached, there will be difficulty in persuading the major Persian Gulf producers that their strictly *economic* interest is best achieved by maximum production *now* rather than *later*.) A peace settlement would seem to be the minimum requirement for increased Arab production.

A real peace would also have two benefits for Israel. First, it would reduce Jerusalem's dependence on Washington. Second, it would involve a new U.S. commitment to Israeli security. Despite the large and diversified Israeli armaments industry, Israel's reliance on the United States has grown with each round of war. New and advanced weapons, precision-guided munitions, aircraft with electronic countermeasures and other specialized equipment have been needed to balance the increasing sophistication of Arab arms and tactics. Stocks that seemed adequate before war have turned out to be smaller than required when war occurred. It is not even certain that current levels are sufficient for all eventualities. Perhaps surprisingly, Israel's nuclear capacities have played little role in deterring limited Arab attacks. Nor would an attempt now to try to make them deter small-scale Arab initiatives be credible. Thus Israel has been thrust back on the United States for conventional arms and support. An end to the ever present threat of war would free Jerusalem from Washington in much the same way that it would free the Arabs from the Soviet embrace.

But while a peace agreement would liberate Israeli energies for economic development and trade, it would also almost certainly offer a new and significant American commitment to Israeli defense. The nature of such a commitment has been much debated. Its form remains unspecified. But it would be a major American contribution to a peace settlement. It could change past assumptions that Israel would absorb all the initial punishment in any war, and that Washington would be ready to offer new supplies only *in extremis*. If such a commitment is given, involving stationing of American troops in Israel, the U.S. would be implicated at the very beginning should a new challenge be presented. Thus, while Jerusalem's foreign policy latitude would be increased, the U.S. stake in Israeli security would be enhanced. It is worth speculating here on possible parallels with Germany. Bonn has U.S. forces on its soil and thus benefits from a well-nigh automatic credibility of U.S. response. Since American fortunes are already committed, Germany is not in the position of having to persuade Washington to help or to send supplies. Not having to defer to Washington to build up goodwill that might be needed in a crisis, Bonn can take independent initiatives on many foreign policy questions. Israel might do so also.

A peace agreement would also help to dispel the Third World's occasional equation of Israel with South Africa. The West Bank would no longer be seen as a kind of Bantustan or worse, with Israel controlling the strings either on stage or from behind the scenes. For this prospect to emerge, however, Israel would have to be ready to withdraw over time from most of the West Bank and to permit the local population to participate in determining its own future. Then an autonomous West Bank linked with Jordan, but with open frontiers to the west, would demonstrate the mutual and freely acknowledged value attached to economic relations, trade, and labor mobility. This part of the tentative Camp David agreement is extremely important. Such an agreement would also solve Israel's demographic problem in the occupied territories: the danger of Arab numerical preponderance in Israel proper and the territories it controls. Indeed, if the Israeli government seeks to assimilate the territories, it will be presented ultimately with a Middle Eastern version of the Rhodesian and South African dilemmas.

Of course a peace agreement may not be attained. Then the United States would either have to support Israel, to some degree at the expense of its other goals, or to acknowledge its failure to reach agreement with Jerusalem and to place greater emphasis upon other objectives. The choice between these alternatives would be difficult and affected by the reasons for the failure of a peace agreement. If the Camp David accords, including both the Egyptian-Israeli peace and the "Framework for Peace in the Middle East" were implemented and if other political groups and nations refused to participate, the onus and responsibility would then be on others. A partial agreement would be consistent with Washington's strong support for Israel and also with her desire to assist President Sādāt. It would make the best of a bad situation and it might not lead to any worsening of relations with the Persian Gulf.

Much less satisfactory would be a situation in which the Camp David accords collapsed because of Egyptian-Israeli disagreement. If the United States then decided to put Israeli security at the very top of its Middle Eastern foreign policy agenda, it would have to discount the oil weapon, to acknowledge greater Soviet influence in the region, and to frustrate the hopes of its closest Middle Eastern associates, Egypt and Jordan. It might mean forcing Egypt back into the Soviet fold and sacrificing President Sādāt. Such a change would probably bring on an Egyptian regime determined to wage another round of war with Israel.

For such a policy to work the United States would have to enact much tighter energy controls and stop subsidizing the price of oil and natural gas. This would entail a *volte face* in energy legislation and administration policy and also in American consuming habits. It certainly would demand a larger oil stockpile than that presently planned. It would involve a considerably heavier commitment to Israeli security in the absence of a peace agreement than the United States has yet made and one which might not be sustained by domestic opinion. It would force acceptance of perpetual tension and occasional war on the U.S. and Middle Eastern nations. For Israel it would probably mean confronting new guerrilla activities launched from Jordan and from Lebanon. It would surely mean greater political activism and terrorism on the West Bank and Gaza.

The United States would never explicitly alter its stance and downgrade Israeli security as a major American foreign policy interest. But to shift greater support to Egypt, Jordan, and Saudi Arabia might indirectly loosen the ties between Washington and Jerusalem. This shift would be speeded by increased American dependence on Middle Eastern oil, and the oil revenues would provide a growing Arab ability to redress Israeli superiority in conventional military terms. If war occurred, Washington might be somewhat less ready to replenish Israeli stockpiles. Israel would be forced to rely to a greater degree on its own production. Jerusalem might strive to extract the maximum deterrence from its nuclear weapons, but whether these would suffice for the low-level challenges that the Arabs and their allies would initially present cannot be determined. It would certainly hasten overt Arab acquisition of nuclear capacities, leaving the conventional balance to tell the tale.

Each of these possibilities would lend a greater consistency to U.S. foreign policy priorities in the Middle East. But the real world does not always provide a nice consistency and most often agrees with Emerson. Thus, an unresolved tension among U.S. goals may continue for a considerable period of time.

Possible Future Orientation

As to actual future scenarios in the Middle East, at least three sets of evolutions can be analyzed: the first is a gradual movement toward Middle East peace, with agreements on the structure of peace between Israel and Egypt, intensive Egyptian-Israeli negotiations to reach a concrete settlement of their own differences, followed or accompanied by drawn-out and difficult discussions between Israel and her other opponents, Jordan (possibly including Palestine Liberation Organization [P.L.O.] members) and Syria. These negotiations may founder on Israeli unwillingness to surrender territory on the West Bank or on Jerusalem's hesitancy to permit the population of the West Bank and Gaza to participate in the determination of its own political future. But many other obstacles could also impede peace, such as an Arab refusal to demilitarize the West Bank, or an insistence that a West Bank state be endowed with full sovereign powers.

A second scenario (if peace negotiations become interminably prolonged or fail and if a partial settlement is ruled out) would be for a continuation of a "no war-no peace" situation in the Middle East. The implications for American policy in such circumstances would inevitably be affected by the respective degrees of intransigence of the Middle Eastern nations most directly involved. Inevitably U.S. governmental and popular opinion would react against the presumed authors of the difficulty in reaching peace.

Aside from the negotiating issues of the moment, however, one must consider what may be long term changes in American domestic opinion on Middle Eastern matters. Figure I gives Gallup Poll results over the past eleven years, charting the rise and fall of American "sympathies" with the Arabs and Israel. As one would expect, each war has brought a temporary increase in support for Israel. Polls have also been affected by setbacks in the negotiating process, as for example in March 1975 and February 1978. Discounting these special circumstances, however, one notes that Israel has gradually lost ground in American opinion while the Arabs have gained. Since 1967 those who basically sympathize with the Arabs have grown by 250 percent while Israel has lost about 40 percent of its previous supporters.

Figure II indicates a similar pattern in the distribution of U.S. arms deliveries. While military deliveries to Israel from the United

States have increased enormously since 1968, those to its Arab and Moslem neighbors have increased even more. When the proposed Arab and Israeli arms sales are approved, the Arab countries will further increase their lead. This pattern is likely to be projected into the future if only because Israel depends upon U.S. foreign aid for a substantial portion of its arms deliveries while the Arabs and oil producers contribute to the U.S. balance of payments by paying in cash. This is not only a potent political advantage; it may be a growing economic advantage if the U.S. Middle Eastern oil bill continues to rise.

A third scenario would see a resumption of war. If Camp David fails either Israeli or Arab participants might seek to gain new political capital through a resort to war. Sādāt, pressed by political opinion in Egypt if his overtures are rejected, may be forced in this direction. He would then return to his checkered alliance with Syria. Jordan and perhaps even Iraq would be brought in. Economic support would be found from Saudi Arabia as well as the Soviet Union. For its own part Israel might be tempted to think that war would be a solution to the diplomatic impasse, that a further display of military potency would strengthen its negotiating position.

The difficulty in both cases, however, would be that war would change little. Could Israel afford new territorial acquisitions? It has a more than sufficient Arab population to police now. New gains at the expense of Syria or Egypt would be forbidden by the Soviet Union. On the other hand, the Arabs could not expect to dislodge Israel from the Golan, Sinai, or the West Bank through war. Major Arab victories would be likely to bring an ultimatum from the United States. Thus war would produce little good and much evil. Farseeing Israelis and Arabs will seek to prevent it. But this does not mean that political leaders will not resort to war if all else fails.

Conclusion

Basic trends over the past twenty years in the Middle East have undermined the happy coexistence of the several U.S. policy goals. The growing complexity of Middle Eastern politics and economics has tended, in the absence of a settlement, to reduce the centrality of American support for Israel. This does not mean that policy makers are any less sympathetic to Jerusalem, but they see themselves in a much more complicated and multi-faceted position. No longer can they assume that support for Israel comports easily with other, increasingly important American objectives.

The more one examines the alternatives to a peace settlement (partial or complete) the less attractive they seem. "No war-no peace" merely projects present trends into the future, confounding both U.S. objectives and possibly witnessing a further decline in the heretofore close Israeli-American relationship. War repeats the cycle we have seen before without producing any vital change in the political, military, and territorial balance.

Perhaps therefore the present stalemate will be seen merely as temporary barriers on the path leading toward peace. It is quite possible that the difficulties are less formidable than they now seem. One can imagine Israelis saying to their American counterparts that one cannot expect Jerusalem to make major concessions to Cairo alone, when concessions would only be fruitful in a multilateral negotiation involving other parties, Syria and Jordan. One does not give away important positions unless one gets concessions in return. Thus Israel may have more concessions prepared than it has yet revealed.

For the U.S. part, America understands Israeli objections to the security problems presented by a sovereign successor regime on the West Bank. Thus, the basic Israeli position on demilitarization, temporary Israeli occupation, and open frontiers can be acknowledged and even accepted. A state endowed with all the political and military trappings of sovereignty would present an intolerable security threat. Nor does Washington expect Israel to return all occupied territories. But a permanent Israeli military presence (even if only initially sanctioned for five years) is not consistent with "autonomy" for the area, to say nothing of participation by its inhabitants in the determination of their own political future. It also does not appear that extraterritorial Israeli settlements are compatible with Arab internal rule. In the longer term and regardless of the outcome of the current negotiations with Egypt, it appears likely that Israel will eventually have to consider two general alternatives to the unresolved contradictions in present arrangements. One would see further settlements in the West Bank and an attempt at physical assimilation of the Arab population with all the attendant difficulties. The other would see Israeli military withdrawal, leaving the area in the hands of moderate Arabs who are satisfied to accept autonomy and demilitarization of the area. The longer it is postponed, the less credible this option becomes. Israeli withdrawal would not only be greatly preferable from the standpoint of U.S. policy objectives in the Middle East, but would, if suitably guaranteed and safeguarded, be in Israel's own longer term interests.

Table I

(See Figure II)

**U.S. Foreign Military Sales Deliveries
to Selected Middle Eastern Countries 1968-77**
Egypt, Iran, Jordan, Kuwait, Lebanon, Saudi Arabia, Syria, Israel
(Dollars in Thousands)

	1968	1969	1970	1971	1972	1973	1974	1975	1976	1977
Egypt	—	—	—	—	—	—	—	—	62	10,469
Iran	56,717	94,881	127,717	78,566	214,807	238,633	510,347	913,267	1,466,767	2,245,899
Jordan	11,999	24,248	53,075	14,445	10,579	15,228	14,629	16,636	72,885	116,440
Kuwait	—	—	—	—	—	—	44	7,563	20,446	88,504
Lebanon	518	980	1,044	1,122	38	1,791	844	943	5,325	1,034
Saudi Arabia	36,856	32,086	51,937	144,049	59,646	86,159	254,971	342,239	1,027,640	1,617,423
Syria	1	—	—	—	—	—	—	—	—	—
	106,091	152,195	233,773	238,182	285,070	341,811	780,835	1,280,648	2,593,125	4,079,769
Israel	28,598	72,486	215,864	303,195	192,499	189,903	977,931	656,547	728,671	875,328
	134,689	224,681	449,637	541,377	477,569	531,714	1,758,766	1,937,195	3,321,796	4,955,097
Ratio =	.212	.322	.480	.560	.403	.357	.556	.338	.219	.176

Figure I

Gallup Poll Results (1967-78)
Sympathies in U.S. Opinion

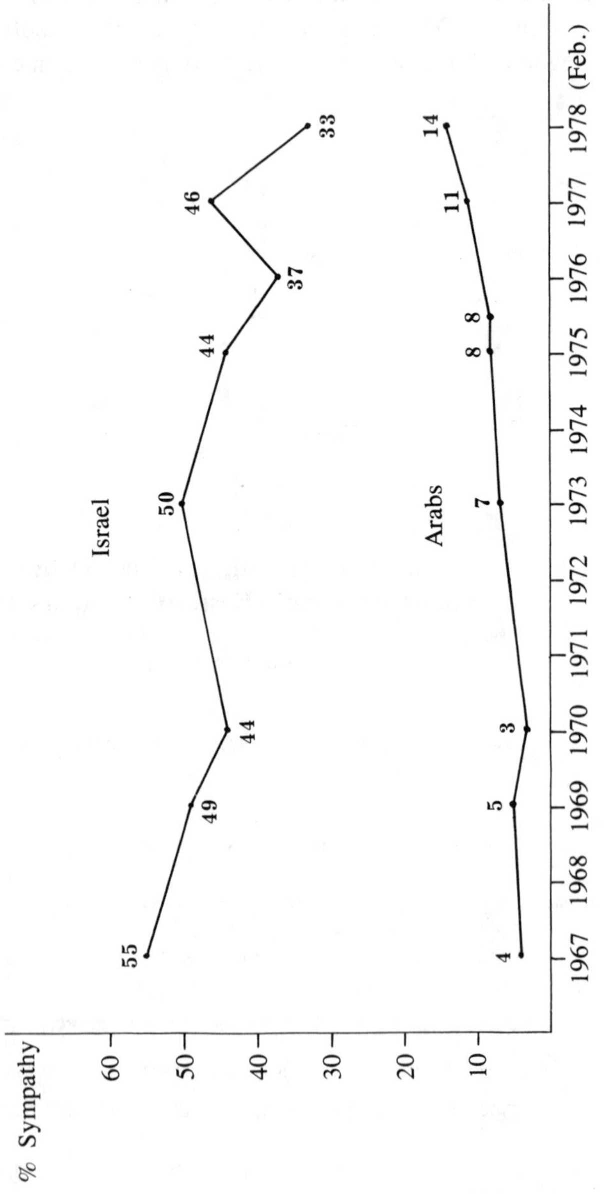

Figure II

U.S. Foreign Military Sales Deliveries to Israel 1968-77 as a Proportion of Total Deliveries to Middle Eastern Countries

(Israel, Egypt, Iran, Jordan, Kuwait, Lebanon, Saudi Arabia, Syria)

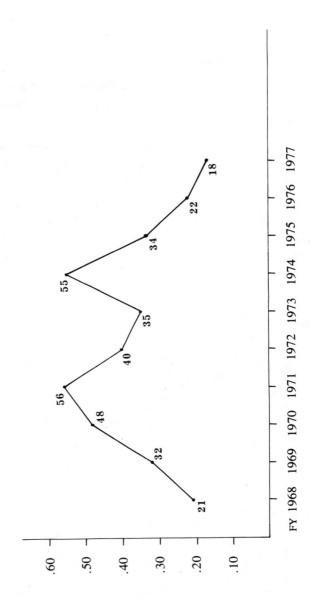

Figure III

Effectiveness of Political Leadership
in Working for Peace in Middle East
(as judged by U.S. opinion)

[Reasonable vs. unreasonable — Harris Poll]
[Excellent-good vs. fair-poor — Gallup Poll]

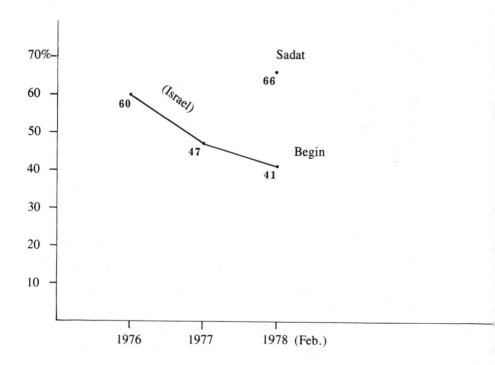

ANNEX

September 17, 1978

A FRAMEWORK FOR PEACE
IN THE MIDDLE EAST
AGREED AT CAMP DAVID

Muhammad Anwar al-Sadat, President of the Arab Republic of Egypt, and Menachem Begin, Prime Minister of Israel, met with Jimmy Carter, President of the United States of America, at Camp David from September 5 to September 17, 1978, and have agreed on the following framework for peace in the Middle East. They invite other parties to the Arab-Israeli conflict to adhere to it.

PREAMBLE

The search for peace in the Middle East must be guided by the following:

— The agreed basis for a peaceful settlement of the conflict between Israel and its neighbors is United Nations Security Council Resolution 242, in all its parts.

— After four wars during thirty years, despite intensive human efforts, the Middle East, which is the cradle of civilization and the birthplace of three great religions, does not yet enjoy the blessings of peace. The people of the Middle East yearn for peace so that the vast human and natural resources of the region can be turned to the pursuits of peace and so that this area can become a model for coexistence and cooperation among nations.

— The historic initiative of President Sadat in visiting Jerusalem and the reception accorded to him by the Parliament, government and people of Israel, and the reciprocal visit of Prime Minister Begin to Ismailia, the peace proposals made by both leaders, as well as the warm reception of these missions by the peoples of both countries, have created an unprecedented opportunity for peace which must not be lost if this generation and future generations are to be spared the tragedies of war.

— The provisions of the Charter of the United Nations and the other accepted norms of international law and legitimacy now provide accepted standards for the conduct of relations among all states.

— To achieve a relationship of peace, in the spirit of Article 2 of the United Nations Charter, future negotiations between Israel and any neighbor prepared to negotiate peace and security with it, are necessary for the purpose of carrying out all the provisions and principles of Resolutions 242 and 338.

— Peace requires respect for the sovereignty, territorial integrity and political independence of every state in the area and their right to live in peace within secure and recognized boundaries free from threats or acts of force. Progress toward that goal can accelerate movement toward a new era of reconciliation in the Middle East marked by cooperation in promoting economic development, in maintaining stability, and in assuring security.

— Security is enhanced by a relationship of peace and by cooperation between nations which enjoy normal relations. In addition, under the terms of peace treaties, the parties can, on the basis of reciprocity, agree to special security arrangements such as demilitarized zones, limited armaments areas, early warning stations, the presence of international forces, liaison, agreed measures for monitoring, and other arrangements that they agree are useful.

FRAMEWORK

Taking these factors into account, the parties are determined to reach a just, comprehensive, and durable settlement of the Middle East conflict through the conclusion of peace treaties based on Security Council Resolutions 242 and 338, in all their parts. Their purpose is to achieve peace and good neighborly relations. They recognize that, for peace to endure, it must involve all those who have been most deeply affected by the conflict. They therefore agree that this framework as appropriate is intended by them to constitute a basis for peace not only between Egypt and Israel, but also between Israel and each of its other neighbors which is prepared to negotiate peace with Israel on this basis. With that objective in mind, they have agreed to proceed as follows:

A. West Bank and Gaza

1. Egypt, Israel, Jordan and the representatives of the Palestinian people should participate in negotiations on the resolution of the Palestinian problem in all its aspects. To achieve that objective, negotiations relating to the West Bank and Gaza should proceed in three stages:

(a) Egypt and Israel agree that, in order to ensure a peaceful and orderly transfer of authority, and taking into account the security concerns of all the parties, there should be transitional arrangements for the West Bank and Gaza for a period not exceeding five years. In order to provide full autonomy to the inhabitants, under these arrangements the Israeli military government and its civilian administration will be withdrawn as soon as a self-governing authority has been freely elected by the inhabitants of these areas to replace the existing military government. To negotiate the details of a transitional arrangement, the Government of Jordan will be invited to join the negotiations on the basis of this framework. These new arrangements should give due consideration both to the principle of self-government by the inhabitants of these territories and to the legitimate security concerns of the parties involved.

(b) Egypt, Israel, and Jordan will agree on the modalities for establishing the elected self-governing authority in the West Bank and Gaza. The delegations of Egypt and Jordan may include Palestinians from the West Bank and Gaza or other Palestinians as mutually agreed. The parties will negotiate an agreement which will define the powers and responsibilities of the self-governing authority to be exercised in the West Bank and Gaza. A withdrawal of Israeli armed forces will take place and there will be a redeployment of the remaining Israeli forces into specified security locations. The agreement will also include arrangements for assuring internal and external security and public order. A strong local police force will be established, which may include Jordanian citizens. In addition, Israeli and Jordanian forces will participate in joint patrols and in the manning of control posts to assure the security of the borders.

(c) When the self-governing authority (administrative council) in the West Bank and Gaza is established and inaugurated, the transitional period of five years will begin. As soon as possible, but not later than the third year after the beginning of the transitional period, negotiations will take place to determine the final status of the West Bank and Gaza and its relationship with its neighbors, and to conclude a peace treaty between Israel and Jordan by the end of the transitional period. These negotiations will be conducted among Egypt, Israel, Jordan, and the elected representatives of the inhabitants of the West Bank and Gaza. Two separate but related committees will be convened, one committee, consisting of representatives of the four parties which will negotiate and agree on the final status of the West Bank and Gaza, and its relationship with its neighbors, and the second committee, consisting of representatives of Israel and representatives of Jordan to be joined by the elected representatives of the inhabitants of the West Bank and Gaza, to negotiate the peace treaty between Israel and Jordan, taking into account the agreement reached on the final status of the West Bank and Gaza. The negotiations shall be based on all the provisions and principles of U.N. Security Council Resolution 242. The negotiations will resolve, among other matters, the location of the boundaries and the nature of the security arrangements. The resolution from the negotiations must also recognize the legitimate rights of the Palestinian people and their just requirements. In this way, the Palestinians will participate in the determination of their own future through:

1) The negotiations among Egypt, Israel, Jordan and the representatives of the inhabitants of the West Bank and Gaza to agree on the final status of the West Bank and Gaza and other outstanding issues by the end of the transitional period.

2) Submitting their agreement to a vote by the elected representatives of the inhabitants of the West Bank and Gaza.

3) Providing for the elected representatives of the inhabitants of the West Bank and Gaza to decide how they shall govern themselves consistent with the provisions of their agreement.

4) Participating as stated above in the work of the committee negotiating the peace treaty between Israel and Jordan.

2. All necessary measures will be taken and provisions made to assure the security of Israel and its neighbors during the transitional period and beyond. To assist in providing such security, a strong local police force will be constituted by the self-governing authority. It will be composed of inhabitants of the West Bank and Gaza. The police will maintain continuing liaison on internal security matters with the designated Israeli, Jordanian, and Egyptian officers.

3. During the transitional period, representatives of Egypt, Israel, Jordan, and the self-governing authority will constitute a continuing committee to decide by agreement on the modalities of admission of persons displaced from the West Bank and Gaza in 1967, together with necessary measures to prevent disruption and disorder. Other matters of common concern may also be dealt with by this committee.

4. Egypt and Israel will work with each other and with other interested parties to establish agreed procedures for a prompt, just and permanent implementation of the resolution of the refugee problem.

B. *Egypt-Israel*

1. Egypt and Israel undertake not to resort to the threat or the use of force to settle disputes. Any disputes shall be settled by peaceful means in accordance with the provisions of Article 33 of the Charter of the United Nations.

2. In order to achieve peace between them, the parties agree to negotiate in good faith with a goal of concluding within three months from the signing of this Framework a peace treaty between them, while inviting the other parties to the conflict to proceed simultaneously to negotiate and conclude similar peace treaties with a view to achieving a comprehensive peace in the area. The Framework for the Conclusion of a Peace Treaty between Egypt and Israel will govern the peace negotiations between them. The parties will agree on the modalities and the timetable for the implementation of their obligations under the treaty.

C. *Associated Principles*

1. Egypt and Israel state that the principles and provisions described below should apply to peace treaties between Israel and each of its neighbors—Egypt, Jordan, Syria and Lebanon.

2. Signatories shall establish among themselves relationships normal to states at peace with one another. To this end, they should undertake to abide by all the provisions of the Charter of the United Nations. Steps to be taken in this respect include:
   (a) full recognition;
   (b) abolishing economic boycotts;
   (c) guaranteeing that under their jurisdiction the citizens of the other parties shall enjoy the protection of the due process of law.

3. Signatories should explore possibilities for economic development in the context of final peace treaties, with the objective of contributing to the atmosphere of peace, cooperation and friendship which is their common goal.

4. Claims Commissions may be established for the mutual settlement of all financial claims.

5. The United States shall be invited to participate in the talks on matters related to the modalities of the implementation of the agreements and working out the timetable for the carrying out of the obligations of the parties.

6. The United Nations Security Council shall be requested to endorse the peace treaties and ensure that their provisions shall not be violated. The permanent members of the Security Council shall be requested to underwrite the peace treaties and ensure respect for their provisions. They shall also be requested to conform their policies and actions with the undertakings contained in this Framework.

For the Government of the   For the Government
Arab Republic of Egypt: of Israel:

Witnessed by:

Jimmy Carter, President
of the United States of America

United States Interests
in the Middle East

Bernard Reich

National interest is a flawed concept, although it provides the basis for U.S. policy and legislation. There are varying perceptions in the executive branch, in the Congress, and in the general public of what is or is not in the national interest, and policy advocates on various sides of an issue tend to invoke the national interest for their diverse proposals. This imprecision and the multiple interpretations will become more apparent as this paper seeks to identify the array of alternative U.S. interests in the Middle East which provide the basis for policy decisions.

The national interest of the United States is the continuation of its existence as an independent state, with its institutions and values safeguarded and with the welfare of its people protected and enhanced. The U.S. seeks not only survival and security but continued existence as a particular type of state. Survival and security is a concept common to all states, since without physical survival (existence) there is little else worthy of attention. For the United States there is also a parallel, rather than subordinate, concern for the survival of a particular kind of system. There is an "American ideology" (probably more accurately referred to as a way of life) that seeks the maintenance and flourishing of its system—with democratic institutions, with a particular western culture, with principles and morality as guidelines of policy, and with liberty (and human rights) for its people and for others. While there is no real debate on the fundamental nature of this concept, the objectives and policies essential for its attainment are often in dispute. Clearly, however, it is essential that the United States seek to create and maintain a world environment conducive to the attainment of these ends. Generally, it is believed that an international system of free and independent states pursuing policies of peace and justice (and respect for the rule of law and human rights) would be most desirable. Prevention of nuclear conflict, limitation of local conflict, and promotion of conditions facilitating economic and social development are components of the approach.

U.S. interests cannot be stated as immutable concepts—they change over time, with reference to different world regions, in method of achievement, and in the view of decision makers. The concept of national purpose (or of national goals) remains elusive and normally elicits responses, from the general population as well as from some of the leaders of public opinion, which can best be described as vague generalizations, pious pronouncements, or platitudes. The specifications must be tested at different times and generalized constructs do not suffice. Security is the primary U.S. national interest (as one might argue that it is for all other states); but its components are constantly in flux. It is axiomatic that the United States seeks its survival and security. However, its methods vary. The interests of the United States are affected by numerous factors and interpreting their precise nature is a complex process. To a significant extent, identifying American interests is a subjective procedure and arriving at a precise and objective assessment is therefore virtually impossible. Yet policy decisions are made on a basis of an assumed, presumed, or proven interest. One technique for identifying interests is to utilize various factors which serve as indicators of a relationship. Thus, for example, military aid is more likely to be provided to a state in which there is an interest than to one in which there is not. This is also the case with economic assistance. The extent of trade between the United States and a given country is also an indicator of interest, as is the level of investment and the earnings on that investment. The presence of American citizens in a foreign nation is an additional factor for consideration, as is the location of American military installations and/or their elimination. Unfortunately, precise information on these factors is not always available and approximations must be utilized. This is particularly apparent in the case of the United States role in the Middle East.

THE EVOLUTION AND DEVELOPMENT OF
UNITED STATES INTERESTS

American interests (that is the official interests of the United States rather than those of a specific and particular segment of its population) in the Middle East were slow to develop and to be supported by policy and commitment. Until after World War II U.S. interests remained primarily private and limited to portions of the region rather than to its entirety.

Limited or specialized interests and activities of Americans in the Middle East may be traced to the first decades after the founding of the republic. In 1803-1804 the marines were involved with the Tripoli coast corsairs who had been preying on American shipping in the Mediterranean. But the major American involvement was not strategic, political, or official, but focused instead on the activities of private American groups. These included the missionaries who began to arrive in the Levant during the first few decades of the nineteenth century.

During the nineteenth century American activities were those of private individuals or groups representing particular interests, but they did not concern the United States as a government and did not involve official policies or decisions relating to political or military matters.[1] American political and strategic interests were not identified and the U.S. virtually abstained from official political involvement or policy in the area. To a significant degree, the United States utilized an existing British proxy and relied on British political agents to maintain a political and strategic environment in which its limited interests and activities could flourish.[2] Commercial interests were also severely circumscribed, although there was some trade in regional commodities, especially agricultural products. Protestant missionaries were active and their educational and philanthropic work led to the establishment of Robert College in Turkey in 1863, the Syrian Protestant College (later the American University of Beirut) in 1866, and the American University of Cairo in 1919. Archaeological activity was undertaken as well. However, primary attention was focused on religious, educational, and, more broadly, cultural and humanitarian pursuits. There was a minor commercial component to the United States position, but no real economic, political or security factor of substance was involved.

Commercial interests of a significant nature developed with the discovery of substantial oil fields in the region. Although the government did not develop an oil interest, the United States began to become involved, through its companies, in the oil industry of the region in the 1920s and 1930s. In the period between World War I and World War II the United States insisted on the application of the "open-door" principle to American commercial interests and sought American participation in commercial activity in the Middle East without disadvantage.[3] Oil became the most important commercial sector.

World War II converted and enhanced the American interest. Oil became a strategic/political concern, since it was seen as indispensable for the military activity designed to assure the security of the United States.[4] The war also affected other American interests: it precipitated a significant American physical presence, strategic involvement and the formation of political policy.[5] As a result, the strategic value of the area became more obvious and the increased interest in the region's resources (especially oil) added to the area's importance.

The United States entered the post-World War II era without a specific or comprehensive plan for the area, despite the increased interest generated by the conflict.[6] Soon, however, the identification of interests, and the policy to achieve them, began to emerge. Among the earliest components was the response to the Soviet threat. In September 1946 Loy W. Henderson, then Director of the Office of Near Eastern and African Affairs of the Department of State, articulated the U.S. position in these terms:

> "The main objective of the United States in the Near and
> Middle East is to prevent rivalries and conflicts of interest
> in that area from developing into open hostilities which
> eventually might lead to a third world war."[7]

The reasons for concern with a Soviet threat which might lead to superpower confrontation became clear with the development of Soviet and Soviet-sponsored activity in the northern tier. The United States sought to prevent hostile (particularly Soviet) domination of Greece, Turkey and Iran through a combination of political pressure and bilateral arrangements which supplemented the Truman Doctrine as the means to assist those states in ensuring their security against Soviet and Soviet-sponsored aggression, subversion and pressure.

The United States perceived an interest in preventing Soviet domination and adopted policies in support of that concern.

This approach to problems in the northern tier was not followed elsewhere in the region, especially not with regard to the Palestine problem, which was becoming increasingly pressing and prominent. The Palestine issue[8] and the Truman policy on Israel generated much debate concerning the relationship of interest and policy in the Arab-Israel zone of the Middle East. Moral and humanitarian considerations and the questions of strategic need seemed to clash as alternate conceptions of the national interest (or interests) of the United States came into play. In the third major sector (that is, the Arabian Peninsula and the Persian Gulf) the U.S. presence remained meager in the years after World War II since it continued to rely on the British presence. That precluded any substantial discussion of the national interest as the commercial concerns of American companies seemed to be effectively safeguarded by the British proxy and the United States open-door economic approach. Thus, in the immediate post-World War II period U.S. interests in the northern tier and Arab-Israel sectors began to generate policy responses, while in the Persian Gulf sector the overriding concern remained private.

The positions developed immediately after the war were given further impetus in the 1950s as the United States began to augment its initial efforts. The basic approach was the one centered in the northern tier, which focused on the defense of the region, both the northern tier and the Middle East as a whole, against Soviet encroachment and domination. In support of that policy the U.S. advanced a series of proposals which involved not only the northern tier states but also some in the Arab world. The purpose was to protect both the region and American interests from the Soviet Union.[9]

In the Arab-Israeli sector, the concern of the United States and its Western allies focused initially on the need to promote peace and stability as an end in itself and as a means to protect other interests. One of the earliest expressions of this approach was the Tripartite Declaration of 25 May 1950, in which the United States, England and France sought to clarify their policy on arms supply and sought to prevent the development of an arms race in the Arab-Israeli sector. However, they also declared

"their deep interest in their desire to promote the establishment and maintenance of peace and stability in the area and their unalterable opposition to the use of force or threat of force between any of the states in that area.''[10]

Thus, within a few years after the beginning of its official involvement and the identification of political and strategic interests, the main lines of U.S. policy in the northern tier and Arab-Israel sectors as well as the non-official involvement in the Persian Gulf sector had been established. The defense of the Middle East against the Soviet Union, the termination of the Arab-Israeli conflict and the stability of the region complemented previously devised policies in support of U.S. interests which included the open-door policy for American firms interested in oil and other commercial opportunities and the continued educational, cultural, philanthropic activity of American missionaries and others of similar ilk.

Between the early 1950s and the 1970s the U.S. developed a generalized view of its interests which focused on a number of themes which were repeated in the statements of government officials (including the president), were referred to legislation, and were rehearsed by observers and analysts. These revolved around the region's strategic significance, its economic-commercial potential, its cultural-historical heritage, and Israel.[11]

Strategic-Political Interests

The overriding American strategic-political interest in the Middle East for more than three decades has been the avoidance of nuclear confrontation with the Soviet Union, a clash which might threaten the very existence of the human race.[12] This very real concern helps to explain the activation of the U.S.-Soviet hotline in 1967 and 1973, the alerting of U.S. forces during the October War, and Kissinger's 1970 comment on the need to expel the Russians from Egypt. World War III scenarios based on Middle East conflicts have long held a fascination for United States and foreign analysts of the area.

While this concern has been apparent since 1945, there also has been a contemporaneous and sometimes conflicting interest in ensuring the prevention of Soviet dominance, which is seen as a threat to the North Atlantic Treaty Organization (NATO) flank and ultimately to U.S. allies and the United States itself.[13] Countering Soviet action was a factor in the United States policy concerning Iran in

1945-46, as well as in numerous activities subsequently designed to respond to the Soviet threat. Both the Truman and Eisenhower Doctrines were clear responses to this interpretation of American interests.[14] The United States has not sought regional dominance or control and it has not acted as an imperial power. But it is clear that these interests will sometimes conflict, presenting the problem of choice, and circumstances will dictate the nature and extent of the effort and the willingness to risk confrontation to ensure denial of dominance.

The strategic significance of the region resulting from its geographic location has also generated U.S. interest.[15] Located at the hub of Europe, Asia, and Africa, the Middle East is a crossroads and a bridge. It is bounded by the Mediterranean Sea, the Red Sea, the Arabian Sea, the Indian Ocean, the Persian Gulf, the Black Sea, and the Caspian Sea. This geographical position was of historical significance for land trade routes and is of contemporary importance for land, sea, and air communications linking Western and Eastern Europe with Eastern Africa, the Indian subcontinent, Southeast Asia, the Far East, and Australasia. These routes are of significance and unimpeded transit is an interest of the United States.

These communications links include the maritime passage through the Suez Canal which is the shortest shipping route between Western Europe and Asia, and a primary route for the shipment of Persian Gulf oil to Western Europe. It is also an important route for shipment of other goods between Europe and Indian-Pacific Ocean locations. Despite its advantageous location and (prior to the June War) continuous increases in number of transits, net tonnage, number of passengers, and revenue earned, the Canal's increasing tolls and technical limitations (especially those creating obstacles to the utilization of the Canal by supertankers) place restrictions on its use. Its vulnerability to air attack and blockage is particularly important in times of conflict.

Unimpeded transit through the Suez Canal, an important element of U.S. policy prior to the June War, declined in importance following the closure of the Canal during the 1967 hostilities. It was realized that the Canal's value as an artery of trade and commerce (and especially for the flow of Middle Eastern oil to Western Europe) was of less importance than had been thought to be the case. Alternative arteries of trade and oil supply developed and these were often of lesser cost and technical difficulty than had been anticipated. Also, after 1967, and especially after the cease-fire of 1970 and the launching of the U.S. plan for an "interim settlement," the Canal took on a new political importance as a major element in the quest for peace in the Arab-Israeli conflict. The United States was less concerned with transit rights than with the utilization of the Canal as an instrument of political leverage and negotiation. In the post-October War disengagement agreements between Israel and Egypt this value was further emphasized.

The Turkish Straits, whose control strengthens any state interested in the Black Sea-Mediterranean area, constitute a second major international waterway in the region. Historically Russia showed an interest in control and dominance of the Straits and the Soviet Union has maintained this concern. Effective control of the Straits can prevent a Black Sea power from having access to the Mediterranean. Alternatively, an outside power can advance toward the heartland of the Soviet Union by traversing the Straits and entering the Black Sea. The Straits also have economic significance as a transport route to and from the Black Sea as well as various world markets.

The importance of the Mediterranean Sea in terms of its peacetime use for trade and its military value for warships and supply ships adds to the strategic significance of the states bounding it. The Gulf of Aqaba, connecting both the Israeli port of Eilat and the Jordanian port of Aqaba with the Red Sea and the Indian Ocean, has an intrinsic value to Israel and Jordan, but its significance also must be judged in terms of the role it played in the 1956 and 1967 Arab-Israeli wars. The Bāb al-Mandab at the southern end of the Red Sea separates southwestern Arabia from the Horn of Africa and is the gate to the southern approaches of the Suez Canal and the Gulf of Aqaba. The Strait of Hormuz is the major transit route for Persian Gulf oil shipped to Europe and Japan.

Middle East air routes provide direct flight paths from Europe to Asia and the Pacific and offer good climatic and geographic conditions. North-to-south air routes from Europe and the Soviet Union also cross the Middle East. The importance of these communications links has grown with the increased participation of African and Asian states in world production, world trade, and international affairs.

The geographic position of the Middle East has made it a logical area for bases and staging posts as it provides a convenient focal point for military activity on three continents and is proximate to the Soviet Union. This has long been recognized and forms part of the rationale for continued attempts at control of the region by outside powers. Although the military need to control these communications bases and to have air bases in the region during conflict has diminished as a result of the increasing range of aircraft and intercontinental missiles, the region retains military importance because it constitutes a segment of the rimland of the Soviet Union and because two states, Turkey and Iran, border directly on the U.S.S.R.

Oil is the major natural resource of the Middle East and a strategic interest, although its value has changed over time. The area is credited with at least 60 percent of the world's proven oil reserves,[16] and a potential remains for future discoveries. Local consumption is low, allowing the bulk of production, which is among the highest in the world,[17] to be exported. During and immediately following World War II, Middle East oil was seen as strategically and politically important to the United States and was one of the arguments advanced, especially by the Pentagon, for determining policies involving the Palestine problem and Israel. This view, however, receded into the background and much of the later discussion revolved around the commercial interest in oil. It was recognized, however, that the oil had a far greater value for United States allies in Western Europe and Japan. There was thus an indirect U.S. strategic/political interest in Middle East oil resources, although it was not significant for the United States itself, which imported virtually no oil from the region. By 1973 this picture had begun to change. Oil remained of significance and even increased in importance for the European and Japanese allies of the United States and thus an indirect interest was maintained (or enhanced). Additionally a direct political/strategic interest developed and generated a concern with the extent of regional reserves and production with the growth of U.S. dependence on Middle East oil, for its own use.

By 1973 the oil factor had begun to loom increasingly large and the October War provided the impetus that linked United States efforts on the Arab-Israeli problem with U.S. concerns regarding the availability and price of Persian Gulf oil for the United States and its allies. After the 1973 war, oil emerged from being essentially a commercial-financial interest of American business and economic interests to become a significant component of the United States national interest affecting political and strategic interests and calculations of policy.

Access to this oil and use of it at reasonable prices are important concerns of the United States, although of greater significance for Western Europe and Japan. Despite technological advances in the energy field particularly in the use of atomic energy, and alternative supply sources in North Africa and those resulting from the North Sea strikes, oil is still an important energy source for the industry and economy of Western Europe. In a speech to the Los Angeles World Affairs Council on 20 February, 1978, Secretary of Defense Harold Brown linked Middle East oil to United States security interests in these terms:

> "Because the area is the world's greatest source of oil, the security of the Middle East and the Persian Gulf cannot be separated from our security and that of NATO and our allies in Asia. Japan, for example, imports 80 percent of her oil from this area. We intend to safeguard the production of oil and its transportation to consumer nations without interference by hostile powers." [18]

The Middle East has been characterized as an area susceptible to great power manipulation, to violence, and to destabilizing changes of regime and alterations in existing systems. These types of changes and the instability of the sector often have a negative effect on the vested interests of outside powers.

Prevention or termination of local conflicts or hostilities which have destabilizing effects, which might escalate to superpower confrontation, or which might have a negative impact on other interests has thus become a concern and policy goal of the United States.

Commercial-Economic Interests

The United States has long pursued an economic "open-door" policy in the Middle East (and elsewhere) which seeks freedom for private American concerns to function in the area. In the commercial realm there has been the desire to explore, produce and distribute oil resources and to participate in other profitable activities.

Trade[19] and investment have been important elements of the economic interest and the earnings on that trade and investment have been important for the U.S. balance of trade and balance of payments.[20] Oil has accounted for a large share of the earnings, in part through jobs for American employees and substantial remittances from their payrolls to the United States. There is an interest in economic development as a means of expanding markets and increasing trade as well as promoting improved local conditions. Prior to the October War, this was seen as a commercial interest of a segment of the American economy rather than as a significant official interest of the United States. Tension often resulted from the differing interpretations of this interest by U.S. officials and representatives of business enterprises. The U.S. government saw its role as that of facilitating the efforts of private concerns rather than of officially involving itself directly in the economic/financial/commercial sector.

Cultural-Historical Interests

The Middle East generated substantial interest for Western states because Judaism, Christianity and Islam had their origins in the area and many of the holy places of these three monotheistic faiths are located there. The Judeo-Christian heritage of Western civilization provides a link between the United States and Western Europe and the Middle East that transcends the purely cultural category of interests.

More tangible cultural interests go back to the early nineteenth century and revolve around missionary-educational-philanthropic activities. Robert College, the American University of Beirut, and the American University of Cairo are prominent examples of longstanding cultural involvement which, in recent years, has had U.S. government financial support. Programs and activities within the United States for expanding and increasing cultural links with the region have flourished since World War II.[21]

U.S. INTERESTS AFTER THE OCTOBER WAR

The October War was a major watershed in U.S. policy and led to an alteration in its approach to and its role in the Middle East. The conflict itself, the potential of U.S.S.R.-U.S. confrontation, the employment of the Arab oil weapon, and the four-fold increase in oil prices—and the ramifications of these developments—contributed to a reassessment of U.S. interests and policies. The United States emerged as the central extraregional power in the search for an Arab-Israeli peace settlement and this coincided with changing regional and international circumstances and with the realities of the strategic/economic role that oil would thereafter play. The nature of U.S. interests and the policies in their support underwent alteration, especially in the Persian Gulf/Arabian Peninsula and Arab-Israel zones of the Middle East.[22]

The Persian Gulf/Arabian Peninsula Zone

When Prime Minister Wilson announced the accelerated British withdrawal east of Suez in 1968, the U.S. posture in the Gulf had evolved considerably from the very limited individual and commercial dealings that characterized its relations with that region in the nineteenth century. The process was a slow one. Even after World War II, when the United States assumed global responsibilities and developed a heightened interest in the Gulf, its policy was to recognize and support the paramount British position and to rely on it to protect Western interests. U.S. consular visits to the region increased, but there was no concerted effort to supplant the British or to enhance the U.S. presence at British expense.

In the 1950s U.S. interests began to develop as a result of increased commercial activity involving oil and a growing awareness of the Soviet threat. These factors contributed to the conclusion of the United States-Saudi Arabian mutual defense assistance agreement of 1951, as well as to the Dhahran air base agreement of 1951. A modest military presence developed, but it was primarily the British presence that assured the security and stability which were essential for U.S. interests in the region.

By the late 1960s U.S. interests reflected the continued growth of United States contact with the region, and were generally expanded or widened variations of interests with historical precedent, especially involvement in the oil industry and commercial enterprise. The interest in the oil industry had three elements: investment in the oil industry and earnings on the investment, shipment of oil for United States consumption at home or abroad, and availability of oil on a dependable basis and at reasonable prices to U.S. allies, particularly in Europe. U.S. participation in the oil industry was extensive. Some twenty American oil firms were involved in the Gulf and accounted for more than half of the oil production of the area. U.S. investment in the petroleum industry of the Middle East was in excess of $1.5 billion and much of this was concentrated in the Gulf states. William D. Brewer, then State Department Country Director for Arabian Peninsula Affairs, described the U.S. oil investment in the Gulf sector in these terms:

> "This American economic stake represents perhaps the highest concentration of American private investment in any comparable region of the world. The Arabian-American Oil Co. (ARAMCO) investment alone is said to be the largest single private investment of one American enterprise outside the continental United States." [23]

The earnings on the investment and their contribution to the balance of payments were impossible to gauge with complete accuracy, but U.S. income from this investment was about $1 billion per year.

The importance of the oil resources to United States security was not precisely determinable—some argued they were vital while others disagreed. At that time the general consensus among government analysts and most outside observers was that the oil was important but not vital. That assessment was conveniently summarized by William D. Brewer in the following observation:

> "Experience has shown that the United States itself needs to import little oil from the Gulf. Less oil is imported now [1968] from this source than a decade ago. Nor were we seriously inconvenienced in 1967 when Arab oil was for several months embargoed for shipment to American, British and West German ports.
>
> Our Western European allies, of course, do depend substantially on Gulf crude . . . while United States commercial interests in Persian Gulf oil remain extensive, our strategic interest thus lies primarily in assuring that Gulf oil remains available on a nondiscriminatory basis." [24]

The view that oil did not constitute a vital interest was not shared by the American oil community, which cited the potential decline of U.S. oil reserves and the resulting increased need for Persian Gulf oil as the prime reason for its view of the importance of Persian Gulf oil. This suggested to the oil industry that U.S. interests in the

Middle East and the Persian Gulf were not getting adequate United States support and that in fact these interests ". . . merit a top priority rating in the formulation of our national policies. . . ." [25] Although the United States itself made little direct use of Middle East oil, assurance of supply to allies was a matter of importance and the focus of United States concern with the oil industry of the Gulf. The major U.S. allies in Western Europe were dependent on the oil for a safe and dependable low-cost supply.

Closely related was the commercial relationship with the Gulf states. In recent years U.S. trade had increased at a rapid pace because of the wealth created by oil. During 1967 goods worth over $600 million were exported to the Gulf. This represented more than four times the amount of exports during 1947. More significantly, because the value of imports from the Gulf was very low. U.S. balance of payments had been positively affected. The United States showed a favorable trade balance of over $400 million in 1967, four times the comparable 1947 figure. This increasingly favorable trade balance seemed likely to continue as long as the prosperity of the Gulf states increased and, along with it, the demand for the types of goods and services the United States could provide. There was an interest in maintaining and developing American commercial relations with the Gulf states.

The U.S. also had a fundamental interest in the Persian Gulf which centered on ensuring the development of a region of mounting prosperity and stability free from outside intervention. As in other parts of the world there was a general desire for peace and stability. The protection and well-being of United States citizens in the littoral states became an increasingly important aspect of U.S. interest as the numbers and involvement of Americans grew. Serious disturbances or violence might harm U.S. commercial interests, disrupt the flow of oil, and endanger United States citizens; therefore a stable economic and political environment was regarded as a prime requirement, if U.S. strategic and commercial interests were to be protected. Toward that end the United States encouraged the Gulf States to settle their differences among themselves and attempted to maintain friendly relations with all of them, regardless of their internal political climate or form of government. The United States had relations with all the states except Iraq, which had severed relations at the time of the June War.

The October War accelerated the process of interest identification and further altered the content of U.S. concern in this sector. The elements which had been identified in the period prior to the conflict took on increased significance and additional factors were incorporated into the equation. By 1975 the Department of State, which after the British withdrawal announcement had argued against precipitous extension or expansion of U.S. diplomatic or military involvement in the Gulf, noted:

> "The area of the Persian Gulf and the Arabian Peninsula is of major importance to the United States in political, economic, and strategic terms. United States policies in the region have a strong impact on both regional and global interests." [26]

The arguments in support of this position were numerous and diverse.[27] The major Arab oil-producing states were regarded as significant elements in the process of achieving a settlement of the Arab-Israeli conflict. They played a role in the financial support of the main confrontation states and their views were important in the effort. They were consulted regularly by both the more directly involved Arab states and by the Palestinians. The oil states, particularly Saudi Arabia,[28] were consulted regularly by the United States concerning both the Arab-Israeli conflict and the price and supply of oil since the 1973 war. This provided the linkage between the Arab-Israel and the Persian Gulf/Arabian Peninsula zones of the Middle East, which was now an acknowledged fact of political and diplomatic calculations in the region.

A second political-strategic concern was the increased significance of the oil produced in the region. In the wake of the October War, and the associated embargo on shipment of oil to the United States, it became clearer that the United States was becoming increasingly dependent on this export. As noted previously, much of the official analysis in the United States prior to the October War focused on the indirect factor—the oil needs of American allies rather than those of the United States. In the wake of the war U.S. dependence on Persian Gulf oil increased to substantial levels and insufficient increases in regional production, or denial of that oil to the United States, would have a significant disruptive effect on the United States economy and its security position.[29]

The continued flow of Persian Gulf oil and U.S. access to it at reasonable prices comprise one element of the oil interest while the economic benefits derived from its sale and the petrodollars earned constitute an additional factor. In the wake of the substantial increase in price which accompanied the October War, a number of the regional states earned vastly increased revenues from their oil sales.[30] These became capital surplus nations, with methods and tools for substantial economic activity abroad.[31] They were thus capable of making substantial overseas investment, undertaking foreign assistance efforts, and of becoming markets of an enormous scope for commercial and, particularly, military sales.

As attractive markets for U.S. goods and services, these states became the object of an intensive marketing effort by American commercial interests. The activities of these firms could be seen as beneficial to the United States balance of trade and balance of payments, especially in the light of growing oil purchases at increasing prices. The market opportunities were enhanced by the fact that these states often imported most of what was consumed locally and also required capital goods for their massive and ambitious development plans. The desire to build military capabilities and the low level of infrastructures and installed equipment created a substantial market for the sale of military equipment, the provision of training, and the construction of infrastructure.[32] In this the United States was often the primary and initial choice of the local states. In the first few years after 1973, this market potential began to become apparent and trade substantially increased.

The financial surpluses and reserves of the Gulf/Peninsula states also increased their ability to serve as foreign aid donors, not only to some of the less fortunate Arab states (such as Egypt), but also to states in other regions (such as the Somalis in the Horn of Africa). This not only created a secondary political effect of providing support for regimes and policies, but it also ensured the consultation of the Gulf states on policy issues and tended to generate Gulf State influence on situations in the Middle East and elsewhere.

The financial surpluses of the Gulf/Peninsula states also have a broader significance which generated a direct United States interest. The surpluses increase the potential for investment in the United States (sometimes subsumed under the broader notion of "recycling petrodollars") and for economic disruption by the shifting of large sums in a precipitous manner. There is an interest not only in securing investment in the United States[33] or a market for U.S. goods and services, but also in ensuring that the monies acquired would be used productively rather than disruptively in the region and elsewhere. In part this interest is determined by the amount of funds involved and by what those funds can accomplish.[34]

Reflecting this increased wealth and improved contacts a resurgence has taken place in the cultural and educational activities which have long been an element of the U.S. interest in the region. The United States has increased both its informational and cultural activity in the region and there has been a significant increase in the number of students coming to the United States from this area. This constitutes an interest in continuing to help the economic, cultural and social development of these states and improve both the American image and influence on positions and views in the area.

Reflecting the increasing interest and contact the diplomatic presence of the United States was expanded. Shortly after their independence, the U.S. recognized Baḥrayn (on August 15, 1971); Qatar, (on September 5, 1971); and the United Arab Emirates (U.A.E.), (on July 1971).[35] The U.S. supported U.N. membership for these states and for Oman. In the winter of 1971-72 William A. Stolzfus, Jr. was appointed ambassador to the Trucial Gulf States.[36] In late 1973 the Department of State recommended augmented diplomatic status with resident ambassadors and expanded staff in recognition of growing stability in the lower Gulf region.[37] In May 1974 the Senate confirmed Joseph W. Twinam as ambassador to Baḥrayn, and Michael Sterner as ambassador to the U.A.E., both of whom speak Arabic and are career State Department officers.[38] In June 1974 Robert P. Paganelli was confirmed ambassador to Qatar.[39]

The strategic-military significance of the Gulf was recognized by the United States during World War II when it launched the program of aid to the Soviet Union and required routes through the Gulf and across Iran for its shipment. The establishment of the Persian Gulf Command and later Middle East Force[40] reflected the continuing military value of the region, which took on added dimensions in the 1970s. In a statement before the Near East and South Asia Subcommittee of the House Foreign Affairs Committee in 1973, James Noyes, Deputy Assistant Secretary of Defense for Near Eastern, African and South Asian Affairs, described United States security interests in the Gulf as follows:

1. Containment of Soviet military power within its present borders
2. Access to Persian Gulf Oil
3. Continued free movement of U.S. ships and aircraft into and out of the area and continued access to logistic support facilities on Baḥrayn for MIDEASTFOR.[41]

The U.S. interest in this sector focuses on three elements. There is an interest in promoting stability and in having these States play a role in the resolution of the Arab-Israeli conflict. There is the value of oil in terms of its commercial impact and its economic force. There is strategic interpretation of an American interest in that oil for its allies and for itself.

The Arab-Israel Zone[42]

U.S. interests in the Arab-Israel zone revolve around the resolution of the conflict and the survival of Israel.

The United States has had, and continued to have, a major interest in the resolution of the Arab-Israeli conflict. All presidents from Truman to Carter have devoted attention to that issue,[43] and although the extent of involvement has varied and has increased substantially in recent years, the main theme has been that peace is essential to ensure other United States interests in the region and elsewhere. Often the Arab-Israel conflict has taken on more ominous overtones and these have intensified the U.S. interest. The "powder keg" view of Nixon in 1969 and the "disastrous consequences" view of Carter in 1977-78 are examples of that perspective. Both were convinced that if the conflict continued there would be an explosion involving the superpowers which would have a tragic worldwide impact and therefore had an overwhelming interest in ending the conflict.

The Carter conception of the interest in a settlement is particularly instructive. He has suggested that the time has never been more propitious to work for a settlement and he sees the continuation of the dispute as catastrophic for the region as well as the international political and economic order.[44] More specifically the argument has been that a just and lasting settlement is essential for a more peaceful world. Such a peace is thus essential for all Americans since "conflict there carries the threat of a global confrontation and runs the risk of nuclear war." [45] It could also have profound economic consequences, given the economic strength and potential of the Arab world. A lasting peace would not only prevent war, but would also help to maintain American influence vis-à-vis the Soviet Union since, short of war, the conflict tends to encourage instability and radicalization in the region which facilitates Soviet policy. In a speech before the Los Angeles World Affairs Council on 13 January, 1978, Secretary of State Cyrus Vance commented: "For our part, we stand ready to help Arabs and Israelis achieve their peace. It is important to our national interests that we do so; our values and character as a people demand no less than our greatest effort to help resolve this tragic conflict." Even a war in which the superpowers did not participate would be costly and would have a negative impact on U.S. interests. Thus, for example, Secretary of State Kissinger noted: "We experienced in 1973 that a Middle East war can have the most drastic consequences. The Middle East war in 1973 cost us about $3 billion directly, about $10-15 billion indirectly. It increased our unemployment and contributed to the deepest recession we have had in the post-war period." [46]

There is also an interest in closer ties with the Arab states and especially in divorcing them from Soviet destabilizing influences, thereby facilitating movement toward a settlement. Kissinger has noted "We believe that it is overwhelmingly in our national interest that Egypt has broken its longstanding intimate ties with the Soviet Union and that it has contributed to a moderate and peaceful evolution in the Middle East." [47]

Beyond the political-strategic consensus there are economic interests. The Suez Canal is an artery for oil shipments and general commerce. The sale of military hardware and other goods and services results in dollar earnings helping the balance of payments and the associated creation of jobs in the United States.

The Israel Interest

Israel has a special position in U.S. Middle East policy unmatched by that of any other state and going beyond the role it plays in the Arab-Israeli conflict.[48] The existence and security of Israel have been central themes of U.S. policy since the establishment of the state, and the United States has provided support throughout the period. The special relationship has grown closer over the years and reached significant new levels of political, economic, and military cooperation and parallelism in the period between the June War and the October War, despite occasional lapses and periods of coolness. This focus has been the subject of controversy, revolving not around suppoit for the existence and security of Israel (which is beyond substantial debate or discussion and which all appear to accept)[49] but around the exclusivity of the relationship, especially in the period between 1967 and 1973. Former United States Ambassador to Egypt John Badeau, who expressed concern about the wisdom of the policy, has argued that Israel represented a priority:

> "Israel represents our oldest direct interest in the area. Before the Truman Doctrine—indeed, before the emergence of the State of Israel—Congress went on record as being favorably inclined toward the plan envisioned by the Balfour Declaration. . . . The continuance of Israel as an independent state certainly represents a basic foreign policy commitment of the United States. . . ."[50]

This view, expressed in the 1950s, indicates the constancy of the U.S. interest in the Arab-Israel zone as compared with the Persian Gulf/Arabian Peninsula zone. Unlike the latter, the U.S. approach to the Arab-Israeli conflict and its interest in Israel have remained essentially steadfast, despite some changes in the policy to achieve the interest and the addition of some new elements to the equation. The contemporary articulation of this interest is well expressed by W. Anthony Lake, Director of the Policy Planning Staff of the Department of State, in these terms:

> ". . . we are committed, as we have been for 30 years, to the reality of a secure and enduring Israel, in peace and harmony with her neighbors. It is a commitment rooted deeply in history, in morality, and in American interest, reaffirmed by every Administration in this country since the State of Israel came into existence."[51]

The American interest in and commitment to the survival and security of Israel and termination of the Arab-Israeli conflict is deeply rooted in history and has been reaffirmed by every administration since Truman. A multitude of factors, including those that are political-security, economic, and cultural-religious (or "ideological'') in nature[52] underlie this interest.

The ideological factor is based on the view that the United States seeks more than mere survival. It believes in the need to ensure that its way of life will be supported and that like-minded states will be encouraged as a means of enhancing the U.S. position. Preservation of the uniquely American way of life requires that other free societies exist for a mutual reinforcement of the democratic ideal. Prevention of the dominance of opposition perspectives becomes an important interest.

There is a broad affinity between the U.S. and Israel. There is in the United States a widespread fund of goodwill toward Israel not restricted to the Jewish community that favored the establishment and consolidation of a Jewish state in Palestine and the continued existence, integrity, and security of Israel. Israel is perceived to be a progressive state with a similar outlook to that of the United States and an example of the type of state the United States would like to see exist all over the world.[53] There is an element of cultural identity which leads to the view that Israel is a ''Western'' state in a sea of feudal, oriental states and is a perpetuator of the Judeo-Christian heritage. It is seen as a free, open, and democratic society—a ''showplace of democracy''—pursuing peace. Israel is perceived as a brave, valiant, gallant, and young state, providing a model of courage and tenacity. Its people are praised for their sacrifice, mettle, industriousness, dedication, determination, and spirit. As a result Israel is seen as having achieved substantial progress and development and as worthy of emulation. There is a historical affinity and similarity of national experience, which includes the immigrant and pioneering nature of the two states and their respective commitments to republicanism and democracy.

There is a religious factor. Some perceive Israel as fulfilling the biblical prophecy that the Jews would return to the promised land. This perception, nurtured in America's Bible-belt fundamentalist Christian areas, is further reinforced by ''Sunday-school stories'' linking the Jews to the Holy Land. In response to the Holocaust and the destruction of large segments of world Jewry in Europe during World War II, there appears to be a ''guilt'' element that Israel's existence helps to assuage. There is a response to the historical persecution of the Jews and the effort to provide for the saving of the remnant of world Jewry through the maintenance of a sanctuary.

This maintenance of a refuge for a persecuted people also helps relieve feelings of guilt associated with traditional Western anti-Semitism and thus provides for a form of atonement. There is also a feeling of moral responsibility for the preservation of Israel because of the American effort that helped to establish the state. Often there is reference to the "natural" ties that have linked these two states, although there is little precision as to what these actually are. There is the sympathy for Israel that derives from the American concern for the weak against the strong (the "underdog" sympathy factor), the moral against the immoral, and the democratic against the less democratic.

Israel is seen as a like-image state whose survival is crucial to the ideological prospering of the United States. This perspective goes beyond the more general concern for all similar states to one associated particularly with Israel:

> "It is unthinkable that the international community could stand idly by, in the atmosphere of Duerrenmatt's terrible vision in *The Visit*, if Israel were in danger of destruction. The moral and political convulsion which such an event would engender is beyond calculation. It could spell the end not only of the Atlantic alliance, but of liberal civilization as we know it." [54]

The ideological interest is buttressed by the political-security interest which regards Israel as a strategic asset. Israel is seen as militarily the most powerful state in the region and as a reliable ally. Former Undersecretary of State Eugene V. Rostow has suggested that "Israel is the only sure access point we have between Western Europe and our partners in the Far East, Australia, New Zealand, Korea and Japan." [55] Admiral Elmo Zumwalt has appraised the military value of Israel to the United States in these terms:

> "Israel's military value to the United States derives not only from its location adjacent to the oil-rich Persian Gulf region, at the junction of three continents, but also from the sophistication and prodigious efficiency of its defense forces. More important than either of these factors, however, is the reliability of the state of Israel as a comrade-in-arms on behalf of the essential interests of the Western world—interests which inevitably harmonize with those

of the Jewish state as a result of the latter's dedication to the principles of democratic government." [56]

Rostow has argued the U.S. interest in Israel in these terms:

"the American and the NATO interest in Israel is of critical importance. It has two aspects. . . . The first is the historical responsibility we share with other nations for the existence of Israel. Israel came into being in reliance on the solemn promises of the world communityt . . . It is morally and politically unthinkable that the U.S. and its allies, and many other nations as well, could stand by and allow Israel to be destroyed. . . . The second aspect of our national and NATO interest in the fate of Israel is the use the Soviet have made of the Arab-Israeli conflict in their programs for gaining control of Western Europe . . . our common interests in the entire region cannot be safeguarded without an Arab-Israeli peace." [57]

Israel has also served as a limiting factor in the efforts of the more radical elements in the Arab world and has thus worked in accord with U.S. efforts to limit destabilizing actions in the region. During the Jordanian civil war (1970) Israeli actions helped reduce the scope of Syrian intervention and during the Lebanese civil war (1975-1977) Israel's position controlled the extent of Syrian activity. In the 1960s Israel reduced the ability of Egypt to pursue Nasser's efforts in the Arabian Peninsula and the Persian Gulf, and this limitation was understood in Iran and Saudi Arabia.

Some have argued the possibility of U.S. military bases in, and logistical support provided by, Israel and that such support facilities might be useful for action against the Soviet Union. Some have suggested that Israel can defend the oil wealth of the region. In the event of an oil embargo or related difficulty (which would threaten the United States and/or its allies in Europe and Japan), Israel is seen as a significant asset in an effort to launch a military action against the oil fields and the producing states.

There is a more direct American concern with the Arab-Israeli conflict and Israel's survival. Israel's fall would most likely increase Soviet prestige and influence. It would further weaken those moderate Arab states, such as Jordan and Saudi Arabia, whose overthrow has been a stated goal of various opposition groups within the Arab world and who would no longer be diverted from their aim by preoccupation with Israel.[58] It would probably facilitate Arab radical pressures which have been destabilizing factors in the Persian Gulf. These achievements would, in turn, negatively affect U.S. ability and effort to maintain regional stability and peace, American economic interests, and the flow of oil to the West. Israel's existence, as a democratic, energetic, and progressive force, thus tends to strengthen other states and regimes whose survival is important to the United States.

It has been suggested that the peace, stability, and security of the Middle East, and American interests in that region, can best be preserved by a strong Israel supported by U.S. arms supply and financial assistance. It was argued, especially after the 1967 war, that support of Israel helped to deter Arab aggression that in turn might have led to a larger conflict affecting American interests or involving the United States in a confrontation with the Soviet Union. In this view Israel represents the only solid foothold for the West, and especially for the United States, in the region. It is, after all, a modern and developed state resembling U.S. allies in Western Europe. It has been argued that Israel acts as a proxy for American interests and thus also by proxy as a countervailing factor to the Soviet presence in some of the Arab states (for example, in Egypt between 1967 and 1973 and in Syria in the post-1973 war period). During the Nixon administration, the emphasis was on self-defense and the doctrine that the United States would help nation-states which acted to meet their own security interests and needs. Israel's high-level security and defense capability and its constant stress on its need for American equipment and economic assistance (but not for American soldiers) to provide for its defense became an important element in assuring American support.

There is also an interest in Israel as a credibility element. Israel is perceived by the Arab world and many of the other members of the international community as benefiting from a strong U.S. security commitment. This perception generates expectations. To ensure the credibility of the United States as an ally (an important security interest) the perceived commitment to Israel must be maintained. Continued support for Israel, at a time when U.S. commitments and dependability as an ally are questioned, helps to reassure other American allies and to ensure the credibility of the U.S. role. Any U.S. action that might be interpreted as backing away from the widely identified commitment to Israel would likely affect and undermine the credibility of U.S. commitments, not only to Israel but elsewhere as well. The argument suggests that should the United States "abandon" Israel, the U.S. role in other situations would be open to question. That credibility, already shaken in other world areas, would be dealt a disastrous blow in the case of Israel, for in that instance the world has perceived a special relationship and commitment that goes beyond that which the United States has had with other states.

In sum, the interest in Israel revolves around two distinct, though related, factors of an ideological and a political-strategic nature. There is an interest in maintaining a like-image, democratic and progressive state—a reliable ally which acts as a bulwark against Soviet penetration and domination and Arab radical expansion in the Middle East.

CONFLICTING INTERESTS AND POLICY CHOICES

The United States has substantial interests in the Middle East. Preventing confrontation with the Soviet Union and preventing Soviet regional domination remain salient elements thirty years after the origin of the Cold War. Israel retains its special position because of the values it espouses and the strategic functions it serves, and the United States remains committed to its survival and security. Resolution of the Arab-Israeli conflict—to prevent its generation of superpower conflict, to reduce its adverse economic and military effects, and to allow regional capabilities to be channeled to more positive accomplishments—is a core policy objective. The assurance of the flow of oil from the Gulf and the Peninsula has taken on added significance (because of U.S. and allied needs), as has the financial power of these states which relate to the price of oil and to the vast sums of petrodollars which have been accumulated by its producers and can affect the stability of the world economic order.

These American interests are clearly interrelated and the October War and subsequent developments have demonstrated the interconnection. Since the October War the United States has approached the region in a manner different from the preceding period.

In the wake of the October War the United States emerged as the central extraregional power in the search for peace, with increased interests and concerns in the region. The U.S. based its postwar efforts to achieve a solution of the Arab-Israeli conflict on a combination of improved and increasingly multifaceted relationships with the Arab states and on continued traditional linkages with Israel (which were formalized to a significant degree by the various component parts of the Sinai II agreements). The United States saw improved ties with the Arab states as a logical consequence of its assessment that the expanding relationships would serve numerous purposes: facilitate movement toward an Arab-Israeli settlement, help to depolarize the region and reduce Soviet influence and destabilizing capability, help to improve the energy situation, help to expand opportunities for the export of United States technology and the sale of goods and services, and further other American interests in the region.

In improving this relationship with the Arabs the United States, almost by necessity, reduced the exclusivity which tended to characterize the U.S.-Israel relationship between 1967 and 1973. Although the U.S.-Israeli and U.S.-Arab relationships are not linked together in a zero-sum game relationship (and an improvement in U.S.-Arab relations is not necessarily to Israel's detriment), there is some correlation between improved U.S.-Arab relations and decreasing closeness or exclusivity in the U.S.-Israeli relationship. Generally, there is no inherent contradiction in the United States maintaining sound relations with both Israel and the Arab states and the United States has been able to do so in the past. Since the October War there has been an incremental change in the U.S. role in the region—ties with Israel have not been reduced by virtue of closer links with some Arab states. But, at the same time, the U.S.-Arab relationship was significantly altered. The United States and several Arab states began a process of establishing links that presage a substantial and multifaceted relationship. These ties involved complex economic interrelationships, including technical and economic assistance and agreements on investment and related matters. A zero-sum game relationship does not exist as there is no necessary choice between the sets of alternative interests and they sometimes act in a mutually supportive manner. Dealing with Israel does not automatically exclude the United States from dealings and relations with the Arab world. Trading with Israel does not necessarily exclude companies from trade in the Arab world, since selectivity has been an important factor in the application of the Arab economic boycott.

At the same time there is also the question of choice and a resulting problem of priority.[59] There is no identified method for maximizing all U.S. interests simultaneously. Neither a priority or hierarchy of interests has been identified. Rather it seems that at different times different choices will be made and different foci will prevail.[60]

U.S. interests in the Middle East today are extremely complex and the policies to achieve them are less than precisely formulated, and often contradictory.

The need to accommodate the conflicting nature of U.S. interests remains the major challenge of United States policy in the Middle East today.

NOTES

1. For a more detailed discussion see David H. Finnie, *Pioneers East: The Early American Experience in the Middle East* (Cambridge, Mass.: Harvard University Press, 1967); Robert L. Daniel, *American Philanthropy in the Near East: 1820-1960* (Athens, Ohio: Ohio University Press, 1970): Joseph L. Grabill, *Protestant Diplomacy and the Near East: Missionary Influence on American Policy, 1810-1927* (Minneapolis, Minn.: University of Minnesota Press, 1971); James A. Field, Jr., *America and the Mediterranean World, 1776-1882* (Princeton, N.J.: Princeton University Press, 1969); and Edward Mead Earle, "American Missions in the Near East," *Foreign Affairs* 7 (April 1929): 398-417.

2. To some extent the Persian Gulf area constituted an exception to this general rule. But even in the Persian Gulf region, the United States began its role in an unofficial, nonpolitical, and nonstrategic way. There was trade in commodities such as dates as early as the 1780s, when American commercial interests in Muscat developed the trade in this item. Along with the commercial activity, American missionaries, concentrating on educational and medical endeavors, established important medical centers in such places as Muscat and Oman, Baḥrayn, Kuwait, and Basra by the end of the nineteenth century. American diplomatic contact in the Persian Gulf area was developed as early as 1833, when the United States signed a treaty of amity and commerce with Muscat and by 1838 appointed its first consul (a British merchant) to protect American citizens, businessmen, and missionaries in the area. For further details see Bernard Reich, et. al., *The*

Persian Gulf (McLean, Va.: Research Analysis Corporation, 1971).

3. Indispensable for the period from the beginning of the twentieth century to World War II is John A. DeNovo, *American Interests and Policies in the Middle East 1900-1939* (Minneapolis: The University of Minnesota Press, 1963).

4. For a contemporary assessment of United States oil needs and oil's impact on U.S. Middle East policy in the late 1940s, see Halford L. Hoskins, *Middle East Oil in United States Foreign Policy* (Washington, D.C.: Legislative Reference Service, Library of Congress, 1950. [Public Affairs Bulletin no. 89]).

5. In 1941 President Roosevelt found that the defense of Turkey was vital to the defense of the United States and made possible Lend-Lease aid to Turkey. See *Foreign Relations of the United States*, Diplomatic Papers, 1941, Volume 3, pp. 928-932. In 1942 a similar finding was made with regard to Iran. See *Foreign Relations of the United States, Diplomatic Papers*, 1942, Volume 4, p. 289. This signalled the beginning of U.S. strategic-political interest in these states of the northern tier which developed further in response to the Soviet threat which became apparent following the war.

6. Professor E. A. Speiser of the University of Pennsylvania noted: "The United States has today very significant interests in the Near East. The foreign policy required to maintain them is as yet unformed. It is a fact that the interests in question are too recent to have produced at this early stage a far-sighted policy, at once self-consistent and mature. But the same interests are also too critical to allow much time for experimenting with policy or for entrusting it to hit-or-miss methods." E. A. Speiser, *The United States and the Near East* (Cambridge, Massachusetts: Harvard University Press, 1947), pp. 220-221.

7. *Middle East Journal* 1 (January 1947): 85.

8. In the interwar period there was some interest in the Palestine question and numerous pronouncements in support of a Jewish homeland in Palestine were made by American officials and official American bodies. But no action to implement the statements was forthcoming.

9. For a detailed examination of this U.S. policy in the decade when it was most prominent (the 1950s) see John C. Campbell, *Defense of the Middle East: Problems of American Policy*, Revised Edition (New York: Frederick A. Praeger, 1960).

10. *Department of State Bulletin*, 5 June 1950, p. 886.

11. In May 1953 John Foster Dulles became the first U.S. Secretary of

State to visit the Middle East. On his return he issued a report in which he surveyed the value of the region in these terms: "The area we visited contains about one-fourth of the world's population. It represents about one-half of the people of the world who are still free of Communist domination. The Near East possesses great strategic importance as the bridge between Europe, Asia, and Africa. The present masters of the Kremlin, following the lead of past military conquerors, covet this position. In 1940 Soviet leaders specified, in secret negotiations with the Nazis, that Soviet territorial aspirations center . . . in the direction of the Indian Ocean and . . . the Persian Gulf. This area contains important resources vital to our welfare—oil, manganese, chrome, mica, and other minerals. About 60 percent of the proven oil reserves of the world are in the Near East. Most important of all, the Near East is the source of three great religions—the Jewish, the Christian, and the Moslem—which have for centuries exerted an immense influence throughout the world. Surely we cannot ignore the fate of the peoples who have first received and then passed on to us the great spiritual truths from which our own society derives its inner strength." Report on the Near and Middle East, Secretary of State John Foster Dulles, June 1, 1953, *Department of State Bulletin*, 15 June 1953, pp. 831-35.

12. This theme was expressed by Nixon at the outset of his tenure in office as follows: "I consider it [i.e. the Middle East] a powder keg, very explosive. It needs to be defused. I am open to any suggestions that may cool it off and reduce the possibility of another explosion, because the next explosion in the Mideast, I think, could involve very well a confrontation between the nuclear powers, which we want to avoid." Press conference, 27 January 1969. During a nationally-televised "Conversation with the President" on 1 July 1970 Nixon said: "I think the Middle East now is terribly dangerous. It is like the Balkans before World War I—where the two superpowers, the United States and the Soviet Union, could be drawn into a confrontation that neither of them wants because of the differences there." Henry Kissinger has noted: "Incidentally, I would have to say that if there is the danger of a general war in this Administration, I do not believe, and we do not believe that it will come from Southeast Asia. . . . But it is possible to conceive situations in the Middle East in which a direct confrontation could arise, unintended, maybe, even by the major contestants." Henry Kissinger, Background Briefing, San Clemente, July 1970. See also the speech by Henry Kissinger, "Global Peace, the Middle East, and the United States," 16 September 1975 in Cincinnati, Ohio. Car-

ter's similarly negative views of the Middle East conflict potential are discussed below.

13. George Ball, in a *New York Times Magazine* article, 28 June 1970, argued: ". . . the south and east coasts of the Mediterranean remain critical to Western survival, and a dominant Soviet position throughout the Arab world would threaten our most vital interests—challenging the ancient concept of the Mediterranean as a safe inland sea; shattering NATO's right-flank defenses by threatening the independence of Turkey and Greece; driving Yugoslavia toward Soviet dependency; stirring the huge Communist parties in Italy and France to new activity; isolating Iran, and imperiling the air passage to India and Pakistan. These are only some of the possible consequences. . . ."—pp. 62-63. Eugene Rostow has suggested "Vital security interests of the United States are in peril. . . . The first and most basic is the geopolitical importance of the Middle East to the defense of Europe. Our alliance with Western Europe is absolutely essential to the balance of world power on which the primordial safety of the United States depends. . . . If the Soviet Union were to achieve domination of the Mediterranean, North Africa and the Middle East, it would outflank the NATO defenses in Central Europe, and threaten Europe from its soft underbelly. . . . It has been painfully obvious since October 1973 that hegemonial control of the oil, the space and the mass of the region by the Soviet Union would carry with it dominion over Western Europe as well. NATO would be dismantled." Eugene V. Rostow, "A Basis for Peace: Where Kissinger Went Wrong," *The New Republic* 5 April 1975, pp. 14-15.

14. Former Ambassador John Badeau has argued: "Certainly the most embracing and fundamental objective of the United States is to keep Soviet Russia out of the area. Whether this means Russian military occupation, . . . or some form of alliance . . . or Soviet penetration . . . we are equally resolute in our determination to prevent Russian incursions in the Middle East." John S. Badeau, "The Middle East: Conflict in Priorities," *Foreign Affairs* 36: 232-240 (January 1958), pp. 233-234. Increasingly, however, the United States has recognized that it would be impossible to "expel" the Russians from the region and, therefore, in the post-October War Israel-Egypt and Israel-Syria disengagement efforts it has sought to prevent their upsetting the process while giving then a semblance of "participation" as a face-saving device. In a press conference on 6 June 1974 Kissinger was asked about his earlier (that is, summer 1970) comment on the objective of expelling the Soviet Union from Egypt and what he saw as the

future Soviet role in the region. He responded: "I believe we were talking about expelling Soviet troops from Egypt. Obviously the Soviet Union is a major power with global interests. Obviously, the Middle East is an area of great concern to the Soviet Union. Therefore we have no intention, indeed we have no capability, of expelling Soviet influence from the Middle East." In the aftermath of Sinai II, as increased interest was exhibited in future Soviet roles and participation, the official U.S. position noted the need to involve the Soviet Union in future efforts to achieve a settlement, although the full extent of that participation was not clearly articulated. However, on 1 October 1977, the United States joined the Soviet Union in a statement on the Arab-Israeli problem that brought Soviet leaders back to the forefront of the negotiating process and enhanced their role.

15. For an early postwar official view see Loy W. Henderson, "American Political and Strategic Interests in the Middle East and Southeastern Europe," *Department of State Bulletin*, 23 November 1947, pp. 996-1000.

16.

World Proved Oil Reserves

(1976 Estimate)

	Billion Barrels	Per Cent of Total
Middle East	396	59.3
Saudi Arabia	178	26.6
Kuwait	79	11.8
Iran	64	9.6
Iraq	35	5.2
United Arab Emirates	6	.9
Qatar	31	4.6
Other	3	.4
Africa	65	9.7
Algeria	7	1.0
Libya	26	3.8
Nigeria	20	3.0
Other	12	1.8
North, Central & South America	91	13.6
United States	40	6.0
Western Europe	29	4.3
Asia-Pacific	22	3.3
Communist World	65	9.7
Soviet Union	40	4.0
WORLD TOTAL	668	100.0

Source: International Economic Report of the President, 1977.

17.

World Crude Oil Production
1975-1976

	1975		1976*	
	Thousand Barrels/Day	Per Cent	Thousand Barrels/Day	Per Cent
Middle East	19,590	36.9	21,710	38.3
Saudi Arabia	7.075	13.3	8,585	15.1
Kuwait	2,085	3.9	2,090	3.7
Iran	5,350	10.1	5,850	10.3
Iraq	2,260	4.3	2,075	3.7
Abu Dhabi	1,370	2.6	1,590	2.8
Qatar	440	.8	495	.9
Other	1,010	1.9	1,025	1.8
Africa	4,990	9.4	5,795	10.2
Algeria	960	1.8	990	1.7
Libya	1,480	2.8	1,970	3.5
Nigeria	1,795	3.4	2,055	3.6
Gabon	225	.4	220	.4
Other	530	1.0	560	1.0
North, Central & South America	14,135	26.6	13,805	24.2
United States	8,370	15.8	8,140	14.3
Western Europe	550	1.0	875	1.5
Asia-Pacific	2,215	4.2	2,485	4.4
Communist World	11,650	21.9	12,170	21.4
Soviet Union	9,630	18.1	10,170	17.9
WORLD TOTAL	53,120	100.0	56,840	100.0

* Estimate

Source: International Economic Report of the President, 1977.

18. Office of Assistant Secretary of Defense (Public Affairs), *News Release*, "Remarks Prepared for Delivery by the Honorable Harold Brown, Secretary of Defense, to the Los Angeles World Affairs Council, 20 February 1978," p. 3.

19.

U.S. Trade with Middle East
(Millions of U.S. Dollars)

Country	1974 Exports	1974 Imports	1975 Exports	1975 Imports	1976 Exports	1976 Imports	1977 Exports	1977 Imports
Bahrayn	80	61	90	115	280	33	156	69
Cyprus	20	1	16	2	21	3	19	5
Egypt	455	70	683	33	810	111	828	168
Iran	1734	2132	3242	1579	2776	1631	2181	2599
Iraq	285	1	310	23	382	123	180	337
Israel	1206	282	1551	326	1409	437	1219	493
Jordan	105	—	195	1	234	2	256	3
Kuwait	209	13	366	126	472	41	457	213
Lebanon	287	30	402	35	49	5	93	42
Oman	37	21	75	58	57	251	46	389
Qatar	34	80	50	64	79	133	94	250
Saudi Arabia	835	1671	1502	2987	2774	5847	2868	6026
Syria	40	2	128	7	275	10	116	16
Turkey	463	141	608	155	451	235	385	125
United Arab Emirates	230	366	372	781	425	1532	433	1500
Yemen(San'ā)	11	1	8	—	25	—	40	—
Yemen(Aden)	12	5	3	1	4	1	31	3

Source: International Monetary Fund

20.

U.S. Earnings by Industry
(Millions of Dollars)

	1975 Total	1975 Middle East	1976 Total	1976 Middle East
All Industries	16,434	1,644	18,843	1,920
Mining and Smelting	636	2	861	2
Petroleum	4,746	1,445	5,157	1,641
Manufacturing:				
Total	6,052	15	7,281	4
Food Products	600	1	587	(*)
Chemicals and Allied Products	1,276	−2	1,409	−8
Primary and Fabricated Metals	335	(*)	363	1
Machinery	2,110	10	2,325	8
Transportation Equipment	630	1	1,472	1
Other Manufacturing	1,101	4	1,125	3
Transportation, Communication, and Public Utilities	189	1	148	1
Trade	1,656	10	1,659	19
Finance and Insurance	2,378	45	2,652	60
Other Industries	778	127	1,085	192

(*) Less than $500,000(±)

Source: Survey of Current Business, August 1977

21. The Israel interest is considered in detail below.

22. The previous discussion provided an overview of the main elements of U.S. interests in the region as a whole. Interests and the policies designed to support them are not always regional in scope and nature. Often they are more specifically related to a given zone or sector or even to specific countries of the area. It is important to note that, for purposes of policy formulation and execution, in the post World War II period the concept "Middle East" is too broad. Although U.S. officials—as well as commentators on and critics of U.S. policy—talk of "United States Middle East policy," in practice the unit is smaller. The United States has differentiated between the northern tier and the other parts of the region and has identified divisions and differences in the Arab world. This section focuses on U.S. interests in two main sectors of the region: Persian Gulf/Arabian Peninsula and Arab-Israel. The Persian Gulf zone refers to Iran, Iraq, Kuwait and Saudi Arabia as well as the smaller states of the Gulf which border on that body of water and have a substantial interest in developments there. The Arab-Israel zone consists of Israel and those states contiguous with it (Egypt, Syria, Jordan, Lebanon) as well as Iraq, which have been directly involved in the Arab-Israeli conflict and have participated in one or more of the wars with substantial amounts of troops and equipment. Saudi Arabia has increasingly been involved in the quest for a settlement and has become a significant element in the process.

23. William D. Brewer, "United States Interests in the Persian Gulf," in Princeton University Conference, *Middle East Focus: The Persian Gulf* (Princeton, N.J.: The Princeton University Conference, n.d. [1968]), pp. 177-178.

24. Ibid.

25. Comments by Elston R. Law, Gulf Oil Corp., in ibid., p. 190.

26. Department of State, *Current Policy: Persian Gulf/Arabian Peninsula*, No. 2, June 1975, p. 1.

27. Many of the following are drawn from the statement of Under Secretary of State for Political Affairs Joseph J. Sisco before the House Special Subcommittee on Investigations of the House International Relations Committee on 10 June 1975.

28. It was, after all, King Faysal who had spearheaded the threats to the United States in the spring and summer of 1973 concerning the relationship of oil supply and continued Israeli occupation of Arab territory and who was a major force in the decisions concerning the oil embargo and price increase.

29. Although the Arab oil embargo against the United States was lifted in the spring of 1974, the price of oil continued to be a matter of concern long after. The price increase imperiled the economic and political stability of some U.S. allies. The vast amounts of foreign exchange gravitating toward the Gulf states also seemed to threaten international economic equilibrium and there was concern that this might have increasingly deleterious effects on the United States. Such considerations generated a good deal of discussion in the media of scenarios for military intervention to ensure the flow of oil should the oil-energy situation threaten to "strangle" the United States. In a press conference on 21 November 1973 Secretary of State Kissinger noted "that if [oil embargo/economic] pressures continue unreasonably and indefinitely, that then the United States will have to consider what counter-measures it may have to take." Middle East oil had become an interest worthy of military action in the view of some analysts and officials. President Carter, in a speech entitled "Preserving Our National Security," delivered at Wake Forest University on 16 March 1978, had noted: "The economic health and well-being of the United States, Western Europe, and Japan depend upon continued access to the oil from the Persian Gulf area."

30.

Oil Revenues
(Millions of Dollars)

	1970	1973	1974	1975	1976
Saudi Arabia	1,200	4,340	22,600	25,700	33,500
Kuwait	895	1,900	7,000	7,500	8,500
Iraq	521	1,840	5,700	7,500	8,500
United Arab Emirates*	233	431	5,500	6,000	7,000
Qatar	122	198	1,600	1,700	2,000
Libya	1,295	1,766	6,000	5,100	7,500
Algeria	325	350	3,700	3,400	4,500
TOTAL	4,591	10,825	52,100	58,600	71,500

* Figures prior to 1975 reflect production by only some members of the U.A.E.

Source: *The Middle East: U.S. Policy, Israel, Oil and the Arabs*, Third Edition (Washington, D.C.: Congressional Quarterly, 1977), p. 129.

31.

Monetary Reserves
(Millions of Dollars)

	1970	1972	1973	1974	1975	1976
Algeria	339	493	1,143	1,689	1,353	1,987
Iraq	462	782	1,553	3,273	2,727	4,601
Kuwait	203	363	501	1,397	1,655	1,929
Libya	1,590	2,925	2,127	3,616	2,195	3,206
Saudi Arabia	662	2,500	3,877	14,285	23,319	27,025

Source: *The Middle East: U.S. Policy, Israel, Oil and the Arabs*, Third Edition (Washington, D.C.,: Congressional Quarterly, 1977), p. 138.

32. See Data Management Division, Comptroller, Defense Security Assistance Agency, *Foreign Military Sales and Military Assistance Facts*, December 1977.

33. At least to date Arab investments in the United States, which come primarily from three oil exporters—Saudi Arabia, Kuwait and the United Arab Emirates—,have been cautious and conservative. In general they have been placed in "safe" areas such as certificates of deposit and U.S. government securities.

Financial Placements in the United States
by Arab Oil Exporters
(Millions of Dollars)

	1974	1975	1976	1977	TOTAL
Treasury Bonds, Bills and Notes	2,292	3,301	4,097	3,718	13,408
Other Domestic Bonds	885	1,553	1,179	1,695	5,312
United States Stocks	362	1,649	1,803	1,390	5,204
Commercial Bank Short-and-Long-Term Liabilities	1,927	1,134	1,794	338	5,193
TOTAL	5,466	7,637	8,873	7,141	29,117

Note: The Commerce Department estimates that at the end of 1977 Arab investments in real estate and other direct holdings did not exceed $250 million "at most."

Source: *New York Times*, 15 June 1978.

34. An indication of the economic and political potential of the vast petrodollar reserves is provided by Peter Iseman: "In 1976 the Saudi oil industry . . . earned about $37.8 billion, or just over $100 million a day. At this rate, the Saudis would be able to buy: All stocks listed on U.S. stock exchange (market value) in 26 years, 5 months, 14 days; The *Fortune* 500 companies (total tangible net worth) in 9 years, 8 months, 9 days; All Central Banks gold (including I.M.F.) as of May 1977, at $145/oz., in 4 years, 5 months, 8 days; All taxable real estate in Manhattan in 5 months, 27 days; General Motors in 4 months, 19 days; Bank of America in 2 weeks, 5 days; De Beers Consolidated Diamond Mines in 13 days, 21 hours; C.B.S. in 7 days, 5 hours; All professional football teams in the United States in 4 days, 1 hour; New York Times Corporation in 1 day, 4 hours, 11 minutes; Lehman Bros., Kuhn Loeb (combined capital) in 18 hours, 5 minutes; Tiffany's in 5 hours, 49 minutes; Seattle Slew (estimated syndication value) in 2 hours, 47 minutes; Velasquez' *Juan de Pareja* (the Metropolitan Museum of Art's most expensive acquisition) in 1 hour, 17 minutes."—Peter A. Iseman, "The Arabian Ethos," *Harper's* 256: 37-56 (February 1978), p. 40.

35. *Department of State Bulletin*, 24 April 1972, p. 607.

36. *Department of State Bulletin*, 27 December 1971, p. 748; 27 March 1972, p. 494.

37. *Department of State Bulletin*, 17 December 1973, p. 726.

38. *Department of State Bulletin*, 10 June 1974, p. 644.

39. *Department of State Bulletin*, 8 July 1974, p. 376.

40. The American military presence in the Gulf has been limited to the naval facility in Jufayr leased from the Baḥrayni government in 1971. This provided homeporting facilities for MIDEASTFOR until June 1977 when the agreement ran out. Under a new arrangement, calls by MIDEASTFOR at Baḥrayn will be allowed and some personnel will remain on shore.

41. House of Representatives, Committee on Foreign Affairs, *Hearings, New Perspectives on the Persian Gulf*, Ninety-Third Congress, First Session, p. 39.

42. In many respects the Arab-Israel zone is the most complex with regard to the formulation of U.S. policy, partly because of the difficulty in identifying the interests and determining their priority. Also, events and developments there often impinge upon and affect activities and interests in other zones of the region and beyond.

43. For a full discussion of these efforts see Bernard Reich, "Evolution of United States Policy in the Arab-Israeli Zone," *Middle East Review* 9:

9-18 (Spring 1977) and Bernard Reich, *Quest for Peace: United States-Israel Relations and the Arab-Israeli Conflict* (New Brunswick, N.J.: Transaction Books, 1977).

44. See e.g., Carter's speech at Notre Dame University, 22 May 1977 and also his address to the General Assembly of the United Nations, 4 October 1977.

45. Speech of Vice-President Mondale, 17 June 1977. See also the speech by W. Anthony Lake, Director of the Department of State Policy Planning Staff, 15 December 1977.

46. In response to a question on 3 February 1976 in *Department of State Bulletin*, 23 February 1976, p. 214.

47. Ibid.

48. It is not our purpose here to argue for or against the special role of Israel in U.S. policy but to identify it.

49. For a sampling of the sentiment on this issue see "Appendix—The American Commitment to Israel: Selected Statements," in Bernard Reich, *Quest for Peace*, pp. 457-464.

50. John S. Badeau, "The Middle East: Conflict in Priorities," *Foreign Affairs* 36: 232-240 (January 1958), p. 235. He went on to suggest, however, that Israel was not a priority in the sense that the Arab-Israeli conflict was a barrier to U.S. influence in the area.

51. The Department of State, "Speech: Prospects for Peace in the Middle East," 15 December 1977, p. 3.

52. Much of the following discussion is drawn from Bernard Reich, *Quest for Peace*.

53. The American perception of Israel has been positive and the comparable image of the Arabs has been negative in many instances. These perceptions have been instrumental in the identification of interests and the formulation of policy. The Arabs and their partisans argue that the images are skewed. It is argued that the factors underlying the U.S.-Israeli relationship are incorrectly and superficially perceived and not the result of appropriate, careful, and accurate analysis. In this view U.S. policy is designed to appeal to domestic political interests and is not taken in the national interest of the United States. It is suggested that American interests lie in the Arab world and that American sympathies and emotions, pressured and swayed by the Jewish presence and the Israel-Zionist lobby, move American policy away from its appropriate objectives. The Jewish factor and the Israel-Zionist lobby are thus attributed considerable power in the formulation and execution of American Middle East policy.

54. Eugene V. Rostow, "The American Stake in Israel," *Commentary* 63: 32-46 (April 1977), p. 46. Joseph Alsop has argued the case in these terms: ". . . anyone can foresee at least one sure effect of the destruction of Israel. . . . This would be the automatic release, here in America, of such a flood of guilt and hatred and recrimination as might fatally corrode the whole fabric of our society. Hence I have long believed that we Americans must assure Israel's survival, if only to assure the survival of those American values that I cherish most." Joseph Alsop, "Open Letter to an Israeli Friend," *New York Times Magazine*, 14 December 1975, pp. 16-17.

55. Rostow, *Commentary*, April 1977, p. 37. Joseph Churba has argued: "We [i.e., the United States] must support Israel primarily because it is—and will remain—of paramount strategic value to the security of the United States."—Joseph Churba, *The Politics of Defeat: America's Decline in the Middle East* (New York and London: Cyrco Press, 1977), p. 6. See also p. 29.

56. Elmo Zumwalt in his Preface to *The Politics of Defeat*, p. 4.

57. Eugene V. Rostow, "A Basis for Peace: Where Kissinger Went Wrong," *New Republic*, 5 April 1975, p. 15. "The United States is supporting Israel in order to protect vital national interests of the United States, and of its allies and friends in Europe, the Middle East, and Asia. All would be mortally threatened by Soviet control of the space and the resources of the great arc which extends from Morocco to Iran." Eugene V. Rostow, Address to American Jewish Committee, 28 October 1973, "The Middle East Conflict in Perspective," p. 1.

58. Thus, for example, in a symposium in Washington on 17 May 1978, Major General George F. Keegan, former chief of United States Air Force intelligence argued: "My interest in a strong Israel these past 15 years has been premised primarily on United States interest, because it has been a strong Israeli capability that, in my opinion, has kept the Soviets at bay in the Middle East, and that thus far has prevented the more radical Arab regimes from capturing and seizing Saudi Arabia. . . . Israel has been a powerful stabilizing force." Quoted in *Near East Report*, 14 June 1978, p. 109.

59. Former Senator Fulbright in an address to the Middle East Institute in October 1975 highlighted this problem in the following comment: "The catalogue of our interests is well known and hardly contested: the survival of Israel; access to oil and the friendship of the Arabs; the avoidance of confrontation with the Soviet Union; and the strengthening of the United

Nations as an international peacekeeping agency. What we evidently do not agree upon among ourselves is the priority of these interests and the appropriate means of reconciling them where they conflict. To the Israeli lobby—if I may use the newspaper term—with its extraordinary influence on our politics, the requirements of Israeli security, as judged by the Israelis themselves, are the commanding objective of American policy. In my view—which is a minority view in Congress and the press but which I have a hunch is more widely shared among the people at large—the commanding American interest in the Middle East is access to oil. Our interest in Israel is emotional and ideological: it is in our interests for Israel to survive because we wish Israel to survive. Our interest in Arab oil is a matter of vital economic necessity, tangible and urgent—more urgent indeed than is now recognized by any but a few energy experts."—"The United States and the Middle East: Changing Relationships" The 29th Annual Conference of the Middle East Institute, Washington, D.C., 3-4 October 1975, p. 3. This view is, as Fulbright suggested, a minority position. The overwhelming perspective is that of trying to accommodate diverse interests to achieve the duality of security and ideology which constitutes the core concern.

60. The issues highlighted in this discussion became more apparent in the debate in the U.S. Senate concerning President Carter's proposal of a package deal for the sale of military equipment to Saudi Arabia, Egypt and Israel and efforts by members of the Congress to disapprove of and prevent that sale. Clearly the alternative interpretations of the national interest, and the identification of the best methods and policies to attain even similarly perceived interests, became a matter of debate and disagreement in the Senate debate. That debate provides a case study of the question of competing interests and the problems of identifying priorities. For the text of the full Senate debate see *Congressional Record*, 15 May 1978, pp. S7373-S7446.

The Carter Approach
to the Arab-Israeli Dispute

Steven L. Spiegel

The Carter administration's approach to the Middle East is distinguished by the absence at its highest levels of personalities who knowledgeably present views sympathetic to Israel. Since Jerusalem is seen as a liability rather than an asset in the framework of international affairs, the requirements of domestic American politics and emotional attachment to the "special relationship" with Israel replace any calculation of interests which would stress the utility of a close American-Israeli connection. This paper seeks to explain the decision-making style and the basic premises of administration leaders and how these approaches have been translated into policy during the first two years of Jimmy Carter's occupancy of the White House.

Decision-Making Style and Organization

As the post World War II international system has become increasingly complex. the elite consensus about foreign policy distinctive at the height of the Cold War has disintegrated. In both major parties factional differences have become more acute and ideological disputes have intensified. As the 1976 presidential campaign began, there were four factions in the foreign policy community of the Democratic Party. A first group consisted largely of individuals in middle age with government experience—men with names like Vance, Brzezinski, Warnke, Ball, and Harold Brown. Many had served in the Vietnam years and had grown to reject the decisions and assumptions of the 1960s. Some were afflicted with a sense of guilt over the war; aspiring to reenter government service, many sought to avoid the negative historical judgment pinned on their former superiors by Halberstam in *The Best and the Brightest*.

The magazine *Foreign Affairs* published by the Council on Foreign Relations was generally representative of this group's views; its editor, William P. Bundy, was a former Assistant Secretary of State for Far Eastern Affairs. In substantive foreign policy matters, this group had a tendency to stress North-South, rather than East-West, relations; a generally accommodationist policy toward the third world was exemplified by arguments in favor of redirecting American policy toward Black Africa, understanding of the Organization of Petroleum-Exporting Countries (OPEC), and, in the Middle East, the satisfaction of Palestinian aspirations.

The second group also consisted largely of individuals of middle age, who had had similar experiences in World War II and during the Cold War to their counterparts in the first group. This faction, however, was affected very differently by the events of the 1960s and 1970s—especially by Vietnam and October 1973. Its members included noted names like Jackson, Moynihan, and Norman Podhoretz, editor of *Commentary*—the magazine most representative of its views. These politicians and analysts were in general centrally concerned with the East-West conflict and with the potential threat of Soviet Communism to American interests. They focused on the deprivation of civil and political rights in the third world to a greater degree than on economic rights. They advocated increases in the American defense budget, were suspicious of OPEC, skeptical of the new fascination with third world nationalism, generally ardently supporting of Israel, and either unaffected by Vietnam or not prepared to see the war as an error.

The third group generally consisted of younger advisors, many of whom had associated with the McGovern campaign in 1972—or at least shared the foreign policy ideology of that short-lived political effort. This faction was even more intensely oriented toward the third world than its older counterparts in group one: its major themes included conciliation toward OPEC and third world aspirations, realignment in Africa, amelioration of the Palestinian condition, deemphasis of the Communist threat. The magazine reflective of this group's perspective was *Foreign Policy*, whose editor at the time, Richard Holbrooke, was a member of the Carter campaign entourage and later became Assistant Secretary of State for Far Eastern Affairs.

The fourth group was a hybrid—representing a part of the views of each of the others. *The New Republic* under Martin Peretz was the magazine most representative of its approach. While this faction was sensitive to third world difficulties encompassing both economic and political problems, and intensely concerned about the fate of the blacks in Southern Africa, it was also pro-Israel, suspicious of OPEC, and skeptical of many third world initiatives at the United Nations. Toward the Soviet Union it took a middle-of-the-road stance, concentrating on human rights issues while also sympathetic to arms limitation.

Carter's participation in the Trilateral Commission, his lack of previous foreign policy experience, and the lottery of the presidential primary sweepstakes produced a collection of advisors around the president-elect who represented only the first and third factions. Contrary to the practice of many previous incoming administrations, no move was made to involve party members of every foreign policy perspective. This singularity of purpose was a result of the unique disposition of Jimmy Carter and his entourage and the increased ideological divisions within the Democratic Party after Vietnam. The consequence was that representatives of the second and fourth factions were notable by their absence.

Even after Vietnam, this particular combination of winners and losers was not foreordained. Though Jimmy Carter's victory clearly made the outcome more likely, emphasis on other factors might have produced different results. For example, the first and second factions both contained largely older individuals who had a shared experience of support for Vietnam and past distrust of the Russians. The second two factions were each younger and more directly affected by the Vietnam experience. Once the factional division occurred as it did, however, the criterion of emphasis on North-South rather than East-West issues was bound to be critical for an understanding of administration policy. This combination also assured that the Middle East would be viewed through a particular perspective: emphasizing oil, North-South questions, and Palestinians. It also meant that from the outset the administration included no figure who had a well-developed and knowledgeable view of American interests in the Middle East which included the conception of Israel as a valuable asset to the United States.

If the new president had been previously exposed to the issue on a practical political basis (for example, if he had served in Congress), he might have come to understand the differences in views existing in the country on Arab-Israeli matters and he might as a consequence have been careful to include individuals of alternate perspectives in his entourage as previous presidents had done. But Carter seems not even to have understood that a difference of views existed among experts and knowledgeable observers. Rather, he seems to have seen the pro-Israeli perspective as primarily political and emotional.

Thus the prevailing assumptions and perspectives developed by the Democratic Party factions which assumed power in January 1977 went unchallenged. Though genuine supporters of Israel, the two highest ranking Jews in the White House—Counsel Robert Lipschutz and Domestic Council Chief Stuart Eizenstadt—both had positions of weighty responsibility in their own right in areas of domestic concern, no foreign policy experience, and little prior connection with established leaders of the Democratic pro-Israeli coalition (e.g., Congressmen, labor officials, Jewish leaders). The vice-president, though noted for his pro-Israeli views in the Senate, occupied a position of weakness since American history is replete with the defeat in political battles of those who have relied on this office. Because the pro-Israeli perspective was seen in political terms and some high administration officials recognized that Middle East policy could cause political fallout, Hamilton Jordan—the President's most trusted lieutenant—became engaged. However, Jordan did not have the background to deal with foreign policy; only the skill to develop means of selling particular policies (including those opposed by partisans of Israel) and to discern when positions should be moderated in order to present them more effectively. Thus, no one in the administration was capable of intellectually countering assumptions about Israel and the Middle East prevailing in the White House and throughout the Washington bureaucracy.

After much public criticism from friends of Israel, Carter did add to his staff in the summer of 1978 Edward Sanders—a Los Angeles attorney and an active national Jewish leader—as a senior advisor on Middle East affairs. Though Sanders did take positions on the Arab-Israeli dispute which were distinct from the Carter foreign policy team, he was hindered by his relative isolation and the general perception of him both inside and outside the White House as a political rather than a policy-oriented official.

This array of forces within the administration is ironic in the light of Zbigniew Brzezinski's comments in the summer of 1976. when he argued that the WASP (White, Anglo-Saxon, Protestant) foreign policy establishment had been replaced after Vietnam.

"Perhaps the most successful ethnic group—replacing the displaced WASP—was now the Jewish (ably represented in key [Nixon] Administration posts), but the dominant pattern was one of greater fluidity and heterogeneity." [1]

Nowhere is the monolithic process by which the administration operates toward the Arab-Israeli dispute clearer than in its decisions on the joint Soviet-American statement of October 1977 and the Middle East arms package of the spring of 1978. It is generally acknowledged that the decision to conclude the statement was reached after the involvement of a very small number of officials, centered around the president, the secretary of state and the national security advisor. Therefore, criticism and cross-examination were not possible. In evaluating their own performance on the issue, high officials concluded that the reason the political firestorm erupted at home was not that the policy was incorrect or based on false assumptions but rather that key officials had failed to consult beforehand with American Jewish leaders, key Congressmen, and even some of its own members. As a consequence, Hamilton Jordan's role in foreign policy formulation was elevated, but the basic approach of the administration was left unaltered.

The effect of the changes which were instituted was to broaden involvement and consultation with outsiders and the new system was applied in the case of the Middle East arms package. But the alterations were merely cosmetic. The decision percolated through Washington for weeks before it was announced instead of being introduced as a shock and opponents outside the administration were "consulted" (that is, they were warned politely). But within the administration, the arguments revolved around numbers, not objectives. The Arms Control and Disarmament Agency opposed the sale of planes to Saudi Arabia and Egypt, but it was also against the sales to Israel. In addition, the Division of Program, Analysis and Evaluation, Office of the Secretary of Defense, is reported to have opposed the sales to Saudi Arabia. No agency or individual argued the case advocated by Israel's friends against F-15s to Saudi Arabia and F-5Es for Egypt and in favor of the full complement of

F-15s and F-16s requested by Israel.

Tragically, the administration did not even recognize the weaknesses of its own decision-making apparatus. As one journalist reported shortly after the announcement,

"... Administration officials argue that the process for reaching their decision over the sales embodied the best features of the Administration's open, collegial and sometimes chaotic approach to policy-making—the effort to expose Mr. Carter to a wide range of departmental views. As such the decision is said to offer a revealing example of how the Administration's loosely structured mode of doing business differs from that of the Nixon-Ford period, when decisions were made in a much more rigid and hierarchical framework." [2]

Pro-Israeli sympathizers in the United States have traditionally had great difficulty in gaining representation in the decision-making process. They could always count on a broad coalition outside the Executive Branch—including American Jewry, Congress, the Labor movement, Democratic and Republican party officials, some key Christian leaders. But most segments of the national security apparatus have usually been unfriendly. There have been exceptions—especially in the Pentagon between 1967 and 1973—but generally Israel and her American backers have had to depend on the president and the members of his own entourage (as a rule that meant the White House staff) to provide the input of their own policy views. In most presidencies this system has produced inconsistent policies, but a broad representation of differing perspectives. Under Truman key officials such as David Niles, General John H. Hilldring, and Clark Clifford did side with the Zionist cause against the State Department and its allies in the military and intelligence communities. Kennedy consciously placed pro-Arab and pro-Israeli figures on his dynamic White House staff, while under Johnson the plethora of Israeli sympathizers assured that Jerusalem's voice would be amply heard. In Nixon's first term the competition between Kissinger and Rogers insured a diversity of views, while after October 1973 both Arabs and Israelis had access to Henry Kissinger, but both were dependent on the preferences and insecurities of this highly complex personality.

Since the establishment of the State of Israel, only under

Eisenhower did a monolithic foreign policy system emerge in which there was no key figure who saw Israel in terms favorable to American interests. Like Eisenhower, Carter had a background in the military and many close associates in business circles skeptical of Israel's utility (for Carter it is the Trilateral Commission) and, like the former president, the current occupant of the Oval Office was not previously a member of Congress. But unlike his Republican predecessor, Carter sees himself as sympathetic to Israel and is dependent on Jewish votes. In addition, it was easier for a pro-Israeli figure to be excluded in the Eisenhower administration because of the dominance of Secretary of State John Foster Dulles in the foreign policy process. As is typical of the Democratic Party, under Carter foreign policy formulation is more collegial—with the accompanying participation of a variety of individuals and agencies.

How, then, can we explain the absence of even one major influential pro-Israeli figure? Unlike any previous administration the Middle East is *the key* foreign policy issue to the Carter team. The president has been prepared to devote more time to this matter than to any other single problem confronting him. As Hamilton Jordan stated in a news broadcast interview, ''There's not a single issue, domestic or foreign policy, that the president has spent more of his time and energy and resources on than his quest to bring peace to the Middle East.'' [3] On secondary issues there can be room for diversity, but it is incomparably more difficult to accept differences of view on any issue in which the president is so personally identified and engaged. Therefore, the best previous analogy in American experience to Carter's Arab-Israeli policy is not Eisenhower on the Middle East, and it is important instead to investigate previous issues which have seemed central to individual presidents.

Such an examination indicates the presence of a ''rigidity syndrome'' in the conduct of American foreign policy. To Truman it was the Soviet Union; to Eisenhower, it was China; to Kennedy, Cuba; to Johnson, Vietnam; and to Nixon, Cambodia. Each of these questions had become critical in the latter period of the previous administration and received great concentration once the new team assumed office. The issue then became a sign of loyalty to the new president—no dissent or debate could be allowed (or so it was mistakenly thought). Not surprisingly, individuals differing with the president on these questions have consistently been fired or resigned or transferred (e.g., Henry Wallace under Truman, the State Department's "old China hands" under Eisenhower; Chester Bowles under Kennedy; a variety of officials under Johnson of whom Robert McNamara was the most prominent; a variety of younger National Security Council (N.S.C.) officials under Nixon over Cambodia). Thus, under Carter, Mark Siegel—Hamilton Jordan's political aide and liaison with the Jews—became the first high official of the Carter administration to resign and the first official ever to resign over policy toward Israel. Press comments suggested that Siegel's disagreement with policy could not allow him to continue, but that was a new development distinctive of the Carter entourage. The Johnson and Nixon administrations—much less permissive of dissent—had allowed fundamental differences on the Middle East. Reflecting differing views within American society and government, disagreements over Arab-Israeli policy had been traditional. But, then, those presidents were not preoccupied with the issue and it was not central to their conduct of United States foreign policy.

In this sense the Johnson experience is particularly instructive, for the key officials who now dominate the American government are not only veterans of Vietnam, but their party and their own personal lives have been seared by the experience. Like Johnson's policy in Vietnam, the administration's approach to the Middle East presents a single-mindedness borne of a false sense of moral rectitude, an inadequate understanding of the history of the area, an absence of sensitivity to the social and political concerns at home over the issue and—most important—an overriding unanimity which prevents that level of discordancy which produces refined policies.

It is almost as if the Young Turks and the Old Guard of the Vietnam era have united to erase the memory of America's blemished foreign record by producing a peace in the Holy Land. In so doing, however, they are pursuing by opposite means similar objectives to the policies of their former superiors a decade earlier. As in the case of Lyndon Johnson, a Southern president, inexperienced in foreign affairs, preoccupied with an overriding issue, possessed of misplaced moral fervor, and handicapped by broken campaign promises, seeks to apply the vision of a unanimous bureaucracy and his own entourage to the affairs of foreign peoples and cultures. It seems hardly to have dawned on official Washington that Brzezinski and Vance are not Kissinger and Rogers but Walt Rostow and Dean Rusk committed ideologically and stubbornly to a highly specific policy approach. The perils of rigidity, of over-concentration on a single issue, of mesmerization with self-conceived political martyrdom are all present in the early developments of Carter Middle East policy. But it is the preoccupation with the Middle East which explains how a diversified foreign policy process can produce singular result and why the administration seems to defy conventional rules on how Middle East policy is pursued.

Premises

Not surprisingly, therefore, the premises, as well as the personalities, are monolithic. Much speculation has occurred, especially in American Jewish circles, on the supposed responsibility of National Security Advisor Zbigniew Brzezinski for the thrust of Carter policy. But this analysis misses the point that in a highly collegial administration there are no dissenters from the primary focus of American Middle East policy. Indeed, since there is less disagreement over Arab-Israeli issues than over other primary foreign policy questions confronting the Carter foreign policy team, the consensus on this problem reinforces the sense within the team that its policy is correct and therefore encourages its determination to withstand domestic pressure. The origins of this unity lie in the fundamental premises of the two factions which populate the administration, and although there are basic tactical differences with Henry Kissinger, the conclusions are not distinct. Affected by the shocks of Vietnam and October 1973, both Kissinger and the Democratic critics who rose to high office agree in their pessimistic belief in the limitation of American power and in its need to adjust to the new forces developing in world politics. Kissinger, by comparison with his successors, concentrated on the Russians more and on third world forces less, but all shared a deep-seated fear on another oil embargo, a fascination with the increase in Saudi power, and the opinion that the future in the Middle East lies with the Arabs.

To Kissinger, however, the key state in the Middle East was Egypt and the central problem facing American policy in the area was to block the Russians from a major role. To Brzezinski and his comrades, on the other hand, the key state in the area is Saudi

Arabia and the central problem, energy. Israel had a role to play in Kissinger's approach, but is of little value to the United States in Brzezinski's.

Prominent Democrats in the two winning factions have written a great deal about the Arab-Israeli dispute and how to solve it, and they have thereby made little secret of their views. The result is a doctrine which in its broad outlines has become the intellectual basis of the current American approach. Labeled by former Under Secretary of State George Ball "How to Save Israel in Spite of Herself," the doctrine proposed that because its proponents were friendly toward Israel they understood better than the Israelis and their supporters themselves what was best for the Jewish State. In one form or another these analysts argued that it is right for Israel to return to the 1967 borders because (1) the Arab confrontation states are ready for peace; (2) the Palestinians deserve a homeland; and (3) a smaller Israel would ensure Middle East stability. Basic to their approach was the conviction that Israel could not have both territory and peace. Many argued that Israel must be pressured to return to the 1967 boundaries because if there were to be no settlement the Arab moderates would lose control, thereby diminishing American influence and/or opening the door to Russian reemergence; the Arabs would start another war and/or there would be another oil embargo. Those who maintained these views argued paradoxically, then, that Israel's interests (and, conveniently America's as well) could be simultaneously secured by taking actions the Arabs favored.[4]

Many observers have claimed that the Brookings Institution report on the Middle East published in December 1975 was the intellectual basis of Carter policy, but the report is primarily important because three of its members received high posts in the Administration: National Security Advisor Zbigniew Brzezinski; his Middle East advisor, William Quandt; and Deputy for National Intelligence at the Central Intelligence Agency (C.I.A.), Robert Bowie.[5]

The report itself is much vaguer on key issues than most newspaper readers realize because of the critically differing views of the participants. It broke significant new ground by stressing a comprehensive approach as opposed to Kissinger's step by step, by emphasizing the importance of normalization of relations as part of a settlement, and by citing the importance of phased territorial withdrawals. Because of its studied ambiguity, however, the importance of the report for later policy depended entirely on the people who were charged with implementing ideas that had been developed between October 1973 and November 1976. One can imagine, for example, policies distinctly more pro-Arab or more pro-Israeli than Carter's being implemented by different members of the Brookings team. As further evidence for this point, I would suggest that three months before the Brookings group met for the first time Brzezinski had already published an article in which he urged the United States to "spell out openly" its conception of a settlement. And what were the "principal components" of such a settlement on which Brzezinski saw a "world-wide consensus"?

"Recognition of Israel's sovereignty by all parties, and peace treaties establishing normal relations; creation of a demilitarized Palestinian state; reinforcement of frontiers, based largely on those existing in 1967, by security zones: retention of United Jerusalem but with two capitals in one and a U.S. guarantee for the above."[6]

In his articles in 1974 and 1975 Brzezinski wrote concerning other aspects of his conception of Middle East policy which would become more familiar once Carter rose to power. His conclusions included an emphasis on American leverage on Israel; the "decoupling" of security from the possession of land; "minor modifications" in the 1967 West Bank-Israeli border and total Israeli withdrawals from the Sinai and the Golan; a redefinition of the phrase, "legitimate rights of the Palestinian people." Brzezinski had other ideas. In 1975 he coauthored an article in which it was admitted that a Palestinian state would "probably" be Palestine Liberation Organization (P.L.O.)-dominated, but that this state would be "inextricably bound" to Israel. In an optimistic statement bordering on messianism he argued, "The relations with a neighbor formidable in economic development as well as in conflict would generate powerful Palestinian opinion in favor of cooperation." He also hinted that Israel alone should not be allowed to choose the Palestinians with whom to negotiate and he argued that the Israelis should speak to the P.L.O.[7]

In his writing on the Middle East Brzezinski frequently stressed the issue of guarantees as an integral element in the peace process. In 1974 he argued that Israel would receive a U.S. guarantee for her concessions even though "In effect, Israel already enjoys such a guarantee. In fact, without it the Jewish State would have foundered long ago."[8] (Of course, if the guarantee already existed Israel was not helped much by receiving it in return for territorial concessions.)

By 1975 he had added the concept of a Soviet-American guarantee, in an idea which would later be specifically reflected in the U.S.-U.S.S.R. statement two years later. Now he favored the ensnaring of the Russians in the process lest they be placed outside the diplomatic framework, support the Arab rejectionists, and obstruct a resolution of the conflict. As part of this approach, he advocated Soviet and American "participation in an international force patrolling safety zones on either sides of the agreed frontiers." Brzezinski proceeded to suggest,

> "Conceivably, . . . the United States and the Soviet Union might together negotiate a statement in which they would announce their willingness to provide a joint guarantee for the 1967 frontiers, while leaving the question of devising a scheme for Israeli and Arab presence in an otherwise united Jerusalem to be negotiated separately. Such a joint declaration would put great pressure on the Arabs and Israelis, especially if it were then endorsed by Western Europe and Japan. This might not have immediate effect on Israeli policy, and Israel would no doubt do all it could through the U.S. Congress to change that policy, but a public U.S. posture in favor of such a settlement would exert powerful influence and would probably gain both domestic and international support."[9]

Finally, Brzezinski, like many others in the administration, has repeatedly linked the energy and Arab-Israeli problems.

> "It is impossible to seek a resolution to the energy problem without tackling head-on—and doing so in an urgent fashion—the Arab-Israeli conflict. Without a settlement of that issue in the near future, any stable arrangement in the energy area is simply not possible."[10]

This linkage of the Arab-Israeli and energy questions means that Saudi Arabia must necessarily be central to any analysis of the administration's approach to the area. Were Saudi Arabia to fall to a Saudi Qadhdhāfī, the economic future of the West could be severely jeopardized. But if the current Saudi leaders were to turn against the

United States by raising prices and/or lowering production in the years ahead, the consequences could also be lethal for the West. Therefore, America must not act in a manner which will lead the Saudis to question their trust in the United States or lead other Arabs to question Saudi policies.

Though Brzezinski does not spell out the consequences of his recommendations, a number of corollaries do result logically. The United States can no longer afford to ignore the radical Arabs, because it must be assumed that they possess the power to ruin the structure of American economic and political power in the area. Hence, for example, Asad should be preferred over Sādāt. A further corollary is an inter-Arab domino theory: any accretion of radical power is a potential threat to the conservatives (that is, the Saudis). This type of thinking produces utter fear of the Arab radicals, but no fear of Israeli hawks who are seen as interfering with progress toward a settlement which will "create the kind of confidence on which the resolution of some of the monetary problems with the oil producers depends."[11] Israeli hawks must, therefore, be viewed with contempt. Brzezinski thought in early 1975 that the "West" might soon have to express its own views about a settlement.

> "Otherwise, there is a very real danger that protracted Arab-Israeli negotiations might snag, that domestic immobilism in Israel might prevent the Israelis from making the needed concessions, and that Arab radicalism and unreality (not to speak of guerrilla outrages) might inflame the situation. The consequences might be a new war and/or new oil embargoes and production curtailments."[12]

The Carter policy toward the Arab-Israeli dispute is not the policy of the Brookings Institution but it is the policy of Brzezinski and Quandt and Secretary of State Vance and Ambassador to the United Nations Andrew Young and Carter himself. Though details of the policy have altered in response to events, the basic *Weltanschauung* has remained and it has been an ambiance in which Jimmy Carter—the engineer and the moralist, the pragmatist and the preacher—could feel at home.

Since Carter was previously a little known former Georgia governor when the campaign began, the only means of predicting his Middle East policy were his campaign statements. In a major address in Elizabeth, New Jersey, on 6 June 1976, he stated,

"Now this change of attitude on the part of Arab states must be reflected in tangible and concrete actions including first of all, the recognition of Israel, which they have not yet done; secondly, diplomatic relations with Israel; third, a peace treaty with Israel; fourth, open frontiers with Israel's neighbors; lastly an end to the embargo and official hostile propaganda against the State of Israel. . . . Final borders between Israel and her neighbors should be determined in direct negotiations between the parties, and they should not be imposed from the outside."[13]

On the Palestinians he was also quite explicit:

"There ought to be territories ceded for the use of the Palestinians. I think they should be part of Jordan and be administered by Jordan. I think half the people in Jordan are Palestinians themselves. And that would be my own preference."[14]

Israel's friends could not have been more pleased with his position on foreign aid, when he claimed, for example, that

"We must supply Israel unequivocally and in the full amount necessary, economic and military aid so Israel can pursue peace from a position of strength and be protected against any foreseeable attack."[15]

On arms Carter also had distinct ideas. Towards the Egyptians he suggested

"It would not be wise at this time to supply strike weapons to Egypt, despite that nation's recent signs of friendship for the United States. With its vast population and deep poverty, Egypt needs housing and jobs and health care far more than offensive weapons such as tanks and planes and missiles."[16]

Towards the then-current debate over the sale of Maverick missiles to Saudi Arabia the candidate also had, it seemed, well-developed notions. "No administration which was sensitive to the climate in the Middle East would let the sale go forward."[17]

However, there was another and less noted side to Carter's statements, a point of view which he seems to have discarded as the campaign became more heated and more attention was paid to him. For example, as late as 8 May 1976, he was stunningly honest about what he intended to do as president:

Regarding the Soviet role, he suggested

"It may be that sometime in the future, after unpublicized negotiations between us and the Soviet Union, we
might jointly make a public proposal of a solution to the
Middle East. ... The Soviet Union is going to have to
participate in a forceful way before Syria will be amenable to any productive negotiations with Israel."[18]

We have here already a glimpse of strategies which would be present in the Soviet-American communiqué of 1 October 1977 and the
early fascination with Syria present from the outset of the administration. Regarding the Palestinians, he argued that

"Ultimately the legitimate interests of the Palestinians
are going to have to be recognized. I would not negotiate
with the P.L.O., nor would I try to force Israel to do
that, until I was convinced that the Palestinians do recognize Israel's right to exist in peace in the Middle East.
After that, negotiations could proceed to meet the needs
of the Palestinians."[19]

Carter does not clarify here how he would be convinced of the
P.L.O.'s genuineness nor does he mention the criteria established
by the September 1975 understanding between the United States and
Israel (P.L.O. recognition of Resolutions 242 and 338, and of
Israel's right to exist).

The doctrine of the Democratic foreign policy community enabled
the relatively inexperienced new president to square the circle inherent in his own confused and contradictory view of the Middle East.
Carter saw himself as emotionally committed to Israel (in part for
religious reasons) and he was fully capable of convincing others of
the genuineness and sincerity of his concerns as when he confronted
fifty-odd Jewish leaders at the White House in early July 1977 or
when he suggested he would rather commit suicide than harm Israel
in a meeting with Congressmen after the Soviet-American communiqué in early October. But he was also fascinated with the Middle East and prepared to spend a greater percentage of his time on
the issue than any previous president. Yet, his lack of expertise on
the subject was glaring. Though he had traveled to Israel in the
spring of 1973 while still governor, he had never met an Arab pri-
vately until he occupied the Oval Office.

This type of president was a prime candidate for the blandishments and briefings of experts and bureaucrats, all the more so because they had developed a concept which argued that by suffering on the political cross for Israel Carter was saving her from herself. Yet, inherent in the experts' briefings is a means for Carter to be reborn politically, even though he is taking terrible risks in the domestic arena. By achieving an Arab-Israeli peace his pro-Israeli opponents will recognize the correctness of his approach. Chastened, they will return to his support. No less than a peace settlement is the answer to Carter's gamble and it explains the extraordinary time and effort his administration is prepared to devote to its cause. In the immediate aftermath of the Camp David summit meeting in September 1978 it appeared to some observers that the Carter administration's calculus at home and abroad had been correct after all, but the underlying basic emphasis on comprehensiveness and Israeli concessions soon reemerged. The players in Washington had not changed and neither had the policy.

The Policy

Given the monolithic decision-making style of the administration and its unified consensus on basic premises, it follows that its policy toward the Arab-Israeli dispute has been both consistent and in a direction not favored by Israel's supporters. For all the apparent meandering and frequent clarifications at news conferences, Carter and his advisors have coherently followed the premises that they carried with them upon entering the White House.

This consistency can be seen in relation to the sense of urgency; the emphasis on the Saudis; the stress on the role of the radicals and the Soviet Union and the preoccupation with the Palestinian question; the exercise of leverage and the perceived need for major territorial compromises by Israel.

Urgency—Not only did the Carter administration assume office with a profound sense of moral superiority and optimism, but its definition of the need to solve the energy question and the linkage of that problem to the Arab-Israeli dispute demanded that attempts be made to solve the conflict immediately. Each new administration since the birth of Israel has tried to undertake some initiative, even if limited, to solve the problem. Impatience and an American penchant for beginning history anew every four years often created mini-crises with the government in Jerusalem. But only Carter saw the issue as the top foreign policy priority.

Conveniently, an Arab-Israeli settlement was seen as possible because of the perceived moderation by all the confrontation states and Israel. Even President Asad has on occasion been labeled by Carter as a "strong supporter in the search for peace." This belief that the Arabs would indeed be prepared to accept a normalization of relations as part of any settlement explains why Carter became the first president to endorse the Israeli claim to a genuine peace rather than a mere arrangement of non-belligerency. As its behavior after Camp David verifies, the administration believes, however, that Israel can only earn normalization with major concessions.

The sense of urgency demanded more than confidence in Arab moderation and it explains Secretary of State Vance's four visits to the area in the first year of the administration; the early and frequent summits in Washington; the repeated presidential statements about territories and Palestinians as well as normalization; the preoccupation in the fall of 1977 with reconvening the Geneva Conference by the end of the year; the constant fear that Sādāt might soon withdraw his peace initiative; the convening of the Camp David summit and the concern over the linkage issue in its aftermath.

The Saudis—An Arab-Israeli settlement was stressed, however, to gain the confidence of the Saudis in American leadership and to maintain, by extension, Arab confidence in what Washington perceived as a growing primary Saudi role in the Arab world. For example, American officials drew lessons from the Lebanese Civil War which were distinct from the conclusions drawn by many of Israel's supporters. The latter now stressed that the P.L.O. was on the wane, but the administration emphasized that Saudi Arabia's key function in bringing the major conflicting Arab parties together in October 1976 demonstrated that Riyād was capable of exercising leadership and constituting a stabilizing influence. The Saudi role in moving Somalia away from the Russians reinforced this stabilizing image. But the crucial significance of this most conservative of Arab monarchies was increased manifold by its perceived function as international banker, oil price regulator, and the world's most critical oil producer.

Thus, on his visit in May Prince Fahd was given a royal welcome, Carter commenting that "so far as I know, between ourselves and Saudi Arabia, there are no disturbing differences at all." Apparently, human rights would have to take a back seat to *Realpolitik*. Thus, the private Saudi claim that they sought a Palestinian state on the West Bank and Gaza Strip was followed up seriously and a flirtation with the P.L.O. undertaken. Thus, Saudi Arabia was the only Arab state included on Carter's original itinerary to the Middle East at the outset of 1978 without even a pretense made of the need to balance the visit with stopovers in other Arab states or Israel. Thus, Sādāt's visit to Jerusalem was at first received cautiously in Washington until the Saudi reaction could be ascertained. At the same time the administration refused to insist on a public Saudi statement of support for Sādāt's initiatives. Instead, the Saudis were promised personally by the president that they would receive F-15 jets and the announcement was made at a delicate point of Egyptian-Israeli negotiations and despite widespread controversy at home because the Saudi government claimed it would judge American willingness to sell the planes as a litmus test of its "special relationship" with the U.S. Thus, the president was prepared to confront Israel's supporters on Capitol Hill and to fight fiercely and vigorously for the acceptance of his Middle East arms package to Saudi Arabia, Egypt, and Israel. Thus, the administration responded cautiously and mildly when Saudi Arabia sought in the interests of Arab unity to wean Sādāt away from his peace initiative in the summer of 1978 and when it reacted negatively to Camp David and joined the Arab radicals at an anti-Sādāt, anti-Camp David summit in Baghdad in early November 1978.

The Radicals—The administration initially stressed Geneva, comprehensiveness, Arab unity, the Palestinians, and even a Russian role in the peace process because it sought an Arab world organized under Saudi leadership as a means of assuring the stability of inter-Arab politics and of oil and monetary flows. This objective meant that a peace settlement would have to be as comprehensive as possible so that no party conceivably involved in the area would have an incentive to undermine the proposed settlement. (Perhaps only Libya, Iraq, and the Palestinian rejectionists would have to be left out in the end.) Comprehensiveness at first meant a "Syrianized" American policy for it was Asad who was the key Arab leader with ties to both moderates and radical camps. This objective also demanded the involvement of the P.L.O. in some manner at a peace conference in order to assure that the organization would not torpedo an accord. It also demanded that the Kremlin as cochairman of Geneva and as Washington's competitor must be neutralized through involvement. The administration optimistically assumed that if both the P.L.O. and the Russians were involved in the process of reaching a settlement an agreement could be reached and they would accept it and abide by its terms. These calculations explain the Soviet-American communiqué of October 1977, the administration's flirtation with the P.L.O., its emphasis on a Palestinian homeland, and its endorsement of the controversial phrase, "the legitimate rights of the Palestinians."

The Carter administration's preoccupation with comprehensiveness also helps to explain its initial hesitancy over the Sādāt visit, its lack of enthusiasm for Sādāt's Cairo Conference in December 1977, and its continued overtures to Asad to join the new peace process. At first the Sādāt visit raised the specter of several developments which had been feared in Washington: a moderate-radical split in the Arab world with a major threat against the conservatives from the radical forces; a Soviet-American split with an accompanying Kremlin effort to ruin a comprehensive peace; a separate peace between Israel and Egypt, which would have strengthened Israel but might have jeopardized the conservatives led by Saudi Arabia and might have led to a permanent state of conflict and radicalization in the Arab world. Therefore, it is not surprising that American doubts about Sādāt lessened as it became clear that he would not accept a separate peace and that he would insist on a declaration covering Palestinian rights in specific form. Sādāt was rapidly rewarded with the sale of fifty F-5Es, the first offensive weapons offered Egypt since 1955.

With Sādāt's position clarified it was now not only possible for the optimistic prophets in Washington to conceive of reinvolving the Jordanians, but they could also dream about future Syrian and Russian participation as well.[20] As for the P.L.O. American discouragement with 'Arafāt was clear; the administration now favored neutralizing the organization through some formula such as a plebiscite on the West Bank and Gaza five years after a United Nations or joint Jordanian-Israeli trusteeship had been instituted. Of course, if the P.L.O. were to accept Resolution 242, an American reassessment was possible.

At Camp David the basis for fulfilling this modified, comprehensive policy was established. The two frameworks applying to an Egyptian-Israeli treaty on the one hand and to a comprehensive arrangement, including the autonomy plan for the West Bank were not integrally interconnected. After the summit, however, Washington in conjunction with Cairo sought to link them as tightly as possible. On the surface, the second framework was consistent with the "Begin Plan" for political autonomy on the West Bank and Gaza Strip. Many provisions, however, could be interpreted consistently with American designs for a Palestinian entity: the five year transition period; the creation of a freely elected administrative council; the reduced Israeli role in administrative and security terms; the opportunity for the elected representatives of the two areas to approve any plan for the final disposition of the West Bank and Gaza. When the Jordanians, West Bankers, and Saudis reacted negatively to the Camp David accords, the administration's incentive for stressing the linkage of the two frameworks was increased in order to maintain the basis for a comprehensive approach.

Leverage—This *Weltanschauung* demanded the exercise of political, economic, and military leverage against Israel in order to precipitate the concessions needed for bringing about a settlement as conceived by the United States to be just. President Carter made no secret of his belief in the need for only "minor adjustments in the pre-1967 borders." As the State Department specifically cautioned the new Israeli government in late June 1977, "no territories, including the West Bank, are automatically excluded from the items to be negotiated."

Despite insistence that he would not impose a peace in the area, in May 1977 Carter told a group of European journalists, "I would not hesitate if I saw clearly a fair and equitable solution to use the full strength of our own country and its persuasive powers to bring those nations to agreement." Brzezinski in an interview a few months later with Canadian television was even blunter, claiming that the United States has a "direct interest" in what happens in the Arab-Israeli conflict, and therefore, "has a legitimate right to exercise its own leverage" to precipitate a settlement. Referring to leverage he stated, "I think the point to bear in mind is that the United States is not just an interested bystander, not even just a benevolent mediator.''

Seen in this light, American-Israeli disputes over settlements in occupied territories, over the future of the West Bank, over the definition of Resolution 242, and over linkage between the Egyptian-Israeli and Palestinian issues after Camp David pointed to the heart of the American position. How could little Israel—viewed by the administration as weak and a liability, heavily indebted to the United States for economic and military assistance—undermine the "architectural" plan (to use one of Brzezinski's favorite terms) conceived for the Middle East by the Carter entourage? These Israeli policies were often controversial, but the administration's willingness to engage in a public confrontation with the Begin government over them is indicative of its movement in a direction which loosened American-Israeli ties in the hopes of gaining greater Arab confidence.

Observers need not point to administration statements; however, there are ample actions to justify the conclusion that the Carter administration is prepared, even eager, to exercise leverage over Israel. Merely a few of many by-now familiar examples will suffice. Thus, for the first time an incoming administration rejected its predecessor's deal with Israel when the sale of concussion bombs was canceled; in addition, the sale of the latest (Forward Looking Infra Red) FLIR night-vision equipment was delayed; despite Ford's initials on an agreement over the transfer of a nuclear reactor to Israel, this deal was also delayed; and despite oral promises by Kissinger, the sale of Israeli-built Kfir jets to Ecuador was vetoed. The latter decision worked out poorly for all originally involved: the Ecuadorians ended by purchasing more expensive French Mirages—thereby reducing American leverage over the South American arms race. On the other hand, the sale of Hawk and Maverick missiles to Saudi Arabia, which the president had criticized during the campaign, was allowed to proceed and American participation in the rebuilding of Egyptian MIG-21 jet engines and airframes was approved.

Meanwhile, several coproduction agreements with Israel were not approved such as an Israeli request on F-16 coproduction and the coproduction of a sophisticated military communications network between American and Israeli firms. Early in the administration the State Department had criticized Israel for oil drilling in the Gulf of

Suez; later the original draft of a Presidential Review Memorandum (P.R.M.-12) limiting U.S. arms sales excluded Israel as a preferred arms recipient. When several key Congressmen protested, the president provided assurances, including a letter informing them that he had "inserted explicit language" in the P.R.M. "which acknowledges our special security relationship with Israel."

Thus, the halving of scaled-down Israeli requests for F-15s and F-16s occurred in the context of what had now become a Carter tradition. Whatever one chooses to call it, leverage was being exercised against Israel, while the administration was seemingly unable even to conceive of means by which leverage might be exercised against the Arabs.

A similar pattern was expressed after Camp David when the administration was reluctant to support Israeli claims for large increases in assistance to help finance the moving of sophisticated equipment and materiel from the Sinai to the Negev (the Israelis were seeking almost $3 billion). Meanwhile, the White House pressured a reluctant Congress to approve $90 million in economic aid for Syria despite President Asad's opposition to the Camp David accords and continuing clashes in Lebanon between Syrian peacekeeping forces and Christian militiamen. The pattern was in turn reinforced by the anti-inflation programs at home, which led high level officials to hesitate about major new foreign aid efforts such as Israel was requesting on the ground that the United States simply could not afford them.

After a peace treaty between Egypt and Israel was signed in March 1979, the administration did finally come forward with a major aid program for both countries. However, the heavy reliance on loans and on high interest rates in the administration offer left serious doubts whether the proposed program was quite as generous as it appeared. Certainly, there would still be ample room for the exercise of leverage against Jerusalem.

Conclusion

In the light of these overlapping consistencies between organization, premises, and policies the pattern of the Carter entourage is clear. The administration has a plan for the Middle East which encompasses both the Arab-Israeli and the energy issues and it is determined to achieve it. As far as political risks at home are concerned, the Carter clan is prepared to accept them, believing that if a showdown with Israel's supporters occurs, it will win (as it did over the sale of F-15s to Saudi Arabia), especially given Sādāt's increasing popularity and Begin's perceived decline. Most important, the Carter team believes that once peace is achieved, the president's accomplishments will be appreciated, especially by Israel's supporters.

In every other administration debates have occurred over objectives as well as tactics in the Middle East involving the Arabs as well as Israel. Was the key objective to be an Arab-Israeli settlement, containing the Communists, preserving oil flows, promoting democracy, settling refugee problems? Under Eisenhower, the last administration where Israel's backers were weak, there was a consensus on the primary objective—containing Communism—but considerable disagreement over tactics. Some officials thought a Western-sponsored pact would contain the Russians, while others believed Egyptian nationalist sensitivities would have to be assuaged if Western interests were to be preserved.

In the Carter administration, however, there is no debate on objectives or basic tactics. Comprehensiveness, involvement of the Palestinians, emphasis on Arab unity, fear of Arab radicals, stress on oil—all lead theoretically to a neat package: resolving the energy crisis by achieving an Arab-Israeli settlement. The problem is that this coherence produces a false sense of rectitude and intellectual rigidity. In this atmosphere there is little room for discussion, for there seem to be no conceptual problems, only political challenges.

It has become almost a cliché to suggest that the United States and Israel are on collision course. Because of a deep inability on the part of key American officials to perceive alternative directions, in a sense the United States and Israel are not even on the same course. The objectives of Israel and her supporters are diametrically different from those of the Carter administration and even the Egyptian-Israeli peace treaty does not overcome dissonance over the meaning of comprehensiveness and future diplomatic steps—especially concerning the Palestinians. If these trends continue, the consequences for Israel, for American interests, for the future of the Carter administration, and for Arab-Israeli peace could all be stark indeed.

NOTES

1. Zbigniew Brzezinski, "America in a Hostile World," *Foreign Policy*, Summer 1976, p. 84.

2. Richard Burt, "The Mideast Plane Sales Package: How U.S. Decision Was Reached," *The New York Times*, 28 February 1978, p. 3.

3. Interview with Hamilton Jordan, "Face the Nation," Columbia Broadcasting System, 12 November 1978.

4. For a sampling of the discussion in American journals at the time, see: Zbigniew Brzezinski, Francois Duchene, Kiichi Saeki, "Peace in an International Framework," *Foreign Policy*, Summer 1975; George W. Ball, "How to Save Israel in Spite of Herself," *Foreign Affairs*, April 1977; Stanley Hoffmann, "A New Policy for Israel," *Foreign Affairs*, April 1975; Richard H. Ullman, "After Rabat: Middle East Risks and American Roles," *Foreign Affairs*, January 1975.

5. The other members were Morroe Berger, John C. Campbell, Najeeb Halaby, Rita Hauser, Alan Horton, Malcolm Kerr, Fred Khouri, Philip Klutznick, Nadav Safran, A. L. Udovitch, Charles W. Yost, and the author.

6. Zbigniew Brzezinski, "Unmanifest Destiny: Where Do We Go from Here?," *New York*, 3 March 1975, p. 55.

7. Zbigniew Brzezinski, "A Plan for Peace in the Middle East," *New Leader*, 7 July 1974, and Zbigniew Brzezinski, Francois Duchene, and Kiichi Saeki, "Peace in an International Framework," *Foreign Policy*, Summer 1975.

8. Zbigniew Brzezinski, "A Plan for Peace in the Middle East," *New Leader*, 7 July 1974, p. 9.

9. Zbigniew Brzezinski, Francois Duchene, and Kiichi Saeki, "Peace in an International Framework," *Foreign Policy*, Summer 1975, p. 16.

10. Zbigniew Brzezinski, "Recognizing the Crisis," *Foreign Policy*, Winter 1974-75, p. 67.

11. Zbigniew Brzezinski, "Unmanifest Destiny: Where Do We Go from Here?," *New York*, 3 March 1975, p. 53.

12. Zbigniew Brzezinski, "Recognizing the Crisis," *Foreign Policy*, Winter 1974-75, p. 70.

All remaining footnotes refer to statements by presidential candidate Jimmy Carter

13. Address in Elizabeth, New Jersey, 6 June 1976.

14. Interview by the Hearst Task Force as reported in *The News American*, 26 July 1976.

15. New Year's Message to the Jewish People, 14 September 1976.

16. Address before the New York Synagogue Council, 1 April 1976.

17. Address to the Conference of Presidents of Major American Jewish Organizations, Boston, Massachusetts, 30 September 1976.

18. Interview with *The Chicago Tribune*, 8 May 1976.

19. Ibid.

20. Shortly after Sādāt's visit to Jerusalem, Brzezinski argued that the Arab-Israeli issue is similar to a series of concentric circles with each stage leading to a further arena for involving the parties of the area. To him the first circle consists of Israel and Egypt plus the United States; the second involves moderate Palestinians and Jordanians; the third circle encompasses Russian and Syrian participation. (Interview with Zbigniew Brzezinski, "Issues and Answers," American Broadcasting Company, 10 December 1977).

The International
Context

The European Community and the United States in the Arab World—Political Competition or Partnership?

Udo Steinbach

1. Pragmatic Mediterranean Policy and the "Global Approach"

The European Economic Community (E.E.C.) has since its inception, in the context of its external economic relations, devoted particular interest to the Mediterranean region. The special position of the regions in North Africa formerly colonized by France and Italy (Morocco, Tunisia and Libya) was recognized by the "Rome Treaties." Algeria, as a French territory, was fully integrated into the sphere of application of the E.E.C. Treaty in 1958, under the terms of Article 227.

The six E.E.C. nations began to play an active role in the Mediterranean when Association Agreements were made with Greece (effective from 1 November 1962) and with Turkey (effective from 1 December 1964). These foresaw a gradual removal of tariffs finally leading for both nations[1] to full membership in the E.E.C. as well as financial support by it. Although these agreements were principally of a financial nature, they acquired a political tinge as the U.S. itself pressed for the conclusion of the agreements. The association embodied the goal of binding the two southeastern NATO partners more closely to Europe, with the prospect of later incorporation into the European economy. During the 1960s and early 1970s, a number of agreements of varying content and economic and politico-economic scope were made, although it must be said that the Turkish and Greek experiment was not repeated. The treaties were largely restricted to the establishment of preferential trade relations. They included agreements with Israel, Lebanon, Morocco and Tunisia, Spain, Malta and Cyprus, as well as Egypt and Portugal.[2]

In making these agreements, the E.E.C. took the pragmatic path of strengthening economic cooperation with the nations of the Mediterranean, at the same time contributing to the political stabilization of the whole region. A conception of the form of relations with third parties in general, or with the Mediterranean nations in particular, had not been worked out in advance. The multiplicity of treaties had become confusing and unmanageable, quite apart from the fact that the individual agreements with different Mediterranean nations resulted in contradictions in the policy of the Community, so that demands for equal treatment began to be heard. That was the situation in the first half of 1972, at which time three Mediterranean problems were on the European Council agenda:

a. the renegotiation of the treaties with Morocco and Tunisia "on an extended basis";

b. the consequences of the extension of the community to Spanish and Israeli foreign trade;

c. the applications of Spain, Israel and Turkey for incorporation into the general preference system.

Since any decision made in these problem areas would necessarily have consequences for the existing treaties and those in the process of negotiation, the Council directed the Commission to provide it with proposals for a "global Mediterranean scheme." The Commission complied with this wish in its statement of 14 July 1972. In November 1972 (i.e., before the onset of the oil crisis), the Council established the basis of a Mediterranean policy: The Community is prepared, in the context of this "global Mediterranean policy," to make full treaties with all states bordering on the Mediterranean (and Jordan), if they so desire. These provide for a complete opening of the Community's market to industrial goods, preferential access for agricultural produce, economic cooperation and, if the occasion arises, financial and technical assistance from the Community. The content and scope of the treaties made with the countries concerned was to be determined according to the particular circumstances of each case.[3]

The "global policy" did not result in extensive agreements between the European Community and its Mediterranean partners. Due to the multiplicity of competing interests—first of all among the European member states, secondly among the Mediterranean nations, and thirdly between individual member states and individual Mediterranean nations—any far-reaching realization of the goals could hardly have been expected.[4]

The guidelines of the global Mediterranean policy were, from the beginning, not intended to apply to the associate relationship with Greece and Turkey. They were designed to apply first and foremost to Spain, Israel, and the Maghreb nations. The first treaty, with Israel, was signed in May 1975, those with the Maghreb nations of Morocco, Algeria and Tunisia in April 1976. The completion of negotiations with the Mashrek nations of Egypt, Syria and Jordan in January 1977 (the agreement with Lebanon was delayed till May because of the internal political crisis there) ended an important phase in the relations of the Community with the Mediterranean region.

The European Community has established a system of agreements with all of the Mediterranean nations (and Jordan) with the exception of Libya and Albania. The arrangements are restricted to economic relations, but at the same time are intended to make a long-term contribution to the realization of two foreign policy goals:

a. the economic and social development of the Mediterranean nations through close economic cooperation, in order to encourage economic and, at the same time, political stability in the region;

b. the establishment of close economic cooperation as a contribution to the establishment and maintenance of a lasting peace.

2. European Political Cooperation (E.P.C.)

The implicit political elements within the Mediterranean treaty policy of the Community did not by any means imply a Mediterranean "policy," but were merely an expression of a natural priority the Community's foreign policy had to accord to this region for a number of reasons. Nor did the E.E.C. have any body able to plan or apply common political measures of any kind whatsoever. Genuinely noteworthy steps to found one were first proposed at the summit conference of member states in December 1969. These came to fruition in the creation of the European Political Cooperation in 1970. In this framework, set by the Davignon Report, an instrument for political negotiations was established. Its most important component is four annual meetings of the foreign ministers of member states, apart from the routine summit meetings. Although formally outside the institutional framework of the Community, the ministers can appear in the E.P.C. as members of the Community. A Political Committee consisting of the political directors of the foreign ministries prepares the ministerial meetings.

It was indicative of the political importance of the Mediterranean and Middle East region that the E.P.C. gave the Middle East and the crisis in that area a political priority alongside the Conference on Security and Cooperation in Europe (C.S.C.E.).

Certainly at that time the political basis for a common standpoint of the six member countries on the most important points of the Middle East problem was still weak: The traditions and interests of the Mediterranean members of the Community in relation to the Arab world differed from those of the North Sea. The political-psychological status of Israel was not the same in all of the partner nations. As permanent members of the U.N. Security Council, France and Great Britain had a special position with regard to the Middle East conflict. Finally, the coordination of positions and of the political role of Western Europe in general with the United States was insufficient. The result of the political consultations within the E.P.C., the report of the Political Committee which the foreign ministers accepted in May 1971, thus led to a variety of reactions in the member states and to considerable reservations and open disapproval from the U.S.A. and Israel.

The Six had reached agreement on the most delicate points of the Middle East conflict: The question of Israel's withdrawal from the areas occupied in 1967 (albeit with "minor modifications"), the modalities of "recognized and guaranteed borders" (international guarantees, demilitarized and internationally controlled security zones), the demand for an "administrative internationalization" of Jerusalem, the settlement of the question of the Palestinian refugees, as well as that of shipping in the Suez Canal and the Gulf of Aqaba. The impression arose that the E.E.C. nations wanted to take their own initiative in negotiations and exercise pressure on Israel over the territorial question. Israel reacted strongly and denied the right and the qualifications of the E.E.C. nations to engage in efforts to settle the conflict. In contrast, the E.P.C. Report was favorably received in the Arab capitals. The U.S. and the Soviet Union had reservations.

Although there was no declared connection between the efforts for a "global" approach in E.E.C. external economic relations with the Mediterranean nations and the attempt to achieve political agreement within the E.P.C., the energy crisis was soon to show that the reordering of economic relations in terms of partnership and equilibrium would be an important element in overall relations between the two areas. This crisis occurred as a result of the imposition of the Arab oil embargo at the end of 1973.

European engagement in the Middle East conflict seemed to meet with resistance for two principal reasons: On the one hand, Western Europe seemed to possess insufficient political weight to make an effective contribution to a solution of the conflict; its "interference" thus seemed only to create confusion. On the other hand, Western Europe's dependence on oil occasioned suspicion that it might side too strongly with the Arabs under the pressure of the "oil weapon" and thereby weaken Israel's bargaining position.

3. The Euro-Arab Dialogue: Preparation and Basis

After the United States and the Soviet Union agreed, in the course of the October crisis (1973), to limit the peace initiatives at the Geneva Conference to themselves and the parties to the conflict, the Nine had to suspend consideration of a Western European contribution to the peace initiative. They then had to press towards a new long-term sphere of activity in Euro-Arab policy outside the realm of the Arab-Israeli conflict.[5]

The idea of a Euro-Arab dialogue, which four Arab ministers presented in Copenhagen in December 1973 on behalf of the twenty member nations of the Arab League, corresponded with European considerations of a new way to organize relations with the Arab region. In view of the particular situation of Western Europe, marked by the double nature of economic and political foreign relations, the different relations between the E.E.C. members with Israel and the

Arab nations, and U.S.-Israeli mistrust of European political initiatives, the dialogue had to be a new form of diplomatic and political contact.

The conception of the "dialogue," which was worked out in the first half of 1974, reflects the efforts of the administrations of the Nine to establish relations with the Arab world on a stable long-term basis of partnership. Thus, it was clear from the outset that the dialogue should not impede the imminent initiatives of the oil politics on a wider international stage and, above all, that it should not interfere with attempts at a peace settlement for the Middle East. That is to say, the conflict was not to be a point on the agenda of the dialogue. This was made clear by the Foreign Minister of the Federal Republic of Germany, Hans-Dietrich Genscher, at the press conference on 11 June 1974, in which he formally confirmed the beginning of the Euro-Arab dialogue. Thus, the dialogue was to be located institutionally outside foreign economic relations with the Middle East nations, which were to be arranged according to the principles of the "global approach," and outside the framework of E.P.C. as well.

Even though political components, especially the Israel-Arab conflict, were excluded from the dialogue by definition, the political background against which the development of its approach is to be understood must not be overlooked.

1. For a long time, a number of Arab states on the Mediterranean have pressed for the acceptance of questions of Mediterranean security into the agenda of the Helsinki C.S.C.E. This was to be done in order to discuss the question of Mediterranean security in relation to European security as well as the problem of peace, stability and security in the Middle East. These efforts found only a limited response from nations meeting in Helsinki. The dominant feeling was that the C.S.C.E. should restrict itself to security in Europe and should not be overwhelmed by peripheral problems of security outside Europe, particularly in the Middle East.

2. The October War (1973) made the studiously ignored connection between the security of both regions dramatically obvious. Not only had the involvement of the two superpowers immediately affected Europe, but the U.S. had even alerted her nuclear forces late in the war and transported military equipment stored in the Federal Republic to Israel, without consulting her allies. This was a

step which was to cause difficulties for the Federal Republic of Germany both with the Arab states and with the U.S.

3. With the application of the oil embargo against most of the European nations, the Arabs tried to shift Western Europe to a statement in favor of their anti-Israel goals. This made it evident how dependent the economic prosperity of the Nine was on a balanced and active policy in the Middle East.

4. The Middle East statement by the Nine on 6 November 1973 did not mean the adoption of an active policy in the Middle East conflict. However, it did make clear that Western Europe had adjusted to the changed situation in the Middle East and was ready to support peace initiatives presented on the basis of internationally recognized facts and resolutions. The intimation that the Nine had allowed themselves to be "compelled" to a pro-Arab position by the pressure of the Arab states is unfounded. On the one hand, their position rests on important elements which were already part of the 1971 working paper of the Six, and on the other hand, as was stated, it follows internationally recognized basic elements of a Middle Eastern peace policy. The bases for a balanced peace program were established by Security Council Resolution 242 of 22 November 1967. Added to this was the principle of respect for the rights of the Palestinians, which was mentioned in the U.N. General Assembly Resolution of 13 December 1972 supported by the Nine. The guidelines of E.E.C. policy, as laid down by the statement mentioned above, are: a balanced consideration of Arab and Israeli interests; no annexation of territory by force and consequently the requirement that Israel end the occupation exercised since the June War of 1967; the occupation to be ended as a result of a process of negotiation leading to the recognition of Israel's right to exist within guaranteed boundaries; following from this, respect for the right to self-determination of the Palestinian people on territory made free for the creation of a national homeland.[6] The Nine also demand international guarantees, but they refrain from making proposals. Finally, the Resolution recalls the various ties which have existed between members of the Community and South- and East-Mediterranean states. In this context, the decision to make balanced, global agreements on economic relations with all Mediterranean nations is once again mentioned.

The European statement made it easier in the bilateral preparatory talks on the Euro-Arab dialogue to show understanding for justified Arab concerns, but at the same time to insist on parity for Israel. Thus the German foreign minister gave notice of a consultation with Israel in the press conference of 11 June 1974 mentioned above, announcing at the same time the beginning of the Euro-Arab dialogue.

4. Conflct of Interest with the U.S.?

The contextual position of the Euro-Arab dialogue has been carefully analysed. On the one hand, it could not be a direct political contribution of the Nine, since it was not planned with such a role in mind; on the other hand, it could not be carried out in a political vacuum. Nevertheless it was possible to disappoint the Arab expectations of converting the success of the "oil front" into political capital, and yet at the same time declare a credible commitment to Arab concerns which seemed adequate to the Arabs too as a basis for the dialogue. However, U.S. resistance to the idea of a dialogue had to be overcome.

The U.S. has never taken a positive view of an active E.E.C. role in the Mediterranean. It encouraged the E.E.C. to make treaties of association with Greece and Turkey, important from a security standpoint, in order to bind the two states closely to the West economically as well. But very soon, with the signing of the subsequent agreements with the Mediterranean states, the Community found itself confronting the constant suspicion of the U.S. which was afraid of losing its share of the market, and as a result pressed for similar concessions in the context of the General Agreement on Tariffs and Trade (GATT). "It would be indicative of the arrogance of power, if the American government, in the name of the citrus fruit millionaires of Arizona and California, were able to achieve the same concessions for the U.S. as the small citrus farmers in Morocco and Tunisia have in Europe. It would also show the arrogance of power if the E.E.C. reversed their own economically balanced agreement, which had been agreed by the Council of Ministers." [7] The extension of these treaties in the context of a "global approach" and the opening of talks which led in early 1975 to the E.E.C.-A.C.P. Treaty of Lomé strengthened American resistance.

The prospect of a close connection with the European Community of 46 developing countries in the African-Caribbean-Pacific (A.C.P.) regions and a parallel network of agreements with almost all of the Mediterranean countries upset the American administration. Eventually, in close consultation, it was possible to convince the U.S. that this initiative was not directed against them, but would rather be a relief to them. By means of the so-called "Soames-Casey Formula" which has never been officially made known, the reservations of the U.S. were eventually removed. According to this, it seems that the U.S. has recognized that the European Community may maintain preferential relations in Europe with the European Free Trade Association (E.F.T.A.) nations, with the Mediterranean states (including Portugal and Jordan) as well as with the A.C.P. countries, in the context of contractual agreements. These concessions could apparently be granted more easily by the U.S. after the E.E.C. relinquished "reciprocal preferences" in talks with the A.C.P. nations, i.e. customs preferences, the removal of custom duties and other advantages which its partners are offered do not commit them to the statutory reciprocity characteristic of GATT. The U.S. would have regarded that as discrimination in the markets of the relevant developing countries.[8]

The preparations for the Euro-Arab dialogue certainly led to an intensification of American reservations against a European Middle East and Mediterranean policy. Discord between Europe and the U.S. had already emerged during the fourth Middle East War. The European nations had refused to be used as a base for arms deliveries to Israel and simultaneously the inadequacies of the consultative mechanism had become apparent to the NATO partners. Thus, inter alia, the U.S. did not consult its allies about the decision on the world-wide nuclear alarm in October 1973.

Beyond their fears that the Euro-Arab dialogue might undermine Kissinger's policy of small steps towards solution of the Middle East conflict, the U.S. had very definite opinions on how the oil policy of the Arab states should be met, namely by a joint coordinated energy policy of Western consumer countries. The plan which led to the creation of the International Energy Agency in late 1974 was developed at that time and the U.S. viewed the Euro-Arab dialogue as a threat to its plan of a coordinated Western energy policy, which it considered to be a means of applying counter-pressure on the Arab states.

Consequently, the American reaction to the announcement, on 4 March 1974, of readiness in principle to begin the Euro-Arab dialogue, was very strong. As early as autumn 1973 Secretary of State Kissinger had already made a statement relating to independent European activities: the quest for a separate European identity would result in a confrontation with the U.S. Now, in a speech in Chicago on 15 March 1974, Richard Nixon, U.S. president at the time, stated that the European Community was conspiring against the U.S. It required intensive talks between the E.E.C. nations and the U.S. before acceptable solutions could be found. Their main content was the omission of energy policy and the oil questions, as well as that of the Arab-Israeli conflict, from the Euro-Arab dialogue. At the same time, in "private talks" between the foreign ministers of the Nine at Schloss Gymnich (20-21 April 1974), agreement was reached on the creation of a scheme for an "organic consultative relationship" which was to ensure that the nine E.E.C. countries would not pass any definitive resolutions which could affect American interests (e.g. especially not American policy in the Middle East) without prior consultation with the U.S. Federal Foreign Minister Hans-Dietrich Genscher gave a comprehensive account of the contents of the "gentleman's agreement of Gymnich" in his press conference on 11 June 1974:

"The ministers were agreed that in elaborating common positions on foreign policy there arises the question of consultations with allied or friendly countries. Such consultations are a matter of course in any modern foreign policy. We decided on a pragmatic approach in each individual case, which means that the country holding the Presidency will be authorized by the other eight partners to hold consultations on behalf of the Nine.

"In practice, therefore, if any member of the E.E.C. raises within the framework of E.P.C. the question of informing and consulting an ally or a friendly state, the Nine will discuss the matter and, upon reaching agreement, authorize the Presidency to proceed on that basis.

"The ministers trust that this gentleman's agreement will also lead to smooth and pragmatic consultations with the United States which will take into account the interests of both sides." [9]

The U.S. has followed the Euro-Arab dialogue with interest and taken the opportunity to indicate this to both sides, perhaps most clearly in November 1975. During the third round of the dialogue in Abu Dhabi (22-27 December 1975), U.S. Under Secretary for Energy Questions Gerald Parsky engaged in talks with the United Arab Emirates on subjects similar to those being discussed at that moment by the European Community (E.C.) within the dialogue.

5. Elements of the Euro-Arab Dialogue

The Euro-Arab dialogue constitutes in effect a framework for political negotiations in which the E.C. in Brussels and the E.P.C. collaborate. While it is true that the E.C. is restricted to economic, trade policy and technical cooperation, and more or less completely excludes the political area, and the E.P.C. as a form of inter-governmental cooperation should be strictly separated from the activities of the Community and has hardly any actual political executive power, the Euro-Arab dialogue is involved in both areas. A European Coordinating Group was constituted as the E.P.C.-E.C. executive body for the dialogue. It consists of special delegates of the nine governments at ambassador level and of representatives of the E.C. commission. It is also the dialogue partner for the Arab side. Both sides are represented in a General Commission, which consists of delegates of the twenty-one states of the Arab League and the nine member countries of the E.C. Its function is to establish the principles of Euro-Arab cooperation and to coordinate the working groups concerned with specific areas of cooperation. Considerable time was to pass, however, before this commission could meet. For even in the inaugural session of the dialogue in Paris on 31 July 1974, it was clear that the Arab side wanted to lay stress on political talks, since agreement over any form of cooperation could not be separated from a comprehensive political agreement. The most delicate problem proved to be the question of representation of the Palestinians. Furthermore, the Arabs expected that the Europeans would put pressure on Israel to withdraw from the territories occupied in 1967. Against this, the European side insisted on the exclusion of political problems from the dialogue.

The removal of political difficulties, which cannot be described in detail, constantly delayed the beginning of the dialogue, until it finally was able to begin at expert level in the summer of 1975. The Europeans had to make clear that in spite of all regard for the Arab position they would not allow themselves to be held for ransom politically nor would they, in the context of the Euro-Arab dialogue, preempt results which would first have to be attained by international agreements at other levels. The Arabs, for their part, by accepting the dialogue, finally recognized its special character as a framework for negotiations devoted primarily to questions of Euro-Arab cooperation in specific areas.

At the first meeting of experts at Cairo in June 1975, working groups were constituted for the areas of agricultural development, industrialization, projects for the infra-structure, development of trade between the two regions, questions of finance, scientific and technical cooperation, and cultural and social cooperation.

The dialogue is an attempt at a new form of diplomacy. Two organizations of states, the E.C. and the Arab League, wish to establish a relationship of structured cooperation. From the European side, the Nine participate as a unit, institutionalized in the committees of the E.E.C. and the E.P.C.; on the Arab side, the member states of the Arab League and the General Secretariat of the Arab League take part. Each of the alliances of states has a different form, and each must be left to determine its own organization. Many reservations have been voiced against the multilateral and collective approach of the dialogue. The multilateral approach is justified in particular because it builds upon the sum total of bilateral relations both between the European nations and between the Arab nations, as well as upon those between the E.C. and the individual Mediterranean countries. The dialogue is an additional enterprise: It is an interregional policy aimed at ordering an overall pattern. As such, it must relate to all the countries of both regions, must be concerned with the overall arrangement of the relationships of both regions—political, economic, cultural—and must work out the common, long-term goals clearly.

The success of the dialogue cannot yet be measured in concrete results. Without a doubt, political agreement and economic cooperation have become closer. In the cultural sphere, too, it was possible for new contacts to be established. Capital involvement and entrepreneurial cooperation have been encouraged, and the opportunity for a permanent dialogue has lessened the chances of short-term, politically motivated actions being undertaken against the interest of the other party. The progress of the working groups and their subgroups (the project groups) is admittedly not overwhelming. Nonetheless, progress has been made, as in the areas of industrialization (extension of the petrochemical industries), infrastructure (including technical education), agricultural, and cultural-scientific cooperation. In other areas, the difficulties seem hardly surmountable: The demand by the Arabs for the opening of the European market for Arab products is just as controversial in this context as a treaty on the protection of capital investment or on parity with European colleagues for the Arab *Gastarbeiter* (guest workers).

In spite of this, the progress of the working groups was sufficient, in the second half of 1975 and early 1976, for the decisive body of the dialogue, the General Commission, to meet on this basis for the first time in May 1976 in Luxembourg. Representatives of the Arab League countries and of the General Secretary of the League, as well as the member countries of the E.C. and a delegate of the E.C. Commission at ambassadorial level took part. There had been a Palestinian representative included in the Arab expert groups, which had acted as unified delegations and now a Palestinian representative in the General Commission was present as well. The agenda of the Luxembourg meeting included an evaluation of the results of the expert meetings to date, the establishment of a time-table and the coordination of the various working and project groups, and an exchange of political statements.

However, no spectacular results could be achieved at the session in Luxembourg either, since it too was marked by Arab attempts to push through the acceptance of fundamental political positions on the Arab-Israeli conflict. This became clear, for example, in the question of the Palestinians: Whereas the European side assumed that the communities as a whole were represented in the delegations, as had been the case in the groups of experts, the Arabs explained in their introduction that the member states were represented individually. Since the Community accepted this silently, a quasi-recognition of the P.L.O. was thereby achieved.

Nonetheless, with this meeting, a succession of sessions was set up, alternating meetings in the working groups which dealt with problems of cooperation, and flanking sessions of the General Commission in which political statements could be exchanged, although this was not the real purpose of the dialogue. As a result, the second session of the General Commission in Tunis (10-12 February 1977) was not only preceded by intensive meetings of all working groups, but also by a political discussion by the foreign ministers of the Nine (London Statement of 31 January 1977). This drew significantly on the Middle East Statement of 6 November 1973, and once more particularly stressed the rights of the Palestinian people. It also announced the readiness of the members of the E.C. to take a concrete part in a peace settlement in the Middle East and to consider the possibility of participation in the guarantees for the security of the participants. It was emphasized that a settlement would have to include the right of the Palestinian people to express their national identity. This later formulation should be interpreted in connection with the statement of the representative of the E.E.C. at the 31st General Assembly of the U.N. (October 1976), that the Palestinian people must be allowed their own territory.[10]

Even though this statement did not satisfy the Arab participants, it created a climate which allowed a development of the relevant questions. The General Commission examined the results of the seven working groups and sixteen project groups. In questions such as the financing of the dialogue and cooperation in the realms of technology transfer, agriculture, and cultural relations, progress could be made. The only political compromise was the agreement to consider the creation of a political committee for the discussion of political questions in the context of the Euro-Arab dialogue.

The Euro-Arab dialogue has been operating in a state of tension between the strong desire for closer cooperation on the one hand and different political attitudes on the other. The third session of the General Commission in October 1977 in Brussels also worked under this tension. Once more, a statement of E.E.C. heads of government (published 29 June 1977) preceded the session, drawing significantly on previous statements, but speaking out more clearly for the creation of a homeland (German = *Heimstatt,* French = *patrie*).

In addition, a politically fortunate coincidence occurred when on 27 October 1977 the member countries of the E.E.C. and of the Arab League voted in the U.N. General Assembly against Israel's settlement policy and for a resolution which determined among other things "that measures and actions taken by Israel in the Palestinian and other Arab territories occupied since 1967 have no legal validity and constitute a serious obstruction of efforts aimed at achieving a just and lasting peace in the Middle East.'' In the working groups, it was already possible to identify common projects, towards the implementation of which feasibility studies could be undertaken as a first step. As a political result, it is noteworthy that the discussion on the creation of a committee for political consultation between the two sides, which was promoted by the Arab side at the second session of the General Commission, was taken a good deal further.

6. *Balanced Double-Tracking*

The progress of the dialogue has shown that, despite the attempt to restrict the content to questions of economic, technical and cultural cooperation, a slowly growing politicization is unavoidable. The political statements of the Nine on the situation in the Middle East, which also reflect the attempt to achieve a common political language for problems in which European interests are involved, have been made outside the context of the Euro-Arab dialogue. Naturally, they have had an impact on the dialogue itself, as we have shown, in particular on the work of the General Commission. The dialogue will certainly be further politicized, should the establishment of a political committee be carried out.

On the other hand, the E.C. has not allowed itself to be pressured into accepting one-sided Arab positions, and has thus followed a fairly balanced policy. It is a misunderstanding of the goals of European policy, and also an overestimation of its role, for Israel to dispute the right of the E.C. to publicly present an independent policy on developments, in the realm of the Middle East conflict. In a region which is of great security importance for Western Europe and in which the E.C. carries out an effective policy of trade and cooperation, Western Europe may and must have its own political conception for its future.

That European Middle East and Mediterranean policy at various levels is not directed against Israel has been emphasized regularly by the Community. The signing of the trade agreement with Israel on 11 May 1975 was the reason for another postponement of the start of the Euro-Arab dialogue. For the Arabs had expected that the

E.C. would take advantage of the signing to put political pressure on Israel, and they blamed the Community for ignoring the opportunity. The E.C. explained to them that they would not allow themselves to be told with whom they could sign agreements. Up to now, it has not proven to be an unfounded expectation that the continual strengthening of economic ties between Western Europe and the Arab states (bilateral, in the context of the "global approach", and multilateral, in the context of the Euro-Arab dialogue) would exercise a certain influence in terms of moderating political goals and of a quest for Arab-Israeli coexistence. Important interests in the area of economic and development policy have been created, in cooperation with the E.E.C., which would suffer set-backs through any renewal of the military dispute. Finally, a credible double-tracking in Middle East policy by the E.E.C. provided the possibility of a more open commitment to the Israeli side. Blacklists and boycott threats should, in the long term, lose their point in such a climate.

7. Consultation with the U.S.

Western Europe and the U.S. have, in general, similar interests in the Mediterranean and the Middle East. Numerous points of political contact result from this.

a. The U.S. is the only power with sufficient means and influence over both sides to be able to work towards the solution of the Middle East conflict in the context of diplomatic initiatives. Since the security of Western Europe depends, to a considerable extent, on the stability of the Middle East, the E.E.C. must support all efforts towards a settlement of the conflict.

b. The states of the region are seeking a diversification of relations and reject any one-sided dependence upon one power or the other. The implication for Western Europe is that, in working out a policy for the Mediterranean and the Middle East, the objective cannot be to create a system of exclusive relations and to "displace" the U.S. Rather, Western Europe must simultaneously make room for achieving its own interests and offer points of contact on the Arab side for the efforts of the U.S. towards a solution of the Middle East conflict.

c. The dependence of Western Europe on the U.S. in the area of security policy also establishes limits to a European solo effort in the Mediterranean and the Middle East. The presence of the Sixth Fleet in the Mediterranean will remain necessary as long as no real détente becomes apparent in the region and no new options to the present situation of the security policy become available. A contradiction between European Mediterranean policy and U.S. interests would, in the last analysis, weaken the overall position of Western Europe in the region.

The growing political independence of the E.E.C., however, has certainly shown that a better coordinating mechanism between the European Community and the United States must be found. From the European side, the E.P.C. appears to be the suitable partner. A complex of shared attitudes and joint measures by the Nine could be a concrete basis for Western European activity in international relations. Compared with the early sixties, the capacity for cooperation in material and organizational respects has grown on the European side.

For the United States, this opens the prospect of some devolution of power and sharing of responsibility. In fact, its readiness to share responsibility in world-wide contingencies thus becomes more credible. Primarily in order to diversify burdens stemming from a commitment, but also because there is widespread realization that the trend is not towards a new climax of "imperial presidency," the management of world diplomacy will no longer be considered a monopoly of the U.S. secretary of state. The new danger lies in shifting responsibilities, particularly if the partners of the U.S. claim competence (like the Europeans in the Mediterranean) without being able to live up to it in a crisis.[11]

It cannot be overstressed, therefore, that the preconditions for cooperation, which are beginning to show signs of improvement in Western Europe and the United States, are not of a comprehensive nature. There are also simultaneous opposing trends (increased dependence, more bilateralism). However, Western Europe should be able to achieve selective cooperation with Washington in the area of diplomacy. Crises have a selective character in any case, and the Nine are in possession of the best organizational basis (comparatively speaking) for such purposes—namely the E.P.C.

Compared with the situation of 15 March 1974 (see above p. 130), certain factors have thus changed in the Western European-

American relationship. The Gymnich Agreement of June 1974 has not been seriously treated in practice to date. It still constitutes the most concrete provision for the relationship between E.P.C. and U.S. diplomacy. It provides a protective modus vivendi, a defensive formula, if one examines the story of its origin. This formula continues to be necessary. However, what is obviously lacking is an offensive formula for constructive cooperation between the E.P.C. and U.S. diplomacy. The present tradition of cooperation is insufficient to avoid lower-level escalations and to fend off long-term or permanent disturbances. Although certain persons are available on both sides for regular contacts between U.S. diplomacy and E.P.C., the "linkage body" (presidential representative of E.P.C. plus representatives of the State Department) has been used rather unilaterally to date: In general, the European side "discusses" the agenda for the next meeting of the Political Committee with the U.S. representative. Why should these meetings not also be used for the discussion of items on the American agenda? The Gymnich formula, if extended to mutuality, might find practical application in Washington as well, where possible contacts between the State Department and E.P.C. ambassadorial meetings have not been fully exploited.

The European Community has made it clear, since the early seventies, that it is going to expand into the Mediterranean, i.e. into a crisis area (the Balkans, Yugoslavia, the Turkish-Greek and the Middle East conflicts, Lebanon, the West Sahara and Gibraltar) in the coming years. For the Europeans, this means new interests and responsibilities in crisis management. They have raised expectations which must be met in the short term, as well as in the long term. The enterprise boils down to investment by the North European member states in their own security. Without the United States, however, the tasks in the Mediterranean cannot be accomplished.

NOTES

1. Cf. Theo M. Loch/Hajo Hasenpflug, *Die Assoziierungs- und Präferenzpolitik der EG*, Bonn 1974; and Udo Steinbach, "Auf dem Wege nach Europa? Die Beziehungen zwischen der Türkei und der Europäischen Gemeinschaft durchlaufen eine kritische Phase," in *Orient*, 1(1977): 79-101.

2. For more details cf. Loch/Hasenpflug, op.cit., passim; H. Andresen, "Über die Verwirklichung einer gemeinschaftlichen Mittelmeerpolitik," in *Europa und die arabische Welt*—Probleme und Perspektiven europäischer Arabienpolitik, Europäische Schriften des Instituts für Europäische Politik, Vol. 41/42, Bonn 1975, pp. 293-326; R. Regul, *Die Europäischen Gemeinschaften und die Mittelmeerländer*, Schriftenreihe Europäische Wirtschaft, Vol. 75. Baden Baden 1977, passim; Avi Shlaim, "The Community and the Mediterranean Basin," in Kenneth J. Twitchett, *Europe and the World*—The External Relations of the Common Market, London 1976, pp. 77-120.

3. Cf. Andresen, op.cit., pp. 304-306.

4. Cf. Loukas Tsoukalis, "The E.E.C. and the Mediterranean: Is 'Global' Policy a Misnomer?" in *International Affairs* (London: July 1977): 422-438.

5. Cf. Günther van Well, "Die Entwicklung einer gemeinsamen Nahost-Politik der Neun," in *Europa-Archiv*, 4(1976): 119-128.

6. For the full text see *Europa-Archiv* 2(1974): D 29 f.

7. Ralf Dahrendorf, *Plädoyer für die Europäische Union* (Munich: Piper Verlag, 1973).

8. Cf. Carl A. Erhardt, "Die EG und der Mittelmeerraum," *Außenpolitik* 2(1976): 224 f.

9. *Europa-Archiv* 18(1974): D 416.

10. Cf. Ursula Braun: "Der europäisch-arabische Dialog—Entwicklung und Zwischenbilanz," *Orient*1(1977): 30-56.

11. In my conclusions I am relying very much on the conclusions drawn by Reinhard Rummel, *The E.P.C. in U.S.-West European Crisis Consultation: The Cyprus Experience*. Stiftung Wissenschaft und Politik, Ebenhausen/Isar, November 1977.

The U.S. Role in the Middle East—
The Soviet Perspective

Yaacov Ro'i

The 1970s have revolutionized the Soviet view of U.S. policy in the Middle East. In the sixties the U.S.A. was depicted as fighting a rearguard action to preserve its position in the area. This it did by virtue of connections with the bastions of conservatism and reaction, whose days were inevitably numbered; through the oil companies, who were suffering increasing limitations on their power and activities and were destined to disappear from the scene in the fore-seeable future as the oil-extracting processes became nationalized; and as. a result of the presence of the Sixth Fleet whose monopoly of the Mediterranean Sea had been meaningfully violated by the growth of a substantial and impressive Soviet squadron. Today, as the 1970s draw to a close, the Soviet Union is clearly worried by the American comeback in the region. The U.S.A. is seen from Moscow as the patron not only of its traditional allies, Saudi Arabia and Israel—and until January 1979, Iran—but also of the largest and most important Arab state, namely Egypt. Moreover, Saudi Arabia has become a major regional power and, together with the other Persian Gulf Arab oil producers, a factor that cannot be ignored in the international arena.

In theory, the Soviets still talk of the "weakness" of U.S. policy in that, for example, it supports the forces of "yesterday" and does not take into account the will of "the liberated peoples, struggling for a happy tomorrow." [1] In fact, however, this seems to be mere lip service to the old formulae and an increasingly unsatisfactory cover for the Kremlin's anxiety at U.S. achievements, the fall of the Shah and some troubles with Saudi Arabia notwithstanding.

A number of developments in particular have been the focus of Soviet concern. The first of these is Washington's relationship with

Riyād which in itself is sufficient to render meaningless the threat of reinvoking the oil embargo or of reapplying the oil weapon against the U.S.A. in any other form. It has also enhanced American leverage in the inter-Arab scene as a concomitant of the growth of Saudi influence. A second cause of anxiety has been the continued and increasing power ensured the U.S.A. as the principal arms supplier of the region, specifically of Israel in the traditional heartland of the Middle East, as well as of Saudi Arabia, with its mounting pretensions to military prowess, of Egypt, so long a purchaser of large quantities of sophisticated Soviet weaponry, and of other states in the area. Thirdly, Moscow is fully aware of the significance of Egypt both as the largest Arab state and as the traditional and perhaps only possible leader of the Arab world. Cairo's entry into the U.S. orbit and rejection of radicalism and Arab socialism have thus not only been a serious blow in themselves, creating inter alia obvious serious difficulties for the simplistic Marxist-Leninist presentation of historical trends and processes; they have also comprised a dangerous precedent for other regimes that had previously been aligned with the radical camp. Last and certainly not least, the Soviet Union has been upset by U.S. attempts to dominate the peacemaking process of the Arab-Israeli conflict, attempts that have been all the more worrying in view of their considerable success. The official commitment to coordinate endeavors between the two superpowers as cochairmen of the Geneva Conference had not been accepted as binding upon U.S. diplomacy, as shown by the Camp David talks in the fall of 1978 and the Egyptian-Israeli peace agreement.

Throughout, too, Moscow presents Washington as bearing in mind the strategic significance of the Middle East in the context of its relations with the U.S.S.R. and desire to undermine "the anti-imperialist national liberation struggle of the peoples." The Near East, the Persian Gulf, the Indian Ocean and Africa, especially East Africa, are all intrinsically connected and by strengthening its position in any one of these, the U.S.A.—and presumably also the U.S.S.R.—improves its position in all. (Soviet terminology differentiates between the Near East, that is, the Eastern Mediterranean lands, and the Persian Gulf; the original differentiation, until the 1960s, was between the Near and Middle East, the latter comprising Turkey, Iran, Iraq and Afghanistan.) The U.S. base in Diego-Garcia in the Indian Ocean and the Seventh Fleet had played an important role in the Middle East; U.S. warships had moved toward the Bāb al-Mandab Straits during the October 1973 war so as to put pressure on the Arab States.[2] The Persian Gulf, the largest oil reservoir in the capitalist world and a vast source of petrodollars, the Soviet argument runs, is a zone of fierce current and potential conflicts— between Iran and Saudi Arabia, Saudi Arabia and Iraq, Iran and Iraq, Saudi Arabia and the People's Democratic Republic of Yemen (P.D.R.Y.). The role of the U.S.A. is to prevent the development there, either in the context of these conflicts or irrespective of them, of antiimperialist trends and to isolate the national-liberation forces from Soviet support. Developments in many states of the Indian Ocean basin too would bear directly on the relation of forces in the world, which was the source of U.S. anxiety at the appearance in the Indian Ocean of the Soviet navy.[3]

These, then, are some of the major issues with which this paper will deal with the intention perhaps also of reading some operative meaning into Soviet comment on U.S. policy and interests in the Middle East.

The post-October 1973 period opened with an almost ecstatic rejoicing in the Soviet media at the extent of the damage effected by the use of the Arab oil weapon against the U.S.A. The panic, the inflation, the closing of industrial plants and the growth of unemployment in the world's leading capitalist power all seemed to promise the coming of the millennium, the longed for crisis of the capitalist economy.[4] The U.S.A.'s domestic problems were, moreover, supplemented by the disputes which erupted between Washington and its European allies, whose fears of the application to Western Europe of oil sanctions led them to express support for the Arabs in their war against Israel.[5] In this context it was clear that one of the most pressing tasks of American policy in the Middle East must be to put an end to the energy crisis precipitated by the invocation of the Arab oil weapon and to make every effort to ensure that it would not again be resorted to. Arab oil had become a weapon which it was impossible not to reckon with in the West in view of the tremendous need for it.[6] Indeed, the U.S.A. was trying "by hook or by crook" to terminate the embargo in the speediest possible fashion.[7]

Apart from this short-term goal, the U.S.A. was thought to be absorbed in more far-reaching strategic planning as regards the Middle East. The growing need for Middle East oil, resulting from the impossibility of increasing oil imports from Venezuela and Canada, meant that the U.S. interests and global strategy would be pivoting on the Persian Gulf before the end of the 1970s. One third of the U.S.A.'s imported oil was said to be coming from the Persian Gulf area.[8] Meanwhile an attempt was being made to intimidate the oil-exporting countries with threats of employing force so as to guarantee the supply of oil to the West. There was also a tendency in the U.S.A. to set up "a kind of anti-OPEC" uniting the developed capitalist oil-consuming countries which could resist the oil producers' "just struggle for greater control over their own reserves." Yet, the Soviets reported, neither of these directions was proving effective. The U.S.A.'s potential partners in a consumers' organization, Japan and Western Europe, were not keen on its establishment for fear of alienating the Arab countries. They also had reservations regarding American plans for expanding in the area as a whole, out of concern for their own oil supplies.[9] Soviet sources pointed out that the oil weapon was far more worrying to Western Europe and Japan than to the U.S.A. which was an oil-producer as well as importer; indeed, the American oil companies had made "enormous profit" from the sale of oil to Western Europe during the embargo.[10] U.S. political, military and economic pressures on the Arab oil-producers to reduce oil prices had led to a decision by the Organization of Petroleum Exporting Countries (OPEC) countries to enhance cooperation among themselves and to consider attempts at intervention in the domestic affairs of any one of them as aggression against all members of the organization.[11]

In 1977 with the advent of Jimmy Carter to the presidency, the U.S.S.R. noted growing U.S. concern regarding oil. The "energy crisis" was said to be considered Washington's "most serious problem after that of preventing a world war. . . . One thing," *Izvestiia* wrote, "is clear: the U.S. oil concerns will precipitate a further penetration of the Near East by all means—economic, political and military—and in this they will act hand in hand with the American authorities. Already, the United States is striving to achieve in this region entire 'strategic zones'." The U.S.A.'s strategic purpose was to establish and preserve "in the oil countries political regimes that suited their interests." The U.S.A. would like "certain Arab conservative regimes to fill the role of a 'regional police force' not only in the Near East area but also on the African continent.'' [12] This applied in particular to Saudi and to an extent also Sudanese interference in the Horn of Africa, including supply of military matériel to Somalia, throughout 1977.[13]

Saudi Arabia enjoyed a central role in this entire scenario. In the winter of 1973-74 the Soviet press stressed in particular Saudi statements that the Arabs were intending to continue the embargo against the U.S.A.[14] Even in early 1975 when Saudi-U.S. relations seemed to have improved, on the basis largely of Riyād's anti-Communism and the common stance against the very phenomenon of the national liberation movement, Washington was reportedly concerned by Saudi policy on the Middle East conflict and settlement, particularly support for the Palestine Liberation Organization (P.L.O.), and on "questions connected with oil." Riyād's participation in OPEC and the Organization of Arab Petroleum Exporting Countries (OAPEC) placed it in opposition to the "imperialist monopolies" and made it a protector of the producers' "sovereignty" over their natural resources. Riyād would agree to lower oil prices only on condition that the U.S.A. pressured Israel to withdraw from "the occupied Arab territories." [15] These topics have continued to preoccupy Soviet thinking. Washington, it was maintained, tried to set Saudi Arabia against the other OPEC countries.[16] Fearing that any further appreciable rise in oil prices would plunge the West's capitalist economy into an even worse recession and knowing that Saudi Arabia was not interested in raising oil prices, Washington used Riyād to exert pressure on OPEC.[17] Earlier optimism that Saudi Arabia might withstand Washington and foil its intentions in the Middle East, however, has receded under the Carter administration. The general trend of the media's comments on U.S.-Saudi relations—comments which have continued to be relatively numerous, particularly in the central press and journals—was to show Saudi inability to maintain an independent line. The U.S.S.R. seemed increasingly convinced that despite the U.S.A.'s need for Saudi Arabia and its oil and petrodollars, Riyād's dependence on Washington is even greater. Its fear of "social change" has made it a servant of imperialist forces. As a result, Saudi policy has played into the hands of American economic and strategic interests without receiving the stipulated quid pro quo in the field of the

Arab-Israeli conflict and settlement.[18] However, there were indications of a shift in the Soviet attitude to Saudi Arabia in the spring of 1979, resulting from growing Soviet criticism of and strained relations with the U.S., and demonstrating a clear Soviet drive for relations with Riyād.[19]

The Persian Gulf was, then, according to the Soviets, becoming the major focus of U.S. attention. The reason for this attention was the U.S. need for oil. The main expression of this attention, its outcome, was the consolidation of the U.S.A.'s military position in the area, largely—though not entirely—through arms supplies. The U.S.A. already had a base in Baḥrayn and was permitted by Oman to use the base on Masira. The Persian Gulf, according to Soviet sources, was to be the westernmost link in a new system of U.S. military bases in Asia that would encircle the entire continent. The Gulf was itself surrounded in a classical pincer movement by American naval units and military bases. U.S. military personnel had already encroached into the area and enjoyed virtual control over most of the forces in the Gulf, largely as a result of the dispatch of military technicians to accompany increasingly sophisticated weapons systems. By 1980, it was estimated, these would number 150,000. Meanwhile the Pentagon had elaborated a plan for the speedy landing of troops in the Gulf, but this was "an extreme measure."

As to arms supplies, a senior Pentagon official was quoted as saying that these were the instrument that would secure continued U.S. control over the Persian Gulf. Once again, Saudi Arabia was the purchaser of war matériel that most attracted Soviet comment. American arms were already being used against the national liberation movement in Zufār and served to give pungency to threats against the P.D.R.Y. The "deepening defense relationship" with states in the Gulf was likely to drag the U.S.A. even against its will into local conflicts. Specifically, Soviet media accused the U.S.A. of violating détente in the Persian Gulf and called for the application of its principles in that area.[20]

It was not, however, to the Gulf states alone that the U.S.A. was supplying arms. Israel continued to be a major recipient of large quantities and great varieties of sophisticated weaponry that were the object of Soviet attention throughout the period under review. Almost every high-level contact between Washington and Jerusalem was alleged to have centered on new Israeli demands for arms with the activating of the Israeli lobby in Washington to press the point and the eventual agreement of the administration and Congress to the satisfaction of most if not all of Israel's requests.[21]

True, the American policy of support for Israel was not necessarily always the direct result of government inclinations or orientations. U.S.-Israeli relations had traditionally been complicated by the strength of the Israeli lobby—supposedly the strongest of Washington's lobbies—and the fact that the Israeli prime minister often enjoyed stronger support in the Senate than did the U.S. president. American diplomacy which sought to improve the U.S. position with the Arabs with their oil wealth and strategic importance was unable to circumvent Israel as a result of the latter's great influence in Washington.[22]

The increasing U.S. arms sales looked particularly sinister in the context of the development of the neutron bomb which was causing great disquiet throughout the world. The purpose of these arms sales was said to be to strengthen Israel, to support the U.S.A.'s " 'friends' in the Arab countries" and to protect its oil interests. The connection between the first two was made explicit by Washington's request to the Israeli government to divert weaponry to the Lebanese Christian Right.[23] The arms sales also made nonsense of American claims that Washington sought peace in the Middle East. Decisions to provide arms undermined attempts at attaining a settlement "because peace and the accumulation of arms are incompatible." [24]

Both the U.S.A.'s military presence in the Persian Gulf area and the influence it attained through its arms sales have been significantly weakened by the Shah's fall, beyond—it would seem —the wildest Soviet expectations. As tensions mounted in Iran in the fall of 1978, the Soviet Union, while itself careful not to do anything to jeopardize its own fairly good relationship with the Shah and his regime until it became virtually certain that his days were numbered, was manifestly aware of the stakes at issue from the point of view of its rival, or fellow, superpower. The plethora of articles that dealt with the Iranian situation from September 1978 through January 1979 all pointed out the great strategic importance of Iran for the U.S., the major interest Washington had in keeping the Shah in power and American plans to intervene to that end. At first the Soviet media dwelt on the tremendous U.S. military and economic investment in Iran, the vast arms sales including the most sophisticated arms such as the "sensational contract" for eighty F-14 fighters and the very large contingent of American "advisers" in Iran said to reach 40-50,000, many of them with overt military and paramilitary assignments.[25] With the deterioration of the Iranian situation, the Soviets became vociferous about alleged American plans and intentions to intervene, even militarily, in Iran's domestic affairs in order to keep the Shah and his regime "afloat";[26] one article was significantly entitled "For the Sake of Oil Washington Is Prepared [to Do] Anything. . ."[27] The mission to Teheran in December of Senate Democratic Party majority leader, Robert Byrd, as personal envoy of President Carter, was said to be to assure the Shah of the U.S. administration's continued support and continued guarantee of Iranian "security."[28] The Soviet press described with manifest satisfaction the grown Iranian protest at American designs to intervene.[29] Brezhnev himself warned Washington that the Soviet Union opposed any external intervention in Iran's domestic affairs "by anyone, in any form and under any pretext." He went on: "It must be clear that any, and especially a military, intervention in Iran's affairs—a state bordering directly on the Soviet Union—would be considered by the Soviet Union as affecting its own security interests."[30]

In the last weeks of the Shah's rule, the U.S.S.R. stepped up its propaganda drive, pointing out the U.S. role in Iranian developments in the fields of military, intelligence and diplomatic activity, including the presence in the Persian Gulf of U.S. naval units.[31] Washington's "initial confidence in the ability of the [Shah's] regime to keep things in hand" was said to have "changed to near-panic as the. . .opposition movement gained ground and increasingly acquired an anti-American character." The Soviets also stressed the U.S. failure "to salvage whatever [could] be saved" and the controversy in the administration as to the desirable course of action. The group headed by George Ball (set up by Carter to study the Iranian situation) advised against "attempts to preserve the status quo" which would reduce the chances of the United States "preserving its influence in Iran, if there is a change of government," while National Security Adviser Brzezinski feared that changes in Iran "could have a demoralizing effect on other Washington-backed regimes and give rise to doubts as to the reliability of alliances with the Americans.'' This reasoning, it was contended, was identical to "the notorious domino theory which served as the 'theoretical basis' for the military intervention in Vietnam.'' In January 1979 the U.S. was said to be supporting the government of Shahpur Bakhtiar by helping it split the opposition; if Bakhtiar failed "to cope with the situation,'' he would be succeeded by "a Right-wing military dictatorship'' which, with the tacit support of Washington, would not stand on ceremony with the opposition.[32]

The new Iranian regime, although certainly not committed to the Soviet Union and far less pro-Soviet than Moscow had hoped, has been widely praised by the U.S.S.R. for refusing "to play the role of [U.S.] policeman in the Persian Gulf area'' as had its predecessor, for withdrawing from the Central Treaty Organization (CENTO), expelling the American advisers, taking over "the electronic espionage bases stretching along the Soviet border,'' obviously manned by Americans, and annulling arms contracts. They have tried to warn Iran's new rulers that the U.S. imperialists "will not easily accept such a staggering defeat,'' as evidenced by calls for an economic boycott of Iran and by the movement of the "nuclear-powered aircraft carrier Constellation. . .in the direction of the Persian Gulf.'' The new rulers were indeed aware of all this. Deputy Premier Abbas Amir Entezam having "disclosed that members of the disbanded State Security and Intelligence Organization (SAVAK), supported by agents of the C.I.A. and the Israeli intelligence service are mounting a campaign of subversion, sabotage and terror.''[33] Whether post-Pahlevi Iran will reach the requisite conclusions and decide on an active pro-Soviet orientation, the necessity for which is clearly implied in the Soviet analysis of the U.S. role, remains to be seen. Today, in the early summer of 1979, it looks most unlikely.

Moreover, Moscow is aware that Washington has not yet relinquished its position in the Persian Gulf as made clear by statements by Defense Secretary Harold Brown and Energy Secretary James Schlesinger. Yet U.S. plans to resume the American military presence in the Gulf by obtaining new military and naval bases in the Arabian Peninsula, "to press American arms and military advisers on the countries of the region and to increase U.S. naval strength in the Indian Ocean and Persian Gulf,'' had been rejected "even'' by

"countries that have closely cooperated with the U.S. for years,"
such as Saudi Arabia and Kuwait.[34] The United States' open support
for North Yemen in its war against the People's Democratic
Republic of Yemen in March 1979 when it openly landed large
quantities of weaponry in Saudi Arabia for this very purpose, was
ample evidence of the more active role Washington was adopting in
the region. The U.S. was said to be undermining "the sovereignty
of the Arab countries [and] striving to intensify the dispute between
the two Yemens."[35]

Meanwhile, the U.S. has been strengthening its position in new
directions. It has made significant headway with some of the traditional allies of the Soviet Union in the Arab world, notably Egypt.
While the Soviets noted on the occasion of Richard Nixon's triumphant tour of the Middle East in June 1974 that both Sādāt and
Nixon referred to the misunderstanding and tension that had characterized bilateral relations between their two countries for many
years, "reactionary propaganda" was said to be taking the opportunity to "belittle in every way the Soviet Union's role in the Middle East settlement" and to undermine Soviet-Arab friendship.[36]
Since the Sinai II agreement of 1 September 1975 and Sādāt's first
visit to the U.S.A. at the end of October of that year this has
become an issue that has caused the Kremlin growing anxiety,
although the main thrust of comment on this has been directed not
against the United States, but against Sādāt for betraying the legacy
of Nasser and the Egyptian "revolution."[37] Nonetheless, Washington was specifically accused of encouraging the Egyptian president
to abrogate unilaterally the Soviet-Egyptian Treaty of Friendship and
Cooperation.[38] There was, too, considerable American capital
investment in Egypt as a result of Sādāt's "open door" policy.[39]
When Secretary of the Treasury William Simon visited Egypt early
in March 1976, TASS reported the agreement he reached with his
hosts for "what he described as a new Marshall Plan." The aim of
this plan was the further growth of the private sector in the Egyptian
economy and the attraction of yet more foreign capital.[40] Washington used its aid so as to influence domestic trends and developments
and to persuade Egypt, and other recipient countries, to increase
trade with the U.S.A.; it sought through aid to preserve economic
backwardness, not wanting to create a base for a national industry.[41]
Soviet comment ridiculed American economic aid to Egypt, claim-

ing that neither its general direction nor its scope held any real hope for solving Egypt's very basic economic problems.[42]

For a long while, Soviet sources have made even more fun of Sādāt's attempts to procure military aid from the United States. Moscow was certainly worried at his recurrent statements that he was indeed variegating his sources of military supplies (his first statement to this effect was made in April 1974), as its own arms policy toward Egypt clearly reflected. At first, however, the Kremlin seems to have believed that there was no chance that the U.S.A. might actually provide the weaponry Sādāt was demanding. The debate in Washington over the six C-130 military transport planes early in 1976 seemed to prove the Soviets' point.[43] When Sādāt made his first visit to the U.S.A. after Carter's election, *Pravda* noted that the discussion of Egypt's "'defense demands'... led to neither concrete solutions nor any U.S. commitments."[44] As late as February 1978, during and following Sādāt's latest trip to Washington, which the Soviets described as having disappointed Cairo,[45] the Soviet position has been that Sādāt's demand of the U.S. administration to obtain the same weaponry as is supplied to Israel is unrealistic, since Washington in fact counts on Israel as its forepost in the Middle East.[46] Even with the announcement that the U.S.A. would be supplying Egypt as well as Saudi Arabia and Israel with sophisticated weapons, the Soviets insisted that there was no basic change in American policy since the greater quantity and better quality of the aircraft in question were designed for Israel and not Egypt (the former was to receive 90 F-15s and F-16s and the latter 50 F-5Es).[47]

With other Arab states, too, the U.S.A. was making significant headway. This was true first and foremost of Sudan and the Yemen Arab Republic which had in the past entertained fairly close connections with the U.S.S.R. It was true even of Syria which the U.S.A. not only renewed diplomatic relations with, but also included in Nixon's Middle Eastern tour. American ties with Syria were reported in very low key.[48]

From the point of view of quantity of comment, it has been the fourth issue, namely, the Arab-Israeli conflict and its settlement, that has drawn the most Soviet attention. The enhanced U.S. position in the area was also reflected in U.S. intervention in the region's other conflicts, notably the Lebanese civil war, on which the

Soviets looked with undisguised anxiety; yet, with all their importance, these were ancillary to the Arab-Israeli conflict.[49] While it is
difficult to isolate this question from the ones I have outlined
above—the Arab oil weapon, U.S. military aid and the relationship
with Saudi Arabia and Egypt, all of which bear directly on what the
Soviets call the Near Eastern settlement—it warrants and even
demands separate discussion. The prospects of Soviet-U.S. cooperation in negotiating, achieving and guaranteeing a settlement within
the framework of the Geneva Conference, that actually came into
being within two months of the termination of the October 1973
war, were the nexus of Soviet hopes for a comeback in a region
where the U.S.S.R.'s power seemed to be in constant and serious
decline in the mid-1970s. This was so much the case that the Soviet
Union was unusually hesitant in castigating American activity in the
course of Arab-Israeli diplomacy. The January 1974 disengagement
agreement between Egypt and Israel that was initiated, mediated and
attained by the U.S.A. to the total exclusion of Moscow was at no
stage an object of censure. The U.S.S.R. was able to force itself
somewhat artificially into the negotiations that led to the Syrian-
Israeli disengagement agreement of May 1974, Gromyko meeting
with Kissinger several times in this connection. The cooperation
of the two superpowers over this question was also a subject of discussion at Brezhnev's two summit meetings of the same year, with
Nixon in Moscow (in June) and with Ford at Vladivostok (in
November). It was only when Kissinger resumed his step-by-step
"shuttle" diplomacy in February 1975 on his first unsuccessful mission,[50] and again in August on the mission that led to the Sinai II
Agreement, that the U.S.S.R. had resort to unqualified attacks upon
U.S. policy. Sinai II was not only achieved as a result of U.S.
initiative and efforts; as the Soviets hardly tired of stressing, it
brought in its wake a U.S. presence in the Sinai Peninsula in the
form of the 200 technicians who were to man the early warning
machinery set up between the Egyptian and Israeli forces.[51] The
agreement was also said to benefit Israel only, leaving ninety percent of Sinai under Israeli control and killing any possible incentives
for further withdrawals on any front by removing the principal
source of pressure on the Israeli government.[52]

The U.S.S.R. insisted that the U.S.A. was not genuinely
interested in peace in the Middle East. On the contrary, it was said

to be slowing down and confusing the peace-making process and ossifying a crisis-ridden situation. The American administration's refusal to accept P.L.O. participation at Geneva from the initial stages not only meant a repudiation of the Palestinians' legitimate representative but also implied an unwillingness to proceed with the Geneva Conference. Its failure to recognize the Palestinian right to self-determination showed that American advocacy of human rights was selective. Washington was merely seeking means to promote its own interests and policies and strengthen its own position. This was the ulterior motive behind attempts to convince the Arabs of the U.S. desire for a rapprochement with them and propaganda stunts to show that the U.S.A. alone was able to resolve the Arab-Israeli conflict. In fact, the U.S.A. was splitting Arab ranks, weakening the Arab states and trying to change political and social processes within them. At the same time, it was preserving for Israel the role of chief partner in the region and not applying pressures for a withdrawal of troops from the occupied territories. Egypt was in reality neutralized in such a way that its army could not participate in military action against Israel—unless the latter actually attacked it—leaving Syria and Jordan to face Israel alone. Washington was using military and economic aid to attain a settlement on its own conditions. Yet the situation was not entirely black. The U.S.A. was isolated over the Palestinian issue. Its Security Council veto of January 1976, of a draft resolution calling for the Palestinian people to be given the right to establish its own independent state, showed that the official U.S. position on a settlement was as negative as before and still coincided with that of Israel. Moreover, there were forces and groupings in the U.S.A. which did not agree with official policy. Some, like Senator Charles Percy, had called for the establishment of an independent Palestinian Arab state, while the Brookings Institution report spoke of the need to discuss a comprehensive (as against a partial) settlement and to solve the Palestinian problem.[53] At least one prominent Soviet commentator admitted that the U.S. desire to prevent a simultaneous recurrence of an energy crisis and Arab-Israeli hostilities and to weaken the Soviet position had led the United States to change the correlation of forces between the sides to the conflict and to neutralize extremist elements inside Israel.[54]

After Sinai II, Moscow for the first time seemed to appreciate that the U.S.A. enjoyed advantages that enabled it to play the role of mediator between the Arabs and Israel. It was this evaluation that led the Soviet Union to take up throughout 1976 a position that was characterized by inherent contradictions on the issue of an Arab-Israeli settlement. This position comprised three main components: (a) insistence on the resumption of the Geneva Conference; (b) efforts to strengthen the P.L.O. and Moscow's relationship with it as the one element directly concerned in the Arab-Israeli conflict with which Washington had no direct working relationship—this included the demand for the P.L.O.'s participation at Geneva from the initial stages and on an equal footing; and (c) attempts to demonstrate the reasonableness of the Soviet proposals for a settlement, that came to include in October 1976 a call for the normalization of Arab-Israeli relations.

This last concession was made with an eye to the approaching U.S. presidential elections in the hope of influencing the incoming administration to forsake the Kissinger policy of step-by-step diplomacy and separate, partial settlements. Indeed the Carter administration quickly announced its commitment to a renewal of the Geneva Conference and a comprehensive settlement. With the induction of the Carter administration and Soviet hopes for cooperation, Soviet sources moderated their approach regarding the U.S. position. Washington, they claimed, increasingly favored a solution of the Palestinian problem as a sine qua non of a peace settlement.[55]

These hopes, however, were soon dashed. Given the tensions between the Soviet Union and the United States that resulted particularly from Carter's commitment to human rights, the Soviet Union continued to attack Washington for its role in the Middle East. The U.S.A., Soviet sources contended, continued to uphold the "special" American relationship with Israel, to supply it with sophisticated weaponry, to support its territorial claims and to refuse to agree to the participation at Geneva of the Palestinians' legitimate representatives. Indeed, its real intention was to put off Geneva once more and to defer all practical measures toward a settlement both as a result of Israeli pressure and in the hope that new internecine conflicts would break out in the Arab world and weaken it still further.[56] Attempts by the Carter administration to make a show of favoring a balanced compromise formula for a settlement were dictated by U.S. needs, specifically dependence on Arab oil. They did not imply any change in policy. Israel remained Washington's main support in the Middle East.[57] Despite rumors concerning divergences of opinion, Carter had stressed that the U.S.A.'s primary goal in its Near East policy was to protect Israel's interests. Begin's first visit to Washington in July saw the discarding of pretenses of even-handedness and showed the unreserved pro-Israeli bent of U.S. policy.[58] Toward the end of September the Soviets were still condemning the U.S.A.'s duplicity.

This changed with the joint Soviet-U.S. statement of 1 October. Although it was clear "that both powers still looked differently at many issues," a greater measure of agreement than ever before had been reached. Both the U.S.A. and the U.S.S.R. were now considering the settlement of the Middle East conflict as an indivisible part of the international détente in which both were interested. This was the termination of the course previously conducted by the U.S.A. of not consulting Moscow nor coordinating efforts with it—of attempting in fact to exclude the Soviet Union from the settlement process—that had reduced the chances of obtaining a settlement. The coincidental standpoint of the two superpowers on important aspects of the settlement opened up reassuring prospects for the establishment of peace and the elimination of a situation threatening explosion in one of the world's main hotbeds of trouble.[59]

This idyllic situation, however, soon changed again. A number of *SShA* that went to press in the second week of October talked of the existence in the U.S.A. of two plans. One reflected a more "realistic approach to solving the crucial problems in the international arena" (Secretary Vance was mentioned in this connection). The other, which operated consistently against normalizing the international climate, now accused Carter of surrendering to the Soviet Union, of applying pressure against Israel, and of letting the U.S.S.R. renew its influence in the Near East.[60] The American-Israeli working paper of 5 October that was formulated in a protracted meeting between Carter and Dayan was said to stymie any continued activity in the direction of implementing the Soviet-American statement. While the administration did not retract the statement, it had "to humor" Israel and that country's American lobbyists who had reacted to the U.S.-Soviet statement with threats of Congressional opposition to all the president's legislative initiatives and defeat in 1980 and with what was described in the American media as "'a strong diplomatic storm'" and "'a political confrontation between Israel's traditional supporters in the U.S.A. and the President'."[61] Less than six weeks after the joint statement, Washington was once more described as "complicating" the question of a settlement.[62]

The Sādāt "initiative" and Washington's position first of active and then of passive support of direct Egyptian-Israeli negotiations once more placed the two superpowers on opposite sides in all that concerned the Arab-Israeli conflict and its settlement. The Sādāt-Begin meeting in Jerusalem was quickly dubbed "a maneuver" undertaken "under American direction." The more involved the U.S.A. became in the Egyptian-Israeli talks, the more villainous its role especially as the U.S.S.R. found itself able to collaborate with a relatively large grouping of Arabs, including Syria, and was again in a position to describe itself with a measure of realism as the protector of the Arab cause, and the U.S.A. as the opponent of that cause. Carter's attempt to persuade other Arabs to support Sādāt's "disruptive" and "separatist" course, Vance's tour of the Arab countries directly concerned in the conflict and finally Ambassador-at-large Alfred Atherton's virtual mediation between Cairo and Jerusalem were portrayed as Washington's return to "shuttle diplomacy," with the intention once again of forcing concessions upon Egypt and the Arabs. Sādāt had directed his entire activity at Washington which he still considered to hold 99% of the cards in all that concerned the settlement of the conflict, but the U.S. administration was not convinced; "the miracle did not happen." Washington's sympathies remained with Israel, particularly over "the Palestinian problem." It announced it would not apply pressure on Israel either by limiting arms supplies or stopping economic support.[63]

With the change of regime in Teheran, the Soviets claimed that Egypt and the new Egyptian-Israeli axis would make up, from the U.S. point of view, for the loss of Iran. Soviet sources explained that "a new structure" would now "replace the pro-American regime in Iran, which collapsed, and the CENTO base which has disintegrated." In the wake of the fall of the Shah, the U.S. was seeking to strengthen its strategic positions in the Middle East. Sādāt had offered his services as American gendarme in the Arab world.[64] There is no scope in this article for following in detail the Soviet reaction to, and view of, the Camp David negotiations in September 1978 and the persistent hope, from the moment that talks there were over through the end of March 1979, that no treaty would in fact emerge from the agreement reached between Carter, Sādāt and Begin. Nor perhaps would a discussion of these developments be relevant in the new era seemingly reshaped by the treaty. Since it was signed, however, the U.S.S.R. has made and frequently reiterated a number of points: a. that "no developing country has yet succeeded in overcoming its lag and ensuring posperity for its people with 'aid' from the U.S. or any other imperialist power," in other words that Egypt was deluding itself into thinking that its economic problems would be solved by American technical and financial assistance; b. "that the U.S. administration. . .will never contribute, nor will it be allowed to contribute to the emergence next to Israel of a truly developed and prosperous (and hence strong) Arab state. It is unlikely that the U.S. and Israel will ever forget the lesson taught their ruling circles by the downfall of the Shah and his regime, which was no less closely associated with them than the present Egyptian regime"; in other words, that since the rapprochement with the U.S. was the personal work of Sādāt and could easily be terminated by his successor, Egypt could not hope for an involvement parallel to that which Israel was enjoying; c. that the treaty "cannot ensure the success of [imperialist] machinations. Washington would do well to realize" the futility of trying "to halt the anti-imperialist liberation movement of the peoples" and to take into account "the strength of the peoples fighting for their freedom and independence and drawing on the support of the mighty revolutionary forces of our time, the vanguard of which is world socialism." The cooperation between the two forces, the Arab national liberation movement and world socialism, had once again been confirmed by Gromyko's visit to Syria from March 24 to 26;[65] d. that the U.S. has been unsuccessful in preventing its traditional friends in the Arab world, the "moderates," from joining the more radical Arab states in their opposition to the treaty. Indeed the entire Arab world is united against the U.S., Egypt and Israel and their treaty, and supported, of course, by the U.S.S.R.[66] The new Soviet attitude toward Saudi Arabia has already been mentioned; e. that in return for its moderation, "Washington will probably get naval bases in the Israeli ports of Haifa and Ashdod and in the

Egyptian port of Sharm al-Shaykh, as well as two air bases in Israel and the Etzion air base in the Sinai."[67] The U.S., the Soviet contended, needed "the separate deal" because "far-reaching plans [were] associated with it in the creation of a pro-American bloc of Israel, Egypt and some other Arab countries to protect U.S. interests in the Middle East;"[68] the U.S.A. was interested in the Middle East as part of its strategic array against the U.S.S.R. and because of its need for oil. In order to promote its interests, it wanted to subordinate to them both the foreign policy and the internal developments of the countries of the region.[69]

In conclusion, I would like to ask what, if anything, we can learn from the increasingly complex picture the Soviets provide of the U.S. role in the Middle East. They no longer propagate the much-worn theory of the days of their own offensive and achievement in the Arab world to the effect that the U.S.S.R. is the sole ally of the forces of progress and national liberation in the Arab world and that Soviet policies march hand in hand with the historical processes and trends. The severance of the Soviet-Egyptian partnership and doubts about the Syrians—not only for their policy in Lebanon but also for leaving options open regarding their own relationship with the U.S.A.—and even the Iraqis, have made such arguments untenable for Moscow. The more ubiquitous and variegated the U.S. successes in the Arab world, the more sophisticated and inconsistent must the Soviet exposition of American intentions and policies become.

True, Washington too has known difficulties and the Soviets have been quick to highlight what they have seen as its traditional mistakes, such as threats of military intervention in the event of any danger jeopardizing its oil imports. They have also stressed American weaknesses, notably U.S. dependence on Arab oil as well as what has appeared at times a major drawback in the settlement-making process, namely the lack of contact between Washington and the P.L.O. For all the frustrations that the U.S.S.R.'s own contacts with the P.L.O. have brought the Kremlin, the dearth of a working relationship has meant for the United States a certain lack of maneuverability. The Soviet leadership has undoubtedly known periods when its own rapport with the P.L.O. has brought it advantage, especially in the euphoria of late 1974 and 1975 in the wake of the Arab summit at Rabat and 'Arafat's appearance at the U.N. General Assembly. Carter's various pronouncements on the Palestinians, intended as they were to mitigate the U.S. stance, have been received by the Soviets as a rather lame attempt to rectify an unsatisfactory situation. The basic Soviet position that the U.S.A. is unable to concede to the Palestinians even their minimum demands has remained unchanged.

Moscow has watched with glee the speedy and abrupt termination of the American-Iranian relationship, and in the zero-sum game of superpower rivalries, an American loss is automatically a Soviet gain. It has noted, too, that Saudi Arabia has shown signs of mounting criticism of the U.S., especially concerning the Egyptian-Israeli treaty. Finally, the Soviets have pointed out that the Egyptian-Israeli treaty contains a number of inherent difficulties which promise to make its implementation a protracted and thorny process. Yet, despite these difficulties and despite American anxiety about the free flow of sufficient Middle Eastern oil to both the U.S. and its allies in Western Europe and the Far East (Japan), the U.S. has clearly taken a positive and far-reaching initiative which—as it hopes and the Soviet Union fears—may turn out to herald a new period in Middle Eastern politics. Moscow, whose own illusions concerning erstwhile and presentday Arab allies have been thoroughly shaken, is certainly worried that, if this is the case, other Arab countries, including its own traditional allies, will move into the U.S. orbit.

The general picture that comes through, however, is one of American success and growing strength and influence and, concomitantly, as an inevitable sequitur thereof, of Soviet weakness and ineffectiveness. The different excuses made for the various manifestations of this trend do not detract from its general validity.

NOTES

This paper was updated in 1979.

1. E.g., *Izvestiia*, 27 July 1976.

2. *Izvestiia*, 15 March 1974.

3. E.M. Primakov, "The Mainsprings of the U.S.A.'s Near Eastern Policy." *SShA*, November 1976: 3-15.

4. Cf. *Izvestiia*, 20 December 1973.

5. *Izvestiia*, 14 and 24 February 1974; *Trud*, 12 March and 9 April 1974.

6. *Izvestiia*, 24 January 1974.

7. *Izvestiia*, 15 March 1974.

8. *Pravda*, 15 June 1977.

9. Y. Yershov, "The 'Energy Crisis' and Oil Diplomacy Manoeuvres," *International Affairs* (Moscow), November 1973: 53-62. In a long article entitled "'Oil Strategy' Boomerangs," *Trud* (1 April 1975) pointed out that the U.S.A.'s Western allies feared that these measures would merely impinge on their economic independence.

10. *Trud*, 15 January 1974. The Soviets made no mention of their own exploitation of the embargo to sell oil to the U.S.A. and Holland.

11. O.S. Bogdanov and S.V. Gorbunov, " 'Petrodollars' and the Currency Problems of Capitalism," *SShA*, April 1975: 25-36.

12. *Izvestiia*, 7 May 1977.

13. E.g., TASS in Russian for abroad, 12 December 1977/BBC, *Summary of World Broadcasts*, Part I, 15 December 1977.

14. *Izvestiia*, 24 February 1974; the reference was to a statement by Saudi Foreign Minister 'Umar al-Saqqāf on a visit to the U.S.A.

15. *New Times*, No. 7, February 1975; and D. Kasatkin, "In the Land of Oil and Sand," *Aziia i Afrika segodnia*, September 1975: 42-45.

16. D. Penzin, "Saudi Arabia—Oil and Development," *Mirovaia ekonomika i mezhdunarodnye otnosheniia*, November 1976: 114-119.

17. *New Times*, No. 3, January 1977.

18. E.g., *Izvestiia*, 11 May 1977; *Pravda*, 9 July and 25 August 1977. The *Izvestiia* article depicted the U.S.-Saudi relationship as part of an American master plan against the developing countries.

19. *Sovetskaia Rossiia* wrote on 27 March, 1979: "contrary to the desire of the Soviet side, there have been no diplomatic missions either in Moscow or in Riyād since [the eve of World War II]. The lack of such mission of course makes our relations largely formal, though there has never been any objective reason for perpetuating what is frankly an abnormal situation" Cf. also R. Moscow in Arabic, 5 March, 1979/*SWB I*, 7 March, 1979.

20. *New Times*, No. 7, February 1975, and No. 2, January 1976, *Aziia i Afrika segodnia*, September 1975; *Krasnaia zvezda*, 18 and 21 November 1975. For Soviet comment on military aid to Iran, see, e.g., *Pravda*, 21 September, 1977.

21. *Trud*, 8 January 1974, and 12 February 1976; *Izvestiia*, 3 April 1974.

22. *Izvestiia*, 19 October 1977.

23. *Izvestiia*, 15 July 1977.

24. *Pravda*, 17 February 1978. This argument had always been rejected by the Soviets when referring to Soviet arms sales.

25. *Za rubezhom*, No. 34, August 1978; *New Times*, Nos. 39, 48, September, November 1978; and *Literaturnaia gazeta*, No. 43, October 1978.

26. *Literaturnaia gazeta*, No. 43, October 1978; *Za rubezhom*, Nos. 46 and 50, November and December 1978; *New Times*, Nos. 47 and 50, November and December 1978.

27. *Za rubezhom*, November 1978.

28. *New Times*, No. 50, December 1978; G. Anatol'ev, "Events in Iran," *Agitator*, January 1979, pp. 45-7.

29. *Za rubezhom*, Nos. 51 and 52, December 1978; and *Agitator*, ibid.

30. *Pravda*, 19 November, 1978. Brezhnev made the statement in reply to a question from a *Pravda* correspondent.

31. *Literaturnaia gazeta*, No. 2, January 1979.

32. *New Times*, No. 4, January 1979.

33. *New Times*, No. 13, March 1979.

34. *New Times*, No. 11, March 1979.

35. R. Moscow in Arabic for the Maghreb, 8 March, 1979, and TASS in Russian for abroad, 12 March 1979/*SWB I*, 12 and 15 March, 1979; *Pravda*, 12 March, 1979.

36. TASS in English, 13 June 1974/*FBIS III*, 14 June 1974, and *Pravda*, 16 June 1974.

37. *Pravda*, 25 October 1974.

38. *Izvestiia*, 4 April 1976; E. M. Primakov, "The Mainsprings of the U.S.A.'s Near Eastern Policy", *SShA*, November 1976: 3-15.

39. TASS, 20 October 1975.

40. TASS, 8 March 1976.

41. A. Vavilov, "U.S. 'Aid' to Arab Countries: Myths and Reality," *Aziia i Afrika segodnia*, October 1974: 38-41.

42. E.g., R. Moscow in Arabic, 25 November 1975/BBC, *Summary of World Broadcasts*, Part I, 27 November 1975.

43. On March 3, 1976, the State Department confirmed that the Ford Administration had started consultations with key Congressional leaders on the sale of the six C-130s as the first step toward ending Washington's long-standing arms embargo to Egypt.

44. *Pravda*, 7 April 1977.

45. R. Moscow, 6 and 9 February 1978/BBC, *Summary of World Broadcasts*, Part I, 9 and 11 February 1978.

46. *Pravda*, 5 February 1978.

47. *Pravda*, 17 February 1978.

48. This held not only for the above mentioned events but also for Foreign Minister 'Abd al-Halīm Khaddām's visit to Washington in June 1975 and President Asad's meeting with Carter in May 1977.

49. Soviet concern over the U.S. role in the Lebanon reached its height in the spring of 1976 with the U.S.-Syrian dialogue over Lebanese developments and the mission to Lebanon of President Ford's special envoy, Dean Brown—e.g., R. Peace and Progress, 13 May 1976/BBC, *Summary of World Broadcasts*, Part I, 15 May 1976.

50. The failure of this mission was said to have convinced many in the U.S.A. of the lack of prospects of step-by-step diplomacy and the bankruptcy of separate agreements—*Izvestiia*, 29 April 1975.

51. The Soviets compared this with the beginning of the U.S. military presence in Vietnam—*Trud*, 3 September 1975; *Pravda*, 25 October 1975.

52. *Izvestiia*, 13 November 1975.

53. *Izvestiia*, 29 May and 13 November 1975 and 30 January, 1 February and 20 May 1976; I. P. Beliaev, "The U.S.A. and the Near Eastern Crisis," *SShA*, March 1976: 16-27.

54. E. M. Primakov, "The Mainsprings of the U.S.A.'s Near Eastern Policy," *SShA*, November 1976: 3-15.

55. *Izvestiia*, 8 February 1977.

56. For Soviet comment in this vein, see, e.g., *Izvestiia*, 23 February, 19 March, 14 April 1977; *Pravda*, 15 June 1977.

57. *Izvestiia*, 11 June, 3 July 1977; *Pravda*, 3 July 1977.

58. *Pravda*, 22 July 1977.

59. *Pravda*, 3 and 4 October 1977; *Izvestiia*, 19 October 1977.

60. A. K. Kislev, "After the Soviet-American Statement on the Near East," *SShA*, December 1977, pp. 43-48.

61. *Izvestiia*, 19 October 1977; *New Times*, No. 47, November 1977.

62. *Pravda*, 10 November 1977.

63. *Izvestiia*, 29 December 1977; *Pravda*, 8 and 10 January 1978, *Za rubezhom*, 1978, No. 7.

64. *Pravda*, 8 and 17 March, 1979; *R. Peace and Progress*, March 9, 1979/SWB I, 12 March, 1979.

65. *New Times*, No. 14, April 1979.

66. *New Times*, No. 16, April 1979.

67. *New Times*, No. 15, April 1979.

68. *New Times*, No. 11, March 1979.

69. *Pravda*, 2 April, 1979.

The Regional
Environment

The United States, Turkey and Iran

Bernard Lewis

"The longest, broadest, and most meaningful step in the nation's history, out beyond the established frontiers of its influence."

In these words, broadcast on 14 March 1947, two days after President Truman's message to Congress embodying what came to be known as the Truman Doctrine, Joseph Harsch gave expression to the sense of shocked awareness of the American people at what was rightly seen as the opening of a new era in their country's foreign policy and the acceptance of new, far-reaching and wholly unprecedented commitments.

To begin with, this new doctrine appeared to be of limited application. Both Britain's abandonment of responsibility and America's acceptance of it were intended to apply only to Greece and Turkey and not to other countries in the Middle East. But there were some who saw immediately that this was the beginning of a larger process and that by her appeal to the United States to take over the burden of supporting Turkey and Greece against Soviet pressure, Britain was in fact abdicating from her position of power and responsibility in the Middle East and was, in a manner of speaking, calling upon the United States to take over as her successor.

The problem of defending Greece and Turkey against pressure from the north was not new to American diplomacy. In November 1945, a U.S. note to Turkey had made clear Washington's interest in preserving the territorial integrity of Turkey against Russian demands, and in a series of diplomatic exchanges during the following months, the United States repeatedly expressed its deep concern on these matters. American support for Turkey was given visible expression in a number of ways as, for example, in April 1946, when the aircraft carrier Missouri was sent to Istanbul, ostensibly to

165

bring the coffin of the Turkish Ambassador Münir Ertegün, who had died in Washington, but clearly also as an encouragement to Turkey and a warning to Russia. At least, so it was seen in Istanbul at the time. The point was made more explicitly in August 1946 in the American answer to a Soviet government statement setting forth Russian claims in the Straits and elsewhere.

But all these fell far short of any kind of commitment or acceptance of responsibility for the defense of the region. Direct American interests in the area had in the past basically been of two kinds—on the one hand, commercial, and on the other, sentimental and philanthropic. American military and political involvement were seen as secondary to Britain's: in the one, the provision of much-needed money and matériel, in the other, the tendering of usually unwelcome advice.

The announcement of the Truman Doctrine gave an entirely new character to American policy in the area. American involvement in the defense of these two countries was made at once more coherent, more direct and more formal. The withdrawal of British power initiated in 1947 and completed in the 1950s and 1960s gave to the United States greater and, for a while, virtually sole responsibility for the defense of the area. Even after the constitution of the North Atlantic Treaty Organization (NATO) the contribution of other NATO countries to the defense and support of the southeastern flank remained minimal.

The promulgation of the Truman Doctrine was followed by a series of other steps. In May and June 1947, the first American military mission arrived in Turkey—the harbinger of a continuing and expanding relationship. On 12 July 1947, an agreement was signed in Ankara between the Turkish Foreign Minister and the American ambassador, Edwin Wilson, regularizing the procedures for American aid to Turkey in accordance with the Truman Doctrine. In the following year, this assistance to Turkey was incorporated within the legal framework of the American Foreign Assistance Act and in July 1947 an agreement was signed in Ankara incorporating Turkey into the provisions of the Economic Cooperation Act, that is to say, bringing her within the scope of Marshall Aid. On 6 November 1949, Turkey and Greece, though still not members of NATO, were included in the Mutual Defense Assistance Act covering American military aid to NATO members. The height of Turco-American cooperation came in 1950 when units of the American Mediterranean fleet visited Istanbul and Izmir and, in November of the same year, a Turkish brigade was sent to Korea where it distinguished itself in combat. So far Turkey and Greece, though cooperating closely with NATO, had not been admitted to membership. This was proposed by the United States on 15 May 1951, and finally approved on 18 February 1952. At this point, for the first time, Turkey and America were formally allied.

The Truman Doctrine applied only to Greece and Turkey. It was however accompanied by a parallel development, albeit along somewhat different lines, whereby American aid and protection were also extended to Iran, menaced in a different way, but by the same adversary.

Iran's experience of the Soviet threat was more direct and more painful than Turkey's. The Turks had been confronted with demands for territorial concessions and for bases on Turkish soil. Iran had endured far more—a partial occupation of Iranian territory and an attempt to set up separatist regimes in both Azerbaijan and Kurdistan. The situation here was somewhat different from that prevailing in Greece and Turkey, where the United States was called upon to take over a burden offered by Britain. Unlike Greece and Turkey in the mid-1940s, Iran was not disposed to trust Britain which, as Iranians saw it, had been twice willing, in 1907 and again in 1941, to sacrifice Iranian interests for the sake of an agreement with Russia. The second time, this had involved a joint military occupation by the two powers.

It was therefore to the United States that the Iranians turned in 1945 and after for assistance in resisting Soviet pressures and threats. With strong American and British support Iran took her complaint about Russian military and other activities in Azerbaijan to the United Nations in March 1946. By skillful diplomacy and with effective American help, the Iranian Prime Minister Qawam as-Saltaneh was able to negotiate an agreement with Russia, securing the withdrawal of Russian troops. This was completed by May 1946. Part of the price of this agreement was Iranian acceptance of a Soviet proposal for a joint Soviet-Iranian oil company with exclusive rights in northern Iran and with 51% Soviet control. The problem of Soviet-sponsored separatism in Iranian Azerbaijan and Kurdistan was for the time being shelved, though it remained a potential danger to the unity of the realm.

The growing threat to the integrity and independence of Iran on the one hand and the increasing support of the United States on the other helped bring about a new reassertion of Iranian rights, culminating in a vote by the Majlis rejecting the Russian oil agreement on 22 October 1947. In June of the same year, the United States had already agreed to grant Iran a credit of $25,000,000 for the purchase of surplus military matériel. Iranian caution however was indicated by a Majlis decision to grant authority to purchase matériel only to the amount of $10,000,000. The U.S. Congress later authorized a further $16,000,000 to cover the handling costs, bringing the total in usable credits to $26,000,000. The first shipment arrived in March 1949.

The interlude of government by Dr. Musaddiq and his National Front led to a rapid growth of anti-Western feeling, directed primarily against Britain but also affecting Britain's allies, and consequently to a reduction in relations between Iran and the United States. This was accompanied by a reinforcement of Soviet influence which, however, came to an end in 1953 with the overthrow of Musaddiq and the return of the Shah. This return led to a new and closer relationship between Iran and the United States.

The adoption of the Truman Doctrine and parallel developments elsewhere thus marked an entirely new departure in the foreign policy of the United States. America had acquired new allies and a new role in the Middle East, extending far beyond its previously somewhat limited and secondary involvement. This role required fresh perceptions and new skills, and necessitated a different approach to the problems of the region and, indeed, of international relations in general.

A point of some importance but one frequently overlooked in the Western world is that, for Turkey and Iran as well as for the United States, the offer and acceptance of American help involved some basic rethinking of positions and policies.

The two countries, Turkey and Iran, have much in common but also differ in several significant respects. Both are Muslim, neither is Arab. Both are old sovereign states with long experience of the conduct of their own affairs and acceptance of responsibility for their own decisions. Both have long experience of Russian expansion; both have suffered great losses of territory in the course of the past centuries and are aware of many millions who share their language, culture and religion still living in provinces acquired by the Russian Empire and retained by the Soviet Union. As nations directly abutting on the Russian frontier, both have an awareness of historic Russian policies which is without parallel further south, at least as yet.

Both are also affected by similar Soviet policies towards them. Since many parts of the Soviet Union, north of the Persian and Turkish borders, are inhabited by Persian and Turkish-speaking Muslims, both countries are seen in Russia as representing a possible threat to Soviet rule—a source of religious, nationalist or other ideological contamination which could sow dissension among the Soviet citizens of the Caucasian and Central Asian Republics and stir them up against the rule of Moscow. In Soviet demonology, pan-Turkism, pan-Iranism and pan-Islamism are dangerous heresies to be detected and extirpated wherever they occur. Their common offense, which they also share with pan-Judaism, or Zionism, is that they offer an identity other than that of the Soviet Union to important groups of Soviet citizens and, furthermore, one with a center outside Soviet control. (Pan-Arabism, incidentally, is still exempt from these strictures and is likely to remain so until one or other Arab country applies for admission to the Soviet family and is accepted.)

Iran and Turkey, lying along the soft southern border of the Soviet Union, are seen as a problem for Soviet security. Even as neutrals they are a potential source of trouble; in alliance with a hostile power they could constitute a serious threat. By their bullying and aggressive policies towards these countries in the mid-1940s, the Soviets themselves created the danger which they were seeking to forestall.

In their long relationship with their northern neighbors—at one time several of them, now only Russia and its dependencies—both Turkey and Iran have often been in need of help, but the two have very different perceptions of the nature of the threat and the best means of countering it.

Turkish experience of this problem is both longer and more extensive than that of Iran and goes back to the latter part of the seventeenth century when the Turks failed in their second attempt to capture Vienna and were forced by the Austrians to retreat through southeastern Europe. For the first time in their long history the Turks were compelled to make peace as a defeated power. On that occasion, they sought and obtained the help of Britain in negotiating somewhat better terms than they might otherwise have got, and first learned the game of using remoter powers to counter their immediate neighbors. The eighteenth century provided further illustrations of this principle which during the nineteenth and early twentieth centuries became the main basis of Turkish foreign policy. The advancing power of Russia was now seen as the principal danger and the rest of Europe as a source from which help might be obtained to counteract it. At first, Turkish eyes were directed mainly towards Western Europe—sometimes to Britain, sometimes to France, sometimes even to both together as in the Crimean War. The consolidation of the Germanic powers in Central Europe and the consequent rapprochement between the West European powers and Russia caused the Turks to look elsewhere. Germany and, to a lesser extent, Austria-Hungary replaced Britain and France as the traditional defenders of "the integrity and independence of the Ottoman Empire" against Russian threats.

Similar considerations underlay the somewhat ambivalent attitude adopted by the Turkish Republic during the Second World War and the Turkish refusal to enter the war despite the treaty of alliance concluded with Britain and France shortly after its outbreak. Ideally, the Turks would have liked to see Russia defeated by Germany and Germany defeated by the Western allies. This however did not occur and, as a result of their long hesitation, the Turks found themselves in a dangerous position of isolation at the end of the war. Britain proving inadequate, a new source of support was required and the United States was seen as the answer.

Turkish policy thus was no improvisation but the culmination of a long and sophisticated diplomatic evolution. Its aim was to maintain the independence and integrity of the country—no longer the Ottoman Empire but now the Turkish Republic. This meant that there was no slack, and that the issue was not the loss of outlying provinces but the survival of the heartland itself. It had been Turkish policy during the nineteenth and until the mid-twentieth century to seek such help and use it as convenient in war or diplomacy or through economic aid, but to avoid adopting policies or entering into situations in which Turkey would be dependent on the provision of aid by foreign allies, that is to say on the faithfulness of foreign friends to their commitments. The aim of the Turks was to avoid such situations rather than to prepare for them; to keep their policies and the commitments in which these policies involved them within the limits of their own unaided forces however inadequate these might be. In this perception foreign help was something to be invoked when needed in an emergency rather than a basis on which to formulate policy. Turkey's military alliance with the Central Powers in 1914 was not a policy but a last-minute improvisation, and its results did not encourage further ventures of the sort. In the results of Turkish involvement in World War I we may see one of the main causes of Turkish isolation in World War II. As the Turkish proverb has it, "The child burnt his tongue on the soup; he blows on the yoghurt."

By the second half of the twentieth century however the situation had changed radically. The increasing sophistication and cost of weaponry and the consequent growing disparity between major and minor powers made such a policy of independent action increasingly difficult. The Turkish involvement with the United States and then with NATO meant in effect that for the first time in her history, Turkey was basing her foreign policy on alliances; that is to say accepting commitments and facing risks, both of which were beyond her own unaided strength and the acceptance of which was predicated on the assumption that her allies would loyally discharge their commitments towards her.

Iran, though similarly affected in the past and similarly threatened in the future by Russian expansion, has nevertheless undergone a different formative experience. Her geopolitical experience of the last 150 years has been largely determined by the expansion of the two greatest European colonial empires, those of Britain and Russia. The advance of the Muscovites to the Caucasus, the Caspian and Central Asia brought them ultimately to the northern borders of Iran which barred their further expansion southward. The consolidation of the British Empire in India made British governments keenly aware of the importance of Iran and also of Afghanistan for the British position and awakened an interest in the affairs of both countries. During the nineteenth and early twentieth centuries, Iranian independence was preserved in the main through an uneasy balance between the two great empires which were her neighbors in the north and south, and Iranian statesmen learned to play them off very skillfully against one another.

Experience taught the Iranians that the greatest dangers to Iran were of two types. One was when the two Empires reached agreement, which happened in 1907 and 1941—on both occasions for the same reason, the need to join forces against a common enemy. And on both occasions the agreements between the two involved a virtual division of Iran between their spheres of influence and a consequent diminution of Iranian independence.

Even greater than the danger of an agreement between the two great neighbors was the disappearance or enfeeblement of one of them, leaving Iran alone face to face with the other. The seriousness of this threat depended very much on who that other happened to be. During the Russian Revolution and Civil War, Russian power was for a while eliminated, but this did not greatly threaten the independence of the country, since British interest was largely defensive, and the British government of India had neither the need nor the inclination to exploit this opportunity to more than a very limited extent.

A much graver danger came in the period immediately following the end of World War II, when Britain withdrew, leaving the Russians alone. The British Empire was coming to an end. Britain could no longer provide a counterweight to the now really formidable Russian power in the north. It soon became clear that this situation placed the integrity and independence of Iran in mortal danger. The new states which emerged in the Indian subcontinent, because of their division, their rivalries, their weakness and their inexperience, were incapable of inheriting the role of the former Indian Empire. The power in the north remained, stronger than ever. An indication of this strength was the steady growth of Soviet influence in Afghanistan, culminating in the pro-Soviet coup of April 1978. The implications for Iran of this change on her eastern frontier were disturbing.

An important new element in the situation is the basic change in Iran's perception of her own role. Until very recently Iran was a minor state and, like other minor states, concerned basically with her own interests and her dialogue with the Great Powers about these interests and about the affairs of the immediately adjoining areas. Recent years, however, have brought important changes. Iran has already developed from a minor to an intermediate power and the Shah tried to make her a major power, at least on a regional basis. Iran is already the most important single power in the Middle East as a whole, with a range of activity and influence extending far beyond her immediate national concerns. Nor is it sufficient to consider Iran merely in a Middle Eastern role. Iran also has frontiers with Soviet Central Asia, Afghanistan and Pakistan and has, to an increasing extent, developed relations with countries beyond these, notably with China and India. The range of Iranian activity—diplomatic, economic and even military—was extended to the Indian Ocean and beyond, to Asia, Africa and even on other levels to Australia, Europe and the Americas.

This new power, based largely though not exclusively on the wealth derived from oil, also created a new vulnerability. Unlike Iraq and Saudi Arabia, Iran has no pipeline leading to the Mediterranean but must rely for the export of her oil from the southwest on sea transport through the Persian Gulf and beyond that across the sea lanes round Arabia to the West. This broke the hitherto almost exclusive concern of Iranian foreign policy with the Soviet threat in the north, and has directed it increasingly towards Iran's neighbors in the south and west. The development in recent years of radical nationalism, sometimes combined with Islamic revivalism, in several Arab countries was seen as confronting Iran with a double problem—an ideological challenge to the stability of the regime and—through Arab claims on the Iranian coast of the Gulf—an irredentist threat to the integrity of the realm. There is some difference of opinion among Iranians on which of these two is the more important. These considerations as well as the perennial threat from the north determine Iran's choice of allies and associates and her expectations from them.

The withdrawal of Britain was not immediately apparent. For a while the issue was obscured by a continuing British presence which proved particularly distracting in Iranian politics during the late 1940s and early 1950s. But the British withdrawal was continuing rapidly—Palestine in 1948, Suez in 1955, Jordan in 1957, Aden in 1967, the Gulf by December 1971. Inevitably there was a tendency to equate the newly arrived American power with the departing British power which it was replacing, the more so because of some similarities of language and institutions between the two countries.

The differences between the British Empire and the United States were not then fully appreciated and this sometimes gave rise to confused thinking. Of the two great empires that had been neighbors of Iran's one had gone and the other remained. Now, not two empires but two superpowers confronted each other in the region and the relationship between the two was very different. Unlike the British Empire, the United States has no firm base in the area comparable with India and other former British possessions in South and Southwest Asia. Unlike imperial Britain or contemporary Russia, the United States has no territorial and only limited naval power in the region. The danger of an American alliance, as some of America's allies are belatedly beginning to perceive, is not American expansion but American loss of interest. There are signs that some Iranians now see China, more than America, as the alternate superpower on the Asian continent, and as the counterweight to Russia. This may be a trend for the future; it has not happened yet.

With the withdrawal and problematic replacement of British power in the south, the position of Russian power in the north became both relatively and absolutely greater. Tsarist Russia was one of several European imperial powers; Soviet Russia is now one of only two, or perhaps potentially three, superpowers. The ideological instruments of Tsarist expansion, the Orthodox Church and pan-Slavism, were of limited appeal and meant nothing to peoples who were neither Orthodox nor Slav. The Marxist orthodoxy and pan-leftism dispensed by the Soviet Union can be used in a much wider range of countries and can threaten a much wider range of regimes. Both in Turkey and in Iran they have already shown an ominous attractiveness to important elements of the population, notably among the youth and more generally among the intellectuals. The most obvious response to such influences is anti-Americanism.

At first, relations between the United States on the one hand and her new allies and associates on the other seemed excellent, and the late 1940s and the 1950s constitute what a recent Turkish diplomatic writer has called "the heroic age of Turco-American friendship." These years saw increasingly close relations between Turkey and the United States on a wide range of topics, a series of visits by the leading statesmen, significant cooperation in the field of foreign policy and, above all, increasingly close military cooperation at all levels. The strength of the Turco-American relationship in this period is demonstrated by the fact that it survived the unsuccessful attempt to create a Middle East Command in 1951, the reluctance of the United States to become a full member of the Middle East Alliance in 1955 and, most searching test of all, the Suez crisis in 1956. U.S.-Turkish cooperation was effective during the Iraqi and Lebanese crises of 1958, in the course of which the United States was able to use its air base near Adana as a staging point in the despatch of troops to Lebanon. This is in striking contrast with the situation in October 1973, when Turkey—like some other European NATO members—denied the Americans facilities in supplying Israel, but allowed Russian planes bound for Egypt and Syria to overfly. The Treaty of Cooperation of 1959 regularized the existing commitments of the United States towards Turkey and was paralleled by similar pacts concluded by the United States with Iran and Pakistan.

Only in the economic sphere was there occasional friction between the two allies. American views did not coincide with those of the Menderes government in Turkey as to the sums needed for investment and the way in which they should be invested. These economic differences did not however in any way affect the continuing harmonious political and military cooperation.

The first note of discord to disturb Turco-American harmony was heard in May 1960 when an American U-2 plane flying from the American base at Incirlik in Turkey was shot down over Soviet Russia. The fact that this plane had been operating out of a base on Turkish soil without the knowledge of the Turkish government caused some disquiet and gave rise to some discussion. The disquiet became greater after the Cuban missile crisis in 1962 when, as part of a compromise agreement between the United States and the Soviet Union, Soviet missiles were withdrawn from Cuba and, in return, American Jupiter missiles which had been based in Turkey since 1959 were withdrawn from that country. The explanation that was given to the Turks at the time—that the Jupiter missiles had lost their value since the introduction of Polaris submarines not long previously—did not entirely convince them. The suspicion that matters of vital interest to Turkey were discussed without her knowledge and settled without her participation, in a direct deal between the two superpowers, was confirmed by the publication of Senator Robert Kennedy's memoirs of the Cuban missile crisis in 1969.

In the meantime, Turco-American friendship suffered a more direct blow through the sending on 5 June 1964 of President Johnson's brusquely worded message to Prime Minister Inönü, warning him against sending Turkish troops to Cyprus. For most Turks this came as a shock and was seen as a betrayal. It initiated a steady deterioration in U.S.-Turkish relations which continued for a long time, notably after the Cyprus crisis of 1974, the despatch of Turkish troops to the island, and the American imposition of an embargo on arms for Turkey. Both the embargo and the failure to lift it occasioned bitter comparisons—with Egypt on the first point, with Saudi Arabia on the second. Egypt attacked in Sinai and was rewarded; Turkey landed troops in Cyprus and was punished. Powerful lobbies opposed the supply of war matériel to both Saudi Arabia and to Turkey. The one, thanks to great efforts by the administration, was overruled; the second for the time being prevailed. Few Turks were willing to believe that the Greek lobby was stronger than the Jewish.

Turkish anger and anxiety were not limited to the immediate question at issue, the problem of Cyprus. There was the larger question that in Turkish eyes the attitude embodied in the Johnson letter of 1964 and the embargo of 1975 nullified the assumption on the basis of which Turkish foreign policy had been realigned, and thus endangered their whole international position. The Turks had made a fundamental change of policy, committing themselves to a long-term alliance and accepting the risks and responsibilities involved in such a decision. For Turkey therefore, the United States was not only the heir of the powers of Central and Western Europe as a counterweight and corrective to Soviet power. It was also assigned a new role that had never really been assumed by any European country in the past—that of an ally and, indeed, the leader of a grand alliance of which Turkey was an active partner. For the Turks this represented a radical change from policies pursued over centuries. This made it easier for them to show some understanding of a similar American unwillingness to become involved in alliances—even in alliances which were largely of American inspiration. As the Turks see it, they have been loyal and active members of both the Central Treaty Organization (CENTO) and NATO, sometimes at considerable cost and risk to themselves. At the time of the Cuban missile crisis they had acquiesced in a script which placed them in the center of the stage but without a speaking role in a major conflict between the superpowers. It now came as a great shock to them to discover that on an issue which to them was one of vital importance, the question of Cyprus, the United States not only disagreed with them but apparently felt in no way bound by the alliances to support or to help them. As they see it, their loyal service to alliances, beginning with the despatch of a brigade to Korea in 1950 and continuing thereafter, went unnoticed, as did also their patience during the years when, in violation of the Zurich Agreements, the Greek majority regime on the island failed to give the Turkish minority the rights which had been accorded to it.

There can be little doubt that the attitude of both Turkey and Iran towards the United States at the present time is largely one of disappointment. Both countries had assigned roles to the United States which it was unable and unwilling to play. But there is another reason for their disappointment, more fundamental than the refusal of the U.S.A. to accept specific foreign policies designed and assigned to it by these countries. This arises from certain fundamental characteristics of American foreign policy which are received with incomprehension in both Turkey and Iran, as well as in some other places. In part this is due to the multiple and varying sources of American decisions. The complexities of the decision-making process in American foreign policy are difficult enough for Americans and other Westerners to understand. They are often impossible for observers brought up in other political cultures.

One difficulty is the apparent unwillingness of the United States to see itself in the role of one power among others, contending in a multilateral conflict in which the U.S. has both allies and enemies, that is to say groups with whom there is a community of interests and others with whom there is a clash of interests. There is a marked tendency in American policy makers, even in dealing with alliances of their own creation and with issues in which they are vitally involved, to try and maintain a position *au dessus de la mêlée* and to see the role of the United States as that of a judge or, at worst, that of an advocate and not that of an interested party. This latter role is assigned to the smaller powers which are variously seen as litigants or as clients—the latter perhaps in both the Roman and contemporary legal senses of the term.

The terms "friends" and "friendship" are sometimes used

loosely to denote a community of interest or cooperation in action between countries. In this sense, however, the words mean something quite different from their normal use in private or personal relationships. In international politics, friendship means some arrangement with a government and the normal questions to be asked about such a relationship would be: Can we get it? Do we want it? How long can we keep it? How much is it worth when we have it?

There is however another sense in which the term friendship can be used between nations—a sense closer to the private and personal meaning of the word. This is where there are not only common interests but genuine affinities—a community of basic beliefs and values, particularly concerning social, political, cultural and economic matters. The Turks believe that they alone among the peoples of the Middle East, with the solitary exception of Israel, can claim such a relationship with the Western world. Turkey's alignment with the West is after all not merely diplomatic. It is an expression of a much profounder movement extending over more than a century of Turkish history and involving an attempt to modernize—and this was understood as meaning Westernize—the economic, political and administrative systems of the country and the basic direction of its culture and aspirations. Already in the 1920s the United States was seen by many Turks as the leader of the Western world and the embodiment of the most advanced form of that Western civilization to which Turkey was aspiring. The Westernization of Turkey has brought profound changes in Turkish society and a gradual, painful but nevertheless genuine development of a Western way of life with a liberal economy and a parliamentary democracy. Despite recurring crises at home, Turkey has retained her commitment to parliamentary government and to democratic values and on this ground alone expects some consideration from the country that has now replaced Western Europe as the leader of the free and democratic world. Indeed, with the collapse or weakening and withdrawal of the Western European powers, the United States in Turkish eyes took over the place which all of them had held and was seen as replacing the British navy, the German army, French culture and the diplomatic roles of all three. For most Turks the United States has not lived up to this ideal.

Whether in the recognition and safeguarding of common interests or in the perception and pursuit of common purposes, they have found the American response disappointing. It is a common assumption of both the militant and fashionable left in most parts of the world that the United States is a force for evil both in its domestic affairs and in its international policies. According to this view, any country or government or group or individual that is well disposed to the United States is suspect and probably vicious. That such views should be expressed by known adversaries of American policy and the American way of life is not surprising. It is however somewhat disconcerting to find that the same assumptions appear to underlie the pronouncements of many leading commentators on international affairs in American media and even, at times, the policies and declarations of the American government. This kind of political masochism, however puzzling and disquieting, is not wholly unfamiliar, and is ominously reminiscent of certain aspects of British foreign policy during the terminal stages of British imperial decline.

The United States does not play the imperial or for that matter the diplomatic game according to the old rules; neither has it yet instructed its fellow players in any new ones. The balance of power, it would seem, no longer applies; the new principle of the balance of deterrence or more precisely of terror is neither accurately understood nor consistently applied. Turks and Iranians, like many others, are baffled by the unique blend of naive cynicism and corrupt idealism which inspire many acts of U.S. foreign policy as well as other American activities abroad. They are puzzled by a Great Power which seems unwilling to differentiate between its friends and its enemies, at least to the former's advantage, and seems at times indeed unable to distinguish between them.

One of the most important factors therefore shaping the policies of these countries at the present time is a growing perplexity about American policy. Even governments which are well aware that their interests march with those of the United States and clash with those of the Soviet Union hesitate to align themselves with a country which, in their eyes, seems fickle and unreliable. The Soviets are near, the U.S. is far. The Soviets, however hostile, are purposeful, consistent, intelligible; since their policies are always and invariably determined by naked self-interest, they are to that extent calculable and predictable. The policies of the United States are changeable and unpredictable. They are often affected or even determined by considerations and attitudes which many abroad find it difficult to understand.

The question must inevitably arise whether the United States does in fact constitute an effective counterbalance to the Soviet Empire. If she does not and if no other countervailing power emerges, then there is nothing to stop eventual Soviet domination over the whole of the Middle East, and simple common sense and self-preservation would impel the rulers of Middle Eastern countries to make the best terms they can with the inevitable.

There is thus considerable importance in their perception and assessment of American policies towards them and, more generally, of American attitudes and policies in the world today.

The Challenge of Diversity:
American Policy and the System of
Inter-Arab Relations, 1973–1977

Itamar Rabinovich

The Arab world presents a peculiar problem to a Great Power interested in the Middle East. The domination of pan-Arab ideology on the one hand and the specific political evolution of several Arab states on the other fashioned a system of inter-Arab relations that is characterized by an intense quest for unity and consensus but fragmented by deep cleavages and bitter rivalries. An external Power formulating a comprehensive Middle Eastern or Arab policy is therefore required to address itself at one and the same time to the Arab system as a collectivity and to the particular positions and policies of individual Arab states. Egypt, to take the most notable example, is a large, important and strategically placed state in its own right. Its importance since World War II has been enhanced immensely by its position of leadership in the Arab world. And yet, its ability to carry with it the Arab world or a large part of it or even to act in its own interest impervious to Arab pressures has remained a moot point.

These issues were first encountered by the United States in the aftermath of World War II when it became seriously involved in the Middle East and gradually inherited Britain's position of primacy in that area. Britain's legacy included also an ambivalent attitude toward an embryonic system of inter-Arab relations which had just been institutionalized in the form of an Arab League. Britain had vacillated between efforts to integrate the Arab states into one system and attempts to base British policy and influence on a direct bilateral relationship with individual Arab states.[1]

When the United States sought in the late 1940s and early 1950s to organize the Arab and other Middle Eastern states into a pro-Western alliance, it shifted between similar alternatives. Thus in February 1948 the American minister in Jidda was told that King Ibn Saud favored the idea of

"... a tripartite agreement under U.N. between U.S., Great Britain and Arab states possibly through Arab League which would attain the same security objectives the British had in their proposed bilateral treaties with Iraq, Saudi Arabia and Egypt. Such an arrangement would ease the problem of those Arab states in making individual arrangements and would facilitate objectives we all sought."

Offering his own opinion in this matter, the minister wrote a few weeks later that:

"General advantages [of] such pact whether multilateral or bilateral in character on our part and Great Britain's are to me very great." [2]

In the event, though, the United States, like Britain, was unable to reconcile the differences and rivalries between various Arab states, particularly between Egypt and Iraq. By 1958 it became clear that both the effort to organize a pro-Western Arab pact or to deal with the Arab world through one chief client had failed.[3]

During the next fifteen years the United States continued to be active in the Middle East but its policies tended to be directed at specific problems and issues rather than at broad regional schemes. The effort to formulate a comprehensive regional policy and to organize an active pro-American coalition in the Arab world was not undertaken again as a high-priority, sustained effort until October 1973.

The decision to embark on such a new policy was motivated by an awareness of the region's vital importance, the nature and extent of the perceived American interests and the unique position gained by the United States with regard to the Arab-Israeli conflict due to the course of the October War. Washington now sought to settle the Arab-Israeli conflict and thereby prevent the danger of renewed war, enhance the American position and limit Soviet influence and achieve several more immediate policy goals such as the uninterrupted flow of oil.[4]

The establishment of a moderate, or pro-Western, Arab coalition was an essential part of the new policy. "U.S.-Egyptian relations," we are told, "were seen as the linchpin of the new American policy in the Middle East, with Saudi Arabia and Jordan playing key supportive roles in favor of Arab moderation."[5] But Egypt, Saudi Arabia and Jordan did not operate in a complete political vacuum; they were part of a broader system of inter-Arab relations and their relationship with the other Arab states raised three operative questions:

a. To what extent could Egypt and her two partners to this prospective coalition further American policy goals in the area as a whole?

b. To what extent, if they could not carry much of the Arab world with them, were these states capable of conducting an autonomous policy, immune to pressures exercised by the rest of the Arab world?

c. To what extent were American successes in the promotion of Arab "moderation" bound to generate counter-pressures by the opponents of such moderation, Arab radicals and the Soviet Union?

The answer to these questions depended to a great extent on the course along which inter-Arab relations were to develop. It was quite clear at the time that in this respect, too, the October War had inaugurated a new phase. The elements of continuity and change represented by this new stage can best be seen with the help of a brief survey of the development of inter-Arab relations during the three previous decades. That period can be conveniently divided into four main phases:

a. 1944-1945. During this formative period the Arab League was established and the pattern of inter-Arab relations became apparent Two rival groupings emerged that fought for supremacy in the Arab world: the Saudi-Egyptian and the Hashemite blocs.

b. 1955-1963. This phase coincided with the heyday of the Nasserist regime and movement. Egypt acquired a position of hegemony in the Arab world and the attainment of Arab union seemed for a brief moment a feasible goal. Inter-Arab relations ceased to be governed primarily by dynastic rivalries as inter-Arab rivalries were also motivated by ideological concerns or were at any rate couched in ideological terms. Inter-Arab conflicts could never be neatly separated from domestic Arab politics and Great Power rivalries, but during this period they came to be intertwined still more closely.

c. 1963-1967. This phase saw the exacerbation of ideological rivalries in the Arab world and the division of the Arab states into three distinct groups: Egypt and her allies, the conservative states and the Ba'thī regimes. The Arab summit conferences replaced the Arab League as the all-Arab forum. A close interplay existed between the dynamics of inter-Arab relations and the course of the Arab-Israeli conflict. The Palestinian problem which had been submerged since the early 1950s resurfaced as an important issue in inter-Arab relations.

d. 1967-1973. The war of June 1967 affected inter-Arab relations in a number of ways. Nasserism suffered a further decline; ideological rivalries were blunted; Egypt, Syria and Jordan, despite obvious differences and rivalries, shared a consensus as to minimal Arab demands in any settlement with Israel and ruled out the possibility of separate settlements; the Palestinians became a more autonomous actor in Arab and regional politics. With further divisions and subdivisions there were no real groupings left in the inter-Arab system which became virtually atomized.[6]

The October War, in part a result of these developments, gave further impetus to some of them. Thus the idea of pragmatic cooperation between Arab states seemed to overshadow the ideal of political union as a more feasible way of expressing Arab unity and solidarity. The position of oil-producing Arab states, particularly Saudi Arabia, became increasingly influential.

A significant structural change was the emergence of a group of four Arab states which, at least for a while, seemed to occupy the center of the new stage: Egypt, Saudi Arabia, Syria and Algeria. Saudi Arabia and Egypt were the architects of a policy which advocated Arab cooperation with the United States and saw this policy as organically linked to a strategy which sought to generate American pressure on Israel in order to force a political solution acceptable to them.[7] Syria was Egypt's war-time partner and together with Algeria it provided an essential nexus to the radical wing of the Arab world. The importance of this quadruple grouping was demonstrated and institutionalized when the leaders of the four states met in February 1974 for a summit conference of their own. It was their cooperation which had made the success of the Algiers Arab Summit in November 1973 possible and prepared the ground in the Arab world for the two disengagement agreements of 1974 and for the convening of the Geneva Conference.

But as Syria's absence from Geneva clearly indicated, all was not well in the realm of inter-Arab relations. In fact, an American policy seeking in 1974 to rely on a supportive Arab coalition faced several serious obstacles:

a. The pro-American "moderate" coalition described above and the quadruple grouping which served as the new (and temporary) establishment of the Arab system overlapped but were not coextensive. Most significant was Jordan's exclusion. Jordan had to pay the actual price for making a new Arab consensus possible. The pre-October 1973 consensus viewed Egypt, Syria and Jordan as equal partners to the 1967 defeat and thus to the settlement that was expected to undo its consequences. But when Egypt and Syria planned the October War they excluded Jordan primarily because they intended to have the West Bank handed over to a Palestinian organization like the Palestine Liberation Organization (P.L.O.). This position was formally adopted by the Algiers summit in November 1973 and Jordan in turn sought to break or alter the new Arab consensus.

b. Syria, for a variety of reasons, distrusted Egypt, Saudi Arabia and the United States. Its endorsement of Egypt and Saudi Arabia's American orientation was very tenuous.

c. Egypt and Saudi Arabia became committed to the preservation of the new Arab solidarity as an asset in itself. The course of the October War and the conditions which obtained in its aftermath persuaded the Egyptian leadership that economic, military and political support by the other Arab states, or at least several of them, remained essential underpinnings of its strategy. Saudi Arabia came to enjoy its new position as the "elder statesman" of Arab politics and its rulers realized that continued inter-Arab cooperation and a certain degree of harmony were necessary for the perpetuation of that position. Consequently, both Egypt and Saudi Arabia were reluctant to pursue or endorse policies that were likely to breed division and bickering in the Arab ranks.

d. The emergence of a "moderate", or "pragmatic" new establishment prompted both the Soviet Union and the radical elements in the Arab world—Iraq, Libya and part of the P.L.O.—to increase and coordinate their counter-efforts. This radical grouping presented the new establishment with a permanent challenge and sought in particular to attract Syria, Algeria and the P.L.O. leadership to its side.

During the first half of 1974 American diplomacy as conducted by Henry Kissinger was able to overcome these obstacles and the other difficulties which confronted it. Israel, Egypt and Syria had direct and important interests involved in the efforts to bring about the first two disengagement agreements. This community of interests was essential to the success of American policy at that stage. But when preparations began for a second phase of American diplomacy in the Middle East in the summer of 1974, still more serious problems appeared. The difficulties were of diverse origins: the incompatibility of the Arab and Israeli outlooks, a change of president in the United States and change of prime minister in Israel, and the general weakening of Washington's international posture. But there is a particular interest in examining the problems facing American policy because of the intricacies of Arab regional politics as the United States sought to effect a dual, Egyptian-Israeli and Jordanian-Israeli, interim agreement. The notion of such a prospective settlement was based on a number of assumptions:

a. That another Arab-Israeli agreement was essential for the maintenance of "momentum" in Dr. Kissinger's "step by step" diplomacy.

b. That the crucial element in such an agreement was a second Egyptian-Israeli accord, but that Egypt could not afford to sign a separate agreement which was likely to be denounced as a violation of Arab solidarity.

c. That it would be very difficult to reach a second Syrian-Israeli agreement with regard to the Golan Heights, so that a repetition of the pattern established during the first half of 1974 (a dual, Egyptian-Israeli, Syrian-Israeli agreement, was difficult to envisage.

d. That there would be two important merits to a Jordanian-Israeli agreement:

1) Jordan, an American client, whose leaders had been pressuring the United States to include them in the settlement program, could finally be made a partner to the peace-making process.[8]

2) A Jordanian-Israeli agreement concerning the West Bank or part of it would address the Palestinian issue without involving,

indeed by preempting, the P.L.O.[9]

In July, then, President Sādāt invited King Ḥusayn to Egypt. After two days of discussions, on 18 July they published a joint communiqué which was clearly designed to pave the way for a Jordanian-Israeli agreement. The relevant passages in the communiqué read as follows:

> "The two sides declared that the P.L.O. was the legitimate representative of the Palestinians except the Palestinians residing in the Hashemite Kingdom of Jordan. . . . The two sides agreed on the need to reach a disengagement agreement on the Jordanian front as a first step towards a just peaceful solution." [10]

The formula used by the two rulers represented an attempt to sidestep the unpublicized resolutions of the Algiers Arab summit which had designated the P.L.O. as the only legitimate representative of the Palestinian people. The formulation adopted in Alexandria was deliberately vague, but could be interpreted to include the West Bank in the Jordanian Hashemite Kingdom and therefore to imply that Jordan had a claim over the West Bank.

But soon after this auspicious start serious problems began to surface. First, Egypt came under a fierce attack by Syria and the P.L.O. precisely because the Alexandria formula was seen by them as an infraction of the new Arab consensus established in November 1973. Both disparaged the notion of a Jordanian-Israeli agreement which they saw as pernicious to their own respective interests. Egypt was accused of committing a treacherous act which threatened to destroy Arab solidarity.[11]

Then, Israeli, Jordanian, Egyptian and Syrian envoys arrived in Washington in succession to discuss the next phase in the efforts to promote a settlement of the Arab-Israeli conflict. Their discussions with American officials revealed great divergences and difficulties. It was hardly surprising that Syria objected to Washington's plans for another interim agreement which, at least initially, excluded Syria and it had been well known that a wide gap separated the Israeli and Jordanian positions.[12] What had not been anticipated was the rapid change in Egypt's attitude toward Jordan and its role in the projected interim agreement. In E. Sheehan's vivid language:

> ". . . Nor did he (King Ḥusayn) reckon upon the intrigues of the Egyptian cousin. Ismāʿīl Fahmī was in

Washington, too. The Egyptians coveted a second Israeli withdrawal in the Sinai and they pleaded their preeminence over the Hashemites.'' [13]

By 20 September the Egyptians had made up their minds. They decided to free themselves from the Jordanians and return to the fold by coordinating their policy with Syria and the P.L.O. On 20 September a joint communiqué was published by Egypt, Syria and the P.L.O. in which Egypt retracted its earlier commitment to Jordan. Furthermore, Egypt publicly undertook to maintain monthly coordination with Syria and periodic coordination with the P.L.O.[14] In retrospect it became evident that the communiqué of 20 September had foreshadowed the resolutions which were adopted a month later at the Rabat Arab Summit.

Seen from an American perspective, the failure to bring about a concerted Egyptian-Israeli-Jordanian agreement could not have been very surprising or even disappointing. Kissinger had been aware of the enormous difficulties involved in such a venture and his own approach to it was described later, probably without too much hindsight, as "half-hearted." [15] But it is clear that he was surprised and dismayed by the resolutions which were adopted at the Rabat summit conference. On the eve of the conference the secretary of state paid another visit to the Middle East and, following the expected formulation of an all-Arab position, planned to continue with the next phase of his "step by step" diplomacy. The Rabat resolutions confronted this American policy with two calculated challenges: Jordan was specifically disqualified as a partner in interim settlements, and the Palestinian problem, a core issue that Kissinger sought to skirt, was thrust to the forefront. Equally serious were the implications for the assumptions which underlay American policy in the Arab world. Saudi Arabia and Egypt were either unwilling or unable to risk friction with other Arab states in order to save some of Jordan's position or to devise a face-saving formula. In an all-Arab forum, relying on the powerful impact of the Palestinian issue, the Syrian-Palestinian axis proved more effective than the Saudi-Egyptian one.

The practical solution to the stalemate produced by the Rabat Summit was to be a virtually separate Egyptian-Israeli agreement. It took almost a year to arrange and, in addition to the obvious benefits, it entailed, due to the circumstances, American-Israeli friction and very costly arrangements. Furthermore, when it was finally signed, Egypt found itself virtually isolated in the Arab world: the Syrian-Palestinian axis led the attack on Egypt, Jordan had by that time drawn close to Damascus, and Saudi Arabia provided no political backing. Kissinger's moderate Arab coalition ceased to exist.

The conclusion which seems to have been drawn in Washington during the last quarter of 1975 as a result of these developments was that American policy had to be reoriented so as to accommodate Syria and to address the Palestinian issue more directly. A message to this effect was relayed when Secretary of State Kissinger spoke on 29 September 1975 to the Arab representatives at the U.N. Among other things he said that "the United States was ready to work for a Syrian-Israeli second step, if that was wanted; that the United States would consider ways of working for an overall settlement and that he would begin to refine his thinking on how the legitimate interests of the Palestinian people could be met."[16]

Later, two important steps were taken which seemed to reflect a shift in the same direction. In October the United States supported a Syrian initiative to discuss the Palestinian issue at the Security Council in January 1976 and to invite the P.L.O. to participate in that discussion. The American support of the Syrian initiative would appear to be rather surprising in view of the fact that it was designed not merely to embarrass both Egypt and Israel but also to underscore the futility of the then recent Sinai Agreement. Then, on 12 November, H.H. Saunders, Deputy Assistant Secretary of State for Near Eastern Affairs in testifying before a congressional committee made several significant references to the Palestinian issue. Saunders presented the Palestinian component of the Arab-Israeli conflict as "the heart of the conflict" and stated that "the legitimate interests of the Palestinians must be taken into account in the negotiating of the Arab-Israeli peace."[17]

Whether or not the policy changes which were implicit in these notions and actions would have been implemented by a reelected Ford Administration is a moot point. The "step by step diplomacy" had been based on the assumption that the core issues of the Arab-Israeli conflict, particularly the Palestinian question, were virtually insoluble. It did not seem worthwhile to enter into a painful confrontation with Israel by trying to force her to accept an overall settlement whose prospects appeared, anyway, to be rather dim. When it seemed after September 1975 that the "piecemeal diplomacy" had reached a dead end, more and more voices were raised within and outside of the administration which called for a change of direction, even if it involved serious friction with Israel. But the beginnings which were apparently being made in September were not pursued later as the United States and the Arab world became preoccupied with, respectively, the protracted presidential election campaign and the Lebanese civil war.

These and other changes, though, were introduced in 1977 by a new administration that embarked on new policies in the Middle East. The origins and directions of these policies are discussed in detail elsewhere in this volume. Here it will suffice to note that emphasis was laid on the quest for a comprehensive settlement and that this entailed also an effort to guarantee Syria's participation, particular attention to the Palestinian issue and a willingness to enter into a confrontation with Israel if the implementation of the new policy so required. These elements which had been implicit in the final phases of the previous administration's Middle Eastern venture were placed at the center of the policy pursued by its successor.

One important consequence of this change was a new American outlook on inter-Arab relations. The emphasis shifted from an attempt to organize and sustain a rather limited "moderate" Arab coalition to an attempt to devise a formula acceptable not only to Saudi Arabia and Jordan but also to Syria and the P.L.O. Syria had a particularly vital role in this scheme. Its own acceptance and the influence it possessed over the P.L.O. were essential to the success of any effort to bring about a comprehensive settlement. The Carter administration was willing to exercise pressure on Israel to accept its version of a comprehensive peace settlement, but there was no point in so doing if some of the prospective Arab participants were likely to reject the American offer.

These considerations were reinforced by two other factors. During the Lebanese civil war Syria had coordinated its policy with the United States, thereby producing in Washington both a sense of indebtedness and a feeling that Syria was a potential partner for other joint ventures as well.[18] Furthermore, Syria was still a Soviet client, but Soviet-Syrian relations were evidently strained during the first months of 1977 and there seemed to be a good prospect of luring Damascus away from the Soviet Union into or at least closer to the American fold.[19]

On the face of it the inter-Arab scene during the first few months of 1977 augured well for such an American policy. During 1976 inter-Arab relations had been governed by the impact of the Lebanese civil war. But the Riyād Summit of October 1976 resulted in a redrawing of Arab alliances and rivalries. Convened by the Saudis in order to anticipate and influence a new American policy in the Middle East, the Summit terminated the active phase of the Lebanese civil war and revived Syrian-Egyptian cooperation. Egypt and Syria agreed to establish a Unified Political Command and the Egyptian War Minister was appointed Supreme Commander of the Egyptian-Syrian front. The efforts to formulate a joint Arab strategy continued in December 1976 and January 1977. They included meetings between Presidents Sādāt and Asad, President Sādāt and King Husayn and the Foreign Ministers of the "confrontation" and Persian Gulf oil-producing states and representatives of the P.L.O. The policy line which emerged from these meetings called for Arab pressure on the U.S., an early reconvening of the Geneva Conference, a modification of the current P.L.O. position that would enable it to participate in this process and some role for Jordan as well.[20]

But the apparent solidarity and cohesion were misleading. The Riyād-Cairo-Damascus axis was sufficiently effective to have the resolutions of the Riyād summit adopted by an all-Arab summit in Cairo a week later and to push through the coordination efforts of December and January. The leaders of Saudi Arabia, Egypt and Syria also met again on 19 May for a coordination of policies on the eve of Prince Fahd's important visit to Washington. But powerful factors militated against a coordination of Arab policies and against an American policy based on the assumption that such a coordination existed or could be brought about. One factor was the limited impact of the Saudi-Egyptian-Syrian axis. The three partners could coordinate their own policies and those of their clients. But a rival "rejectionist" bloc continued to exist and to pursue its counter policy. Furthermore, the P.L.O. and Jordan, both germane to any Arab policy in the conflict with Israel, conducted policies of their own.

Their ability to do so derived also from the continuation, though in subtler form, of the Syrian-Egyptian rivalry. The military and political coordination which had been agreed upon in 1976 did not materialize in 1977 and although the propaganda war between the two countries was not renewed before September 1977, their mutual suspicions had been felt in the preceding months. Syria suspected that in its dealings with the U.S. (and eventually with Israel) Egypt was willing to go well beyond the positions acceptable to Damascus and that it was not averse to another separate agreement with Israel. Egypt suspected that beyond Syria's radical positions there lurked a scheme for Syrian aggrandizement, the objects of which were Lebanon, Jordan and a future Palestinian entity, and felt that Syria's conduct obstructed the execution of the strategy agreed upon in Riyād.

These tensions were manifested throughout 1977 in Syria and Egypt's divergent attitudes toward the form and procedure of Arab-Israeli negotiations. Syria insisted that the Arabs should be represented in Geneva by a unified delegation; Egypt resented the idea precisely because it perceived a Syrian suspiciousness and a desire to prevent separate negotiations between Egyptians and Israelis. In August during Secretary Vance's second tour of the area Egypt suggested that the United States convene an Arab-Israeli "working group" that would meet in the United States to prepare for a Geneva Conference, but the idea was openly rejected by Syria. About a month later Syria suggested at an Arab League meeting that a radical line be adopted at the U.N. while Egypt objected that Syria's position amounted to an "insistence on the impossible." [21]

The Syrian-Egyptian rivalry in 1977 was also reflected—and intensified—by the two countries' conflicting outlooks on the Palestinian question and its possible settlement. In theory, both Syria and Egypt shared in the Arab consensus which called for the establishment of a Palestinian state in the West Bank and the Gaza Strip and for the P.L.O.'s participation at the Geneva Conference. In practice both deviated from this consensus, but in different ways and for different purposes. Egypt proposed that a Palestinian state should have formal links with Jordan so as to make its establishment more palatable to Israel and Jordan. Syria's position was much more complex. Early in 1977 it did exercise overt pressure on the P.L.O. to accept and support the joint Arab strategy that had been worked out in Riyād. Yet, Syria continued throughout 1977 to allude to the possibility of an entirely different solution to the Palestinian problem—one inspired and administered by itself. Thus, the Syrian Ba'th recommended in the spring of 1977 that the P.L.O. examine various forms of a Palestinian entity linked to Jordan or to Jordan and "other confrontation states." This was a clear reference to the group of states dominated by Damascus that Syria had been trying to form since 1975.[22]

It is only against this background that Washington's failure in the latter part of 1977 to cope with the Palestinian dimension of the Arab-Israeli conflict can be understood. The Carter administration began to expound the importance of the Palestinian component in a Middle East settlement in March 1977. Until the end of July American statements focused on the notion of a Palestinian "homeland." Being vague and failing to specify the precise nature of that "homeland" at this phase, they served mainly to exacerbate tensions in American-Israeli relations. But this situation changed at the end of July as the emphasis shifted to Palestinian participation in Geneva and to the P.L.O. as a prospective participant. Israel's objections did not diminish but their relative importance declined as the issue became a matter of inter-Arab rivalries during Secretary Vance's second tour of the Middle East in August.

The secretary of state as well as the president himself invested efforts to have the P.L.O. endorse Security Council Resolution 242 in order to make its participation at the Geneva Conference possible. Their eagerness served to underline American helplessness in contending with the complexities of Palestinian Arab politics. Thus, during Cyrus Vance's visit to the Middle East, the three major partners to the Riyād Summit were pulling the Palestinian cart in different directions:

a. A Syrian-inspired radio report had it on 2 August that Damascus and the P.L.O. had reached an agreement according to which "there shall be no links between the (Palestinian) state and Jordan before the Geneva Conference . . . ; moreover, any links with Jordan later on should be in the form of a federation between Syria, Palestine and Jordan."

b. Egypt, in turn, sought to underscore its own approach and the relevance of its position by convening the Higher Joint Egyptian-Palestinian Committee (whose membership included Yāssir

'Arafāt). The Egyptian media claimed that Cairo's policies had P.L.O. support and that Egypt had been preparing the ground for American contacts with the P.L.O.

c. Saudi Arabia, too, tried to appear as playing the key role in bringing about an American-Palestinian understanding. It was from Saudi Arabia that the Secretary of State notified the President that the P.L.O. was willing to accept (a watered-down version of) Security Council Resolution 242.[23]

In the event, though, these countervailing pressures, in addition to its own domestic politics and the influence of the "rejectionist" Arab states and other extraneous actors, now led the P.L.O. on 28 August once again to reject Resolution 242. Consequently, on 9 September President Carter had to define the P.L.O.'s position as "an obstacle in the way of our efforts to convene a peace conference." But he expressed hope that the organization "would reexamine its position on this matter." [24]

Washington's efforts to overcome these problems continued during the next two months through the ill-fated Soviet-American joint statement of 1 October and the subsequent American-Israeli working paper of 6 October. But the policy line which underlay these efforts became outdated through the opening of a direct, overt Egyptian-Israeli dialogue in November. It was ironic that the embarrassment which affected the Carter administration as a result of this *volte face* was in part the consequence of its own policies. President Sādāt's decision to go to Jerusalem in November 1977 was the result of several long term processes and immediate pressures. But as he himself indicated in his speeches at the time, the desire to reassert Egypt's preeminence and freedom of action in the Arab world was an essential component of his new policy.[25] This reassertion was clearly a reaction to Washington's Arab policy which throughout 1977 seemed to give Syria preference over Egypt and which, by addressing the Arab world as a collectivity, served to endow Syria and the P.L.O. with a virtual veto power over Egyptian policy in the Arab-Israeli conflict. Nor was it surprising that Washington's immediate public response to the opening of the Egyptian-Israeli dialogue revealed a preoccupation with its impact on the Arab system. This was one of the more important reasons which led the Carter administration to hesitate and wait before granting a belated endorsement to the bilateral Egyptian-Israeli negotiations. The role played by the U.S. in these negotiations will have to be dealt with when a better perspective and richer documentation become available.

NOTES

1. See E. Kedourie, *The Chatham House Version* (N.Y. 1970), pp. 213-235. "Pan Arabism and British Policy" in France's approach to the same issue was markedly different (for obvious historical reasons). Thus the French Foreign Minister, when the Saudi and Iraqı emissaries Fu'ād Hamza and Tawfīq Suwaydī raised the question of Syria with him in 1938, responded that: "Quand au règlement de nos rapports avec la Syrie, il devrait rester entre elle et nous un problème circonscrit par les frontières du pays et relevant de ses donnés propres." See *Documents Diplomatiques Français, 1932-1939*, 2 Série (1966-9), Tome XI, Paris 1977, p. 224.

2. *Foreign Relations of the United States, 1948*, vol. 5, part I (Washington 1975) pp. 224, 228.

3. J. C. Campbell, *Defense of the Middle East* (Revised edition, New York 1960), Chaps. 3-9.

4. W. B. Quandt, *Decade of Decisions* (Berkeley 1977), pp. 208-214 and B. Reich, *Quest for Peace* (New Brunswick, N.J. 1977, pp. 241-268.

5. Quandt, p. 210.

6. P. Y. Hammond and S. Alexander, *Political Dynamics in the Middle East* (New York 1972), pp. 31-52; and P. J. Vatikiotis, "Inter-Arab Relations" in A. L. Udovitch, *The Middle East, Oil, Conflict and Hope* (Lexington, Mass. 1976), pp. 145-179.

7. See E. Sheehan, *The Arabs, Israelis and Kissinger* (New York 1976), pp. 64-69.

8. For a description of the pressure exercised by Jordan on the American government, see Quandt, p. 234.

9. See also *The Economist*, 24 August 1974.

10. Radio Cairo, Voice of the Arabs, 18 July 1974.

11. See for instance the statement issued by the P.L.O. Executive Committee on 25 July 1974. Radio Algiers, Voice of Palestine in Arabic, 26 July 1974.

12. See Reich, pp. 298-299. There were differences of opinion within the Israeli government over the feasibility and desirability of a Jordanian-Israeli agreement. M. Golan in *The Secret Conversations of*

Henry Kissinger (New York 1976) reflects the views of Prime Minister Rabin's critics. Other Israeli politicians and officials who were interviewed by the present writer claimed that there was no serious effort to bring about an Israeli-Jordanian agreement at that time.

13. Sheehan, p. 148.

14. Radio Cairo, Voice of the Arabs, 21 September 1974.

15. Quandt, p. 256.

16. Quandt, p. 276, n. 32; Sheehan, p. 202.

17. Reich, pp. 400-401 and Quandt, p. 278.

18. For a very cautious description of American-Syrian coordination in Lebanon see Quandt, pp. 281-284. Additional information is to be found in J. Bulloch's journalistic account *Death of a Country* (London 1977), passim.

19. G. Golan and I. Rabinovitch, "The Soviet Union and Syria: The Limits of Co-operation" in Y. Ro'i (ed.), *The Limits of Power* (London 1979), pp. 213-231.

20. M. Gammar, "The Arab-Israeli Conflict: A Chronology and Commentary on Political Developments (October 1976-October 1977)" in C. Legum (ed.), *Middle East Contemporary Survey*, vol. I, 1976-7 (N.Y. 1978), pp. 123-144.

21. D. Dishon, "Inter-Arab Relations," in Legum, pp. 147-178.

22. I. Rabinovich, "Syria," in Legum, p. 616.

23. Dishon, ibid.

24. Gammar, ibid.

25. On several occasions during the final weeks of 1977 President Sādāt reiterated that "the key to war and peace is here" (implying at the same time that it was not to be found in Damascus).

Libya and the United States —
A Relationship of
Self-Fulfilling Expectations?

Gideon Gera

If one cared to reflect on the opening line of the well-known anthem of the U.S. Marine Corps, "From the halls of Montezuma to the shores of Tripoli," one would be immediately reminded that there is a historical precedent to the increasingly hostile political relations between the U.S. and Libya since 1969. In the variety of relations the U.S. entertains with the nations of the Middle East, some of which have anti-Western military and semi-military regimes, the relations with Qadhdhāfī's Libya are noteworthy because of the ongoing U.S. antagonism towards that regime.

This is in marked contrast to the much publicized new openness of the Carter administration towards developing nations and their international concerns. This paper outlines the main developments in the relations between the U.S. and Libya and attempts to explore the sources of the animosity between them.

After attaining independence in 1951 the Kingdom of Libya developed a close relationship with the U.S. In exchange for financial and other aid urgently needed by the very poor new state, Libya leased the U.S. military facilities, the main one being Wheelus Air Base near Tripoli. American oil companies had a major share in exploring and later on exploiting Libyan oil, the discovery of which in 1959 totally changed the economic perspective of the country. Libya continued in its pro-Western foreign policy and was considered a strategic, political and economic asset by the West. Obviously the main Western countries involved in Libya—Britain and the U.S.—were interested and involved in the internal stability and security of the monarchy. Thus they were aware of the widespread corruption in the government and the growing weakness of the king.

The generation of young educated Libyans (that is, those educated since 1943) not only regarded the monarchy as reactionary and corrupt but also as foreign-dominated (thus evoking memories of the Italian period). This stratum was deeply influenced by neighboring Nasserite Egypt, both through the latter's propaganda and the pervasive Egyptian presence in the school system. Already in 1964 student unrest led the Libyan government to ask the U.S. to reconsider whether it really required military bases in Libya. The Six Day War aggravated the issue, as many Libyans believed the Egyptian allegation that aircraft from the British and American bases in Libya had participated in the attack on Egypt. Not only was the foreign military presence considered an affront to Libyan independence and a symbol of "imperialist" aggression, but the close ties between the monarchy and the U.S. and Britain led to the popular belief that the main purpose of the bases was to safeguard the regime.

These views were shared in a most radical way by the group of young officers which had formed around Qadhdhāfī in 1964. The group professed a militant Nasserism, in which Pan-Arab, fundamentalist Islamic tradition and "socialist" ideas combined to fuel revolutionary ardor. After the 1967 war the group decided, in unique departure from its conspiratorial ways, to join some civilian extremists in their attempt to sabotage the foreign bases, an operation which was never carried out. The view that in an emergency the bases would serve as supports of the regime led Qadhdhāfī to deploy some artillery units around Wheelus on the night of his *coup d'état*, in order to prevent possible moves from there.

Thus, the overthrow of the Libyan monarchy and the proclamation of the Libyan Arab Republic by a group of junior officers on 1 September 1969 did not bode well for the relations between Libya and the United States.

Whatever its feelings on the matter, the U.S. government recognized the new Libyan regime on 6 September 1969 (together with Britain and France, two days after the U.S.S.R.). A new U.S. ambassador presented his credentials on 16 September 1969. The expected Libyan demand to terminate the U.S. military presence was officially made on 30 October 1969 and presented as a necessary preliminary to relations based on mutual respect. But already on 22 September 1969 the Libyan Foreign Ministry voiced concern about American deliveries of F-4 aircraft to Israel, saying they could harm Libyan relations with the U.S. Indeed, the subject of military supplies to Israel became one of the most voiced Libyan grievances against the U.S.

Negotiations on the evacuation of the American bases were rapid and successful; they commenced on 15 December and an agreement was signed on 23 December 1969. The next day a Libyan request to hand over intact the fixed installations of the bases was granted. However, the future shape of mutual relations was outlined by Qadhdhāfī in his statement opening the negotiations: Not only did he demand full and speedy evacuation but insisted that Libya, as a non-aligned state, would not tolerate the continued presence of military installations belonging to a nation engaged in a bloody war against the Vietnamese and which could serve for North Atlantic Treaty Organization (NATO) aggression. Qadhdhāfī did however thank the U.S. for the aid extended to Libya and hailed the American people as "leaders in modern technology and conquerors of space." [1] These were the last kind public words Americans heard from Qadhdhāfī for a long while.

Wheelus Base was duly evacuated on 11 June 1970. A few days later, in a speech celebrating the event, Qadhdhāfī said that now Arabs should talk from the position of the victor. No equal relations between Libya and the U.S. were possible as long as the U.S. "holds one hand to us and with the other provides arms to Israel, in order to hit us in Palestine or other Arab regions." Furthermore, "the hand held out to us should be clean of the blood of the people of Vietnam and Indochina struggling for their liberty." [2]

Thus, once the restraint that the U.S. military presence itself had imposed on Qadhdhāfī seemed no longer necessary, he proceeded to build up an image of the U.S. as Libya's main enemy. Like many similar regimes Qadhdhāfī's needed an enemy-figure, the struggle against which in the name of sacred values would serve to legitimize and enhance the regime. This figure had to be important enough to be accepted as a credible threat but not actually and immediately dangerous. Qadhdhāfī not only adopted the ideology of Nasserism but also its definitions of the enemy—Imperialism and Zionism. By equating the U.S. with Imperialism, Qadhdhāfī presented himself as successfully combatting a mighty adversary ("forcing" him to evacuate the bases), thereby inflating his own importance.

Open antagonism towards the U.S. accorded with Qadhdhāfī's Arab policies (his animosity towards conservative regimes), his radical position on the Israel-Arab conflict and his non-alignment in international politics. Furthermore, his militant stand on oil prices—forcing oil companies to augment payments to the Libyan government—set in motion the process which culminated in the quintupling of oil prices in 1974.

In his speech on the first anniversary of the evacuation, Qadhdhāfī declared that repeated Libyan attempts to open a new page in the relations with the U.S. had come to nothing, as this could not be achieved at the expense of the Arab nation and the Palestine problem. The continuous American arms supplies to Israel signified that the U.S. was party to an international conspiracy against the Arabs. In the same speech he announced the recognition of the People's Republic of China.[3]

A year later Qadhdhāfī felt secure enough to openly espouse more radical policies. Not only did he declare Libyan support of the Moro rebellion in the Philippines and of the Irish Republican Army in its struggle against the British; he also stated that "following the evacuation of the base, the struggle is now carried into the heart of America, as Libya announces her support of the Movement of the Blacks. Libya stands faithfully by 25 million black Americans who requested this. It is only logical that after Imperialism quit our region, we would pursue it to its home . . . We side with five million Black Muslims who lead the Black Movement in the U.S. Today America faces a counterattack."[4]

For some time it seemed that Qadhdhāfī had successfully separated his political posture from practical dealings with the U.S. As late as September 1972 the Libyans allocated some $20 million for the procurement of eight C-130 military transport aircraft in the U.S. However, later in 1972, the U.S. demonstrated its displeasure with Qadhdhāfī by reducing the level of its diplomatic representation in Tripoli from the ambassadorial level. Qadhdhāfī reacted by violently attacking the U.S. in a speech made in Tunis on 16 December 1972. After mentioning U.S. arms supplies to Israel and Libyan support of the Black Muslims, he said: "As the U.S. had provoked us to challenge it, we decided to cooperate with the Latin

American organizations opposed to the U.S. so that it would learn that we were capable of carrying the battle to her borders."[5] Although this cooperation was never publicly elaborated, it heralded the Libyan involvement in international terrorism.

Since then Libyan relations with the U.S. have deteriorated. Qadhdhāfī was publicly implicated by President Numayrī of Sudan in the Palestinian attack on the Saudi Embassy in Khartoum, in which two senior American diplomats were killed (1 March 1973). Three weeks later a U.S. naval aircraft was intercepted by Libyan fighters over the open Mediterranean. Libya then claimed control of the airspace to a distance of 185 kilometers from its coast (a claim which had it been sustained would have seriously hampered the routine air activities of the Sixth Fleet).

After the Yom Kippur War and the deterioration of its relations with Egypt, Libya became an important member of the Arab "rejectionist front." Vehemently opposed to any political settlement of the Arab-Israeli conflict, Libya considered Sādāt's agreements with Israel treasonable and the growing U.S. role a threat to the Arabs. The more the U.S. seemed to progress in the "political process," the more Sādāt turned to the U.S., the more hostile Qadhdhāfī became—by now actively encouraged and supported by the U.S.S.R. Qadhdhāfī began to support the Popular Front for the Liberation of Palestine (P.F.L.P.) and other radical Palestinian groups, which he had harshly denounced a few months earlier. Such support meant a growing Libyan involvement in international terrorism, a field in which Libya, as mentioned above, made its debut before the 1973 war (by Palestinian proxies who utilized various organizational labels). This led, among other things, to attacks on American airliners and to the loss of American lives. In their campaign against Qadhdhāfī the Egyptians underlined his part in terrorist activities (such as the attack on the Organization of Petroleum-Exporting Countries [OPEC] conference in Vienna in December 1975),[6] causing the Libyan leader and other Libyan spokesmen to deny any connection with terrorism and to condemn hijackings. However, Qadhdhāfī carefully pointed out that Liberation Movements were not terrorist but Zionism and the U.S. were also engaging in terrorism.

This Libyan involvement led the U.S. to consider practical steps against Libya. In 1974 the delivery of eight C-130 aircraft was blocked, although the deal was already paid for. Libyan protests and denunciations by Qadhdhāfī that this was a hostile act were of no avail.

Eventually the Ford administration ranked Libya fourth in a list of potential enemies included in its last annual Defence Department report of early 1977. After discussing the U.S.S.R. and China, the report says that "other and lesser powers may also choose to challenge U.S. interests and friends. North Korea, Libya and Cuba are only the most obviously bellicose of the candidates . . . The incidence of terrorism, occasionally fostered by irresponsible foreign leaders, could also increase." [7] Press reports connected Libya and Qadhdhāfī with the second sentence.

Since Qadhdhāfī repeatedly mentioned this achievement of fourth place among enemies of the U.S., he seemed to have considered this a kind of compliment. At any rate it endorsed his status as an important adversary of the U.S.[8] However, on the advent of the Carter administration, which announced a policy of better relations with the Third World, Qadhdhāfī tried to explore the possibility of a corresponding change in its attitude towards him, which might ameliorate his relations with the U.S. without any change of policy on his part. A member of his staff came twice to Washington during the spring of 1977, but to no avail.

In a speech on the seventh anniversary of the evacuation of Wheelus Base (11 June 1977) Qadhdhāfī publicly called on President Carter to change the "unjust U.S. policy towards us," if he wanted to show his good intentions towards Libya. Libya wanted to normalize relations, to reestablish diplomatic representation on the ambassadorial level and, most of all, to get her aircraft, even if it had to convert them into civilian transports.[9] The asked-for change did not materialize. After her four-day war with Egypt, Libya publicly accused the U.S. of supplying combat intelligence to the Egyptians.

Qadhdhāfī gave vent to his disappointment with the Carter administration and its Middle Eastern policy in a speech on 7 October 1977 (the anniversary of the expulsion of the Italians): "The U.S. is waging a war against nationalists in which Washington replaces Rome, both ancient Rome of the days of Carthage and that of the Italian Libyan war . . . Washington today is the ancient Imperialist Rome, it carries the banners of war against Arab nation-

alism, against the East and against the civilization of the East.'' [10]
Obviously, American support of Sādāt's peace initiative in
November 1977 further envenomed the Libyan attitude towards the
U.S. Qadhdhāfī described it, in an interview on ABC television, as
the leader of international terrorism (although he refrained from personal attacks on President Carter). During January 1978 the U.S.
administration redressed one Libyan grievance: it refunded the
money the Libyans had paid for the eight C-130 aircraft. However,
in late February it was announced that the U.S. would no longer
maintain American-made Libyan military transport aircraft (a few
C-130s) and had blocked the delivery of two Boeing 727 airliners to
Libya.[11] Preventing the delivery of civilian aircraft was considered
an escalation in U.S. steps against Libya. However, in November
1978 the administration relented somewhat, permitting the delivery
of the two Boeing 727 airliners and some seventy million dollars'
worth of heavy trucks.

Quite apart from the strained political climate, economic relations
between the two countries continued to develop. Once American oil
corporations adjusted to the regime and to the nationalization of
their local assets, they continued to profit from Libyan dependence
on their skills and from increasing U.S. oil imports. In fact the U.S.
ran up a major trade deficit with Libya (which grew from $1,267
million in 1974 to $1,965 million in 1976 and more than $2 billion
in 1977).[12] The main Libyan import from the U.S. was technology:
Boeing airliners, a Westinghouse power and desalination plant and
advanced agricultural technologies for development projects.[13] In the
fall of 1977 a Libyan mission came to Idaho, bought some five million dollars' worth of wheat and negotiated further and bigger deals.

This separation between business and politics (and ideology)
worked mainly to the advantage of the Libyans, who probably could
not hope for a similar situation in their tightening relationship with
the U.S.S.R. Thus Qadhdhāfī had the best of both worlds.
Regarded by the U.S. as its fourth ranking global enemy,[14] while
profiting from its need for his oil, he has gained in international
prestige (or notoriety) and enhanced his internal position. Libyans
are rather pleased with their country's new international importance
after centuries of oblivion and are probably not averse to nostalgi-
cally remembering their corsair or camel-raiding ancestors.

The sources of Qadhdhāfī's conduct towards the U.S. are quite clear: He views the U.S. as both an ideological and a concrete enemy. On the ideological level, the U.S. is part of the hostile West, which has a long history of political, cultural and religious conflict with the Arabs. Indeed, for centuries the Libyan shore was in the frontline of this struggle. In this conflict the U.S. had a record of military and political intervention, which has no parallel in other Arab countries: From 1803 to 1813 the U.S. retaliated militarily and later politically to the seizure of American ships and crews by Tripolitanian corsairs, finally forcing the ruler of Tripoli to release all his Christian captives. Contrary to the prevailing Western point of view, piracy was considered in Tripolitania, as along the whole Barbary Coast, not only as a major source of revenue but also as a legitimate form of warfare against the infidel. Indeed, reading repeated Libyan statements that "struggles of liberation are not terrorism," one could perceive a certain continuity of opinion. On the concrete level the U.S. is, in Qadhdhāfī's eyes, the major Imperialist power, the main supporter of Israel and lately of his neighbor and adversary Sādāt. As the former occupant of a military base in Libya and as presently deploying a considerable naval force near Libyan shores (the Sixth Fleet), the U.S. is also regarded as a permanent threat to the regime (a threat that evokes historical memories). Thus, in a recent interview Jallūd—the second-ranking personality of the regime—asked the rhetorical question: "What do you call the presence of imperialist fleet near our shores other than international terrorism?" [15]

However, Qadhdhāfī distinguishes very well between Western culture and values, which he rejects and western science and technology which he urges the Arab to adopt and utilize (it being after all the outgrowth of the Arab contribution to medieval Europe). The import of U.S. technology, indeed trade with the West, does not contradict the historical tradition described above: the Barbary coast entertained a lively trade with Europe.

As to the Unitated States, one may attribute its growing coolness towards Qadhdhāfī not just to a natural reaction to his abuse, but mainly to his continued and active support of international terrorism (which caused the loss of American lives), to Libyan efforts, however insignificant, to interfere in internal U.S. affairs (support of the Black Muslims), to his support of subversion in countries allied with the U.S. (as the Philippines) and his tightening relationship with the Soviets (and Cubans). U.S. policy towards Libya has not changed with the advent of the Carter administration; the understanding and support shown by it towards other African and Third World countries seems not to apply to Libya (as compared, for instance, with Algeria or even Ethiopia).

One should however question the present U.S. policy towards Libya, on which Qadhdhāfī seems to thrive. Surely a more effective U.S. way of dealing with Qadhdhāfī could have been devised during the last eight years.

A more realistic evaluation of Libya's capabilities and vulnerabilities would have led either to an acquiescent acceptance of Qadhdhāfī as a necessary nuisance or an equally quiet cutting him down to size (something many of his Arab neighbors wish dearly). However, by publicly overreacting to him without really harming him, the U.S. is continuing to build Qadhdhāfī up, even in the eyes of his Arab enemies. Would it be too far-fetched to look for some emotional residue of the image of piratical Barbary which tried to taunt the U.S., impeding a more rational approach to the problem presented by Qadhdhāfī to the international community?

NOTES

1. Al-Jumhūriyya al-'Arabiyya al-Lībiyya, *Thawrat al-Sha'b al-'Arabī al-Lībī: Min Aqwāl al-Akh al-'Aqīd Mu'ammar al-Qadhāfī* (Tripoli, 1972-1973), vol. 1, pp. 153-154.

2. *Thawrat al-Sha'b*, vol. 2, p. 61 (22 June 1970).

3. Ibid., vol. 3, pp. 55-56, passim.

4. Ibid., vol. 1, p. 209 (11 June 1972).

5. Ibid., vol. 2, p. 169.

6. Qadhdhāfī's involvement in international terrorism was repeatedly stressed by Sādāt (see his interviews with *Akhbār al-Yawm* (Cairo), 10 July 1976, and *al-Siyāsa* (Kuwait), 13 August 1977. His part in the Vienna operation was specified in an Egyptian note to the Arab League dated 16 April 1971. *BBC*, 18 April 1977.

7. U.S. Government, *Annual Defense Department Report, FY 1978.* (U.S. General Printing Office, Washington, 1977), p. 13.

8. An editorial in *Arab Dawn*, a monthly published by the Libyans in London, proudly mentioned this status as late as October 1977.

9. *Radio Tripoli*, 11 June 1977 (*DR*, 13 June 1977).

10. *Radio Tripoli*, 11 June 1977 (*DR*, 13 June 1977).

11. *Al-Fajr al-Jadīd* (Tripoli), 4 March 1978.

12. *MEED*, November 1977, pp. 13, 79.

13. See for instance, *Business Week*, 20 September 1976, p. 35.

14. This view of Libya seems to have remained unchanged under the Carter administration. As recently as 5 April 1978 a State Department official described Libya as one of the countries "now supporting international terrorism." (*International Herald Tribune*, 6 April 1978).

15. *Arab Dawn*, October 1977, p. 7. For a clear but somewhat disingenuous summary of the Libyan view of relations with the U.S. see: Mansūr Kikhyā, "America and Arabs," in *Libya, the United States and Britain* (London: Arab Dawn Report No. 1, n.d. [1977]), pp. 12-19, esp. pp. 16-19.

Oil and
Economics

The Economics of Interdependence: the United States and the Arab World, 1973–1977

Gad G. Gilbar

The phenomenon of highly developed, sophisticated economies being dependent for their growth rates, their degree of stability and affluence on economies just commencing their process of transformation from the traditional to the modern pattern is fairly rare in the twentieth century. Such dependence has been particularly conspicuous by its absence during the historic development of the United States economy. In the late 1960s, however, a certain dependence between the growth and affluence of the American economy and a number of Middle Eastern and North African oil economies began to be apparent. Since 1973 there have been a number of overt and substantial manifestations of this trend, and their significance extends beyond the economic sphere. Concurrently, the development of the Arab oil economies in particular and of the other Arab economies in general have come to depend on the United States economy. The aim of this paper is to present the various expressions of this interdependence, as it developed from 1973 till the beginning of 1978.[1]

The question of American economic dependence on the Arab oil economies has been frequently discussed in recent years, especially in the daily press, in the United States and elsewhere, for the obvious reason that such dependence constitutes one of the most important factors in shaping the policy of the American administration vis-à-vis most of the states of the Middle East. Discussions of the dependence question and its possible repercussions have often tended to develop into heated arguments, in which one side claims

209

that no such dependence actually exists, and that to create the impression that the American economy is beholden to the Arab oil economies is to practice fraud and deception which serve the interests of a number of pressure groups in the United States itself as well as the rulers of the Arab oil states. The other side asserts that the dimensions of American economic dependence on the Arab oil states have increased to such an extent that "a number of sheikhs hold the mighty American economy by its throat." Cartoons lampooning this state of affairs have abounded in the American and West European press. The main weakness of these treatments is that references to quantitative data, that ought properly serve as a basis and a point of departure for any discussion of the dependence question, have been either casual or selective. Thus the conclusions reached by various commentators could hardly be well-founded or balanced.

This article is devoted mainly to a presentation of available data relevant to the subject at issue. The economic ties between the parties concerned will be traced first from the American vantage-point and then from that of the Arab economies. Each of these two sections will include a survey of the flow of goods (visible imports and exports), transactions in the services sector (invisible imports and exports), aid and unilateral transfers, and finally the flow of factors of production (capital, manpower and technology). On the basis of these figures, the last part of the essay will be devoted to an attempt to assess the nature of the economic relations between the United States and the Arab world during the period under review, and the repercussions arising therefrom.

I. UNITED STATES ECONOMIC DEPENDENCE ON THE ARAB STATES

Obviously, the ever increasing importation of oil has been basic to United States economic dependence on the Arab world. In a matter of years, the proportion of oil imported from members of the Organization of Arab Petroleum Exporting Countries (OAPEC) out of total American oil consumption (crude and refined products) has sharply increased, from 5 percent in 1972 to 20 percent in 1977. The proportion of OAPEC oil out of total oil imports into the United States rose from 17 percent in 1972 to 43 percent in 1977 (see Table 1). By mid-1977, the OAPEC states were supplying almost half the quantity of crude oil imported into the United States (see Table 2). Three Arab oil exporters contributed to this development: Saudi Arabia first and foremost (about 19 percent of total oil imports to the United States in 1976), Libya (7 percent) and Algeria (6 percent) (see Table 3). In 1976 Saudi Arabia was the biggest oil supplier of the United States, taking precedence over Venezuela, Nigeria and Canada (see Table 4).

The reasons for this rapid development in the American oil market are known and therefore need merely to be restated: 1) Annual growth rates of consumption outstripped growth rates of oil production in the United States itself; 2) Proven reserves dwindled and the quantity annually produced declined in Venezuela, which had been the biggest "traditional" oil supplier of the United States; 3) There was an increase in proven reserves, real production capacity and quantity actually produced in a number of Arab oil states in the Middle East.

It is not within the scope of this work to discuss the findings of the production and consumption forecasts as regards crude oil in the world market in general and the United States in particular up to the end of the 1980s. Yet one cannot fail to point out that most of these forecasts postulate that the forces and factors responsible for the rapid change in the breakdown of oil supply to the American market in terms of sources will continue to exist at least until the mid-1980s, so that a further absolute and relative increase may be anticipated in American dependence on Arab oil.[2]

The increase, in absolute terms, in the imports of OAPEC oil to the United States, from 0.8 million barrels a day in 1972 to 3.8 million barrels a day in 1977, and the sharp rises in the price of crude oil on the world market in October 1973 and in January 1974 led to a steep increase in American expenditure for the import of this oil. Payments to the OAPEC economies, totaling some $0.6 billion in 1972, jumped to about $16.5 billion in 1977 (at current prices).[3] This development gave rise to a chain reaction which comprised efforts to bring about an increase in the visible exports of the United States to the Arab oil economies, an increase in United States income from the supply of services to the OAPEC economies and a rise in the nominal and real value of Arab assets in the American economy.

The greatly increased imports of Arab oil into the United States brought about a profound change in the U.S. balance of trade with the Arab economies between 1973 and 1977. The proportion accounted for by Arab economies in the visible imports of the United States rose from 1 percent in 1972 to over 11 percent in 1977. This leap having been effectuated solely by the increase in oil imports and the rise in the price of oil, the federal administration and various factors in the American private sector were impelled to take steps to increase exports to the OAPEC economies, which in 1974 and 1975 started on the execution of development plans on a large scale, the most far-flung and ambitious of which was the Saudi Arabian five-year plan (1975-80), providing for an overall expenditure of $142 billion (at 1975 prices). These plans opened up new possibilities, and very largely explain the increase in the United State visible exports to the Arab states from $1.2 billion in 1972 to $7.1 billion in 1976 and to $8.2 billion in 1977 (at current prices). The proportion of United States visible exports to the Arab world increased in those years from some 2.5 percent to some 7.0 percent (see Table 5).

The breakdown of United States visible exports by destination shows that throughout the period under review Saudi Arabia maintained its position as the biggest customer in the Arab world for American-made goods. There was an impressive increase in American exports to Saudi Arabia from $0.3 billion in 1972 to $2.8 billion in 1976 and to $3.5 billion in 1977 (at current prices). The relative share of American visible exports to Saudi Arabia in total American visible exports rose from 0.6 percent to 2.9 percent during 1972-77. Kuwait, which in 1972 was the second largest consumer in the Arab world of American manufactured goods, was superseded in the mid-1970s by Egypt, which in 1977 imported goods from the United States to the value of over $1.0 billion. This development resulted from the considerable increase in economic aid rendered by the United States government to Egypt during 1975-77.[4]

The breakdown of American visible exports to the Arab states by product (data for 1976) shows that the major part of the exports, some 74 percent, was finished industrial products, while the second largest item, some 17 percent, was foodstuffs (see Table 6).

A radical change has thus taken place in the American balance of trade with the Arab economies. To be sure, both imports and exports grew considerably in both absolute and relative terms, but the annual growth rates of imports were higher than the annual growth rates of exports. Whereas imports in 1972-77 increased 27.5 times, exports increased only 7.0 times. The lower annual growth rates of exports are explained by the limited capacity for the absorption of industrial products on the part of most of the Arab oil economies, and also by the stiff competition of manufacturers from other industrialized economies in the West and in Japan.[5] The outcome of this was that the United States, which until 1973 had enjoyed a surplus in its balance of trade with the Arab states, began suffering a growing deficit in its trade with these countries. During 1976 and 1977 the American visible imports surplus in its trade with the Arab economies totaled $5.8 billion and $8.4 billion respectively, and the rate of visible imports surplus of total visible imports from the Arab countries in 1977 reached some 51 percent. Hence, the increase, in absolute terms, in the deficit in the balance of trade with the Arab states made a significant contribution to the deficit in the overall U.S. balance of trade, which totaled $14.6 billion in 1976 and some $27 billion in 1977.

American invisible imports from the Arab economies and invisible exports to them also reached considerable proportions during the period in question. The most important item of invisible imports was the payments on account of interest and profits, deriving from assets in the United States of the Arab oil states (in both the public and the private sectors), and especially of Saudi Arabia.[6] The estimated expenditure of the American economy under this heading during 1974-77 was some $12 billion.[7] On the invisible exports side are two main items: net profit from the activities of the American oil companies in the Arab states,[8] and the net profit of the American construction and engineering companies,[9] which in 1975 and 1976 were awarded comprehensive contracts for the execution of projects, mostly in the oil states of the Arabian Peninsula, whose outlay was estimated at some $19 billion.[10] Our estimate regarding the aggregate net income during 1974-76 of the United States economy from these two sources totals some $16-17 billion.[11] In the absence of data on the other invisible trade items, it cannot be determined whether in that account too the United States has come to register a deficit in its commerce with the Arab economies, which previously recorded a considerable surplus. At the same time it may plausibly be assumed that even if the United States had a surplus in its balance of invisible trade, this surplus would not be such as to offset the deficit in the balance of trade and maintain a balanced current account with the Arab economies.

Likewise in the sphere of economic aid and unilateral transfers from the United States to the Arab economies, a considerable change took place in the years in question. After a long period of aid (grants, loans and technical assistance) on a very limited scale, the administration in Washington began pouring large-scale aid into a number of Arab economies. Total aid (economic and military) that was approved for the Arab states rose from $127 million in the 1973 (American) fiscal year to about $1.4 billion in the 1978 fiscal year, and the total aid approved during the 1974-78 fiscal years reached some $5.5 billion. Most of the aid flowed to Egypt ($3.2 billion, representing 59 percent of total aid to the Arab world) and to Jordan ($1.0 billion, representing 19 percent of the total aid). Other Arab states that received aid from the United States were Syria, Lebanon, Sudan, Morocco, Tunisia and finally also Yemen (San'ā), Baḥrayn and Libya. Eighty percent of the total aid to the Arab economies was given to finance needs and projects in the civilian sector, long-term loans for the financing of foodstuffs imports, grants and loans for the financing of development projects and also for covering deficits in the current accounts of the recipient economies (see Table 7).

Unilateral transfers from the Arab states to institutions and individuals in the United States came from two main sources: the governments of the oil economies and American citizens employed in the Arab world. The governments of Saudi Arabia, the United Arab Emirates (U.A.E.), Kuwait and Libya made direct and indirect grants, during the period under review, to universities, research institutes and other institutions that have a hand in shaping public opinion and also participate in the political decision-making process in the United States. The cumulative size of these transfers obviously cannot be estimated, but on the basis of partial data published, it may be assumed that the amount in question is in the range of many tens of millions of dollars.[12] Similarly it is not possible to determine the cumulative total of the transfers made by some ninety thousand United States nationals (including military personnel) that in late 1977 were in administrative, advisory, instructional and supervisory positions in Saudi Arabia and in the other Arab states.[13]

More than in any other sphere, excepting actual American dependence on OAPEC oil supply, the economic relations between the United States and the Arab world are influenced by the flow of investments of a number of Arab oil economies into the United States, and in this sphere too, Saudi Arabia is in the lead. Six Arab oil-producers (Saudi Arabia, Kuwait, the U.A.E., Libya, Iraq and Qatar) managed, as a result of the generation of surpluses in their current accounts, to accumulate foreign assets whose real value was estimated in December 1976 at $107 billion, and in December 1977 at $135 billion. Out of this amount, the foreign assets of Saudi Arabia alone were estimated at the end of 1977 at $68 billion (see Table 8).[14] A pall of secrecy enshrouds the information connected with the patterns of use of these surpluses and their breakdown throughout the major money markets. Various sources however indicate that the total Arab investments (deriving from governments, companies and individuals) in the United States during 1974-77 amounted to $60-70 billion at the least.[15] The largest share of these investments is owned by the Saudi Arabian government. Out of this amount, $17.2 billion in 1976 and some $23 billion in 1977 were invested in United States bonds and long-term, non-negotiable treasury notes.[16] Although no published information is available as to the breakdown of the balance between bank deposits, corporate bonds and stocks of companies and real estate assets, there are grounds for asserting that a sharp decline has taken place in the relative share of long term bonds in the portfolio of U.S. assets of Saudi Arabia in particular and of the Arab oil exporters in general.[17] As against the very considerable investments of the Arab oil states in the United States in 1977, according to an estimate of the U.S. Department of Commerce, American companies invested only $2.9 billion in the Arab states. The estimate of investments for previous years was much lower.[18]

Assuming that our figure for the total Arab investments in the United States is not an overestimation, the aggregate inflow to the U.S. of dollars originating in the Arab states was in 1974-77 several tens of billions of dollars greater than the outflow of dollars from the United States to the Arab economies. In other words, capital export from the Arab oil countries to the United States, rather more than offset the deficit in the balance of trade and the possible deficit in the balance of invisible trade between the United States and the OAPEC economies and the flow of net unilateral transfers and the economic aid of the United States to the Arab world. It goes without saying that taking into consideration the deficit in the overall current account of the United States and the weakness of the dollar in the world market in 1977 and most of 1978, this fact is of great importance.

In concluding this chapter, mention ought to be made of three additional facts that are relevant to the question of American economic dependence on the Arab world. First, fixing the price of crude oil trafficked on the world market has since October 1973 been the province of a group of Arab oil exporters, who during the years in question produced over 60 percent of the oil of the Organization of Petroleum Exporting Countries (OPEC). Moreover, the size of its proven reserves and real production capacity have, since 1976, made Saudi Arabia the main factor fixing the price of OPEC oil, and it could reasonably be argued that the very existence of this organization, as a cartel, will in the late 1970s and early 1980s come to depend on the oil policy of the Saudi Arabian government. Secondly, the major U.S. allies in Western Europe and Japan, with whom it maintains the most ramified economic relations, themselves depend on OAPEC oil supplies at even higher rates than does the United States itself (see Table 9). Thirdly, the increase in and the diversification of the economic relations of the United States with the Arab states also has an important micro-economic aspect, deriving from the data presented above. According to unofficial figures, during the mid-1970s some five hundred American companies in various branches of heavy and light industry, construction and engineering, minerals, banking and transportation and so forth, maintained offices and staffs in the Arab states.[19] Many of these companies are among the largest in their line, and many are among the hundred biggest companies in the United States. These five hundred companies in turn provide orders for many hundreds of other American companies. Hence American economic ties with the Arab states ensure employment for hundreds of thousands of workers in the industrial and service branches in the United States, and they have contributed their share to the growth of business turnover and the increase in the amount and rate of profit of hundreds of companies.[20] All these have created strong interests among wide and diverse groups in the American economy, beginning with the shareholders and managements of the said companies and ending with the production line workers, in strengthening the economic ties with the Arab economies, and especially with Saudi Arabia.

II. ECONOMIC DEPENDENCE OF THE ARAB STATES ON THE UNITED STATES

The high dependence rate of a number of Arab economies on income deriving from the export of oil has given rise to the argument that these economies depend to a considerable extent on the rate of oil consumption in the United States, that country being, in absolute terms, the next largest consumer of OAPEC oil, after Japan. This argument needs qualifying. It does not apply in periods of excess demand (''a sellers' market'') in the world oil market. But even in periods of excess supply (''a buyers' market'') in the world oil market, this argument is meaningful only in relation to two Arab oil exporters, Algeria and Libya. The relative share of the crude oil exports of each of these countries to the United States rose to 41 percent of total oil exports for Algeria and 23 percent of total oil exports for Libya in 1976. Algerian dependence on American demand for its oil is particularly conspicuous because of the deficit characterizing both its balance of trade and its current account during the period under review.[21] The rate of crude oil exports of the rest of OAPEC members to the United States during that year was lower and did not exceed 15 percent, and the rate of total crude oil exports of all OAPEC countries to the United States did not exceed 13 percent (2.4 million barrels a day out of 18.8 million barrels; see Table 10). The breakdown of the exports of crude oil and refined products by OAPEC members suggests an identical conclusion with regard to the extent of their dependence on the United States as customer. To add items of visible exports deriving from the non-oil sector of the Arab states to the United States does nothing to alter the conclusion that the American market as consumer is of secondary importance for the Arab economies, the exceptions being Algeria and Libya, the relative share of whose visible exports to the

United States out of their total visible exports amounted in 1976 to about 43 percent and 27 percent respectively. It is interesting that the relative share of the visible exports of the oil economies of Kuwait and Iraq, and also of the economies of Syria, Lebanon, Jordan and Morocco to the United States in 1976 totaled a mere 1 percent or less for each (see Table 11).

The picture is somewhat different as regards the significance of the American economy as a source of visible imports for the Arab states. With the exception of Algeria, Libya, Baḥrayn, Oman and Tunisia, in all the other Arab economies, the relative share of visible imports from the United States exceeded the relative share of visible exports to that country. The Arab world's biggest importer from the United States in both absolute and relative terms was Saudi Arabia, which in 1976 imported goods to an overall value of about $3.1 billion which constituted some 26 percent of its total visible imports. Egypt was the second biggest importer in the Arab world from the United States with about $900 million that constituted some 18 percent of its total visible imports in 1976 (see Table 11). A high degree of interrelationship is apparent between the volume and the rate of visible exports to the United States and the investments in that country by Saudi Arabia and the U.A.E., and the volume and rate of the visible imports of these economies from the United States, and also between the amounts of American aid to Egypt and the volume of Egyptian visible imports from the United States. On the other hand, there is a low degree of interrelationship between the high rates of visible exports by Algeria and Libya to the United States, and the low rates of visible imports by those two economies from the United States, while the opposite is true with regard to Kuwait, which has a low rate of visible exports to the United States, but a high rate of visible imports from that economy.

As noted above, about 74 percent of the visible imports of the Arab states from the United States is in finished industrial products (including arms) and some 17 percent consists of agricultural produce (foodstuffs). This breakdown of the Arab visible imports from the United States has produced the claim that the Arab states' dependence on the industry and agriculture of the United States is comprehensive and profound. An analysis of the relevant data leads to the conclusion that this argument too is in need of qualification. The rate of imports of industrial products from the United States out of the total industrial imports is a high one only in Saudi Arabia, which in 1976 imported 25 percent of its industrial products from the United States. In the other Arab economies this rate is lower (see Table 6). Also with regard to Saudi Arabia, the degree of dependence on the American industry is not great because apart from a limited number of products, mainly in the sphere of arms, substitutes for the U.S. import items which are close in quality and either identical or cheaper in price are available in other industrialized economies in Western Europe and Japan. Moreover, the relatively high share of industrial imports of Saudi Arabia from the United States does not derive from economic factors only. As stated, from 1975 on, the competition between American companies and manufacturers in Japan, Britain, France, Germany, Italy, Holland and other countries for orders for industrial products by the Saudi Arabian government has become fiercer. In many fields, the manufacturers in those countries have obvious advantages over their American counterparts. If, notwithstanding, American companies do obtain more orders for industrial products than the companies of any other industrialized state, this is also due to the encouragement and support that American manufacturers are given by their government in their activity in Saudi Arabia, and because the regime in Riyād is more exposed to American pressures than to those that can be exerted by any other industrialized state.

Another claim that needs to be qualified posits the dependence of the Arab world on the imports of wheat from the United States. During the mid-1970s the Arab economies together imported over half their total wheat consumption. The United States was in fact the main purveyor of wheat to the Arab world, but still imports from the United States did not amount to more than 15-20 percent of total consumption. The breakdown of the imports of wheat from the United States by country shows that only Algeria, Jordan and Saudi Arabia imported 30 percent or more of their total consumption from the United States (see Table 12). Moreover, there can be no doubt that in good years other big wheat exporters of the world—Canada, Australia and Argentine—can supply the total Arab demand for wheat without any drastic change occurring in its price. To this one might add that even in the short term, there are substitutes for wheat, such as cornflour, rice and potatoes. No great similarity can, therefore, be shown between the quality and character of

American dependence on Arab oil, and the Arab economies' dependence on industrial products or agricultural produce from the United States. Our conclusion would of course have been different if the comparison had been between the Arab states on the one hand and all the Western economies, including Japan, on the other hand, and not with the United States alone.

The degree of dependence of the Arab states on the United States in all matters connected with the acquisition of up-to-date know-how and technology and the training of highly skilled manpower is of course a pivotal question in the economic relationship between the two. At the same time it should be emphasized that an assessment of this dependence cannot be expressed in quantitative terms only. As stated, about ninety thousand United States citizens were engaged as experts and other employees in the Arab states during 1977. Of these about seventy thousand were in Saudi Arabia. This manpower was employed in planning, administration and supervision of the execution of various projects, beginning with infrastructural projects in the transportation sector and ending with the establishment and operation of research institutes and universities. As in most other fields discussed so far, here too there are substitutes in other industrialized economies approximating the know-how and skill offered by the United States. It is however important to note that among the bodies responsible for economic development in a number of Arab states, and especially the oil states, there is a prevalent attitude that the substitutes more often than not fall below the U.S. standard. Similarly, the dependence on having Arab academicians trained in the United States is not unequivocal. An estimate of the total number of students from the Arab states who studied for academic degrees in the United States in 1977 amounted to about thirty thousand, of whom about 8,000 hailed from Saudi Arabia.[22] Even if the various universities in the Western world apart from the United States could absorb that number of Arab students, it would not have been within their power to offer the curricula available in the United States and which are sought after by the governments supporting the students abroad. It should also be stressed that there is an obvious affinity between the scope of activity of American companies in the Arab states and the number of nationals of those countries acquiring their technical and higher education in the United States, for the reason that often enough the work methods in use in these companies are distinctive, and exclusive.

It has already been pointed out that the economic aid that the American government granted to Egypt and to Jordan up to the end of the 1977 fiscal year was of great importance for the financing of development projects and for the reduction of deficits in the current accounts of those two economies. However, the relative share of American aid in the total economic aid that flowed to Egypt and to Jordan is worth reviewing. During 1974-77 the relative share of American governmental aid to the two above-mentioned economies did not exceed 20-25 percent each, whereas the relative share of the aid granted by the Arab oil states to each of the two economies was in excess of 50 percent.[23]

The aggregate value of the assets held by the Arab accumulation states, headed by Saudi Arabia, in the United States, gave them a vested interest in the monetary stability and high growth rate of the American economy. A high rate of inflation in the United States means a decline in the real value of securities, bonds and Treasury notes, since they are not linked to any index. A slowdown in the economic activity of the United States could, in this context, prove injurious to the rates of return on the shares. A decline in the exchange rate of the dollar would mean a lessening of the external value of the assets in the United States. The Saudi interest in the existence of monetary stability in the United States economy found expression in the first months of 1978, when there was a decline in the exchange rate of the dollar. In these months the Saudi Arabian government was the main factor in preventing the other OPEC members from taking any steps to compensate for this decline, which adversely affected the real income of the oil exporters. This policy was initiated by the Riyād government, because to have taken compensatory measures, such as switching from a dollar base to another currency or basket of currencies in calculating payments for oil, would without doubt have caused further weakening and decline in the external value of the U.S. dollar. In Riyād it was thought that the United States government should be given some extension of time, so as to succeed in what seemed to be a policy aimed at strengthening the dollar. The Saudi economic interest in the maintenance of monetary stability and high growth rates in the United States explains, at least partially, also the Saudi policy in 1976-77 in regard to the fixing of crude oil prices on the world market and also to the production of oil within its boundaries. During 1976-77, Saudi Arabia threw its entire weight, at the OPEC Oil Ministers Conferences, against sharp rises in the price of crude oil. In most cases this stand of Riyād's was opposed to the stand of most OPEC members. A number of factors explain this price policy, and there is no doubt that one of them was the wish to avoid causing further difficulties to the economies of the West in general, and the economy of the United States in particular. In order to ensure that OPEC oil prices did not rise beyond what had been decided, the Saudi Arabian government adopted a production policy that prevented the emergence of a state of excess demand for crude oil on the world market, as had happened during 1971-73.

Important as Saudi assets in the United States for its future development are, there is no doubt that Saudi Arabia is not dependent on these assets and on their rates of return for the fulfillment of its second five-year plan. Moreover, according to current forecasts, Saudi Arabia will continue to accumulate surpluses in its current accounts in the early 1980s too, even if the comprehensive economic development policy continues.

Finally, the efforts of the administration in Washington to channel a major portion of the surpluses in the current accounts of the Arab accumulation states into the American economy have yielded a two-fold gain: first, there was a massive inflow of petro-dollars into the American money market and secondly, no less important, the largest Arab oil producer, Saudi Arabia, developed an interest in the maintenance of the monetary stability and high growth rate of the American economy. Even assuming that the Saudi Arabian government should in the future adopt a more balanced policy in distributing its external assets, and make purchases on a large scale in other industrialized economies, this will not alter its dependence on the stability and affluence of the American economy, since a considerable part of its assets in the United States is invested in non-negotiable long-term securities. Some scholars seek to suggest that because of these investments Saudi Arabia will find it difficult to take part in another oil embargo against the West, since a move of this sort could provoke retaliatory steps in the form of nationalization of its assets in the United States.

To conclude, three groups having different degrees of economic dependence on the United States are distinguishable among the Arab countries: 1) economies with a high rate of dependence—including Algeria (the American oil market), Egypt and Jordan (economic aid), Saudi Arabia and the U.A.E. (industrial imports, technology and investments in the United States); 2) economies with a low rate of dependence—including Iraq, Sudan and South Yemen; and 3) other economies in which, although some dependence exists, it is neither high in degree nor of great significance. In this group are Libya, Qatar, Oman and Baḥrayn, Syria and Lebanon, Tunisia, Morocco and Yemen (San'ā). As stated, the dependence on the American economy of even the countries belonging to the first group is not basically of vital importance for their future economic development.

III. AN ASYMMETRICAL ECONOMIC INTERDEPENDENCE

Data on the economic relationship between the United States and the Arab states make it clear that since 1973 not only have these relations increasingly widened, but also an unprecedented economic interdependence between the two has evolved, finding expression in many and various fields. At the same time however it is obvious that this interdependence is asymmetrical in form, since American economic dependence on the Arab states is more profound, and perhaps more crucial, than the economic dependence of the Arab countries on the United States. The difference in the level of dependence arises from the specific contribution made by the factors that created the dependence and from the degree of their substitution.

The dependence of the United States on the Arab world centers on the importation of a raw material whose needfulness and centrality to the economic system of an industrialized and sophisticated economy, the biggest energy consumer in the world in both absolute and relative terms, scarcely need to be expounded. There are of course no suitable substitutes for this raw material, as regards either uses or price, in the short term. Hence American dependence on the Arab world focuses on Saudi Arabia, which has become the biggest oil supplier for the American economy. On the other hand, although Arab economies depend on the United States in a number of fields, this dependence does not contain the rare and menacing combination of needfulness and centrality, and absence of suitable substitutes. The asymmetry is expressed in the fact that, all other things being equal, the American economy is not capable of functioning properly without the imports of Arab oil, while the Arab economies, including Saudi Arabia, bereft of their economic relations with the United States, would only be partially, and certainly not fatally, damaged.

The United States government is aware of this asymmetry and the grave consequences liable to derive therefrom. It is fortunate for the United States and its allies in the West that the political conditions on the Arabian Peninsula in particular and the Middle East in general opened up possibilities for offsetting this economic asymmetry. The inherent weakness of the oil state regimes of the Arabian peninsula, their hostility towards and fear of the growing threat of radical forces from within and of the Soviet Union and its protégés in the Middle East from without, has prompted them to strengthen their political ties with the United States. The survival and stability of these regimes, according to their leaders, depend to an ever increasing extent on the political and military support of the United States. The administration in Washington then responded with unqualified enthusiasm to this orientation on the part of the oil states in the Arabian peninsula, led by Saudi Arabia. In May 1977 sources of known reliability reported a secret informal military-economic agreement between the United States and Saudi Arabia. Contacts relevant to this agreement and its signing took place as the Ford administration came to its end, and Carter came into office. Under the terms of the agreement the United States government undertook to guarantee the security of Saudi Arabia and the maintenance of its present regime against all threats from home and abroad. In return for this commitment, the Saudi Arabian government undertook to invest in the American economy the major part of the surpluses that would accumulate in its current accounts, and to refrain from raising the price of crude oil by more than 5 percent per annum until the end of 1984.[24] Commentators have found various phenomena supporting the existence of such an informal agreement and among other things pointed to the fact that Saudi Arabia has become the biggest customer in the world for the American arms industry, and that the Carter administration had consented to approve the sale to Riyād of most sophisticated types of weaponry, reserved exclusively for America's closest allies or friends. Thus it would seem that in

1977 a situation developed in which the asymmetry of American economic dependence on Arab oil in the Arabian Peninsula was off-set by an asymmetry in the political dependence of these oil states on the United States.

It should be stressed that this system of dependence and counter-dependence might ensure the economic interests of the United States on condition that the existing regimes in the oil states of the Arabian peninsula remain in power. Far-reaching changes in the character of these regimes would of course blunt the effectiveness of the balance of asymmetries that has been created in such a way that the economic asymmetry alone would remain, to the detriment of the United States. A number of developments in the oil economies, and in other parts of the world, such as the social and demographic developments in Saudi Arabia, Kuwait and the U.A.E., the changes some oil economists anticipate in the 1980s in the balance of consumption and production of oil in the Soviet Union, and the political changes in the Horn of Africa, Iran, etc. render ever more dubious the prospects for the present regimes of the Arabian peninsula to hold their own and survive.[25] Radical regimes in the oil economies, should they arise, would probably adopt a foreign policy and economic policy greatly opposed to those being pursued by the present regimes. Examples of sudden shifts of policy as a result of the accession to power of radical regimes are by no means lacking in the contemporary history of the Arab world (Qāsim, Qadhdhāfī). Nor is there any lack of examples of recent cases in which the American administration, along with its intelligence community, was taken by surprise and unprepared for events that occurred in the Middle East, in 1977-78 as well. Hence, because of the importance of the economic interests of the United States in the Arab world, the securing of which depends on regimes whose chances of survival into the median and distant future appear most dubious, and because there is no guarantee that the new rulers will continue with the economic policy pursued so far, since no symmetry exists in economic dependence between the United States and these economies, it is essential that the United States adopt a policy that will make provisions for possible political developments in the Arabian peninsula in the 1980s, and that will be worked out on the basis of long-term considerations. Such a policy will foster achievements that will become meaningful in coming decades and not in the immediate time range only, and will strive to ensure the enhancement and reinforcement of the pro-Western potential existing in the Middle East, whose orientation, for obvious reasons, is not likely to undergo radical changes.

NOTES

1. a. The Arab economies discussed in this study are (in alphabetical order): Algeria, Baḥrayn, Egypt, Iraq, Jordan, Kuwait, Lebanon, Libya, Morocco, Oman, Qatar, Saudi Arabia, Sudan, Syria, Tunisia, the United Arab Emirates, Yemen (San'ā) and South Yemen (Aden). b. The data here presented for 1977 are tentative.

2. See, e.g., U.S. Congressional Research Service, *Project Interdependence: U.S. and World Energy Outlook through 1990*, Washington, 1977; U.S. General Accounting Office, *More Attention Should Be Paid to Making the U.S. Less Vulnerable to Foreign Oil Price and Supply Decisions*, Washington, January 1978; Rockefeller Foundation, *International Energy Supply: A Perspective from the Industrial World*, May 1978. It should be noted that these forecasts had been made before the considerable additional proven oil reserves were discovered in Mexico in late 1978; Also, a number of scholars have questioned the assumptions underlying these forecasts, particularly with regard to the anticipated development of the Soviet petroleum industry, and the expected growth in the GNP of Western industrial economies in the 1980s.

3. U.S. Department of Commerce, FT 135.

4. On U.S. aid to Egypt see p. 214 and Table 7 below.

5. "Japan scores with cheaper goods delivered faster", *MEED*, Special Report, Japan, October 1977, p. ix; Gardiner Brown, "Rising costs of oil imports challenge US export lead", *MEED*, Special Report, Arab-American Commerce, November 1977, p. 14. See also ibid., p. 64.

6. For an estimate of the real value of the Arab oil countries' assets in the United States, see p. 221 ff. and Table 8 below.

7. Our estimate is based on data published in SAMA, *Statistical Summary, 1975/6*; IMF, *International Financial Statistics*, vol. 29, no. 12 (December 1976); *Middle East Currency Reports*, vol. 3, no. 7 (May 1977); U.S. Federal Reserve Bulletin, February 1977; Morgan Guaranty Trust Company, *World Financial Markets*, November 1977.

8. See the list of American oil companies operating in Arab countries, *MEED*, Special Report, November 1977, pp. 31-33.

9. See the list of leading American construction companies operating in Arab countries, ibid., p. 22.

10. Ibid., pp. 3, 18-27.

11. Our estimate is based on data published in *Oil and Gas International Yearbook 1977; Engineering News Record*, 15 April, 1976 and 14 April, 1977; *Petroleum Economist*, vol. 44 (1977), pp. 92-93, 177-178, 242, 362, 363. See also *MEED*, Special Report, November 1977, p. 14.

12. See, e.g., *Petroeconomic File*, no. 14, March 1978.

13. U.S. Senate Committee on Energy and Natural Resources, *Access to Oil—The United States Relationships with Saudi Arabia and Iran*, no. 95-70, December 1977, p. 40; *MEED*, Special Report, November 1977, p. 68; *New York Times*, 8 January, 1978.

14. Cf. *MEED*, 20 January, 1978, p. 4.

15. *al-Sayyād* (Lebanon), 19 February, 1976; IMF, *World Economic Outlook*, 2 March, 1977; *Middle East Currency Reports*, vol. 3, no. 7 (May 1977), pp. 29-32.

16. *Middle East Currency Reports*, vol. 3, no. 7 (May 1977), pp. 29-32; *MEED*, 20 January, 1978, p. 4.

17. *Middle East Currency Reports*, vol. 3, no. 7 (May 1977), pp. 31-32.

18. *MEED*, Special Report, November 1977, p. 13.

19. Ibid., p. 11.

20. According to estimates widely held by U.S. businessmen in 1977. U.S. companies would obtain Arab orders totaling $30 billion between 1978 and 1981. See ibid., p. 13.

21. IMF, *Direction of Trade, Annual 1970-1976*, August 1977, p. 63; IMF, *Balance of Payments Yearbook*, 1975-1977.

22. *MEED*, Special Report, November 1977, p. 77; *Time*, 29 May, 1978, p. 19; *Tishrīn* (Damascus), 25 and 27 February, 1978. The figure on the total number of students from Arab countries studying in the United States does not include students of Arab descent who are American citizens.

23. IMF, *Balance of Payments Yearbook*, 1975-1977; *al-Ahrām* (Cairo), 27 February, and 28 June, 1976.

24. For details of this agreement see *International Currency Review*, vol. 9, no. 2 (May 1977), pp. 5-18; *Middle East Currency Reports*, vol. 3, no. 7 (May 1977), pp. 29-30; *Far Eastern Economic Review*, 13 May, 1977, p. 51.

25. According to reports published in the West, Palestinians sabotaged

oil installations at the Abqayq oil field in the Eastern Desert in May 1977 by setting a fire that raged for three days and caused a 30 percent reduction in Aramco oil production for several weeks. See *Middle East Currency Reports*, vol. 3, no. 7 (May 1977), p. 34; *London Currency Report*, 17 July, 1977.

* I am grateful to Professors Bernard Lewis, Bernard Reich, Steven L. Spiegel, and John Waterbury who took part in the Colloquium for their comments. My thanks are also due to the Institute of Middle Eastern Studies, University of Haifa, for its help in the preparation of this paper.

Table I: U.S. consumption and imports of crude oil and refined products, 1970-1977
(millions of barrels a day and percentages)

	1970	1971	1972	1973	1974	1975	1976	1977[1]
Total consumption	14.6	15.1	16.2	17.4	16.6	16.3	17.4	19.1
Total imports	3.4	3.9	4.7	6.3	6.1	6.0	7.3	8.9
Imports from OAPEC	0.3	0.4	0.8	1.4	1.3	1.8	2.8	3.8
Imports from OAPEC as % of consumption	2	3	5	8	8	11	16	20
Imports from OAPEC as % of total imports	9	10	17	22	21	30	38	43

Note:
1 Tentative figures.

Sources: U.S. Bureau of Mines; U.S. Department of Energy, *Monthly Petroleum Statistics Reports*, 1977.

Table 2: **U.S. imports of crude oil from OAPEC, 1973-1977**

	September 1973[1]		1974 Average		1975 Average		1976 Average		May 1977[2]	
	'000 b/d	%	'000 b/d	%	'000 b/d	%	'000 b/d	%	'000 b/d	%
Algeria	124	3.6	180	5.2	264	6.4	408	7.7	381	5.6
Egypt	—	—	9	0.3	5	0.1	17	0.3	82	1.2
Iraq	17	0.5	—	—	2	..	26	0.5	168	2.5
Kuwait	44	1.3	5	0.1	4	0.1	1	..	51	0.8
Libya	153	4.4	4	0.1	223	5.4	444	8.4	749	11.0
Qatar	41	1.2	17	0.5	18	0.4	24	0.5	94	1.4
Saudi Arabia	599	17.3	438	12.6	701	17.1	1,222	23.1	1,716	25.2
United Arab Emirates	88	2.5	69	2.0	117	2.9	255	4.8	237	3.5
Total OAPEC	1,066	30.7[3]	722	20.8	1,334	32.5[3]	2,397	45.3	3,478	51.0[3]
Total imports	3,471	100.0	3,477	100.0	4,105	100.0	5,287	100.0	6,821	100.0

Notes:
1 Pre-crisis level (prior to the oil embargo).
2 Tentative figures.
3 Components do not add up to totals because of rounding.

Sources: U.S. Bureau of Mines; U.S. Department of Energy, *Monthly Petroleum Statistics Reports*, 1977.

Table 3: U.S. imports of crude oil and refined products from OAPEC, 1975-1976
(estimates)

	1975		1976	
	'000 b/d	%	'000 b/d	%
Algeria	290	4.8	437	6.0
Iraq	10	0.2	38	0.5
Kuwait	30	0.5	9	0.1
Libya	330	5.5	532	7.3
Saudi Arabia	850	14.1	1,371	18.8
United Arab Emirates	170	2.8	319	4.4
Others[1]	90	1.5	90	1.2
Total OAPEC	1,770	29.4	2,796	38.3
Total imports	6,030	100.0	7,295	100.0

Note:
1 Including Baḥrayn, Egypt, Qatar and Syria.

Sources: U.S. Bureau of Mines; U.S. Department of Energy, 1977.

Table 4: Eight leading oil exporters (crude and refined products) to the U.S., 1975-1976
(estimates)

	1975		1976	
	'000 b/d	%	'000 b/d	%
Venezuela	1,040	17.2	985	13.5
Saudi Arabia	850	14.1	1,371	18.8
Nigeria	820	13.6	1,124	15.4
Canada	800	13.3	599	8.2
Iran	500	8.3	548	7.5
Indonesia	450	7.5	573	7.8
Libya	330	5.5	532	7.3
Algeria	290	4.8	437	6.0
Total eight exporters	5,080	84.2	6,169	84.6
Total U.S. imports	6,030	100.0	7,295	100.0

Sources: U.S. Bureau of Mines; U.S. Department of Energy, 1977.

Table 5: U.S. visible trade with Arab countries, 1972-1977
(millions of dollars)

	IMPORTS						EXPORTS					
	1972	1973	1974	1975	1976	1977	1972	1973	1974	1975	1976	1977
Algeria	104.4	215.1	1,090.6	1,358.6	2,343.7	3,064.5	97.7	160.5	315.1	631.8	487.0	526.5
Bahrayn	20.0	16.6	60.7	100.4	33.1	74.4	26.5	41.4	79.7	90.2	279.5	203.3
Egypt	16.9	25.9	69.8	27.5	111.0	170.0	76.1	225.4	455.2	682.7	810.0	982.4
Iraq	9.5	15.8	0.9	19.1	123.2	381.5	23.3	55.9	284.7	309.7	381.8	210.9
Jordan	0.3	0.3	0.2	0.8	1.5	3.2	65.2	79.4	105.2	195.4	234.0	301.8
Kuwait	49.0	64.9	13.4	111.4	41.1	214.5	111.3	119.5	208.5	366.1	471.5	547.8
Lebanon	20.6	32.7	29.9	33.3	4.9	42.5	130.2	161.6	286.9	402.3	48.5	123.8
Libya	116.2	215.8	1.4	1,044.6	2,406.2	3,796.1	85.1	103.7	139.4	231.5	276.6	313.7
Morocco	11.4	13.7	19.7	10.2	18.4	21.0	57.8	112.9	184.0	199.5	297.0	371.6
Oman	2.8	24.0	20.8	52.7	251.1	424.3	6.6	9.1	36.5	74.7	57.1	56.9
Qatar	5.3	13.3	79.6	56.5	132.7	292.2	13.5	18.8	33.6	50.3	78.7	113.1
Saudi Arabia	193.6	514.5	1,671.2	2,623.3	5,846.8	6,358.5	314.2	441.9	835.2	1,501.8	2,774.1	3,575.3
Sudan	12.2	8.8	26.8	8.1	24.2	19.0	18.2	38.5	64.3	102.6	105.7	87.1
Syria	2.9	5.8	2.1	7.0	10.3	16.2	19.7	20.7	39.6	127.8	272.2	133.6
Tunisia	8.3	32.6	21.4	26.0	59.2	11.2	54.6	60.2	86.9	90.8	82.4	111.3
United Arab Emirates	26.9	67.2	366.3	682.3	1,531.7	1,640.8	69.2	121.1	229.7	371.5	424.8	515.1
Yemen (San'a)	0.2	0.2	0.6	0.2	0.3	0.6	2.2	9.6	1.5	8.3	25.4	46.4
South Yemen	2.7	3.8	5.0	0.6	0.8	2.8	0.9	2.6	12.3	2.8	4.4	30.9
Arab countries total	603.2	1,271.0	3,480.4	6,162.6	12,940.2	16,533.3	1,172.3	1,782.8	3,398.3	5,439.8	7,109.9	8,251.5
World total	55,555.2	69,475.7	100,972.3	96,940.3	120,677.4	146,816.7	49,675.7	71,338.8	98,506.3	107,651.8	114,807.1	120,163.2
Arab countries as % of world	1.1	1.8	3.4	6.4	10.7	11.3	2.4	2.5	3.4	5.0	6.2	6.9

Source: U.S. Department of Commerce, 1978.

Table 6: **U.S. visible exports by main commodity groups to Arab countries, 1976**
(million of dollars)

	Food and animals	Beverages and tobacco	Crude materials[1]	Mineral fuels[2]	Animal and vegetable oils and fats	Chemicals	Manufactured goods	Machinery and transport equipment	Miscellaneous manufactured goods	Unclassified items
Algeria	94.4	0.6	1.1	0.4	16.7	9.6	62.0	288.4	5.7	0.7
Bahrayn	4.9	4.4	0.2	6.3	0.3	4.8	10.8	235.2	6.3	5.6
Egypt	304.8	22.4	18.5	18.4	133.1	17.0	46.0	230.6	13.9	2.9
Iraq	54.1	2.2	2.9	0.9	4.9	6.7	10.9	287.1	8.1	3.0
Jordan	26.3	1.5	1.2	2.7	0.7	3.6	10.2	77.5	5.1	3.2
Kuwait	11.7	18.5	0.9	3.3	1.3	7.6	38.1	349.0	29.0	2.9
Lebanon	15.2	5.9	3.9	—	1.1	1.4	2.8	16.4	1.1	0.4
Libya	5.9	7.4	2.9	0.5	—	7.3	18.6	201.3	16.1	6.3
Morocco	93.9	5.0	8.5	0.2	9.5	2.9	9.0	117.1	2.8	1.5
Oman	1.0	0.6	0.1	—	—	1.6	3.4	40.4	2.7	1.1
Qatar	1.4	0.4	0.5	0.2	—	2.9	5.9	62.6	3.4	0.9
Saudi Arabia	153.3	21.8	13.3	18.9	10.1	44.9	303.9	1,881.0	134.1	23.7
Sudan	24.5	0.1	0.2	0.2	1.1	4.9	4.1	68.1	1.5	1.1
Syria	18.2	35.7	1.6	0.1	2.9	3.8	14.3	189.6	3.7	1.9
Tunisia	15.5	0.5	4.6	—	1.9	2.5	2.1	52.2	1.6	0.5
United Arab Emirates	11.1	14.4	3.2	1.7	0.6	20.7	56.8	291.6	16.7	4.7
Yemen (San'a)	14.1	—	0.2	—	0.4	0.2	1.2	8.8	0.3	0.3
South Yemen (Aden)	1.2	—	—	—	0.3	0.1	0.2	1.7	—	0.1
Arab countries total	851.6	141.7	64.0	53.9	185.0	142.2	600.3	4,398.7	252.1	60.8
World total	15,709.7	1,523.3	10,891.4	4,226.1	978.1	9,958.1	11,204.8	49,509.9	6,572.2	2,749.4
Arab countries as % of world	5.4	9.3	0.6	1.3	18.9	1.4	5.4	8.9	3.8	2.2

Notes:
1 Excluding fuels.
2 Including lubricants.

Table 7: **U.S. aid to Arab countries, 1974-1978[1]**
(authorized grants, loans and technical assistance)

	1974		1975		1976[2]		1977		1978		Total 1974-1978	
	$ mn	%	$ mn	%	$ mn	%	$ mn	%	$ mn	%	$ mn	%
Egypt												
Economic	21		371		1,032		898		919		3,241	
Military	—		—		—		—		—		—	
Total	21	11.5	371	37.1	1,032	65.0	898	66.8	919	67.7	3,241	59.2
Jordan												
Economic	65		99		144		75		99		482	
Military	42		105		133		145		132		557	
Total	107	58.8	204	20.4	277	17.4	220	16.4	231	17.0	1,039	19.0
Syria												
Economic	—		104		114		98		106		422	
Military	—		—		—		—		—		—	
Total	—	—	104	10.4	114	7.2	98	7.3	106	7.8	422	7.7
Lebanon												
Economic	5		—		10		46		54		115	
Military	10		—		—		—		25		35	
Total	15	8.2	—	—	10	0.6	46	3.4	79	5.8	150	2.7
Others[3]												
Economic	29		21		30		36		30		146	
Military	10		300		125		46		—		481	
Total	39	21.4	321	32.1	155	9.8	82	6.1	30	2.2	627	11.4
Total												
Economic	120		595		1,330		1,153		1,200		4,406	
Military	62		405		258		191		157		1,073	
Total	182	100.0	1,000	100.0	1,588	100.0	1,344	100.0	1,357	100.0	5,479	100.0

Notes:
1 U.S. fiscal years.
2 Includes interim quarter (1 July-30 September 1976).
3 Partial data, includes mainly Morocco and Sudan.

Table 8: **Net external assets of Arab oil
exporting countries, 1976-1978[1]**
(billions of dollars)

	1976[2]	1977[2]	1978[3]
Saudi Arabia	56	68	77
Kuwait	25	31	38
United Arab Emirates	12	16	21
Libya	6	8	9
Iraq	5	7	8
Qatar	4	5	5
Total[4]	107	135	158

Notes:
1 Figures for the end of the calendar year.
2 Estimates.
3 Forecast.
4 Components may not add up to totals because of rounding.

Source: Morgan Guaranty Trust Company, World Financial Markets, November 1977.

Table 9: **Western Europe and Japan's imports of crude oil
and refined products from OAPEC, 1975-1976**
(estimates)

	1975			1976		
	Total imports	Imports from OAPEC		Total imports	Imports from OAPEC	
	'000 b/d	'000 b/d	%	'000 b/d	'000 b/d	%
	1	2	3(=1÷2)	4	5	6(=4÷5)
Britain	1,830	990	54.1	2,052	965	47.0
France	2,190	1,550	70.8	2,598	1,805	69.5
West Germany	1,970	1,170	59.4	2,809	1,276	45.4
Italy	1,990	1,420	71.4	2,268	1,196	52.7
Netherlands	1,200	580	48.3	1,435	691	48.2
Western Europe total[1]	12,080	7,520	62.3	13,528	8,292	61.3
Japan	5,010	2,540	50.7	5,235	2,909	55.6

Note:
1 In addition to the five countries listed, includes also Belgium, Luxembourg, Spain,
Portugal, Austria, Switzerland, Denmark, Sweden and Norway.

Source: U.S. Department of Energy, 1977.

Table 10: OAPEC crude oil exports—totals and to U.S., 1973-1977
(annual averages)

		1973[1]		1974		1975		1976		1977[2]	
		'000 b/d	%	'000 b/d	%	'000 b/d	%	'000 b/d	%	'000 b/d	%
Algeria	Total	1,070	100.0	960	100.0	960	100.0	990	100.0	1,000	100.0
	to U.S.	124	11.6	180	18.8	264	27.5	408	41.2	555	55.5
Egypt	Total	165	100.0	145	100.0	250	100.0	330	100.0	440	100.0
	to U.S.	—	—	9	6.2	5	2.0	17	5.2	..	..
Iraq	Total	2,020	100.0	1,970	100.0	2,260	100.0	2,415	100.0	2,000	100.0
	to U.S.	17	0.8	—	—	2	0.1	26	1.1	100	5.0
Kuwait	Total	3,020	100.0	2,545	100.0	2,085	100.0	2,145	100.0	1,630	100.0
	to U.S.	44	1.5	5	0.2	4	0.2	1	0.1	50	3.1
Libya	Total	2,175	100.0	1,520	100.0	1,480	100.0	1,935	100.0	1,890	100.0
	to U.S.	153	7.0	4	0.3	223	15.1	444	22.9	625	33.1
Qatar	Total	570	100.0	520	100.0	440	100.0	495	100.0	390	100.0
	to U.S.	41	7.2	17	3.3	18	4.1	24	4.8	90	23.1
Saudi Arabia	Total	7,595	100.0	8,480	100.0	7,075	100.0	8,575	100.0	9,800	100.0
	to U.S.	599	7.9	438	5.2	701	9.9	1,222	14.3	1,342	13.7
United Arab Emirates	Total	1,535	100.0	1,680	100.0	1,665	100.0	1,935	100.0	2,050	100.0
	to U.S.	88	5.7	69	4.1	117	7.0	255	13.2	280	13.7
OAPEC	Total	18,150	100.0	17,820	100.0	16,215	100.0	18,820	100.0	19,200	100.0
	to U.S.	1,066	5.9	722	4.1	1,334	8.2	2,397	12.7	3,042	15.8

Notes:
1 Figures for oil exports to U.S. are averages for September 1973 (pre-crisis level).
2 Figures for total exports and exports to U.S. are averages for July 1977. Tentative data.

Sources: U.S. Bureau of Mines; U.S. Department of Energy, Monthly Petroleum Statistics Reports, 1977.

Table 11: Arab countries' visible trade—totals and with U.S., 1972-1976

IMPORTS[1]

		1972		1973		1974		1975[3]		1976[3]	
		$ mn	%	$ mn	%	$ mn	%	$ mn	%	$ mn	%
Algeria	Total	1,471.9	100.0	2,251.0	100.0	4,358.1	100.0	5,917.8	100.0	5,313.0	100.0
	U.S.	103.0	7.0	185.0	8.2	346.2	7.9	695.0	11.7	632.1	11.9
Bahrayn	Total	323.4	100.0	509.4	100.0	1,131.7	100.0	1,188.9	100.0	1,664.0	100.0
	U.S.	29.2	9.0	43.9	8.6	80.3	7.1	91.8	7.7	145.1	8.7
Egypt	Total	888.8	100.0	908.3	100.0	2,351.7	100.0	3,534.0	100.0	4,983.7	100.0
	U.S.	78.1	8.8	115.4	12.7	389.0	16.5	580.9	16.4	891.1	17.9
Iraq	Total	717.2	100.0	904.9	100.0	2,364.4	100.0	4,202.9	100.0	3,277.8	100.0
	U.S.	29.1	4.1	50.3	5.6	188.2	8.0	370.3	8.8	163.2	5.0
Jordan	Total	270.9	100.0	327.7	100.0	432.2	100.0	732.6	100.0	925.3	100.0
	U.S.	47.3	17.5	34.0	10.4	54.5	11.3	56.8	7.8	82.4	8.9
Kuwait	Total	797.0	100.0	1,043.0	100.0	1,556.0	100.0	2,388.0	100.0	3,648.0	100.0
	U.S.	104.0	13.0	147.0	14.1	219.0	14.1	430.0	18.0	510.0	14.0
Lebanon	Total	859.6	100.0	1,252.5	100.0	2,438.9	100.0	2,141.4	100.0	820.4	100.0
	U.S.	106.5	12.4	146.8	11.7	315.5	12.9	405.3	18.9	53.6	6.5
Libya	Total	1,044.5	100.0	1,722.9	100.0	2,762.8	100.0	4,035.3	100.0	4,774.9	100.0
	U.S.	65.8	6.3	93.8	5.4	107.1	3.9	174.5	4.3	304.4	6.4
Morocco	Total	779.0	100.0	1,144.3	100.0	1,910.0	100.0	2,567.4	100.0	2,837.4	100.0
	U.S.	58.9	7.6	120.6	10.5	170.2	8.9	196.9	7.7	241.5	8.5
Oman	Total	185.9	100.0	162.6	100.0	458.0	100.0	669.4	100.0	667.3	100.0
	U.S.	7.3	3.9	10.2	6.3	40.5	8.8	64.6	9.6	44.0	6.6

		1972 $ mn	1972 %	1973 $ mn	1973 %	1974 $ mn	1974 %	1975³ $ mn	1975³ %	1976³ $ mn	1976³ %
Qatar	Total	138.4	100.0	194.4	100.0	270.9	100.0	577.4	100.0	973.4	100.0
	U.S.	14.4	10.4	19.9	10.2	27.7	10.2	55.3	9.6	84.6	8.7
Saudi Arabia	Total	1,136.0	100.0	1,961.0	100.0	2,858.0	100.0	7,060.0	100.0	11,812.0	100.0
	U.S.	221.0	19.5	380.0	19.4	489.0	17.1	1,652.0	23.4	3,051.0	25.8
Sudan	Total	338.6	100.0	436.1	100.0	710.7	100.0	1,033.4	100.0	980.5	100.0
	U.S.	13.8	4.1	33.2	7.6	63.6	8.9	88.2	8.5	92.1	9.4
Syria	Total	539.6	100.0	613.2	100.0	1,229.7	100.0	1,685.5	100.0	2,428.1	100.0
	U.S.	24.2	4.5	22.6	3.7	35.9	2.9	109.3	6.5	129.8	5.3
Tunisia	Total	459.6	100.0	606.3	100.0	1,135.6	100.0	1,421.8	100.0	1,493.9	100.0
	U.S.	55.1	12.0	56.4	9.3	92.5	8.1	96.0	6.8	92.5	6.2
U.A.E	Total	495.6	100.0	838.7	100.0	1,781.8	100.0	2,754.5	100.0	3,419.7	100.0
	U.S.	69.4	14.0	133.0	15.9	232.3	13.0	415.2	15.1	459.0	13.4
Yemen (San'a)	Total	80.8	100.0	122.3	100.0	189.8	100.0	293.9	100.0	412.4	100.0
	U.S.	1.1	1.4	1.3	1.1	4.4	2.3	5.2	1.8	15.5	3.8
South Yemen	Total	105.5	100.0	107.4	100.0	268.3	100.0	171.3	100.0	253.9	100.0
	U.S.	1.0	0.9	3.3	3.1	13.6	5.1	3.1	1.8	5.5	2.2
Arab Countries	Total	10,632.3	100.0	15,106.0	100.0	28,258.6	100.0	42,375.5	100.0	50,685.5	100.0
	U.S.	1,029.2	9.7	1,596.7	10.6	2,869.5	10.2	5,490.4	13.0	6,997.4	13.8

Notes:
1. C.i.f. or f.o.b., according to the countries' reports to the IMF.
2 F.o.b.
3 Estimates.

Source: IMF, *Direction of Trade, Annual 1970-76, 1977.*

EXPORTS[2]

		1972 $ mn	1972 %	1973 $ mn	1973 %	1974 $ mn	1974 %	1975[3] $ mn	1975[3] %	1976[3] $ mn	1976[3] %
Algeria	Total	1,287.4	100.0	1,895.6	100.0	4,313.3	100.0	4,201.3	100.0	4,972.3	100.0
	U.S.	108.8	8.5	210.0	11.1	1,091.1	25.3	1,359.6	32.4	2,111.2	42.5
Baḥrayn	Total	201.3	100.0	309.4	100.0	1,170.4	100.0	1,107.3	100.0	1,248.2	100.0
	U.S.	20.0	9.9	18.1	5.8	129.3	11.0	251.7	22.7	119.0	9.5
Egypt	Total	825.2	100.0	1,124.7	100.0	1,516.3	100.0	1,576.3	100.0	2,285.7	100.0
	U.S.	11.9	1.4	17.2	1.5	11.5	0.8	15.2	1.0	100.5	4.4
Iraq	Total	1,211.4	100.0	1,829.4	100.0	5,839.0	100.0	7,293.9	100.0	8,296.3	100.0
	U.S.	16.3	1.3	16.7	0.9	2.0	—	20.7	0.3	111.8	1.3
Jordan	Total	47.6	100.0	57.4	100.0	153.4	100.0	152.6	100.0	207.1	100.0
	U.S.	—	—	—	—	—	—	—	—	—	—
Kuwait	Total	2,906.0	100.0	3,790.0	100.0	10,961.0	100.0	9,186.0	100.0	8,256.0	100.0
	U.S.	49.0	1.7	59.0	1.6	55.0	0.5	79.0	0.9	28.0	0.3
Lebanon	Total	354.4	100.0	608.4	100.0	1,455.4	100.0	1,206.8	100.0	795.5	100.0
	U.S.	23.4	6.6	27.6	4.5	29.6	2.0	32.8	2.7	4.9	0.6
Libya	Total	2,308.2	100.0	3,996.3	100.0	8,260.8	100.0	5,866.1	100.0	8,232.3	100.0
	U.S.	178.1	7.7	309.4	7.7	7.1	0.1	1,190.3	20.3	2,187.5	26.6
Morocco	Total	640.2	100.0	912.8	100.0	1,703.2	100.0	1,542.7	100.0	1,260.5	100.0
	U.S.	10.4	1.6	12.7	1.4	18.1	1.1	11.4	0.7	14.2	1.1
Oman	Total	231.1	100.0	325.9	100.0	1,133.3	100.0	1,445.0	100.0	1,571.7	100.0
	U.S.	6.7	2.9	6.1	1.9	33.1	2.9	127.2	8.8	248.0	15.8
Qatar	Total	394.2	100.0	622.5	100.0	1,524.1	100.0	1,422.6	100.0	1,989.4	100.0
	U.S.	2.8	0.7	23.7	3.8	80.6	5.3	57.0	4.0	120.3	6.0

		1972 $ mn	1972 %	1973 $ mn	1973 %	1974 $ mn	1974 %	1975[3] $ mn	1975[3] %	1976[3] $ mn	1976[3] %
Saudi Arabia	Total	4,519.0	100.0	7,696.0	100.0	30,992.0	100.0	28,959.0	100.0	36,361.0	100.0
	U.S.	224.0	5.0	376.0	4.9	1,085.0	3.5	2,623.0	9.1	5,315.0	14.6
Sudan	Total	357.9	100.0	436.7	100.0	350.4	100.0	439.4	100.0	554.2	100.0
	U.S.	10.6	3.0	8.4	1.9	19.8	5.7	9.6	2.2	21.7	3.9
Syria	Total	287.3	100.0	351.0	100.0	784.3	100.0	930.0	100.0	1,045.2	100.0
	U.S.	1.9	0.7	2.6	0.7	2.5	0.3	6.0	0.6	10.3	1.0
Tunisia	Total	310.9	100.0	384.4	100.0	925.9	100.0	857.5	100.0	787.3	100.0
	U.S.	11.4	3.7	56.8	14.8	47.7	5.2	88.1	10.3	85.6	10.9
U.A.E	Total	803.5	100.0	1,575.0	100.0	5,274.0	100.0	5,947.0	100.0	8,507.3	100.0
	U.S.	26.9	3.3	66.4	4.2	366.7	7.0	681.6	11.5	1,006.9	11.8
Yemen (San'ā)	Total	4.4	100.0	7.8	100.0	13.3	100.0	10.9	100.0	7.7	100.0
	U.S.	—	—	—	—	—	—	0.2	1.8	—	—
South Yemen	Total	39.8	100.0	84.7	100.0	230.0	100.0	282.3	100.0	288.5	100.0
	U.S.	2.7	6.8	4.0	4.7	6.8	3.0	1.4	0.5	0.9	0.3
Arab Countries	Total	16,729.8	100.0	26,008.0	100.0	76,600.1	100.0	72,426.7	100.0	86,666.2	100.0
	U.S.	704.9	4.2	1,214.7	4.7	2,986.0	3.8	6,554.9	9.0	11,485.9	13.3

Notes:
1. C.i.f. or f.o.b., according to the countries' reports to the IMF.
2 F.o.b.
3 Estimates.

Source: IMF, *Direction of Trade, Annual 1970-76*, 1977.

Table 12: Arab countries' wheat consumption and imports, 1973/74-1974/75[1]

	1973/74					1974/75				
	Total consumption	Total net imports[2] '000	Imports from U.S. tons	Imports from U.S. as % of total consumption	Imports from U.S. as % of total wheat imports	Total consumption	Total net imports[2] '000	Imports from U.S. tons	Imports from U.S. as % of total consumption	Imports from U.S. as % of total wheat imports
	1	2	3	4(=3÷1)	5(=3÷2)	1	2	3	4(=3÷1)	5(=3÷2)
Algeria	2,575	1,600	1,046	40.6	65.4	2,849	1,924	717	25.2	37.3
Bahrayn	8	8	—	—	—	..	..	..	..	..
Egypt	5,049	3,189	798	15.8	25.0	5,397	3,489	750	13.9	21.5
Iraq	1,724	576	459	26.6	79.7	1,948	856	—	—	—
Jordan	232	122	71	30.6	58.2	276	150	95	34.4	63.3
Kuwait	112	112	—	—	—	115	115	—	—	—
Lebanon	522	457	148	28.4	32.4	707	634	95	13.4	15.0
Libya	442	285	15	3.4	5.3	562	417	—	—	—
Qatar	14	14	—	—	—	11	11	—	—	—
Saudi Arabia	510	348	154	30.2	44.3	751	576	287	38.2	49.8
Syria	1,336	225	—	—	—	1,924	334	91	4.7	27.2
Total	12,524	6,936	2,691	21.5	38.8	14,540	8,506	2,035	14.0	23.9

Notes:
1 Agricultural years.
2 Total net imports = total imports less total exports.

Sources: F.A.O., World Wheat Statistics, 1976; U.S., Foreign Agricultural Trade Statistics, 1976.

The Short-Term Effectiveness of an Arab Oil Embargo

Uzi B. Arad

Characteristics of the Arab "Oil Weapon"

Few issues on the world's agenda of current affairs demonstrate as great a divergence of views as those related to the politics and economics of oil, and such is also the case with the plethora of treatments of the so-called Arab "oil weapon." At the root of such diversity of views often lie differing definitions of the term "oil weapon." Clearly, the obvious analogy with instruments of war suggests more than just the mere exercise of influence; there is a strong implication of an ability to coerce as well. In other words, the ability not only to affect the stance of others but also to actually force their hand is at the core of this lever of power politics; the analysis of the "oil weapon" is therefore the analysis of a political interaction *par excellence*, a strategic interaction involving political as well as commercial processes. It is perhaps this dual nature of the "oil weapon" which tends to confuse. For the "oil weapon" is but a particular case subsumed within the general type of activity commonly described as economic warfare. However, this rather special form of warfare may be much discussed but is little understood, as James Schlesinger[1] once noted. The point usually ignored, according to him, is that the very use of an economic weapon tends to blunt its cutting edge. As will be argued below, that comment seems also to be borne out when surveying the effectiveness over time of the Arab "oil weapon." Failure to understand the dialectical nature of economic weapons is often preceded by a basic misunderstanding of the relationships involved within that mixture of economics and politics. There are those purely commercial processes which simply involve the employment of economic means (e.g., trade) to secure economic gains (e.g., money). Such activities should never be construed as economic warfare unless their aims change from the purely economic to the purely political.[2] It is the initiator's purpose which determines whether the manipulation of economic activities is to be viewed as normal commercial intercourse or straight power politics. Economic warfare, then, should not be equated with any politicized economic process, particularly at a time when almost none of the internationally significant economic processes is devoid of such politicization. It is only when such politicization takes the form of a blatant and declared attempt at coercion in pursuit of a patently non-economic goal that one can speak of economic warfare.

As an instrument of economic warfare, then, the "oil weapon" can be defined as the ability credibly to threaten to withhold the supply of oil from certain oil-importing nations in order coercibly to effect a change in their political stance.[3] Such a definition also covers interference with the transportation of oil, as was carried out by Arab nations in 1956 and, to a lesser degree, in 1967. Moreover, it should be clear that the ability credibly to threaten is directly related to the ability to actualize the threat. Our concern, then, is with the ability to manipulate supply primarily through an embargo.

While this focus may seem to restrict the range of the inquiry, it hardly makes it less difficult. The major impediment in the way of clear analysis has to do with the near identity between market conditions which call for supply restrictions out of purely economic motivations and those facilitating restrictions initially aimed at political objectives. Generally speaking, the less competitive the trade in a given commodity, the more supply restrictions serve as a way to maximize profits, up to a certain point. But a non-competitive market controlled by few exporters is also a necessary condition for economic sanctions through export curtailment. Conceptually, then, economic warfare may exist as a separate and neat analytical category; in reality, however, it usually appears in a mixture whereby economic interests are enmeshed with political ones, often merging so as to become indistinguishable. Adelman stated this point plainly when claiming that monopoly entails control of supply, hence the ability to stop it. For him, high prices and insecure supply are two sides of the same coin.[4] To possess an "oil weapon," then, is simply to dominate monopolistically the world oil market. But the degrees to which such control is possessed may vary over time; more importantly, the exact relationship between the political benefits obtainable from a monopoly and the economic ones has never been adequately clarified. Nonetheless, it seems certain that in a situation which presents a monopolist with the need to further tighten supply, it may be quite tempting for him to attach a rider in the form of political claims. The way to go about this is to move to tighten supply in accordance with whatever economic considerations there are for such a step, and then go on to present such measures as a prelude for what is to follow unless certain political demands are met. These tactics have the effect of backing the threat with a demonstration of will and ability, thereby increasing its credibility, and, consequently, the likelihood of eventual political success. Complications may, of course, arise if and when the recipient of such threats genuinely expects the monopolist to exercise his power with moderation so long as his political demands are satisfactorily fulfilled. The prospects for such monopolistic restraint invariably depend upon the monopolist's propensity for trading off his economic goals, or compromising them, against his political ones. Many observers, particularly those trained in economics, do not expect nations to rise above their immediate pecuniary interests. Others, committing the opposite fallacy, sometimes tend to ignore the mundane economic realities which often affect nations or constrain their actions. Be that as it may, the ability "to be patriotic and make a buck at the same time," as one Arab economist once put it, is directly related to the ability to monopolistically—or oligopolistically, for that matter—control the market. This is also the essence of the management of the "oil weapon."

It is in this context that the Schlesinger observation quoted above should be understood. The fact that the frequent use of an economic weapon gradually diminished its effectiveness is attributed to the prerequisite that, for an economic weapon to be successfully exploited by an alliance of nations, such an alliance must form an effective cartel. Such a grouping, however, is usually subject to strong centrifugal forces, especially when it occurs on the international level. In abstract terms, then, the successful and continuous use of economic weapons over an extended period of time by a number of nations acting in unison requires that many rather difficult conditions be met. That may be the principal reason why such an event is a rare occurrence indeed.

The 1973 Arab oil embargo was nonetheless such an event. Its success is undeniable, although the exact measure and precise manifestations of its substantive accomplishments are debatable.[5] The embargo instituted by the Organization of Arab Petroleum Exporting Countries (OAPEC) in October of that year expediently dovetailed with the thrust of the Organization of Petroleum Exporting Countries (OPEC) to bolster its monopolistic control over the market and drive prices up, a process which had begun a few years earlier. For a brief moment during the winter of 1973, both economic and political justifications for supply curtailment on the part of OAPEC seemed to converge. OPEC's bargaining posture needed such a demonstration of unilateral ability to determine prices, and the Egyptian-Syrian military campaign against Israel evidently needed the backing of the "oil weapon," especially in the aftermath of their military debacle and during the intense diplomatic negotiations which ensued. Some observers who followed OAPEC's decision closely claim that during that fortuitous convergence of interests, the Arab producers' economic interests, more often than not, took precedence over their political ones.[6] Their argument implies that were OAPEC genuinely intent only on deriving the maximum political benefits obtainable from its "oil weapon" as defined under the declared aims of the embargo, it should have restricted itself to supply manipulations and clearly linked the embargo to the political positions taken by the oil-importing countries. At the same time, it should have refrained from initiating price manipulations designed to gain economic benefits from the situation. Such tactics would have kept the demand for oil high, assured long-term dependence on Arab oil, and demonstrated unambiguously that OAPEC was bent upon achieving its political objectives while transcending the temptation to reap any economic benefits accruing from a tightened supply situation.

As happened in 1973-1974, OAPEC adopted an almost opposite strategy. Far from adhering to the explicit threat to sustain the embargo in an escalating form "until such time as total evacuation of Israeli forces from all Arab territories occupied during the June 1967 War is completed and the legitimate rights of the Palestinian people are restored . . . ,"[7] OAPEC lifted the embargo primarily when market conditions and commercial objectives so required.

Some would go as far as to suggest that the embargo was actually imposed for economic reasons. At any rate, as soon as the newly quadrupled prices took hold, OAPEC moved to resume full production. It seems, then, that the embargo actually lasted as long as the shortages served an economic purpose; the moment political gains had to be traded off against economic ones, OAPEC unhesitatingly opted for the latter. Thus, by early December, OAPEC's ministers substantially modified their political expectations and hastened to join their OPEC partners in doubling the price of oil for the second time in less than two months.

Will such a situation, where economic and political interests so expediently combine to bring about supply restrictions, develop again? That is undoubtedly the fundamental factor determining the probability of another oil embargo. A repetition of the kind of supply curtailments which make the "oil weapon" an instrument of diplomacy ultimately depends on the simultaneous recurrence of the economic conditions which warrant such restrictions together with the politico-strategic conditions which may necessitate, justify, or provide a convenient pretext for their application. The former is evidently tied to OPEC's general policy on production programing, or to individual countries' specific production plans; the latter, to the Arab countries' policy vis-à-vis Israel, particularly to their war option.

There is no real need to try to estimate here just how likely it is that these two sets of conditions will simultaneously transpire again. Suffice it to note that with the Arab-Israeli conflict still unresolved, and as long as OPEC keeps on trying to firm up its hold on the market, such conditions may indeed develop once more, and surprisingly quickly at that. It may be useful, therefore, to turn this discussion to an analysis of the probable effectiveness that can be expected from another activation of the "oil weapon" in the form of an embargo, were such conditions to materialize within the next couple of years.

While the scope of this discussion does not allow for more than a cursory examination of each of the elements determining the effectiveness of such an embargo, we shall note that there are four groups of pertinent factors: first, those relevant to the potency of the "oil weapon" as measured by its potential for damage; second, the lower and upper limits which constrain the scope of an embargo;

third, those elements which affect the precision with which an embargo can be aimed at and hit target countries; and fourth, the various aspects of the timing of the embargo, particularly its synchronization with the dynamics of the unfolding political developments at a time of a Middle East crisis.

Assessing the Effectiveness of an Embargo

It has already been argued that OAPEC's "oil weapon" is but a derivative of OPEC's monopoly power. Everything else being equal, an improvement in OPEC's position on the world oil market will increase the efficacy of OAPEC's "oil weapon," whereas a reduction in the cartel's power is likely to diminish it.

It is instructive, therefore, to note that OPEC's market share, as it is projected into the short-term future (i.e., through 1982), is actually expected to decline relative to its all-time high of 1974, when two thirds of non-Communist oil consumption was supplied by OPEC members. The anticipated decrease in OPEC's share of the global oil demand for this time frame is a trend almost no one seriously disputes; opinions vary only with regard to the extent of such a decline. Exxon's rather conservative estimate foresees OPEC controlling 61 percent of the non-Communist world oil supply by 1980, a comparatively moderate decline over past levels, but a study published by the Irving Trust Co. puts that figure at 51 percent and projects a further dramatic contraction to the level of 47 percent in 1982.[8] The expected decline in OPEC's market share is inevitably accompanied by a decline in OAPEC's share. If in 1974, 52 percent of the non-Communist oil production came from Arab countries, in 1976 that share fell to 41 percent, and it is projected by one major American oil company to decline further to 37 percent in 1980.[9]

There is yet another factor which accounts for OPEC's declining power relative to 1974. In that year, the cartel was producing 30.8 million barrels daily, and had some 4.8 million barrels daily of underutilized capacity. Underutilization of capacity by 1980 is likely to be almost double that figure, and will probably reach some 9 million barrels daily. Put differently; in 1974, OPEC had one-seventh of its productive capacity underutilized, by 1980, it is likely to have almost a third of its productive capacity underutilized.[10] That situation, which will probably last throughout the early 1980s, reflects the relative abundance of world oil supplies caused by the slackening oil demand and the increase in non-OPEC supplies. The currently soft world oil market could begin to tighten again within a few years, but between now and then the demand for OPEC oil is likely to stay constant and hover around 30 million barrels daily. This is attributed to additional oil supplies from the North Sea, Alaska, Mexico, and other non-OPEC sources.[11]

That these additional non-OPEC supplies have already affected OPEC's monopolistic power is clearly manifested in the cartel's inability to prevent, or correct, the gradual worsening of its terms of trade since 1977. In mid-April 1978, OPEC's terms of trade were 10 percent below the 1974 and 1977 averages.[12] To sum up this point, it seems that to the extent that OPEC's monopoly strength constitutes the backbone of OAPEC's "oil weapon," the latter organization can no longer rely on as tight a market and as firm a monopolistic position as it enjoyed in 1973-1974; this immeasurable, yet noticeable, retrogression in its power will probably continue for several years.

The market attribute which analysts most commonly refer to in appraising the potential of an Arab oil embargo and Western vulnerability to it relates to the degree to which Western Europe, Japan, and especially the United States, rely on imported oil, or, more specifically, on Arab imports. Many of these analysts view with particular alarm the continuing trend of rising American dependence on imported oil. In 1973, direct and indirect oil imports into the U.S. totaled 6.3 million barrels daily, of which 70 percent came from OPEC countries, including 21 percent from Arab countries. Four years later, the U.S. was importing 8.7 million barrels daily, and its dependence on OPEC grew to 84 percent, including some 40 percent of its imports coming from Arab countries. President Carter's goal of reducing imports to 6 million barrels daily by 1985 notwithstanding, it is now generally believed that for the short and medium term, the United States will continue to be much more heavily dependent on imported oil than at any time in the past. By 1980, it may be importing some 10 million barrels daily, half of which will originate in the Middle East.[13] One comparatively pessimistic projection by an oil firm sees this trend continuing well into the next decade, reaching 73 percent dependence on OAPEC oil by 1990.[14] Not all forecasters concur on the inevitability of such a trend for the long run or about the gravity of the situation, claiming the trend could be reversed within a few years.[15] As to the short term, however, it must be assumed that the United States will see no quick and drastic alleviation of its present relatively moderate, albeit historically unprecedented, degree of dependence on foreign oil.[16]

A completely different and considerably brighter picture is to be found in Western Europe. General import dependence in 1980 is likely to be significantly lower than it was in 1974. In that year, according to the Organization for Economic Cooperation and Development (O.E.C.D.), Europe's net imports amounted to 14.1 million barrels daily, or 61 percent of its total energy requirements. By 1980, net imports are expected to decline to 12.4 million barrels daily, or 45 percent of Europe's total energy requirements. Such a decline in import dependence more than offsets American as well as Japanese growing dependence, thus rendering the O.E.C.D. or the International Energy Agency (I.E.A.) group as a whole slightly less import-dependent in 1980 than it was in 1974, and commensurately less dependent on Arab oil. Net imports of oil and natural liquefied gas (N.L.G.) by the O.E.C.D. averaged 37 percent of total energy requirements in 1974. By 1980, that share is projected to level off slightly and fall to 36 percent. The same picture obtains for the I.E.A. group, the more relevant aggregate as far as vulnerability to an embargo is concerned. In 1974, net oil imports for the I.E.A. members reached 35 percent of total energy requirements; in 1980, that figure is to decrease to 34 percent.[17] The anticipated decline in dependence on Arab oil imports can be expected to be only slightly more pronounced, from 16 percent for the O.E.C.D. group in 1974 to some 14 percent in 1980.

The psychological, and therefore political, impact of this trend may be of even greater significance than its economic consequence. For, although these figures may suggest only a negligible reduction in the total O.E.C.D./I.E.A. exposure to imported oil between 1974 and 1980, they indicate that the process of a relentlessly growing dependence on imported oil on the part of most O.E.C.D. countries, characteristic of the third quarter of this century, has been at least temporarily halted.

The leveling off and relative decline in the Western world's dependence on Arab oil is the result of two developments. First, there has been a slowing down in the growth rate of oil consumption in the industrial countries. This is caused by the slowdown in the rate of economic growth as well as by more restrained and efficient energy consumption following the rise in oil prices. Second, non-OPEC oil production is rising, the largest relative increase coming from expanded Alaskan, North Sea, and Mexican output, whose combined production may reach seven million barrels daily in 1980.

There is yet a third parameter influencing the likelihood and potential impact of an oil embargo. All too often ignored in analyses of the balance of power between the oil-importing and oil-exporting countries is the complex state of interdependence between these two groups, particularly between the Arab oil countries and the Western economies most likely to be embargoed, a mutable factor that needs to be periodically assessed. One aspect of this relationship, that of dependence on oil imports, has already been discussed above. However, the relationship is two-sided, for, as in all economic processes, there is a measure of reciprocal need as manifested in the mutual interest in trading. Just as figures for import dependence partly measure the extent of need for a particular commodity felt by the importing countries and the degree of their reliance on its uninterrupted supply, so there should be measures of export dependence which could convey the degree to which the exporting nations depend upon uninterrupted trade of the same commodity for their own economic well-being, that is, as a source of revenue, employment, and the like. In the abstract, it can be postulated that the higher the degree of import dependence for a certain internationally traded good as felt by its importers and the lower the degree of export dependence experienced by its exporters, the more amenable that commodity is to being employed as a political instrument. An acutely asymmetrical interdependence of a highly essential commodity is the prerequisite for an effective act of economic warfare such as an export embargo.[18] In the absence of commonly accepted indices for this equally important component in the relationship between importers and exporters as it affects the likelihood of another oil embargo, and as it determines the relative power position of the protagonists, all one can do is to observe the few differences between the indicators of export dependence present in 1973-1974 with those projected for 1980.

The trends here are somewhat more ambiguous and so are their implications. On the one hand, there has been a steady growth in the net external assets of all major OAPEC members, thus facilitating a dabble in economic warfare even if the associated acts of self-denial do not prove economically profitable as they happened to be in 1973. Table 1 illustrates this process of accumulation.

Table 1: **Net External Assets of Key OAPEC Countries**
(billions of dollars, at end of year)

	1976	1977	1978
Saudi Arabia	56	68	77
Kuwait	25	31	38
U.A.E.	21	16	21
Libya	6	8	9
Iraq	5	7	8
Qatar	4	5	5
Algeria	−3	−4	−6
Total	105	131	152

SOURCE: Adapted from estimates and projections (for 1978) in the Morgan Guaranty Trust's *World Financial Markets*, November 1977.

But the outlook for the next three years is for a continuous annual decline in the current account surpluses of all OAPEC members. Saudi Arabia, for one, is expected to see a smaller rise in its net external assets relative to the recent past, probably reaching 84 billion dollars in 1980.[19]

Clearly, such large external assets (a high portion of which are liquid) could cushion the possible adverse effects of an oil embargo with its consequent disruption of revenues. (The Saudis must have vivid memories from their 1967 experiment in economic warfare, when no such reserves were available to sustain the embargo, and it predictably ended in a fiasco.) It is less obvious, however, whether that capability has markedly improved relative to 1973-74. While in 1973 the key Arab oil countries had nowhere near the amount of accumulated external assets they have at present, neither were their expenditures as extravagant as they have since become. Saudi Arabia's average annual growth in import payments, in nominal terms, between 1974 and 1976, was 80 percent; it was 30 percent for 1977, and it is expected to rise roughly by 22 percent during the 1978-1980 period. This would bring total Saudi imports to almost $47 billion by 1980. The expected rise in imports between 1978 and 1980 will be more rapid than the rise in exports, causing a sharp decline in the balance of goods and services, as follows (excluding investment income): from $14.5 billion in 1977 to around $6 billion in 1978 and to only about $1 billion in 1980.[20] In other words, over the years, Saudi Arabia has acquired a need for imports at quite a fast pace, and the same is true for Kuwait and the United Arab Emirates (U.A.E.), those countries which were presumably the "low absorbers" of revenue among OAPEC members. However, countries like Iraq and Algeria were always identified as "high absorbers" and their balance of trade is negative, or nearly so.

Even if one assumed that in the next few years the Arab countries will be able to forego oil revenues during an oil embargo, that cannot signify that export dependence is to remain low indefinitely. It will remain so only until such time as reserves are exhausted. At that moment the pendulum, so to speak, will immediately swing to the other side, that of an extremely high degree of export dependence, because the oil sector for all major OAPEC members is the predominant if not the sole source of foreign revenue. Defining this as long-run export dependence (that is, long in relation to the period imports are covered by financial reserves), it may be conjectured that the OAPEC countries can hardly take much comfort in the nominal rise in their net assets over the last few years, for this is paralleled by an even sharper rise in their import needs, and by no reduction at all in their singularly high long-run export dependence.

Taking a still broader view of the concept of export dependence, it appears clear that while the dependence of the oil-importing countries on OAPEC has remained confined to the importation of oil and natural gas (and to a much lesser degree on OAPEC's investments), the dependence of the Arab oil exporting countries on the West has expanded vastly to include commodities and services of critical importance, most notably in the technological and military fields.

In 1973-1974 this last ingredient was not as significant as it has since become, especially for Saudi Arabia. We thus find here the common paradox of development: that on the way to independence a country has to accept periods of even greater dependence. For Saudi Arabia, for example, this means that "the assertion of independence and new power in the form of military and industrial strength is taking place through a process that in fact increases dependence on the West and particularly the United States".[21] Though such dependence on military and technical supply, instruction, and expert personnel may be temporary, it will probably reach its apex in the next five years or so, the relevant time-frame of this discussion. Moreover, the irony of Saudi Arabia's unique position as an investor and saver on a global scale is that it can now least afford to rock the boat. Its stake in the well-being of the Western economies has grown enormously compared to the 1973-1974 period, thus proportionately reducing the effectiveness and credibility of an embargo, a mechanism whose essence is to threaten to damage these very economies. At the very least, this consideration sets an upper limit that OAPEC can allow its "oil weapon" if applied in the form of an actual embargo (more below about this "ceiling" on the effectiveness of the "oil weapon"). The net effect of this consideration could be to entirely rule out an embargo as being counterproductive.

One final word about the matter of interdependence. There certainly seems to be at least some validity in the following statement made recently in a report issued by the American comptroller general:

". . . an illusion of U.S. impotence has been created by policymakers' fixation on its petroleum marketplace weakness, rather than on its many strengths outside the trade of dollars for oil."[22]

The report then goes on to list these strengths: the U.S. being the home country of five of the seven major oil companies, its market for oil being 20 percent of OPEC exports; its being a leading innovator and supplier of high technology and managerial know-how; its offering large and secure opportunities for capital investments; its occupying a commanding position in the international flow of loans, loan guarantees, and aid; and its ability to offer security. These strengths, coming on top of its political and military prowess, have always provided the U.S. with sufficient bargaining capability to counter much of OAPEC's advantages. It is noteworthy, therefore, to point out that most of these elements of strength have been on the ascendance in terms of significance since 1974.

It can thus be concluded that, in the final analysis, OAPEC has not improved its position in the balance of interdependence. While the dependence of the Western economies on Arab oil imports may somewhat decline within the next few years, the dependence of Arab oil exporters on the Western economies will actually rise. The practice of power politics among interdependent actors is a function of the degree of asymmetry between them. Much of the success of the 1973-1974 embargo had to do with the rather lop-sided nature of that balance at the time. At present, and as far as one can tell for the short-range future, the relationship between the Arab oil exporters and Western importers is no longer so one-sided. As it is not really necessary to argue that the balance has actually been tipped in the latter's favor, suffice it to say that no longer is there as acute an asymmetrical interdependence as in 1973-1974. Thus, the Arabs' maneuvering space for power politics has been not insignificantly curtailed.

Perhaps the most serious technical weakness to plague an embargo as a form of a weapon is its severely limited targetability. Hans Maull analyzed it as the problem of precision.[23] This shortcoming, typical of most economic weapons, seriously limits the political usefulness of that instrument much in the same way as any weapon without a proper guidance mechanism would be inherently defective. This is so because, as *The Petroleum Economist* put it at the height of the 1973 crisis:

> "The successful use of weapons of war rests on the ability to distinguish between friend and foe, and to ensure that strategic gains are reaped by the user. The oil weapon, by its very nature, cannot do this. In practice, the severe production cuts are spreading indiscriminate damage far and wide, thus threatening to stir up general ill will that will do great harm to the Arab cause."[24]

Apparently, this was not the real political product of that contest, indicating perhaps that the outcome of the embargo had less to do with the objective impact of the oil weapon and more with the Western will to resist it and other political predilections.

OAPEC planners are quite familiar with this technical deficiency of the "oil weapon." Declarations of selective embargoes and pretensions to precision notwithstanding, the lack of ability to point the weapon at a target without causing large collateral damage poses great difficulties for OAPEC. The imprecision of the weapon stems from several objective conditions. Foremost among them is the natural diversity of dependency on Arab oil among different countries for purely geo-political and economic reasons. The ideal situation in which all foes are highly dependent, and all friends are not, does not exist in reality, nor can it, since the more dependent countries can be assumed to be better disposed politically toward the Arab position to begin with than those less dependent on Arab oil. It is no coincidence, therefore, that the countries less vulnerable to oil losses (such as the United States, Canada, Britain, the Netherlands, and West Germany) have an "even-handed" approach to Arab-Israeli issues, whereas countries which are likely to suffer more from a given oil shortage (such as Japan, Italy, Spain and Sweden) tilt toward the Arabs.[25] True, as noted above, higher American dependence on Arab oil imports and lower European rates suggest that the diversity in import-dependence conditions has been somewhat mitigated, and that there seems to be a leveling process of sorts within the O.E.C.D. However, substantial differences between the United States, Europe, and Japan still remain. The share of imported oil in total energy requirements for Europe is likely to stay two to three times that of the United States and, for Japan, at three to four times.

The second source of the chronic imprecision of an Arab oil embargo originates in the fact that OAPEC does not have control over the distribution system. Without such control, there is no way by which the Arab countries can effectively determine the destination of oil shipments once they leave Arab ports. The complex distribution system, particularly the tanker fleets, is in the hands of non-Arab private companies and foreign governments. The power of OAPEC, for all practical purposes, can be said to end at the water's edge.

Realizing this disadvantage, Arab planners have spoken at various times of improving their control over the market and the targetability of the "oil weapon" by integrating downwards, that is, by acquiring control over downstream oil operations. With the large financial surpluses at their disposal and the currently bargain tanker prices, an OAPEC move to purchase larger slices of the world's tanker tonnage would make both good politics and even better business. Yet, in fact, more than five years after the tactical lesson should have sunk in, OAPEC is in no better position of real control over the distribution system than it was in 1973. The few direct Arab orders for tankers, together with several joint ventures, add up to no more than a negligible degree of such control. Total Arab deadweight tonnage in service at the beginning of 1978 was 6.6 million (with orders for an additional 1.8 million), amounting to only about two percent.[26] In other words, so far the massive growth in the purchasing power of the key OAPEC nations has not been translated into earnest efforts at vertical integration, and there has thus been no real improvement in their ability to apply the "oil weapon" with any greater precision than in the past.

The third factor limiting the targetability of an embargo is the existence of the I.E.A. emergency sharing scheme. The formation of the I.E.A. in 1974, and the drawing up of the sharing agreement, do not in themselves guarantee smooth performance and full compliance with the scheme at all times, as the mixed historical record of such international agreements attests. Besides, the adoption of the oil-sharing agreement subsequent to the last supply crisis did not introduce a hitherto entirely novel concept into the equation. The international oil companies, for their own reasons, adopted a similar policy in 1973 and implemented it rather well, thereby circumventing the selectivity of the embargo. The voluntary sharing on the part of the oil companies in 1973-1974 was not formally codified at the time, and OAPEC could have treated that contingency as not necessarily automatic. Such corporate flexibility has not been completely discarded by the adoption of the I.E.A. scheme. All in all, then, the I.E.A. group of nations seems to have closed ranks since the last embargo in an effort to foil potential threats of future selective embargoes. The establishment of an international official body charged with counteracting oil embargoes and the adoption of the sharing scheme not only blunt the targetability of the oil weapon, but make that function almost automatic and force OAPEC to start an embargo with considerably higher production cuts if it wants the desired target to be ultimately hit through shock waves across the I.E.A. camp. As a result, the I.E.A. has elevated the lower limit of the effectiveness of the "oil weapon" (to be discussed below), thereby raising the costs of such embargo to the participating Arab nations.

OAPEC, therefore, is in the position of having been left with a weapon with no guidance mechanism. A selective embargo, which had at least nominal justification last time around, has been turned into a totally implausible option. Consequently, OAPEC will be compelled, if and when it again decides on an oil embargo, to turn all the I.E.A. nations—in fact, all importers of oil—into one target. This awkward approach cannot but affect the political utility of the "oil-weapon." Present trends in the world oil trade do not portend any easy way out of the dilemma such a situation poses for OAPEC.

The Western alliance has thus shown some ability to close ranks in the aftermath of the disarray displayed during the 1973 crisis, though such unity is still to be tested. On the other hand, there are no signs that unity among the nations that compose the OAPEC alliance has been correspondingly strengthened. As far as one can tell, the opposite may be the case. Certainly, the Saudi-led alliance which operated the 1973 embargo worked remarkably well, better, in fact, than most observers had predicted. True, there was some cheating: Iraq went its own way and did not cut back its production, and there was substantial leakage of Arab oil into the U.S. (Actually, despite the total ban on deliveries to the U.S., an average of some 30 percent of pre-embargo quantities did reach the U.S. between November 1973 and February 1974.[27]) On the whole, however, with Saudi Arabia carrying the main burden of production cuts, the Arab alliance performed surprisingly well in 1973. It is questionable, however, whether such cooperation will be maintained in the future. At least one observer of the oil scene maintains that divisions among Arab oil exporters might well resurface in a future embargo, and goes as far as surmising that Saudi Arabia, the leader of the alliance and the country without which no embargo would be practical, may choose not to participate.[28] It seems, then, that compared to the last embargo, of the two opposing camps it is that of the oil importing countries which is likely to demonstrate some improvement in alliance cohesiveness and not that of the Arab oil exporters.

If all of the above properties of the "oil weapon" and its context are spatial attributes by character, there are two additional elements of temporal nature. They, too, are relevant and they, too, exhibit some contraction in the potential effectiveness of the "oil weapon." The first is an aspect of timing connected with the element of surprise. It is clear that most governments were caught by surprise by the 1973 embargo. Many of the repercussions commonly attributed to the embargo were actually a result of the havoc this surprise created and the effect it had in reinforcing the tendency to panic and over-react, so characteristic of governments confronted in times of crisis with threats which they were insufficiently prepared for. The hasty establishment of the Federal Energy Office (F.E.O.) in the United States and its hurried allocation orders, for instance, unnecessarily aggravated the shortage there.[29]

Much of the unpleasantness felt in Western Europe was also self-induced, either as a result of faulty stockpile management or through arbitrary regulations that did more harm than good. The paradox of the matter is that a major reason for the success of the 1973 oil embargo was the laxity and state of unpreparedness the Western governments allowed themselves, probably in the light of the totally ineffectual 1967 embargo. In the years ahead, however, it is the memory of the considerably more effective 1973 embargo which is going to prevail. This collective memory has already led to contingency planning and to other precautions designed to minimize the adverse effects of surprise. While the memory may assist OAPEC in that it lends itself to be exploited in the form of continuous putative economic warfare—that is, by *threatening* but *not effecting* production cuts—it diminishes the utility of actual cuts, as OAPEC is not likely to see a repetition of the extent of unpreparedness for such eventualities as it encountered in 1973, at least not the next time around. For the time being, the 1973 precedent and its relative success has taken away the element of surprise from OAPEC, and this is no mean loss.

A much more critical temporal factor is the time lag between the day of export reduction and the day the import shortage cannot be made up. The significance of this time lag for the operation of an embargo is twofold. First, it is in the nature of all bargaining situations and strategic interactions of similar kinds that they involve in effect a contest of strength and staying power. Often the party that wins such contests is the one with the longer staying power. Second, just as with any major military move, for an economic weapon to achieve maximum effectiveness, the impact of the weapon must be synchronized with the political events its possessors want to influence. The advantages of adequate synchronization in the political context are particularly essential for successful economic warfare, as economic weapons are of inherently slow impact. A longer time lag of the sort described above simply implies greater staying power for the oil importers and an exacerbation of the synchronization problem of the oil exporters. It is arguable, of course, that in the mere anticipation of future impact, immediate political dividends may accrue. This may be true, but, clearly, the longer the time lag as it is perceived, the smaller those instant dividends. It is crucial, therefore, to compare the time lag allowed by the 1973 oil system with the one that can be expected if and when another deliberate curtailment of supply is initiated.

This potential time lag is a function of several factors: flexibility in the tanker market; conservation possibilities; optional shut-in capacity outside the embargoing nations; and, the measure specifically designed to provide such cushion, the stockage situation in the potentially affected countries. Upon examination, it turns out that in all these factors there has been an improvement relative to 1973, thus contributing to a considerable prolongation of the likely time lag. The role of oil stockpiles is of particular interest in this connection.

All members of the I.E.A. were obligated under the 1974 agreement to increase by 1980 their national oil stockpiles to 90 days of their net oil imports of the previous year. The United States, Japan, and Germany have moved most determinedly to augment their emergency storage. Although the U.S. will probably not be able to complete the hoped-for one-billion-barrel National Strategic Reserve by 1981, it will have in its strategic stockpile of crude oil some 250 million barrels by mid-1979 and 500 million by the end of 1980.[30] Assuming that by that time it will be importing five million barrels daily from Arab countries, the emergency storage will be equivalent to a 100-day supply of Arab oil. This would come on top of working stocks estimated at two months or so of total imports. Taken together, this would give the United States a reserve equivalent to seven months or so of its Arab oil imports. Japan is considering building up to thirteen days in early 1980, but must overcome storage obstacles even to attain the 90-day figure by 1980. Germany may have a little more than 90 days of net imports by 1980, but European countries should not be looked at individually. Overall stocks in Europe will apparently be built up to the 90-day requirement. Assuming that roughly two-thirds of European and Japanese imports originate from Arab sources, a 90-day stock level would give each the equivalent of more than four months of Arab oil imports.[31]

These figures indicate a real increase relative to 1973 in the length of time that the I.E.A. as a group, or its individual members, could withstand a given level of oil loss. It may be doubtful whether the Arab countries would be deterred from imposing an embargo simply because they would have to hold a reduction in exports a few months longer. Nevertheless, the lengthened time lag will provide oil importers with greater breathing space and is bound to complicate the synchronization problem OAPEC faces.

The Arab "oil weapon" has traditionally been held in abeyance for the eventuality of an outbreak of hostilities with Israel. But Middle East wars in all past activations of the "oil weapon" lasted less than the operative time lag needed for optimal use of the "oil weapon." This predicament confronts OAPEC with another dilemma: either to start the squeeze well in advance of war, in the hope of achieving maximum impact when it breaks out, or to patiently sit pat and wait for hostilities to begin. If the "oil weapon" is applied well in advance of a war it would signal the coming of hostilities and possibly compromise the chances of attaining military surprise. Furthermore, such an "out of the blue" squeeze in peacetime would seem to lack a proper pretext, and would certainly annoy even those governments sympathetic to the Arab cause. Unless, of course, an unrelated cause for a production cutback, perhaps of economic or domestic nature, conveniently presents itself. If the timing of the "oil weapon" is tied to the opening of hostilities, the limited gain in legitimacy may be more than offset by the missed opportunity to have the full weight of production cuts coincide with the critical moments of the political-military crisis.

In disappointment over the less than optimal performance in 1973, some OAPEC planners have been contemplating opting for the former gambit. In the words of 'Abd al-Amīr Kubba, an Iraq oil official, ". . . oil will add to . . . (the war's) ferocity and widen its scope. With one difference. The use of the oil weapon will precede the coming war instead of lagging behind it."[32]

Be that as it may, the present glut in the world oil market makes it no easy feat to apply such a squeeze, and the improvement of the stockage situation in the West has only compounded the difficulty.

In effect, OAPEC has thus been deprived of the capability of making optimal political use of the "oil weapon." It would have to choose between either placing its trust in the political-military offensive and letting oil supply manipulation assume a secondary role, or carrying out a major economic offensive while resigned to the fact that military operations, if begun at all, would be conducted without the exceedingly important advantage of surprise.[33]

As regards the practical staying power that the I.E.A. nations could acquire by 1980 in the face of a possible Arab oil embargo, the key variable would be in the size and duration of cuts in Arab production, as far as the embargoing nations are concerned. For the importers' part, the question is whether the I.E.A. sharing mechanism will be activated. It is conceivable, for example, that under certain political circumstances, the United States, for practical political reasons, may voluntarily seek not to activate the sharing mechanism and elect to confront OAPEC alone. In addition, the real time lag will be determined by the policies adopted by importing governments on measures to restrain demand and on stock drawdowns. If the governments are willing to cut demand "to the bone" before beginning to deplete stocks, that would significantly prolong the period over which a deliberate curtailment of supply would have to be maintained before the targeted economies are seriously affected. At any rate, stock levels being what they are, such a period could last for months even if OAPEC decides on a complete shutdown.

Edward Krapels tried to estimate how long 45 days of emergency reserves (that is, excluding working stocks drawdown, which will presumably be very problematic) would last in various kinds of supply disruptions (assuming 60 percent overall I.E.A. import dependence and compliance with the I.E.A. provisions). These calculations are depicted in Table 2.

Table 2: **The Effects of Various Levels of Oil Loss on I.E.A. Stocks**

Supply loss %	Demand restraint %	Emergency reserve drawdown obligation		Number of days required to deplete 45 days of net imports in stocks
		1. as % of consumption	2. as % of imports	
7	7	0	0	
10	7	3	5	900
15	10	5	8	541
20	10	10	17	264
25	10	15	25	180

SOURCE: E. Krapels, "What Security Are Oil Stockpiles?"

These calculations show that to deplete fully the 45 days' strategic storage in less than six months—that is, to have a relatively quick direct impact on the I.E.A. oil economy—the embargoing alliance has to create a supply loss of 25 percent or more. Table 3, relying on oil data pertinent to 1977, shows that in order to create such a supply loss, OAPEC would have to reduce its exports by more than two-thirds, almost three times as much as it did in 1973.

Table 3: **Export Reduction Required to Cause Various Levels of I.E.A. Supply Loss**

Exporting Countries	I.E.A. Supply Loss		
	10%	20%	30%
Saudia Arabia/Kuwait/UAE	37%	73%	n.p.
Arab OPEC	30%	60%	90%
OPEC	18%	36%	54%

SOURCE: E. Krapels, "What Security Are Oil Stockpiles?"

Cutbacks on the order of magnitude applied in 1973 would allow the Western economies almost three years of consumption at pre-embargo levels, probably an unacceptable long period for OAPEC and clearly a comfortable one for the I.E.A. countries to consider appropriate countermeasures, if they are still needed.

The prospect of a protracted embargo—considerably longer than that managed in 1973-1974—must seem disenchanting to OAPEC, not only because of the difficulty this creates for OAPEC in its possible attempt to link the "oil weapon" to the political bargaining context, but for other reasons as well, chiefly the ultimately adverse consequences of a long and continuous embargo to the Arab countries themselves. The alternative to a protracted embargo would have the same effect. For if OAPEC desires to inflict roughly the same degree of damage on Western economies it achieved in 1973-1974, it would have to escalate its production cuts several fold. The possible need to escalate so as to retain the same level of impact is a disadvantage for the "oil weapon," making it quite expensive, as far as political instruments go, perhaps even prohibitively so.

It could very well be, therefore, that the ultimate consequence of the 1973 embargo was to make another embargo unlikely. This is so because the "floor" of production cutbacks necessary for impact, as discussed above, has been elevated, and also because the "ceiling" to which such cutbacks could rise has been correspondingly lowered, possibly to the point of intersecting the "floor."[34]

In other words, the "oil weapon" may become permissible and affordable at levels that render it ineffective; on becoming effective it may also become too costly. The lowering of the "ceiling" is the result of two developments. The first of the constraints which puts an upper limit on the effectiveness of the "oil weapon" is the threat of military invasion if the damage threatened by an embargo might lead to "strangulation." That this level has not been carefully determined, and that the threat of military invasion may not seem wholly credible to some, is beside the point. The point is that in 1973 OAPEC was not confronted at all with explicit threats of military (or economic) retaliatory action. Their official introduction into the equation only after 1973 must have added a modicum of deterrent effect.[35]

Much more persuasive, however, is the second constraint, and that is the self-deterring effect created by OAPEC's growing dependence on Western economic stability and prosperity. With approximately three-fourths of the total identifiable OPEC investments (that is, mostly current account surplus incurred by OAPEC) going into U.S. dollar denominated assets in 1976 and 1977, the principal Arab oil-producing countries have been assuming yet another form of dependence, primarily on the United States. It is not only that such investments can be designated as hostage money, but that through them OAPEC is acquiring a positive stake in the strength of the American economy. Applying an embargo against that country may, therefore, not only alienate an ally but also jeopardise current oil revenues and endanger the security and/or value of assets held in Europe and in the United States. Robert Tucker put it quite simply, "Why . . . should the oil cartel wish to kill—or, for that matter even seriously injure—the Western goose that lays the golden eggs?"[36] Let alone OAPEC, which has no alternative but to trust the goose, so to speak, with some of those eggs.

Deliberate Western reprisals, economic or military, may or may not be credible, but that a too effective embargo is likely to be economically counterproductive seems a virtual certainty. This realization alone places a rather low "ceiling" on the level to which OAPEC could go in escalating its production cutbacks.

Noting that there is too much Arab money invested in the United States, which could be frozen, and that plans have been drawn up for invading the oil fields, Haykal, the Egyptian journalist, announced last year that the Arab "oil weapon" is dead.[37] Such news may indeed be exaggerated, but it is obviously becoming very difficult for OAPEC leaders to find the golden mean, if there is one, between an empty embargo threat because of half-hearted efforts due to too small production cuts, on one hand, and too severe cuts bound to result in multiple and costly backlashes, on the other.

Conclusion

This discussion has turned on the seemingly *objective* political potential of an Arab oil embargo. There certainly is, however, an important *subjective* dimension, which should not be left ignored. Admittedly, for an instrument of influence to be effective, the fundamental variable is not just how powerful it is in the abstract, but how powerful it is perceived to be, particularly in the eyes of its intended victims. It could even be said that unrecognized realities are irrelevant politically, at least as long as they remain unperceived or perceived differently. But this argument should not be pushed too far. Perceptions cannot be divorced from realities. Realities make themselves felt through experience, and perceptions change through a learning process. To focus an analysis on the objective realities rather than subjective perceptions is therefore not a fallacious approach. It is particularly not so when the purpose of the analysis is to correct what seems to be a faulty perception, in this case that of a growing Western vulnerability to an Arab oil embargo.[38]

This is not the proper place to try to estimate which political demands on the part of the Arabs may be palatable to Western leaders in the future and which will appear exaggerated. It is the success of the last embargo which again may be hindering the success of a future one. The recently signed Camp David accords go a long way toward satisfying most Arab demands for a settlement of the conflict. These accords certainly fulfill the conditions for a settlement set forth by the 1973 E.E.C. resolutions regarded by many as the typical pro-Arab shift brought about by the embargo. This may seem like saying that OAPEC will not have much use for its "oil weapon" in the aftermath of Camp David. It could alternatively mean that OAPEC is also nearing a feasibility limit to its possible political claims, beyond which even the most vulnerable Western country would not go. The political success of the 1973 embargo manifested itself in that it brought the West, primarily the U.S., virtually to dictate its terms of a settlement to Israel. Now that Israel has willy-nilly gone along and largely adjusted itself to the American formula, a major effort would be required on the part of OAPEC if it were to seek to pursue the struggle against Israel to yet another stage, say the resurrection of the 1947 partition plan. The countries of the West have proven themselves not to care much about taking positions calling for a full Israeli withdrawal to the 1967 borders. Further Arab demands, however, may encounter a much less cavalier Western willingness to require additional Israeli concessions.

On balance, it seems then that the net effect of conditions and trends now present suggests a potential retreat compared to 1973-1974 in the overall effectiveness of the Arab "oil weapon," if it is to be unleashed again. However, that such an assessment is not commonly accepted indicates that it could serve the Arab oil-exporting countries to continue to operate the weapon on the putative level and benefit from the prevalent awe with which it is still regarded in many quarters, while avoiding putting it to the test for as long as possible. A putative strategy—namely, brandishing the weapon and just threatening its utilization—may bring greater political payoffs, at a much lesser cost, than the alternative of implementing the threat. At the same time, it is not so clear that such threats, in the absence of actual demonstrations of capability, could adequately gain all the desired political concessions, especially if they are ambitious and happen to be difficult to extract from the governments of the oil-importing countries. The less modest Arab political demands are, the stronger is the leverage required. In such a case, a putative strategy may simply not suffice.

Some OAPEC leaders, in facing up to these problems, have conceded that while not dead, the "oil weapon" as it was applied in 1973-1974 is outmoded. Some of them urge that it should take a new form, not of outright production cutbacks, but of a freeze of production levels or of the adoption of production-rate controls.[39] At first sight, this may seem a more promising as well as a more sophisticated use of the oil power in that it bypasses some of the difficulties and risks discussed above. A second look, however, reveals that this option, in itself a departure from the coercive modality of the "oil weapon," solves a few problems but gives rise to others. Its most obvious shortcoming is that it would be even slower in impact than the "oil weapon" in its traditional form. As one authoritative oil publication put it, a Saudi decision to curb exports "could be momentous, even though its immediate impact in the current world oil surplus might be slight." [40]

The world oil market is indeed likely to remain soft for at least a few more years; a mere Saudi curb on production will lack the necessary political punch that an outright embargo might deliver. This situation may change sometime towards the end of the next decade and is, therefore, only a long-term proposition. The important point is that while as far as the risks of an embargo are concerned things may get worse in the long-term, they have been getting better lately and are likely to remain so for quite a while.

NOTES

* A previous version of this paper had been published by the Center for Strategic Studies (CCS) at Tel Aviv University as CSS Papers: No. 1 (August, 1978).

1. Schlesinger, an economist himself, but one with a keen political sense, is well placed to make such an observation. See his *Political Economy of National Security* (New York: Praeger, 1960). A more recent discussion of the interface between economics and politics in world affairs is Klaus Knorr's *The Power of Nations* (New York: Basic Books, Inc., 1975), particularly pp. 134-165.

2. The converse relationship, that of *political* means to advance *economic* objectives, is equally baffling to many, as the multiplicity of interpretations of the processes of imperialism attest.

3. Hans Maull, in his "Oil and Influence: The Oil Weapon Examined," (*Adelphi Papers*, No. 117, Summer 1975) offers a more general definition:

"any manipulation of the price and/or supply of oil by exporting nations with the intention of changing the political behaviour of the consumer nations."

This seems, however, a dismayingly imprecise definition, particularly because it places price manipulations on an equal level with supply manipulations. The latter should have been singled out, for they are often the means to apply the former. A survey of the political situations in which application of the "oil weapon" can be made is to be found in *Oil, the*

Arab-Israel Dispute, and the Industrial World, edited by J. C. Hurewitz (Boulder, Colo; Westview Press, 1976); Dankwart A. Rustow, "U.S.-Saudi Relations and the Oil Crisis of the 1980s," *Foreign Affairs*, vol. 55, no. 3, April 1977, pp. 499-516; John Campbell, "Oil Power in the Middle East," *Foreign Affairs*, vol. 56, no. 1, October 1977, pp. 89-110; and the exchange in *Foreign Policy*, no. 30, Spring 1978, between S. Fred Singer ("Limits to Arab Oil Power," pp. 53-82) and Robert S. Pindyck ("OPEC's Threat to the West," pp. 36-52).

4. See, for instance, his testimony to that effect in U.S. Congress, Senate Hearing before the Committee on Interior and Insular Affairs, *Oil and Gas Import Issues*, pursuant to S. Res. 45, a National Fuel and Energy Policy Study, 93rd Cong., 1st. Sess., 1971, pp. 1055-58. The direct causal relationship between monopoly and economic power is also lucidly discussed by Klaus Knorr in his "Foreign Oil and National Security," in Frank Trager (ed.), *Oil, Divestiture and National Security* (New York: Crane, Russak & Co., Inc., 1976), pp. 106-123.

5. For differing interpretations of the 1973 embargo, its background, legality and political results, see the following works: Jordan J. Paust, Albert P. Blaustein, with Adele Higgins, *The Arab Oil Weapon* (Dobbs Ferry, N.Y.: Oceana Publications, Inc., 1977); Naiem A. Sherbiny and Mark A. Tessler (eds.), *Arab Oil* (New York: Praeger Pub., 1976); Richard Chadbourn Weisberg, *The Politics of Crude Oil Pricing in the Middle East, 1970-1975* (Berkeley, Calif.: Institute of International Studies, University of California, 1977), and the author's *World Energy Interdependence and the Security of Supply* (unpublished Ph.D. dissertation, Princeton University, 1975).

6. This argument is favored by Israeli economists, (e.g., Shmuel Yaari's "The Basic Economics of Arab Oil Actions," *Middle East Information Series*, XXVI-XXVII, Spring/Summer 1974), pp. 77-83. Even if it may seem to be a self-serving proposition, there is some merit to it. The opposite thesis, that politics supersedes economics in Arab oil decision making, is all too often stated with an equally self-serving ulterior motive. The connection between Arab-Israeli politics and the economics of oil is certainly there, but it seems rather a circumstantial relation than a causal one.

7. Quoted in Yaari, op. cit., p. 80.

8. Exxon's forecast for OPEC production in 1980 is 35 million barrels daily, out of a non-Communist world supply of 57 million barrels daily; (*Oil and Gas Journal*, 1 May 1978.) The official Organization for Economic Cooperation and Development (O.E.C.D.) estimate for 1980 is

slightly lower: 33.5 million barrels daily (Organization for Economic Cooperation and Development, *World Energy Outlook*, Paris 1977). Another major American oil company, according to the *Oil and Gas Journal* (10 October 1977), projected an OPEC production level of 31.7 million barrels daily. Irving Trust Co. obviously has the lowest figure of OPEC's expected 1980 production: 28 million barrels only (*Oil and Gas Journal*, 2 January 1978).

9. Reported in *Oil and Gas Journal*, 10 October 1977.

10. These calculations are based on O.E.C.D. estimates (*World Energy Outlook*) with two modifications: Saudi Arabia was assumed to have a productive capacity of 12.5 and not 15 million barrels daily as assumed by the O.E.C.D., and demand for OPEC oil was assumed to be 30.5 and not 33.5 million barrels daily.

11. This is also the argument made by a joint International Energy Agency (I.E.A.)—Rockefeller Foundation Study (to which contributions came from Shell's Geoffrey Chandler, Vincent Labowret of the Compagnie Française des Pétroles [C.F.P.]), and Giuseppe M. Sgligiotti of Azienda generale italiana petrole [Agip], and Walter Levy) as reported in the *Oil and Gas Journal*, 8 May 1978.

12. As measured by Morgan Guaranty Trust, *World Financial Markets*, April 1978.

13. A rather comprehensive collection of analyses of the future U.S. energy situation can be found in the Congressional Research Service of the Library of Congress report entitled "Project Interdependence: U.S. and World Energy Outlook through 1990," U.S. Government Printing Office, Washington, D.C., 1977.

14. The source for this forecast is Shell, quoted in the *Oil and Gas Journal*, 20 February 1978.

15. It is interesting to note in this connection that in the first quarter of 1978, U.S. imports were down after more than two years of steep quarterly rises. Running at around 8 million barrels daily, oil imports in the first quarter of 1978 made up 43 percent of the overall U.S. supply, down from 45.1 percent for all of 1977 and nearly 48 percent for the first quarter of 1977 (Frank Niering, "Short-term Supply Improvement," *Petroleum Economist*, May 1978).

16. Analysts critical of the approach taken by Washington in managing its foreign oil imports usually point out, first, that importation levels could be lowered through a variety of measures, and second, and perhaps more important, that as long as the United States has to rely on foreign oil it

should seek to minimize dependence on insecure sources (i.e., Middle Eastern or Arab oil) and turn as much as it can to other suppliers. For an excellent presentation of this argument see Horst Mendershausen's "Evaluating Reliable Sources of Supply: Persian Gulf and Elsewhere," a RAND Corporation study performed for the Defense Advanced Research Projects Agency, WN-8583-ARPA, January 1974. Since this policy seems such a perfectly sensible one, it strikes one as very bizarre that the United States is currently gleefully plunging into ever growing dependence on the least reliable sources of all, as if no alternative sources were available. *Business Week*, too, was probably baffled by that policy when it recently detected "A Perplexing U.S. Coolness toward Mexican Oil" (29 May 1978, p. 50). With official estimates of proven reserves stated as 16 billion barrels and potential reserves as high as 120 billion barrels (*Petroleum Economist*, May 1978), Mexico surely is a natural supplier for the U.S. Although Mexican production is rising sharply, much faster than previously anticipated (production by end-1978 is expected to have risen to 1.6 million barrels daily and to 2.3 million barrels daily by 1980 instead of the originally forecast date of 1982), there seems to be curiously little American interest in benefiting from these non-OPEC supplies that would avoid dependence on more distant and hence less secure suppliers. American diplomats have stated that the U.S. would not be concerned if Mexico reduced its exports to the U.S. The Mexican president has thus been forced to travel to Moscow to discuss a possible triangular oil supply deal involving Mexico, the U.S.S.R., and Cuba. Such equanimity on Washington's part could, of course, be explained if there were a comprehensive long-term deal between Saudi Arabia and the United States. But questions as to the wisdom and propriety of such an agreement aside, if there is such an agreement, and its terms are such that they justify neglecting Mexican options, why the urge to constantly appease the Saudis?

    17. These data are reproduced from O.E.C.D. *World Energy Outlook*, Paris, 1977. The forecasts for 1980 can be expected to err on the conservative side, since they were based on higher economic growth assumptions than already experienced through 1977 or now projected for the next couple of years. Therefore, it can be surmised that the extent of joint European, American, and Japanese dependence on Arab oil will be even lower than indicated above.

    18. A thoughtful discussion of the dynamics of complex international interdependencies is Robert O. Keohane and Joseph S. Nye's, *Power and Interdependence* (Boston: Little Brown & Co., 1977). A more detailed

analysis of the prerequisites for effective mobilization of resource power can be found in R. W. Arad et. al., *Sharing Global Resources* (New York: McGraw Hill, 1979) pp. 27-52.

19. For a discussion of Saudi Arabia's finances see the Morgan Guaranty Trust's *World Financial Markets*, April 1978.

20. Morgan Guaranty Trust, *World Financial Markets*, April 1978.

21. Campbell, p. 102.

22. This is the tenor of the comptroller general's Report to the Congress titled "More Attention Should Be Given to Making the U.S. Less Vulnerable to Foreign Oil Price and Supply Decisions," Washington, D.C. 3 January 1978.

23. Maull, p. 12.

24. "A Dangerous Weapon," *The Petroleum Economist*, November 1973.

25. For an elaboration on that dichotomy and its origin see Edward N. Krapels, "Oil and Security: Problems and Prospects of Importing Countries," *Adelphi Papers*, No. 136, Summer 1977.

26. For their own economic reasons, the Arabs are not interested in providing large-scale tanker funding. When urged by Westerners to invest in ships, one Arab executive retorted that the Westerners are "asking the Arabs to establish a charitable organization to save various industries in crisis . . . Arabs are living in under-developed conditions. We ought to consider priorities. Should we pay $5 billion to resolve a crisis not remotely the fault of the Arabs?" (*The London Times*, 13 January 1978). The large excess of tanker tonnage over requirements is certainly partly the Arabs' fault, since they abruptly raised the price of oil in concert with their OPEC partners. The interesting point is, however, that improving the targetability of the oil weapon seems not to figure at all as a high-priority Arab objective.

27. Calculated by the author, *World Energy Interdependence and the Security of Supply*, p. 167.

28. This is argued by Shaykh Rustum 'Alī, in his *Saudi Arabia and Oil Diplomacy* (New York: Praeger Publishers, 1976), p. 157. 'Alī's reasoning rests on an assumption that the Saudis, in a future embargo, may find themselves not only carrying the main burden of production cuts again, but also taking the highest risks. He thinks they might find that combination unacceptable. Singer (pp. 61-62) makes a similar point. He thus reaches the conclusion that an Arab oil embargo is not likely at all.

29. Singer quotes from Paul MacAvoy's piece in the M.I.T. *Technology*

Review (May 1975) to this effect. For a similar argument and a critical analysis of the F.E.O.'s role during the embargo see Richard B. Mancke's *Performance of the Federal Energy Office*, (Washington, D.C.: The American Enterprise Institute, 1975).

30. *Petroleum Intelligence Weekly*, 24 April 1978.

31. See similar calculations of emergency reserves in Krapels, pp. 7-11 and Singer, pp. 58-59. Also important in this respect in Edward N. Krapel's article "What Security Are Oil Stockpiles?" in the July 1978 *Petroleum Economist*, pp. 291-294.

32. OPEC—*Past and Present* (Vienna, Austria: Petro-Economic Research Center, 1974), pp. 100-101.

33. Dankwart A. Rustow finds this element alone substantially to curtail the political utility of an oil embargo linked to a Arab-Israeli conflagration. His summary of the possibility and likely effectiveness of a new embargo runs as follows: ". . . the threat of an effective extended Arab oil embargo is real but limited. It is quite unlikely in the absence of an actual armed Arab-Israeli conflict; it is likely but by no means certain in case of such a conflict; and it would probably have to be maintained well beyond the duration of the conflict to cause major damage." See his contribution to John H. Lichtblau and Helmut J. Frank's, *The Outlook for World Oil into the 21st Century, with Emphasis on the Period to 1990* (New York: Petroleum Industry Research Foundation, Inc., May 1978), p. A-12.

34. The concept of a "ceiling" to the "oil weapon" was introduced by Hans Maull (pp. 14-16); the concept of "floor" refers to the threshhold above which production cutbacks will actually be felt as supply shortfalls.

35. For a compilation of such threats immediately following the last embargo, see U.S. House of Representatives, Committee on International Relations, "Oil Fields as Military Objectives," Washington, D.C.: August, 1975.

36. "Oil and American Power—Three Years Later," *Commentary*, Vol. 63, No. 1, January 1971, p. 35.

37. Quoted in *Events*, 7 October 1977.

38. Singer, in his excellent evaluation of the effectiveness of Arab oil power, emphasizes the psychological component of an embargo threat. This is sensible, because the effectiveness of such a threat indeed hinges on how it is perceived. Singer believes the likelihood of another embargo also depends on such perception (p. 58): "If (Americans) appear convinced that they will be hurt, then an embargo will become more probable." Obviously, as long as people overestimate Arab oil power, a putative

strategy will present certain advantages over a strategy of actual reductions.

39. For instance, Charles Holley, "The Real 'Oil Weapon': Production Rate Control and Not Total Embargo," *The Middle East*, July 1977.

40. *Petroleum Intelligence Weekly*, 19 September 1977. The manipulation of petrodollars is seen by some as another replacement to the outmoded "oil weapon." Though outside the framework of this discussion, it would seem that the petrodollar option, in addition to being circumscribed by all the deficiencies typical of economic weapons, has even less political utility. For further discussion of the limits to Arab financial power, see Singer, pp. 62-65.

Cairo and
Washington

Egypt's Reorientation Towards the U.S.—Factors and Conditions of Decision Making

Shimon Shamir

I

Egypt's reorientation towards the U.S. in the 1970s, which was accompanied by a deep rift with the Soviet Union, was one of the salient developments in the international relations of the decade. The complete return to the West was unprecedented among those Arab states that had after World War II produced "antiimperialistic," revolutionary regimes. Sādāt's exclusive collaboration with the Americans signified a marked departure from the basic beliefs of the "generation of the Revolution" (*jīl al-thawra*) to which Sādāt himself belonged, and a manifest disregard for the platform of the Revolution in which the dictum of neutralism remained an article of faith under Sādāt as well.[1]

This remarkable shift of foreign policy orientation exceeded by far the import of the rapprochement with Kennedy attempted in the early 1960s by Nasser, which did not yield substantial results and was soon replaced by a reconsolidation and gradual intensification of relations with Moscow. It does however resemble the dramatic turn towards the Soviet Union in the mid-1950s, which also effected a comprehensive change in Egypt's position and in the whole Middle Eastern subordinate system.

The vicissitudes in Egypt's orientation seem to indicate that while Cairo's commitment to any orientation is never irrevocable, it has no escape from the need to have a commitment, at almost any given time, to a one-power orientation. Neutralism, i.e., the ability to maneuver between the two superpowers and benefit simultaneously from both, has been a Third World ideal which is never easily realized. Certain circumstances, such as those that existed at the height of the Cold War, sometimes facilitate a neutralist posture, but, as the experience of Egypt has shown, these opportunities may be short-lived. In the final analysis, it appears that a stable neutralist policy cannot realistically be maintained in those states, like Egypt, where there is a convergence of two major constraining conditions: first, a severe shortage of economic resources preventing the government from meeting the needs of development and the expectations of the public, and making it dependent on large-scale economic aid from a world power; and second, a deep involvement in regional conflicts, due to either strategic vulnerability or political aspirations, which necessitate the kind of strategic backing and armaments that only a great power can provide. While Third World states have been known sometimes to manage one such constraint and draw extensive support without accepting an exclusive association with their principal benefactor, the combination of the two generates dynamics of tightening relations with one superpower to the exclusion of the other.

This type of association, which for lack of a better word is here termed *orientation*, falls short of *alignment*, which implies a level of political and strategic commitment that is almost universally resented in the Third World. Nor does it carry all the implications of the term *clientage*, which presumes a level of "influence" on the part of the "patron" that experience often showed to have been exaggerated.[2] The relationship expressed by the term orientation does imply a certain level of "dependence" on the supporting power but—due to the constraints of the international system—it does not guarantee that power, beyond what it may derive from its mere involvement in the assisted state, much more than the latter's receptivity to cooperation—which may sometimes be quite extensive, but is always substantially qualified.

Despite these limitations, the superpowers' interest in gaining Egypt's orientation, whose political and strategic import extended beyond Egypt's immediate area, is self-evident. The question of what determines Egypt's choice of benefactor at any given time and how decisions on this are made has, consequently, aroused great interest among statesmen, commentators and scholars alike. Many have tended to assume a wide range of choices before Egypt and regard as the key to its adoption of one or another orientation the success or failure of interpersonal contacts between representatives and leaders of the great powers and the Egyptian president. This proposition has been attractive particularly in the light of the centralization of decision-making power in the president's hands.

An interesting case in point is Miles Copeland's version, which connects Egypt's turning to the U.S.S.R. in 1955 with a series of diplomatic and bureaucratic blunders committed by the Americans then working with Nasser. Copeland argues that when the American ambassador, Henry Byroade, began to discuss the supply of American weapons to Egypt with Nasser, "there was no indication that the problems, whatever they were, would not be resolved at the end, leaving Byroade and Nasser to work out a solid Egyptian-American friendship and an arrangement for cooperation whereby the pressing problems of the whole area could be solved."[3] Failure to realize the goal, concludes Copeland, was the outcome of the erratic American performance. A similar approach to the problem may also be found, explicitly or implicitly, in the writing of other observers, especially those focusing upon the sequence of diplomatic contacts.

Needless to say, the input into the process of decision making, on such a critical question as the choice between the superpowers, comprises much more than the dynamics of interaction between the personalities involved; and the multiplicity of the factors having a bearing on such a decision certainly constrains the freedom of choice of decision makers. Even in such a highly centralized system as the Egyptian polity, decisions are not made arbitrarily in a vacuum. There is no need to subscribe to deterministic frameworks of analysis in order to accept the observation that by and large major political decisions reflect—in some way that has never adequately been explained—the historical conditions and trends of development of the moment, and that the essence of what political leaders accomplish is no more and no less than—to use a Hegelian concept—"the actualization of their times."

Political scientists, seeking a methodological expression of this process in workable models, and focusing on the factors in the more immediate political setting, have come up with various possibilities of categorization. Thus, for example, K.J. Holsti lists seven categories of factors influencing the choice between foreign policy options: images, attitudes, values and beliefs of policy makers; structure and conditions of the international system; the "national role"; domestic needs; objectives and capabilities; the functions of public opinion and interest groups; and organizational values, needs and traditions.[4] A good many of the factors listed in such attempts at categorization can easily be divided into those emanating from the "operational environment" and those constituting the "psychological prism" of the decision makers, as is indeed suggested by H. and M. Sprout, J. Frankel and M. Brecher.[5] How the factors in the external setting filter through that prism to produce a decision and, more broadly, which factors operate as the determining ones in each case, are open questions, but the fact remains that no analysis of foreign policy decisions can be adequately made any longer without scrutinizing the whole range of influencing factors in order to identify the relevant inputs.

Another methodological concept that must be borne in mind in the analysis of the problem under discussion is the distinction between "core" objectives and subordinate ones. Foreign policy interests and goals are rarely amenable to clear and unequivocal articulation in the form of an orderly hierarchy, but at least some relationships among objectives can always be established. In the case of Egypt, one of the interesting patterns that can be noted in the political behavior of the regime, in the last three decades, is the total subordination of the issue of great-power orientation to other issue areas that rank higher in its priorities. Orientation to East or West has not been regarded of high significance per se, and not determined on its own merit. *In principle*, the Egyptian decision makers, political elite and public at large can accommodate both a Soviet and an American orientation, and the choice in each case is made and justified in terms of predominant "core" interests and national goals./

The dependence of this choice on other factors and objectives can clearly be seen in the case of Nasser's orientation to Moscow. The Soviet Union as such held no great attraction for Nasser who was more comfortable with the Western way of life and regarded with great suspicion both the power politics and the Communism of the Soviet regime. Nevertheless a Soviet orientation was dictated by the *totality* of Nasser's policies and the very nature of Nasserism. Evolving as a messianic pan-Arab movement, nourished by the traumas of a century and a half of West-European hegemony and proposing a vision of ultimate vindication and redemption, Nasserism was from its very start on a collision course with the Western powers. For Nasser's radical-nationalist regime, the conditions of the international system in that period—the culmination of the decolonization process and the height of the Cold War—were conducive to an anti-Washington and pro-Moscow posture. Its commitment to a "national role" of uprooting the remaining footholds of "Western imperialism" meant a large-scale campaign against American interests, strategic bases and alliances in the region and close cooperation with the Soviets.

As an Arab *thawra*, Nasserism aspired to revolutionary polarization and radical transformation of the existing order whose foundation had been laid by the West. Its interests thus converged with those of the Soviet Union which sought to ride the wave of *thawra*s in order to penetrate the Arab world. The desire to gain international prestige and influence by playing an active role in the leadership of the Afro-Asian bloc led to the adoption of "positive neutralism," which was imbued with an anti-Western spirit and backed by the Communist powers. The ambitious goals of Nasserism necessitated the building of a huge military machine which only the Soviet Union was then willing and able to arm. The aspiration to impose Egyptian hegemony over other Arab states clashed with the Western backing of the conservative Arab regimes. The campaign against Israel to which Nasser was deeply committed was conceptualized in terms of the struggle against imperialism; it created frictions in the relations with the U.S. and was a major incentive for close collaboration with the Soviet Union. The domestic needs of the regime, i.e., political mobilization and legitimization, the restructuring of the social base, and the state-directed development schemes called for an "anti-reactionary" campaign—particularly after the collapse of the Union with Syria—which was conducted in semi-Marxist terminology and was naturally approved by the Soviet Union. The Nasserist one-party system was unpalatable to the West but suited the requirements of cooperation with Moscow's Communists, who welcomed the formation of party-to-party channels to reinforce diplomatic relations. Similarly, the regime's measures for the nationalization and control of the economy were disdained in the West but cheered in Moscow as "the non-capitalistic way of development."

The subordination of Nasser's great-power orientation to the totality of these factors was best demonstrated when a change in that orientation was attempted. When Nasser showed readiness, in the Kennedy era, to turn over a new leaf in relations with the United States, the inertial weight of the basic policy factors eventually caused his overture to the West to fail, despite the dispute with Moscow over the issues of Communist parties and Arab unification, and despite American efforts "to come to terms with Nasser." These persistent factors were reflected in a series of Egyptian moves that necessarily engendered frictions and even confrontations with the U.S.: the continuation of the war in Yemen, the attempts to undermine the Saudi regime, the liquidation of private enterprise in Egypt, the support for the rebels in the Congo, the pressure against Western bases in Libya, and the reliance of domestic propaganda on anti-Western themes, which found expression in Nasser's declaration, in 1964, that the Americans could "go and drink the Mediterranean." Thus, the intrinsic dynamics of Nasserism itself eventually returned Egypt to the Soviet camp: the Kennedy-Nasser rapprochement was short-lived and the Soviet-Egyptian connection soon revived and even acquired new strength.

It may very well be that the same fate awaited Nasser's second attempt at rapprochement in May 1970. Realizing that Soviet support would not restore the lost territories, and following explorative talks with Sisco in April, Nasser openly addressed Nixon calling upon him to choose between "an eternal rift or a new, serious and definite beginning."[6] Three months later he accepted the Rogers initiative. Yet, the return of tension in his relations with Washington, following the violation of the cease-fire agreement at the Suez Canal front, shortly before his death, indicated that Nasserist dynamics would have once again hampered a complete change of orientation.

What follows is an attempt to discuss—by necessity in concised form only—the reorientation towards the U.S., which eventually materialized under Sādāt, as facilitated and determined by the factors operating in the Sādāt era.

II

Egypt's turn to the U.S. was effected as a means to advance the solution of the problems with Israel, which constituted the uppermost concern in Sādāt's priorities throughout the 1970s. An examination of the actual evolvement of the reorientation towards the U.S.[7] shows that it was this factor that provided the context of the shift, determined its timing and pace, and constituted its main substance and purpose.

The first steps taken by Sādāt towards the U.S., the feelers he sent to Nixon in November-December 1970 expressing his interest in a peaceful solution to the problems in the Arab-Israeli arena,[8] were in fact an attempt to revive Nasser's abortive shift, half a year earlier, to a reliance on American diplomacy. Similarly, Sādāt's 4 February 1971 "initiative," in the form of a proposal (on the 4th at the National Assembly) to conclude a partial agreement on the Suez Canal zone, or an expression of readiness (on the 15th in the reply to Jarring's note) for a comprehensive peace agreement with Israel, were designed primarily to activate American diplomacy.

At that time a U.S.-sponsored diplomatic solution was, in Sādāt's policy, only one of two options, the second being the resumption of military pressures with the help of more advanced weapons that the Soviets were expected to supply. To solve his problem with Israel Sādāt was willing to go a long way in the direction of either superpower; and just as he signalled to Washington that firmer diplomatic action and pressure on Israel to break the status quo would lead to that "new, serious and definite beginning" in Egyptian-American relations heralded by Nasser's May Day message, so did he pledge to the Soviets that strengthening Egypt militarily would augment Egyptian-Soviet cooperation and the "common strategy" against American schemes in the region.[9]

Working on both options simultaneously was seen in Cairo as sound tactics and a promising avenue, for they were conceived, at least for the time being, as mutually complementary. But eventually these tactics misfired, and by mid-1972 both courses had reached a dead end. Washington, which underestimated Sādāt and was preoccupied with the Vietnam war and the relations with China and the Soviet Union, was not too disturbed by the protraction of the existing situation; while Moscow, which held a similar view of Sādāt and focused on its other global and regional priorities, was not anxious to precipitate another dangerous conflagration in the Middle East.

The expulsion of the Soviets in July 1972, even though it had been often demanded by the Americans as the pre-condition for diplomatic collaboration, did not affect a change in the American posture—as the talks between Ḥāfiz Ismāʿīl and Kissinger-Nixon in February 1973, clearly demonstrated. Not having any perceptible usefulness for Egypt's objectives in the conflict with Israel, a reorientation towards the U.S.—which was widely expected after the Soviet exodus—was for Sādāt out of the question. Paradoxically enough, the expulsion effected a partial change in the *Soviet* posture, inducing Moscow to supply Egypt with some of the long required weapons, and thus facilitating the outbreak of the war which it had regarded so apprehensively.

The very same interest for which a U.S. orientation had been considered unhelpful, or even obstructive, *before* the war, made this orientation indispensable *after* the war. Since Egypt lacked the capability of imposing a solution on Israel by force, it was inevitable that the war should culminate in a diplomatic offensive; and in this sphere, the U.S. with its special and exclusive relations with Israel held, as Sādāt put it, "99 per cent of the cards." Sādāt had completely endorsed the thesis that "the Soviet Union can give the Egyptians arms, but only the U.S. can give them a fair solution by which the occupied territories will be restored."[10]

The sharp shift from Moscow to Washington, even while the guns had not completely fallen silent, took some explaining. Sādāt took pains to elaborate why Egypt should turn to the Americans, who only recently had still been sharply denounced as the enemies of the Arabs and the imperialistic patrons of Israel, and who in the course of the war and after it only stepped up their aid to Israel.

Sādāt's chosen formula was: "The American position is new without having changed radically,"[11] and it was based on an elaborate rationale. First, the circumstances have changed, and in the aftermath of the October War, working through American diplomacy would consolidate a situation of Arab superiority and not one of defeat. Second, the American position itself was not entirely what it had been before the war. Indeed, without withdrawing its commitment to Israel, Washington now spoke of the need "to play a much more active role in the Middle East in pursuing a settlement than has been the case previously, and. . .to take into account the legitimate concerns of both sides."[12] The U.S. had reassessed its position, upgraded its interest in the Middle East and—proportionately—in Egypt, and was determined to work energetically and systematically even without the collaboration of the Soviet Union to achieve a settlement which would inevitably be based on Israeli withdrawal.

The changes were not entirely one-sided, for Sādāt himself gradually modified some elements of the Egyptian policy in order to accommodate the requirements of cooperation with the U.S. as the means of solving the problem. First and foremost, Sādāt abandoned the Nasserite concepts that American support for Israel and Arab-American rapprochement were mutually exclusive, that U.S. policies were inherently opposed to those of the "progressive Arabs," and that basically the only way to achieve some American cooperation was by modifying this imperialistic pro-Israeli position through pressure on American interests. Sādāt on his part was ready to accept U.S. commitment and assistance to Israel, not only by necessity but also because they could facilitate the conclusion of a settlement and would thus be complementary and not contradictory to American cooperation with Egypt. Sādāt was willing to regard the U.S. as the "big wasṭa," the traditional arbiter whose mediation is expected to be effective precisely because both sides respect him and are obliged to him (and therefore can make concessions without losing face).

Second, and as a direct consequence of the first point, Sādāt was increasingly ready for a settlement under an umbrella of exclusive American hegemony which would be tantamount to a new political order in the region. Third, Sādāt adopted a gradualist concept of the American involvement—not insisting on extensive formal commitments to Egypt at the outset of the process, but trusting the dynamics of the process itself to create greater and greater symmetry between relations with Egypt and Israel, and to upgrade the American involvement to "full partnership." Fourth, Sādāt endorsed Kissinger's "step-by-step" method which also meant giving precedence to the solution of the Egyptian problems over those of the other Arabs. And, fifth, he recognized by degrees that "non-belligerency" would not suffice to reciprocate for the return of the occupied territories and that Egypt must commit itself to progress towards genuine peace with Israel.

The evolvement of a U.S.-sponsored settlement of the dispute with Israel, thus facilitated by mutual policy modifications, completely regulated the evolution of the Egyptian orientation towards the U.S. The foundations of this orientation were laid by the arrangement of the 22 October cease-fire (which prevented an Egyptian defeat), the subsequent six-point agreement accepted at the 7 November crucial meeting between Kissinger and Sādāt (which saved the Egyptian Third Army), and the 18 January 1974 Separation of Forces Agreement (which returned to Egypt the territories it lost in the second half of the war). Following these agreements, diplomatic relations with the U.S. were reestablished. Egypt once again became a recipient of American aid and the Suez Canal was reopened with American help. Following the 1 September Sinai II agreement, political relations were further tightened, economic aid was stepped up to surpass the volume of Arab aid, and the first arms deal was concluded between the two countries (covering six C-130 planes). The peace talks, culminating in the 17 September 1978 Camp David agreements and the 26 March 1979 Peace Treaty, brought relations to a new height: Egypt was now given lethal weapons and the modernization of its army was put on an American footing. The Arab boycott led to complete reliance on American economic aid, and Egypt was now universally regarded as part and parcel of the Western camp.

The Arab-Israeli conflict was the decisive factor not only in Egypt's shift to the U.S. but also in its rift with the Soviet Union. Moscow had shown that it could tolerate many affronts from its friends in the area: the expulsion of its personnel, attacks on its global and regional policies, non-payment of debts, the purge of pro-Soviet and Communist elements, and even some two-timing with Moscow's rivals, but it could not tolerate a settlement in the Middle Eastern conflict which was tantamount to a Pax Americana. Thus, while Sādāt clearly desired the continuation of relations with Moscow, in order to give some counterbalance to his growing dependence on Washington,[13] the cancellation of Brezhnev's visit to Cairo, originally scheduled for January 1975, signalled the severity with which the Soviets regarded the U.S.-orchestrated diplomacy in the Middle Eastern arena, and their total refusal to play along with it. After the conclusion of Sinai II, the dispute became an open confrontation, leading in March 1976 to the cancellation of the Soviet-Egyptian Treaty. With the signature of the peace agreements, the polarization had been completed, and it was repeatedly manifested on all levels of Egyptian policies—global, regional and domestic.

A second high-priority policy objective which generated the interest in turning to the U.S. was financial recovery and economic development. True, economic considerations have hardly ever determined major political decisions in the Egyptian regime and, anyway, the reorientation to the U.S., as seen above, could be fully explained by the exigencies of the conflict with Israel alone. However, in this case the economic problem, due to its acuteness, carried a particularly heavy weight, not only as an autonomous second factor, but also as one of the considerations nourishing the principal factor—namely, Sādāt's resolution to terminate the costly conflict with Israel. Economic progress, being a salient motive for seeking a U.S.-sponsored peace with Israel, has become a crucial test for the success and fruition of that policy. The economic factor thus loomed larger and larger as the settlement process evolved, and it was completely interlocked with the first factor—the two together driving Egypt towards an American orientation.

The realization that Egypt's economic problems cannot be tackled without turning to the Western, and particularly the American economies—at least in equilibrium with the economic ties to the East—took place a long time before the peace process. It can be traced back to Nasser's economists (notably 'Abd al-'Azīz Ḥijāzī) who in the second half of the 1960s recommended changes in the economic policies in order to accommodate closer relations with the industrialized West. In the Sādāt period, the emergence of *infitāḥ*, the "open door" policy, began earlier than is generally assumed. Its basic elements had already been outlined as early as September 1971. At the end of that year, Prime Minister Fawzī, presenting the government's program at the National Assembly, expounded the principle of "economic openness and cooperation with Arab and foreign investors" as the first among the five principles of Sādāt's reform.[14] However, full-fledged *infitāḥ* was launched only with the economic liberalization measures and legislation introduced after the appointment of Ḥijāzī as Deputy Prime Minister in April 1973, and substantial implementation began after the October War.

The economic liberalization and other steps taken to attract foreign investment and financial aid were not merely a measure of Sādāt's reordering of the national priorities or his response to the public's expectations in the wake of the October War, but constituted in fact an emergency effort to cope with the sudden growth of the current account deficit, caused mainly by the sharp rise in the prices of imported food, raw materials and other vital commodities after 1973. In 1975 the deficit reached $2.5 billion and in 1976, for all practical purpose, Egypt reached insolvency.

Egypt's economic problems did not end with the growing deficit. It was clear that if the regime wanted not merely to balance its existing accounts but to cope with population increase and poverty, and initiate extensive development schemes (such as the "New Valley" project, the North-West development scheme, the Suez Canal Zone projects, and the new town-building plans) it needed additional capital import on the order of $1-2 billion, bringing the total need of capital imports to $3-5 billion per year.

In the face of needs of such proportions, the Soviet Union could confidently be discounted as the remedy to the problem. Even if it had been ready to waive the Egyptian debt of over $4 billion—which it was not—it could hardly be expected to provide the financial aid, the food supplies and the technologies that the Americans now provided, directly or indirectly. The level of the Soviets' financial aid in the 1960s and the type of large-scale prestige projects that they helped Nasser to execute appeared now to Cairo quite obsolete.

In addition, the ties with the Soviet Union were not compatible with the expectations of Arab oil money which seemed to be a much more significant factor. Indeed, financial aid from this source actually saved the Egyptian economy in the first three years after the war. However, in 1976 it begun to decline sharply and by the time the 1979 boycott was declared, little of it was left to be cancelled.

Dependence on U.S. economic aid has thus been continuously growing and Egypt has become the largest recipient of U.S. civilian aid in the world. The American aid, which since 1976 stood at the level of approximately $1 billion per year, was increased in 1979 and there was talk of an extensive "Marshall Plan" to provide a long-range program for alleviating Egypt's economic hardships.

A great variety of American business concerns and government agencies now offered to Egypt the expertise and technologies which were so central in the new development concept that had replaced the Nasserite "Arab Socialist" corporatist system. The U.S. assistance also brought to the fore and encouraged the growth of bureaucracies and business groups in Egypt who had a vested interest in the continuation of the "open door" policy and the American orientation in foreign policy. The American aid thus generated a momentum of its own, gradually growing in importance in relation to all other factors.

A third major consideration that must be included among the factors of reorientation is the strategic interest, namely the need for advanced weaponry systems and the convergence of Egyptian and American objectives in Egypt's strategic environment. However, unlike the two interests discussed so far, the strategic interest can hardly be considered a primary factor. Rather than motivating the shift to the Americans, strategic cooperation with them was the inevitable outcome of it. It was the dispute with Moscow over the U.S.-sponsored peace process that brought about the Soviet arms embargo and intensified the Soviet strategic support to Egypt's radical neighbors, thus compelling Sādāt to resort to the U.S. and, in turn, alienate the Soviets even further. The spiral escalation process that was thus generated created a sharp polarization leading Moscow to an all-out assault on the Sādāt regime which it denounced as "the policemen of American imperialism." Concomitantly, Sādāt, who initially wished only to remove the Soviets from the diplomatic process of the search for a settlement with Israel, later developed an interest in removing them from the region altogether.

In the mid-1970s Sādāt's Egypt was increasingly drawn into what Haykal ironically called "the new Middle East system": an unwritten and unacknowledged quasi-alliance of states that were opposed to the Soviet penetration of the region and sought greater stability by close collaboration with the U.S. This pro-U.S. system comprised the Shah's regime in Iran and the Saudi regime in Arabia, and in an indirect way it also included the State of Israel, thus closing the circle and providing an additional incentive to Egypt's desire to settle its dispute with Israel which was the prime mover of the U.S. orientation in the first place.

Sādāt felt that the Soviet build-up in the radical arch around Egypt—Libya–Ethiopia–South Yemen—was a grave strategic threat. For sure, the huge Soviet arsenal in Qadhdhāfī's Libya was a part of the Soviet campaign against the Egyptian-American peace diplomacy and it was designed to strengthen Sādāt's avowed adversary across Egypt's western border—a potential "second front" for Egypt. Egyptian sensitivity towards the Soviet presence in the Horn of Africa was intensified by the upgrading of Africa and the "Nile Valley" in Cairo's outlook, which came about not only from the growing sense of Egyptianism, but mainly in reaction to the Arabs' rejection of Egypt's peace policies and the isolation of Egypt in the Arab world. Hence Cairo's concept that any Soviet-backed presence in the Sudan was a threat to Egypt's "strategic depth," and the close support given by Sādāt to the Numayrī regime. Egypt also sought to contain pressures from Soviet-backed radical forces by lending support, in various forms, to Somalia, Eritrea, Zaire, Chad, Yemen and Oman.

True, the Soviet build-up in the regions south of Egypt would have taken place regardless of the developments in Moscow-Cairo relations, and it is plausible that anyway Egypt would have regarded with great concern the entrenchment of the Soviets at the entrance to the Red Sea, near the sources of the Nile and in the African hinterland in general. But without the dispute with Moscow, Cairo would probably have contented itself with striking some balance between its Soviet and American strategic relations and would have avoided full affiliation with the anti-Soviet camp.

Similarly, it may well be that even without the controversy with the Soviets, Egypt would have tried to achieve what Sādāt called "the diversification of the sources of arms supply." But here too, the stress would have been on equilibrium and not on an extensive transfer of the armed forces to U.S.-Western weapons systems.

That being the case, Sādāt sought to derive the maximal benefit from the unpremeditated strategic affiliation with the American camp, and he played it up in his appeals for further U.S. assistance and collaboration.

III

To summarize, the priority objectives that generated the dynamics of the reorientation process were first and foremost the exigencies of the dispute with Israel and, second, the economic constraints. To these two primary ones, the strategic concerns that developed in the course of the process may be added. However, in order to arrive at a fuller explanation of the reorientation decisions, it would be necessary to scrutinize, as mentioned above, a much broader spectrum of factors and look into the elements of the operational and psychological environment that nourished the decisions. As stimuli to the process they operated less directly than the three listed above, but their importance should not be minimized: if the three direct factors represented the problems that the U.S. orientation was expected to solve, the indirect factors represented the conditions that facili- tated the choice of this particular solution.

The structure and conditions of the international system in the 1970s, on both the global and regional levels, were no longer those which in the 1950s and 1960s steered Cairo towards a Soviet orientation. Détente, with all its limitations and false promises, was not the cold war relationship that could entertain a Nasserist-type "positive neutralism." The Third World, on which that neutralism had so extensively relied, no longer exercised the leverage and international prestige it had enjoyed after the Bandung Conference. Although the U.S. was considerably handicapped by the defeat in Vietnam and the scandals in its domestic politics, it was nevertheless gradually recovering from these traumas and even strengthened its commitments in selective areas, notably the Middle East. The Soviet Union, on the other hand, had lost much of its credibility in the region and it could not conceal the limitations on its influence, even in the two major Soviet-oriented regimes in the Arab world, Syria and Iraq. A dramatic growth took place in the power of the oil-producing countries, the majority of which were linked to the Western economic systems and determined to keep the Soviets out of the area. Within the Arab states, the wave of political upheavals and military coups which the Soviets had ridden to penetrate the region had subsided, doctrinaire revolutionaries were losing ground to technocrats, and stabilization became the keyword in most of the regimes.

Moreover, the Soviet Union began to be seen in Cairo as a severe restraint on Egypt's freedom of action and even its sovereignty. The Soviet connection, once associated with the process of liberation and decolonization, was increasingly suspected of, in fact, indicating the opposite. For the Cairo regime, which cherished the evacuation of British troops from Egypt (*al-Jalā'*) as the great historic accomplishment of the Revolution, the Soviet military presence was extremely embarrassing. During the War of Attrition, this presence had grown enormously and come to include, in addition to thousands of Soviet advisors, regular anti-aircraft units, four air bases, and naval bases in three Egyptian ports. It outnumbered in size the British military presence as laid down in the 1936 Anglo-Egyptian Treaty and invoked the concept of foreign bases which was so antithetical to the values of post-1952 Egypt. Although the Soviet presence, having been invited by Egypt, was described by the authorities as completely subservient to Egyptian sovereignty, it was widely suspected that such might not be the case. Sādāt recounted in one of his speeches that when he asked Brezhnev, late in 1970, to recall eighteen teams of SAM-3 missile operators in order to permit their replacement with Egyptians, the Soviet leader said that such a move would damage his country's international standing for it discredited the "Soviet presence." This response, said Sādāt, led him to think: "What does this 'Soviet presence' mean? Does it mean that he who comes to Egypt will never quit?"[15]

Despite frequent reassuring pronouncements, the Soviets had not always refrained from interfering in Egypt's internal affairs. Although they behaved with great caution and even sacrificed the Egyptian Communist Party in order to gain Egyptian confidence,[16] they evidently worked behind the scenes to prepare for greater influence in the future. They sought to establish direct ties with key Egyptian officials and pressured the Egyptian leadership to remove some of those who harbored anti-Soviet attitudes. According to an Egyptian memorandum prepared at the end of the Nasser era, the Soviets pushed for changes in the political institutions of the regime and for the removal of army officers who seemed to them to be hostile.[17] Eventually, Sādāt complained openly about Soviet ties with Nasserist "centers of power" and about "suspicious activity" among students and labor organizations. The Soviets were accused of supporting attempts to turn the Arab Socialist Union into a more avant-garde, cadre-type party and of viewing with favor, in this connection, the political activities and organizational manipulations of 'Alī Sabrī. The latter, though occasioning some reservations on the part of the Soviets, was universally regarded as "Moscow's man" in Cairo, an impression that was enhanced by the Soviet intervention in his favor, in July 1970, which compelled Nasser to cancel his dismissal and upgrade his official position. A similar impression was made by the Soviets' edgy reaction to the arrest of Sabrī, along with the other "centers of power," in May 1971. In the Treaty of Friendship and Cooperation, which that purge prompted them to conclude with Sādāt, the Egyptians asserted their commitment to the Socialist course as a basis for Egyptian-Soviet cooperation (Art. 2), thus implying that questions relating to the domestic regime in Egypt, and not only to its foreign and military affairs, were a legitimate concern of the Soviet Union. The Soviet attempt to support the abortive Communist coup in the Sudan in July 1971 gave some substance to these apprehensions and increased suspicions regarding Moscow's ultimate goals in the region.

Against this background, the interpersonal frictions between Russians and Egyptians—emanating from the differences in cultural values, belief systems, professional codes and norms of behavior—acquired some importance. The heavyhanded and rigid behavior of Soviet personnel did not accord very well with the open and easygoing personality of their Egyptian counterparts. For the Egyptians, the Soviets were too condescending, demanding and lacking in awareness of nationalist and Islamic sensitivities. The antagonism towards the Soviets could be felt not only in the public mood but more significantly within the upper echelon of the Egyptian technocracy—the Foreign Office, the managerial class and particularly the officers of the armed forces.

This applied also to the attitude of the chief decision maker in Egypt, the president himself. Sādāt was deeply offended by the overbearing attitude of the Soviet leaders and their tendency to take him for granted. Their behavior, as he later put it, "made his blood boil."[18] Normally such frictions and irritations could not be expected to erode effective cooperation, as long as it was solidly based on a convergence of interests. But once the utilitarian basis of cooperation was shaken, the element of attitude added its weight to those causing deterioration of relations and hampered attempts at reconciliation. It is quite plausible that the deep distrust between the Egyptian and Soviet leaderships was one of the obstacles that after the 1973 War prevented a compromise settlement of the disputes over military supplies and the Egyptian debt.

In broad terms it may be said that the foundation of Soviet-Egyptian cooperation was disrupted when it no longer appeared to serve Egypt's "national role." The Soviet orientation, which as seen above originally so well complemented the Nasserist conception of national aggrandizement and regional *thawra*, did not live up to expectations. In the final analysis, Soviet aid always fell short of what was needed to establish Egyptian hegemony in a unified Arab bloc. It was Nasser himself, according to Sādāt's version, who concluded shortly before his death that the Soviets were "a hopeless case."[19]

Furthermore, under Sādāt the conception of the "national role" was undergoing transformation, and the tenets of Nasserism were being abandoned one by one. Sādāt needed new concepts not only because he wanted to rid himself of the shadow of Nasser and put his own mark on the history of his country, but also because the Nasserist system he faced upon his accession was almost completely shattered: Egypt's position in the Arab world was at a low ebb, "positive neutralism" had become a dead letter, the Egyptian army was defeated, the internal political system was losing its effectiveness and authority, economic development and growth had stopped completely, and the "Arab Socialist" revolution had reached a dead end.[20] Because of the Nasserist-Soviet symbiosis, the ensuing de-Nasserization process became by necessity coupled with de-Sovietization. (For the same reason, diehard Nasserists like Haykal came out strongly against the rift with Moscow, just as the Soviets sharply criticized the de-Nasserization measures.[21])

Directly or indirectly, most of Sādāt's de-Nasserization steps took Egypt away from the Soviet Union. The liquidation of the Nasserite "centers of power" removed the pro-Moscow clique from power. The dismantling of the A.S.U. cancelled the "party-to-party" channel which the Soviets had developed to parallel "government-to-government" relations. The reinterpretation of the National Charter weeded out the semi-Marxist concepts that had been endorsed by the Soviets. The reinstitution of the private sector diminished ties with the economies of the Eastern bloc. Liberalization in internal politics legitimized socio-political forces of the *ancien régime* which resented the pro-Soviet orientation. The denunciation of Nasser's ideological campaigns in the Arab world, which had been based on polarization between "progressives" and "reactionaries," in fact condemned the basic Soviet strategy in the region. And the abandonment of the Nasserist policy of perpetual struggle against Israel negated the main instrument of Soviet penetration into the area.

Sādāt's own perception of the "national role" was quite different from that of Nasser, in spite of their common ideological background and long-enduring collaboration. Sādāt's vision, as expressed by him and elaborated on by his spokesmen, visualized an Egypt that would indeed enjoy international prestige and regional influence, but would mainly be self-centered, aspiring to social evolution, economic development and "civilizational" progress. Sādāt wanted an Egypt of *infitāh*, a concept meaning not only an economic open door but also political liberalization and openness towards the external world. One of the favorite themes in his speeches was the repudiation of the previous regime's doctrinairism, which had led not only to internal repression but also to isolation from most of the world. The "openness" Sadat wanted was described in his October Paper as facing both East and West, but he left no doubt about the real thrust of this concept: a marked inclination towards the Western world. The whole nomenclature of *infitāh* pointed to the West, and terms such as free trade, enterprise, technological sophistication, open society, and civil rights were generously scattered throughout Sādāt's programatic literature. In his public speeches Sādāt sometimes declared that he had "brought Egypt back to the civilized world"; and just as the Khedive Ismāʿīl, a little over a century earlier, defined the premises of his modernization schemes by the declaration that "Egypt has become part of Europe," so did these declarations of Sādāt identify the advancement of Egypt in his time with close interaction with the Western world. Sādāt's political language was heavily imbued with the symbols, slogans and heroes of the pre-1952 period, thus overleaping the Soviet-oriented Nasserist period and drawing directly from the period in which Egypt was indisputably part of the Western camp.

Unlike Nasser, Sādāt did not seek to change the established order inside and outside Egypt, but to find a way to live with it effectively. For him, international politics was not a series of heroic combats and crucial, zero-sum struggles, but a process of collective bargaining in search of deals that could benefit all parties. Unlike Nasserism, which thrived on political upheavals, Sādāt's policy aimed at stability and sought the cooperation of forces that were so inclined. Sādāt had a realistic perception of Egypt's capabilities and was determined not to return to the disastrous overextension effected by the Nasserist-Soviet venture.

Sādāt's "attitudinal prism" fitted in well with the sober mood of the Egyptian urban classes, whose attention focused in the 1970s almost entirely on practical domestic problems. It was congruent with the widespread mistrust of dogmatic development formulas ("the alliance of the working forces of the people," "the turn towards Socialism" etc.), and the wish to benefit from the affluence associated with Western pragmatism.

Sādāt's outlook was quite close to the elements of the public sector technocracy and the upper strata of the private sector who spearheaded this trend. When Nasser's state-guided and self-sufficiency-oriented development schemes were stranded in the mid-1960s, these groups started propagating an alternative policy based on extensive foreign investment and financing, new managerial technics, and sophisticated technologies, all of which were concomitant with growing consumerism and led directly to a process of tightening economic relations with the West. As seen above, this process generated a momentum of its own and expanded the constituency which had a vested interest in it.

Sādāt also fully shared the intensification of Egyptianism—at the expense of Arabism—as the dominant collective identity, which had already begun to spread among the intelligentsia and other middle class groups in the 1960s and became quite popular in the 1970s. This issue was not irrelevant to the question of relations with the West. Arabism was predicated on *polarity* with Western civilization. It perceived its history as a sequence of great confrontations with Europe (from Byzantium at the birth of the Arab-Islamic *umma*, through the Crusades and the Reconquista, to European imperialism in modern times). Egyptianism, on the other hand, had always prided itself on its immense contribution to world civilization within the sphere of the Mediterranean basin which was conceived as the *foundation* of Western civilization.

Indeed, the deep-rooted hostility to the West, bred by the traumas of Western domination, was diminishing perceptibly. Two decades now separated Sādāt's Egypt from the 1952 revolution which drew on these currents and sought to give them political expression. By the 1970s, the traumas of Western colonialization had somewhat receded into the background and a younger generation emerged which had hardly ever experienced them. In a dialogue between two generations of intellectuals held at the close of the Nasserist period, Aḥmad Hāshim Sharīf, a young writer, exclaimed: "We did not take part in the demonstrations for the *jalā'* (evacuation); our reality began after the Revolution." He proceeded to explain that for his generation the real Egyptian problems were cultural backwardness, underdevelopment and illiteracy, not those that had preoccupied the previous generation.[22]

Perceptive observers of the Egyptian scene have noted that among Egyptian bureaucrats and intellectuals self-confidence vis-à-vis the West was growing, sometimes manifested in statements such as: "the Americans are manageable." In these circumstances, had any leader tried to repeat Nasser's vitriolic attack on the Americans— inviting them, as Nasser did, "to choke in their fury"—he would probably have aroused more bewilderment than the kind of euphoric elation and mass hysteria which that rhetoric aroused in the 1950s. The conditions were thus ripe for turning over a new leaf in Egypt's relations with the West.

IV

Egypt's turn to the U.S. has thus been founded on much more than the personal relations of trust and confidence established between Sādāt and Kissinger in their 7 November 1973 tête-à-tête. The great variety of factors and conditions that went into that decision are not, perhaps, free of internal contradictions—as is always the case in such circumstances—but they are all essential for providing the causality system that explains the actualization of this reorientation. Some of the components of this system can be traced back to the Nasser era, but basically they constitute a self-contained "package" that characterizes Sādāt's Egypt of the 1970s and differs sharply from the Nasser "package" which at that time obliged a Soviet orientation. This was not, of course, a total departure from the previous period, for the continuity of political culture and other "long-term structures" manifested itself in a great many ways, but it did delineate a new phase.

To sum up, the salient features of the Sādāt "package" were: the *core objectives* of relief from the burden imposed by the conflict with Israel, of economic recovery and development, and of the defense of Egypt's strategic interests particularly in the African environment; the *policies* of "openness" which allows qualified liberalization and favors the new public and private sector elite, and of close collaboration with the conservative Arab oil-producers; the *attitude* of distrust towards the Soviets and their ultimate designs, and of disenchantment with the Nasserist experience, its quasi-Marxist revolutionism, Third-World pseudo-neutralism and pan-Arab interventionism; the *belief* in pragmatic evolution, in compromise and in stability as a prerequisite for achievements; the *values* of indigenous tradition, of Egyptianism and of "civilizational progress"; and an *image* of the West which is basically positive, regards the West as manageable, and is relatively free of the residues of the traumatic clash with it. All these elements combined together to effect, through gradual interaction, the turn to the U.S.

The experience of Egypt seems to suggest that in the case of countries similarly constrained, a process of reorientation towards a great power assumes an accelerating pace, with the various factors nourishing each other and creating growing commitment to, and dependence on the assisting power. There is no evidence to show that initially Sādāt contemplated, at any point, a full turn to the U.S. On the contrary, many of his statements and actions registered an intention to maintain some balance between East and West in his economic, political and strategic relations. It was the dynamics of the process itself which made that impossible and involved him deeper and deeper in an exclusive orientation. In a way, it could be compared to the famous "quagmire model" in which a series of partial, situational decisions, each appearing to be the only one possible in the circumstances, eventually build up to a major historical outcome.[23]

The crucial question is to what extent such a process can be expected to escalate beyond the point of no return. Here the Egyptian case seems to suggest that the process is definitely reversible. The revocability of the process ensues from its two inevitable attributes: the fact that growing dependence creates, in any society imbued with a nationalist spirit, its own antidotes; and the fact that the efforts of the assisting power are bound to frustrate the assisted society, because the solution of the problems of a country like Egypt is obviously unfeasible within the range of such a limited political phase.

Just as Egypt's growing dependence on the Soviet Union gradually bred antagonism towards the Russians and disappointment with the worth of their aid, thus leading to an open rupture, so does the American orientation face the threat of a backlash. The far-reaching reliance on Washington may cause growing embarrassment to Sādāt's regime both in domestic and foreign policies. American-sponsored development, based on the influx of capital and the importation of new technologies, can create—as the case of Iran has clearly shown—an intensification of social tensions and internal difficulties. The process almost inevitably entails a dislocation of the masses; inflation and other hardships for the lower classes; an agitation of growing expectations; consumerism, corruption and rapid enrichment among those who have access to the incoming funds; and an assault on traditional norms and values.

In the two issue-areas which were the raison d'être of the turn to the U.S. and constitute its ultimate test, the reorientation has registered impressive achievements: in the Arab-Israeli arena the Egyptians have achieved a peace settlement that is restoring to them the territories of Sinai and could open for them a new era of uninterrupted concentration on the advancement of their own affairs; in the economy, the Egyptians have managed in the wake of the war, to resume economic growth, after a decade of stagnation, and introduce perceptible improvements in their infrastructure. However, none of these two achievements has yet gone beyond the critical line so as to be considered an accomplished success. The consolidation of the peace with Israel will depend on the participation of other Arabs in it and this is still not in the offing, thus putting Sādāt's regime under a heavy strain. Similarly, it is difficult to see how the regime will manage to raise the funds necessary for the ambitious development schemes, whether it will succeed in putting the available sums to good use and when they will bear fruit to effect substantial improvements in the Egyptian economic conditions. The manifestations of the political and economic constraints under which Washington operates have already shown that the Egyptians cannot set their expectations too high with regard to the U.S. diplomatic and strategic backing or the subsidization of the Egyptian economy. To the extent that they do, the threat of the backlash will be more imminent.

It stands to reason that President Sādāt has not been unaware of the threat presented by these limitations when he made the decisions that carried Egypt to an American orientation. His acts, however, inevitably followed the pattern which was so well described by Daniel Ellsberg: "Decision makers follow certain paths not because they *will* work, work better, cheaper or faster, but because such policy *might* work and the alternative would fail."[24]

NOTES

1. Sādāt expressed rejection of alignment with the U.S. throughout the 1970s. See for example his speech in Nikla al-'Inab on 15 May, 1979, and at the People's Assembly on 5 April 1979.

2. On the inadequacies of the term "influence," see the Introduction and Ch. 10 in Alvin Z. Rubinstein, *Red Star on the Nile* (Princeton 1977).

3. Miles Copeland, *The Game of Nations* (New York 1979), p. 155.

4. K. J. Holsti, *International Politics* (Englewood Cliffs, N.J. 1967), pp. 127 ff.

5. See M. Brecher, B. Steinberg and I. Stein, "A Framework for Research on Foreign Policy Behavior," *J. of Conflict Resolution* 13 (1969): 75-101.

6. Nasser's speech in Helwan, 1 May 1970. The same appeal was repeated in Nasser's letter to Nixon, see William B. Quandt, *Decade of Decision* (Berkeley 1977), p. 98 n. 36.

7. A detailed presentation of the sequence of events in this process appears in the forthcoming Hebrew version of this article published in I. Rabinovich and H. Shaked (eds.), *The Middle East and the United States*.

8. Quandt, pp. 133-134.

9. Mohamed Heikal, *Sphinx and Commissar* (London 1978), pp. 234-235.

10. Kissinger to Haykal, as reported by Haykal, *al-Ahrām*, 16

November 1973.

11. Sādāt at a press conference in Algiers, *Washington Post*, 23 January 1974.

12. Kissinger at a press conference in Washington on 22 January 1974. See Bernard Reich, *Quest for Peace* (New Brunswick, N.J. 1971), p. 288 n. 117.

13. See, for example, his speech at the People's Assembly, 18 April 1974.

14. Dr. Muḥammad Fawzī at the National Assembly, 29 December 1971, referring to Sādāt's speech of 16 September 1971.

15. Sādāt's speech on the fifth anniversary of Nasser's death, 28 September 1975.

16. See S. Shamir, "The Marxists in Egypt," in M. Confino and S. Shamir (eds.), *The USSR and the Middle East* (New York 1973), pp. 293-319.

17. Heikal, *Sphinx*, pp. 200-202.

18. Sādāt's speech, ibid. On the frictions with the Soviets see Fū'ad Matar, *Rūsyā al-nāṣiriyya wa-miṣr al-miṣriyya* (Beirut 1972).

19. Sādāt, quoting Nasser's remark upon his return from his last trip to Moscow, interview to *al-Ḥawādith*, 26 April 1974.

20. For the balance sheet of Nasserism see S. Shamir, "Sheqi'at ha-meshīhiyut ha-nāseristith", in S. Shamir (ed.), *Yerīdat ha-nāserism* (Tel Aviv 1978), pp. 1-60.

21. Interview with Haykal, *Middle East*, February 1979, pp. 47-52; Rubinstein, pp. 318-320.

22. *Rūz al-Yūsuf*, 8 December 1969.

23. See Michael P. Sullivan, in D.S. McLellan *et al.* (eds.), *The Theory and Practice of International Relations* (Englewood Cliffs, N.J. 1974), pp. 173-186.

24. Quoted in Sullivan's article, ibid., p. 181.

A Stereotype Illustrated:
An Egyptian Cartoonist's Perception
of the United States

Haim Shaked

"Art critics who study high culture sometimes call a bad painting a 'mere cartoon'; they have largely ignored...political cartoons. Historians think of cartoons only when book publishers demand illustrations to enliven their text. The art critic is puzzled by political history, and the historian deals with words and statistics rather than pictures." This somewhat trite but true observation is contained in a brief introduction to a catalogue entitled *The Image of America in Caricature and Cartoon*,[1] which accompanied an exhibition held a few years ago in the United States.

Indeed, while the cartoon has come to occupy a prominent place in daily newspapers and weekly magazines all over the world, the study of its substance, function and influence is still in the embryonic stage.[2] Moreover, the utilization of caricatures and cartoons as legitimate, historical source material does not seem to have emerged from the stage of conception.[3] This paper is not intended to be a comprehensive, let alone a definitive, study of either the artistic form of the political cartoon or of its attributes and function as a communications medium. Rather, it should be viewed as an *experimental* attempt to shed some light—through a type of source material not frequently utilized by political historians—on a very significant issue in contemporary Egyptian foreign policy. Its objective is twofold: firstly, to reconstruct and interpret by means of content analysis the image of the United States as perceived and portrayed by one very important Egyptian cartoonist and secondly, to provide a stimulus for a more comprehensive and systematic study of this type of source material by historians of the modern Middle East.

A few words of caution appear to be appropriate at this stage. Both conceptually and methodologically, the data collected in this paper do not provide a sufficiently strong basis to support bold or general conclusions. A few questions, to which there are still no fully developed answers, will illustrate the difficulties. There is first the question of definition: one recognizes a cartoon immediately when one sees it, but what is a cartoon? And how does it differ from kindred representations? Second, are political cartoons different from other types of cartoons, and if so, how? Third, what is/are the function(s) or effect(s) of political cartoons? Should the political cartoon be dismissed as mere light, marginal commentary or can it be viewed as having a significant impact, particularly in a society which is subjected to strict censorship? What is the relative impact of one cartoonist as compared with that of his fellow cartoonists? Fourth, do popular cartoons such as appear regularly in an important newspaper *create* a stereotype, enhance it, or merely reflect a stereotype which exists independently? Fifth, how does one make a content analysis of political cartoons: What is the language of such cartoons? What is their symbolic code? What should be the basic units for the analysis, and how should they be counted, weighed and compared?

The methodology of cartoons analysis has not yet solved these problems satisfactorily. Likewise, the next question can be answered only very tentatively. What do Jāhīn's cartoons on the U.S. really mean and how do they relate to Egyptian government policies and popular feelings concerning the United States?

The collection of cartoons which forms the corpus for this study was drawn by Salāh Jāhīn and published by the Egyptian daily, *al-Ahrām* over a period beginning on 2 March 1962 and ending on 20 March 1978.[4]

The total number of *al-Ahrām* issues which appeared during that period was 5923. Out of that number, the Shiloah Center's Documentation System holds 5342, of which 4192 carry cartoons. The cartoons were published almost daily with a few relatively long intervals.[5] Thus, the collection studied here is not only large quantitatively, and spread over a long span of time, but also traces the many vicissitudes of Egypt's politics and policies throughout a period which was by no means tranquil or static.

The highlights of the years that elapsed between 1962 and 1978 include very significant changes in the international arena and in the American scene. In the United States five different presidents were in office: Kennedy, Johnson, Nixon, Ford, and Carter. All of them are represented in Salāḥ Jāhīn's cartoons. The same period also saw important changes in Egypt's inter-Arab status. Insofar as the Arab-Israeli conflict was concerned, during that period, the Egyptians found themselves on the crest of anti-Israeli waves stirred up by the 1967 and 1973 wars and the 1969-1970 War of Attrition; towards the end of the period, however, the same people experienced the expectation of attaining peace with Israel. Dramatic fluctuations were not limited to the Egyptian-Israeli setting. Domestically, the highly-charged period of Nasser's rule ended abruptly with his sudden death in September 1970 and, as indicated elsewhere in this volume, his succession by President Anwar al-Sādāt meant much more than a mere changing of the guard. The profound policy changes made by President Sādāt affected the domestic scene as well as the Arab-Israeli conflict and both were interwoven with an equally important change in Egypt's international orientation. The influence of, and special relationship with, the Soviet Union, which rose to its zenith in the late 1960s, particularly between 1969 and 1971, reached its nadir in 1972-1973, first with the expulsion of the Soviet experts in 1972 and then in the aftermath of the October 1973 war. On the other hand, and to some extent simultaneously, since 1972 but in particular after the October War and President Nixon's visit to Egypt in June 1974, the relationship between Egypt and the United States improved by leaps and bounds, amounting to significant changes in the Egyptian as well as the American outlooks with respect to each other, and in the role each allocated to the other in its own politico-strategic designs.

All these as well as other processes and events were reflected in different ways in the reportage of the Middle Eastern press, in which the veteran Arabic daily al-Ahrām occupied a very special position. During the whole period, its importance exceeded by far that of other Arabic daily newspapers. Many years before the rise of Nasser to power, al-Ahrām had already attained a very prominent place in the Arab world. The close relationship between its editor, Muḥammad Ḥasanayn Haykal, and Nasser strongly enhanced this position and turned the already legendary newspaper into a household name in many non-Middle Eastern capitals. The change in fortune of *al-Ahrām*'s all-powerful editor during Sādāt's time and his removal from the newspaper's editorial board on 1 February 1974 certainly terminated the automatic association of the newspaper with the Egyptian political establishment. Thus far, however, *al-Ahrām* remains an outstanding newspaper which continues to occupy a prominent position in the Arab press in general and the Egyptian press in particular. As for its cartoonist, Salāḥ Jāhīn, in spite of all the inquiries the present author has made, unfortunately less could be learned about him than was desired; yet enough data has been collected to provide for the drawing of a very rudimentary biographical sketch.[6]

Salāḥ Jāhīn—poet,[7] composer, author, scriptwriter, and film director—is best known for the cartoons that he has been drawing for so many years, and celebrated for his witty, courageous, and creative personality. Born in 1934, in 1956 Jāhīn began to draw cartoons for the then newly-established Egyptian newspaper, *Sabbāḥ al-Khayr*, which was an enterprise of the *Rūz al-Yūsuf* Publishing House. In 1962, apparently recruited by Muḥammad Ḥasanayn Haykal, Salāḥ Jāhīn moved to *Al-Ahrām* and on 2 March that newspaper first published his drawings in a very prominent place, on the page opposite the famous Friday editorial (*Bisarāḥā*) written by Haykal. From that day on, Jāhīn's political cartoons have been appearing daily in a fixed corner of the "opinion" (*Ra'y al-Ahrām*) page of the newspaper (page 5 or 7).[8] The following highlights provide an interesting background to Jāhīn's personality and would appear to be of importance for a proper understanding of his outlook and cartoons. In May 1964, he went to the United States for a period of two months.[9] Upon his return, his eighteen handwritten "air letters from the U.S."[10] appeared consecutively in his regular corner.

In July 1971, he went to the U.S.S.R. for neurological treatment.[11] Next we hear of Jāhīn in January 1973, when together with celebrated Egyptian authors he signed a memorandum addressed to members of the Egyptian government, criticizing the authorities and demanding a full inquiry into the causes of the student riots which had taken place a while before.[12] The next significant event was also connected with Jāhīn's criticism of the regime. Early in November 1974 on two consecutive days he published two cartoons, both dealing with water pollution in Cairo. His poignant, witty criticism created a furor within the administration and involved Jāhīn in a formal investigation by the Cairo police. The investigation in turn became a major public issue provoking the dispatch of a memorandum by the Journalists' Union and long debates in the Egyptian *Majlis al-Umma*, on freedom of speech, freedom of the press and the jurisdiction of the Justice authorities.[13]

In an interview granted to an Israeli television correspondent in Cairo in January 1978, Jāhīn mentioned that an experienced cartoonist from India once told him that he should be cautious and ambiguous in his drawings. That way, if the policy of the government were to change, he could easily change the stereotypes of his cartoons accordingly. Following that advice, he "lowered his tone" and his art then became a little milder, so that he could mould it in accordance with the changing winds of state policy. The interviewer was impressed with Jāhīn's "very good feel for the current political line," so that it was rather seldom that his cartoons were censored.[14] Another informant added that when a cartoon by Jāhīn was censored, the next day "the whole of Cairo" would speak of its contents or the point it was trying to make.

The wide range of issues, domestic as well as foreign, which Sālāh Jāhīn touched upon in his cartoons deserves a special in-depth study but is outside the scope of this paper, which is limited to the analysis of the image of the U.S. he perceived and presented. For this purpose, all of his political cartoons published in *al-Ahrām* have been examined. On the assumption that every cartoon could be defined as a " 'super sign,' a framework which unites various secondary signs into one coherent unit of meaning," [15] all available political cartoons by Jāhīn have been examined and all the cartoons in which the United States appears as either a dominant, or a secondary or tertiary sign[16] have been considered as items which together form the source material for this study.

The collection of Jāhīn's cartoons available to, and reviewed by the author of this paper includes 4192 items.[17] In 644 of these cartoons (15.3%) the U.S. appears as a dominant, secondary or tertiary sign. A complementary and even more interesting figure relates to temporal frequency of the appearance of the U.S. in Jāhīn's cartoons. From the graph on page 306 it is evident that, firstly, the relative frequency of cartoons dealing with the U.S. fluctuates over the years as a function of the degree of American involvement in

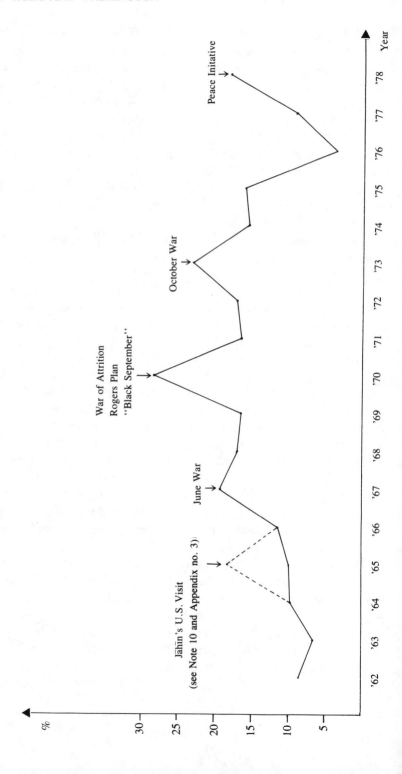

the Middle East. Thus, the relative frequency of the U.S.-related cartoons was under or around 10% until 1967, the year of the June War and has been substantially higher since, averaging 16.7% a year. Secondly, the peak periods are: the end of 1969[18] and the whole of 1970 (28.5%), the year of the Rogers Plan, the War of Attrition, the cease-fire between Egypt and Israel, and the "Black September" crisis in Jordan; 1973 (22.9%), the year of the October War; 1967-1968 (19.3% and 17.3%, respectively), the years of the June War and its immediate aftermath; and 1978 (18.1%, during less than one quarter of the year!), the year of the Peace Initiative. On the other hand, the low in 1976 (3.7%) and 1977 (9.0%) could be attributed to the relatively low profile maintained by the U.S. in the region during the presidential election year of 1976 and while the newly-elected Carter administration was settling in.

While for the purpose of this paper all 644 cartoons which deal with the U.S. constitute one body of source material, their contents should be analyzed in detail if any conclusions are to be drawn concerning Jāhīn's perception of the U.S. In this regard, three interrelated questions need to be raised: (a) what are the specific symbols that represent the U.S.?; (b) What are the main attributes of the U.S.?; and (c) What issues or themes are reflected in Jāhīn's U.S.-related cartoons. To be answered in full, these questions should be tackled by a twofold analytical approach: the static analysis, providing a composite picture, the components of which are weighted relative to each other; and the dynamic analysis which investigates the development of Jāhīn's usage and its fluctuations over time. The attempt to answer the above questions is made through a "concrete content coding" designed to discover what properties the data itself could yield that might be of interest to the historian. The cartoons are thus subjected to an "intrinsic rather than extrinsic kind of analysis," that is, of what they tell us rather than what people who view them tell us about them.[19]

Symbols Representing the U.S.

A count of the dominant, secondary or tertiary symbols which represent the U.S. in Jāhīn's cartoons resulted in a list of fifty-five different symbols which recur 649 times in the cartoons.[20] Table 1 (see page 308) lists these symbols, classified under four headings:

Table 1: Symbols Representing the U.S.

A. Human Figures

1. President of the U.S.:
   256 + (25) = 281[1]
2. Uncle Sam: 134
3. Political leaders, Senators,
   Secretary of State: 67
4. Male: 24
5. Military figure, Policeman:
   16 + (4) = 20
6. Woman: 18 + (1) = 19
7. Astronaut: 8 + (1) = 9
8. Gangster: 8
9. Cowboy: 5 + (2) = 7

10. Magician: (2) + [1] = 3
11. Indian: 3
12. American tourist: 3
13. Nazi: (2)
14. Negro: 2
15. Diplomat: 1
16. Physician: (1)
17. Caveman: (1)
18. Santa Claus: (1)
19. Bullfighter: (1)
20. Knife thrower: (1)
21. Swordsman: [1]

B. Animals

22. Snake: 2
23. Horse: 2
24. Parrot: 1
25. Worm: 1
26. Cow: (1)
27. Camel: (1)

28. Wolf: (1)
29. Cat: (1)
30. Loch Ness monster: (1)
31. Tiger: [1]
32. Mighty Mouse: [1]

C. Artifacts

33. Hat: 15
34. Flag: 14
35. Spaceship: 9
36. Fighter plane: 6
37. Statue of Liberty: 3
38. Skyscraper: 2
39. Apple: 1
40. Car: 1
41. Nuclear bomb: 1
42. Pistol: 1

43. Tightrope: 1
44. Globe: 1
45. Ship: 1
46. House: 1
47. Embassy: 1
48. Lincoln's statue: 1
49. Flashlight: 1
50. Sword
51. Artillery shell: (1)

D. Miscellaneous

52. $ (symbol or word): 5
53. Hand: 2
54. Question mark: (1)
55. Plague: (1)

1. The figure indicates the number of times the symbol recurs in the collection. The figures in brackets represent cases in which the face of the President of the U.S. appears either with a body other than that of a simple male body or with an unusual attire (e.g., as a woman, a cowboy, a wolf). Figures in square brackets represent various forms in which Henry Kissinger is presented.

Given the political content of the cartoons and the common stereotype of the U.S., it is not surprising that the two most frequent symbols are those of the President of the U.S. (43.3%) and the wicked, demonic figure of Uncle Sam (20.6%). Jāhīn's frequent use of the American president's face as a symbol results, obviously, from the fact that he is immediately recognizable and identifiable with the U.S. This feature is of particular importance for a cartoon, the meaning and message of which has to be grasped at a glance. It may also attest, however, to the importance attributed by Jāhīn to American presidential decisions concerning the Middle East and the Arab-Israeli conflict. Interestingly, representations of President Nixon's figure greatly outnumber those of all other American presidents who served during the period covered by Jāhīn's cartoons. Out of the 281 times that a presidential figure is used as a symbol, Nixon appears 186 times (66.1%), Johnson 48 (17%), Kennedy 19 (6.7%), Ford 15 (5.3%) and Carter 13 (4.6%).[21]

President Nixon's image is by far the most unsympathetic of all five American presidents. While caricature almost always deliberately distorts and mocks the persons it portrays, it is obvious that Nixon is treated much less benevolently in Jāhīn's drawings than other American presidents. This is exemplified by Nixon's facial features, as well as by the association of his face with the body of a Nazi (twice, see, e.g. fig. 1),[22] an artillery shell,[23] a caveman,[24] a military man or policeman (three times),[25] a cat,[26] a plague,[27] the Loch Ness monster[28] and Golda Meir.[29] Nixon almost invariably appears with a "five o'clock shadow" on his face (fig. 2), except during his visit to Egypt in June 1974, when he is shown as clean-shaven and rather kindly (fig. 3).

Like the figure of President Nixon, that of Secretary of State Kissinger occupies a major and disproportionate place among the figures grouped above (Table 1) under "Political leaders, Senators and Secretaries of State." During many months (particularly from November 1973 through March 1975), he even surpassed the president in frequency and number of appearances. While President Ford appears in fifteen cartoons, Kissinger appears in nineteen during the same period. More significantly, while President Nixon's facial expression and/or the situation he appears in always communicates a basically negative image, Kissinger's convey a rather positive atmosphere and even a certain sympathy. He is the only American figure who is depicted as Mighty Mouse.[30]

This finding tallies with another fact, that the most negative symbols—like that of the Nazi which appears twice[31] (fig. 1) or the two-headed snake (fig. 4)—completely disappear in the summer or 1973. In fact, animal symbols cease to depict the U.S. in Jāhīn's cartoons as of July 1973.[32] Two facts are of interest in this context. Firstly, the American eagle does not appear among the nine different animals used as symbols of the U.S. The only exception is one cartoon, where Jāhīn does make fun of the American eagle turned parrot (fig. 5). Secondly, the only time an animal symbol appears after July 1973 is one year later, in a cartoon that refers to the appearance of "the American worm for the first time in the fields of Egyptian cotton." It depicts a person (an Egyptian?) with a padlock instead of a head, who points at an "American worm" in a cotton plant. The caption of the cartoon reads: "See? This is what *infitāḥ* brought upon us".[33]

The Attributes of the U.S.

The eighteen "air letters" (e.g., fig. 6) published in *al-Ahrām* in the summer of 1964 after Jāhīn's U.S. visit form a consecutive series of sparsely illustrated texts which deals exclusively and in detail with the U.S. As such, the series presents a very clear and concise picture of Jāhīn's direct impressions of America and enables us to reconstruct his "early image" of the U.S. In the first two letters, Jāhīn relates his confusion at his "discovery of America." He says that since he does not wish to generalize he is not sure whether he could call the U.S. the country of freedom, or the country of capitalists and bourgeoisie, or perhaps describe it as bloodsucking and cannibalistic.[34] What, he asks in his second letter, is the first picture that the simple man in the street visualizes when he says "American"? The answer is: skyscrapers; children wearing wide-brimmed hats, riding horses and throwing lassos and shooting; red-headed or blonde girls wearing shorts or bathing suits, having cold drinks on the beach, or driving a twelve-meter long roofless car. The truth is, he goes on to say, that the America he saw was very different from this vision: 99 percent of its houses are one storied, there are no horses, and the distances he traveled were seven times longer than that between Cairo and Aswān. Jāhīn adds that he did see shorts and bathing suits but a mere three percent of the girls wearing them were blondes. Most of the cars do have roofs and they are not parked on the beach. Rather, they are driven at excessive speeds through forests of billboards. "This is America." [35] All but two of the topics which are alluded to in his other "air letters" are American domestic issues.[36] Of particular interest are three of these "air letters" which further illuminate the stereotype: in one, Jāhīn warns that he might become "Americanized," not by turning into a cowboy or wearing flowered blouses and giving three-day long whiskey and watermelon parties, but by becoming a dog-lover.[37] In another "air letter" he records an imaginary dialogue between Goldwater and Johnson—at that time rival candidates for the presidency—in which they coordinate in detail a point which the two of them would omit in their election campaigns.[38] The third is the only cartoon-letter in which American-Egyptian relations are mentioned. It is a dialogue between an American and an Egyptian (Jāhīn) in which the American says that he wishes to go to Egypt to see the pyramid before it is flooded. In the course of the conversation a reference is made to the American refusal to finance the Aswān Dam, a poke at the hypocritical U.S. concern for the damage the dam might do to archeological sites.[39]

There is a profound discrepancy between the composite picture of the U.S. which emerges from these "air letters" and the picture that can be gleaned from all other U.S.-related cartoons which Jāhīn published after 1964. To begin with, the "air letters" focus almost exclusively on American domestic matters, which other U.S.-related cartoons very seldom do. Furthermore, in their rather naive way the "air letters" portray a positive and "nice" America, while later cartoons communicate a negative and "evil" image of the U.S.

As of the second half of 1967 and during 1968 (i.e., following the June War) as well as during 1970, the following attributes dominate the U.S.-related cartoons: international subversion by the Central Intelligence Agency (C.I.A.; fig. 7), murder (fig. 8), warmongering, aggression, and neo-imperialism which is based on treaties (fig. 9). President Nixon, for instance, is associated with immorality (fig. 10), and President Ford and Uncle Sam with hypocrisy (fig. 11) and double standards (fig. 12). Domestically, the U.S. is depicted as violent (fig. 13), racist and entirely controlled by capitalism (fig. 14).

From the end of 1972 on, the number of negative traits gradually diminishes until, in mid-1973, they disappear almost completely. No trace of such attributes can be found in Jāhīn's U.S.-related cartoons after September 1973 (except an isolated case in January-February 1975 when four cartoons depict negative attributes, aggression in three cases and hypocrisy in one). Although the very lack of overtly negative attributes does project—over time—a more sympathetic America than the U.S. of the cartoons of the late 1960s and early 1970s, this image is not compounded of positive traits. Of even greater significance is the fact that some traits normally associated with the American stereotype are completely absent in all of Jāhīn's U.S.-related cartoons except the eighteen "air letters." That no mention whatsoever is made of American democracy, freedom of speech, etc., is not surprising, given the autocratic Egyptian political system and its sensitivity to such themes. The absence of two other features, American wealth and aid, is less easily explained. It is accepted as a commonplace that whenever poor, Third-World countries seek close relations with the U.S., they do so in the hope of benefiting from American advanced technology, technical know-how and foreign aid. This is connected with the sometimes exaggerated image of American wealth, perceived as vast enough to provide Americans with a very high standard of living and sustain an extensive foreign aid program. Elsewhere in this volume, John Waterbury has defined the fate of President Sādāt's policy of *infitāh* as "indissolubly linked," both from the popular and governmental perspectives, "to the U.S., and great expectations of diplomatic and economic rescue were raised that have been only marginally eroded in the years since. In this sense there is a fundamental imbalance or lack of reciprocity in expectations between the two countries with the U.S. looking for dividends in one among several regions in which it is active, while Egypt looks for *nothing short of national salvation*." [40] The cartoon which comes closest to expressing American bounty is fig. 15, which deals with the War of Attrition and hits at the limitless American aid pouring into Israel. This, however, is much less than one would expect to find in light of the profound changes which occurred in recent years in Egyptian domestic policy and international orientation. It may be that for Jāhīn the U.S. role is associated with power politics to the virtual exclusion of anything else, or that for the Egyptian public—whose feelings Jāhīn's cartoons supposedly reflect—the U.S. does not really represent primarily a potential source of significant help, let alone "salvation," to the Egyptian economy or a source of inspiration for the reorganization of the domestic political system in Egypt. But the evidence which has accumulated thus far does not fully support either of these two hypotheses.

Issues and Themes in U.S.-related Cartoons

The lists of symbols and attributes expose only the most superficial layer of Jāhīn's portrayal of the U.S. It is only their combination with the themes of his U.S.-related cartoons and the issues which they treat that provide an insight into the deeper layers of Jāhīn's image of the U.S.

In terms of content, the U.S.-related cartoons can be grouped under the following headings (arranged in order of the frequency of their appearance):

Table 2: Themes in U.S.-related Cartoons

No.	Theme	Number of instances	Percent of all themes counted (rounded)	Percent of U.S.-related cartoons
1	The U.S. and Israel	291	30	45
		305	31	47
1a	The U.S. and American (Zionist) Jewry	14	1	2
2	The U.S. and the Arab-Israeli conflict	167	17	26
3	The U.S. and the Arab (and Islamic) world	153	16	24
4	American domestic affairs	132	13	20
5	The U.S. and the Powers	120	12	19
6	The U.S. and the world (excluding the Powers)	106	11	16
		983[1]	100	152

[1] This figure represents the number of appearances of the themes in the 644 U.S.-related cartoons.

While in the early 1960s (particularly in 1962-1965) the most salient theme in Jāhīn's U.S.-related cartoons concerns American domestic matters, by 1968, the themes of American-Israeli relations and the U.S. and the Arab-Israeli conflict are preponderant as major themes among the cartoons. This is hardly surprising in light of the changes that took place in the Middle East and the growing involvement of the U.S. therein during the period covered.

The U.S. and Israel [291 (+14) cartoons]

The relationship between Israel and the U.S. is undoubtedly the most elaborate of the six major themes recurring in Jāhīn's cartoons. It is this theme which seems to occupy Jāhīn's mind the most when treating the U.S. The American-Israeli relationship is depicted on three levels simultaneously: normal bilateral relations; American support to Israel; and American pressure exerted on Israel.

Insofar as bilateral relations are concerned, Jāhīn equally presents Israel as a tool in American hands (fig. 16), and the U.S. as the master being led by his dog (=Israel; fig. 17). In many cases, particularly between 1967 and 1973, Jāhīn points to an identity of interests, and close cooperation, between the two (figs. 18, 19, 20). In other cases, mostly after 1973, he refers to tension between them (figs. 21, 22).

Jāhīn is very fond of drawing cartoons on the theme of American support for Israel. This is expressed by supplies of sophisticated American arms (fig. 23) and money (fig. 24) to Israel, or the exercise of the right of veto at the U.N. Security Council (fig. 25). As for American pressure on Israel, in most of the cartoons (14 out of 18) it is dismissed as unserious, imaginary pressure (fig. 26).

While a detailed study of the image of Israel in Jāhīn's cartoons is outside the scope of this paper, Israel's presentation in the context of the U.S.-related cartoons in general and those cartoons dealing specifically with American-Israeli relations is of interest. The cartoons do not convey a homogeneous profile of Israel. The majority of them (140 out of 213 = 65.7%) represent Israel by an Israeli political leader (mostly the prime minister). There are, however, also thirty-six cartoons in which Israel appears as a Stürmer-type *Jude* (particularly frequent from September 1967 through 1971).[41] One exceptional but very striking cartoon depicts Israel as the living embodiment of Nazism, transplanted into the Israeli body by the surgeon, Uncle Sam (fig. 27).[42] Rather surprisingly, relatively few cartoons refer to the subject of American Jewry and its alleged overwhelming influence on American decision making, a subject so frequently brought up by Arab media in their discussion of American Middle Eastern policy.

The U.S. and the Arab-Israeli Conflict (167 cartoons)

The theme of the U.S. and the Arab-Israeli conflict, which figures much less prominently than that of the bilateral American-Israeli relationship (17% as against 31%), includes three types of American connections: the U.S. as a directly involved power; the U.S. as mediator (fig. 29); and the U.S. as instigator (fig. 30). All three become relatively prominent only after 1967, but while the U.S. as mediator becomes more salient in 1973 and afterwards, the frequency of the appearance of the U.S. as instigator drops considerably after 1970. After 1973, a new, important ingredient is added to this category: the U.S. as peacemaker (fig. 31, Kissinger; fig. 32, Nixon; fig. 33, Carter).

Other Themes

The other themes listed in Table 2 constitute a large body of the total number of cartoons. Figs. 34, 35, 36 and 37 are representative of Jāhīn's perception of the relationship of the U.S. with the Arab (and Islamic) world up to 1973 (153 cartoons) while figs. 38 and 39 are typical of the euphoric feelings exaggerating the potency of the oil weapon in the wake of the October War. As for American domestic affairs (132 cartoons), this theme appears at random all along the period surveyed. More often than not these cartoons relate to major events such as presidential elections, the Watergate affair, the American landing on the moon, etc. All of them, except the "air letters" from the U.S., have a political punchline and present a negative image of the U.S. as corrupt, if not always weak.

The remaining 226 cartoons refer to the relations of the U.S. with the Great Powers (120 cartoons) and with other parts of the world (106 cartoons). While the predominant issue in the cartoons dealing with the U.S. and the world is, from 1962 through 1967, that of subversion and C.I.A. activities, this gives way, from 1968 through 1973, mainly to the Vietnam issue. Typical of Jāhīn's outlook on the U.S. and the world (presented by the symbol of the U.N. buildings in New York, a favorite symbol of Jāhīn's) are figs. 40 and 41, which express the U.S. terrorization of, and disregard for, world public opinion.

Throughout the entire period covered, Jāhīn refers to the theme of American relations with the world powers: in 1969-1970 he alludes to the "four power" talks (fig. 42) but in a majority of cartoons (63 out of 120) he elaborates on American-Russian relations. Both are depicted as unreliable and unsympathetic: the two do not seek a solution to the Middle Eastern conflict (fig. 43) and both endanger world peace (fig. 44). It is very illuminating, in this context, to compare the presentation of Israel's relationship with the U.S. as in fig. 46 with that of the P.L.O.'s relationship with the U.S.S.R. as in fig. 45. The similarity of the two cartoons is striking.

Conclusion

The fluctuation in the relative number of appearances of U.S.-related cartoons during the years surveyed by this paper as well as the changing image of the U.S. depicted by them seem to be directly related to the growing involvement of the U.S. in Middle Eastern affairs since the mid-1960s. The changing U.S. role resulted in a profound change, for the worse, in the American image, at least as perceived by Salāḥ Jāhīn. From a lively, sympathetic society and state, the U.S. came to be regarded as a threat and a demon. It became a political abstraction embodied in symbols which were designed to reflect its destructive impact. Jāhīn, like many of fellow journalists and commentators who wished to survive totalitarian regimes, took care to reflect the regime's orientation and outlook. Thus, he was very quick to grasp the new winds which began to blow just before the October 1973 War and continued afterwards. Either because, as an artist, he was sensitive enough, or because the Sādāt regime so signaled, Jāhīn's images of the U.S. gradually changed so as to suit Egypt's international re-orientation. Therefore, one could argue figuratively that Jāhīn's cartoons reflect faithfully the changing Egyptian mood. As such, they can serve as a rich and independent data source for Egyptian perceptions of the

U.S. and of Egyptian-American relations.

In a criticism of those who "attribute some measure of impact of caricature on an audience without evidence," Lawrence H. Streicher rightly argues that "a few cartoonists do not a nation make and caricature may only be relevant for penetrating restricted milieux and locales and subcultures or limited ideational systems." [43] Bearing this warning in mind one can still make the following observations. During the greater part of the period covered here and until recently, al-Ahrām was a very influential newspaper and Salāḥ Jāhīn a very popular cartoonist. In her article on the cartoon in Egypt, Afaf Lutfi al-Sayyid Marsot reports impressionistically that "today a large majority of al-Ahrām's readers turn to the inner page to glance at Salāḥ Jāhīn's cartoon before they even look at the front page, for his cartoon is not only funny, but is 'news in brief' and gives the gist of what preoccupied people most." [44] Promptly adding that it is very difficult to determine who influences whom, the artist or the public, Dr. Marsot points out that "the cartoon has become an element of public opinion in Egypt, if not a measure" thereof.[45] Apparently, Jāhīn's reputation rests not only on the well-established journalistic forum that he has been part of but also on his ability to hit upon just those issues that preoccupy the Egyptian reading public. Last but not least, a very important component of Jāhīn's popularity would seem to be his extensive use of the vernacular in the texts of his cartoons, as well as his great success in adapting his cartoons to the inordinate Egyptian fondness for the nukta, a combination of criticism, wisecrack, joke and anecdote.[46]

As a source for an historical study of the American image in Egyptian eyes, Jāhīn's political cartoons are deficient in many ways. Being cartoons, they emphasize the grotesque, the negative and the unpleasant, thereby distorting the resulting image of the U.S. Furthermore, the content analyst who juxtaposes them and thereby creates a "single frame" or even a succession of frames in motion, like those of a film, risks adding elements which are neither perceived by the cartoonist himself nor by the readers of the newspaper his cartoons appear in.

On the other hand, however, it should be borne in mind that the political cartoon does have some advantages over the regular newspaper commentary, which has become a commonly accepted source by political historians. Since its contents have to be absorbed at a glance, and its point made immediately. The political cartoon can neither be ambiguous nor play with shades of grey: it has to be simple, short, clear-cut, and snappy. It is thus stereotypic, and hence its importance: It is a stereotype which in a vicious circle produces stereotypes and then proceeds to feed on them! As such, it is undoubtedly a powerful medium deserving close attention and investigation. " 'Boss' Tweed, corrupt Tammany chief of the 1860s raised little objection when muckraking reporters prowled [the New York] city hall. What the papers wrote had no meaning, Tweed liked to boast; his constituency was illiterate. The only criticism that ever bothered or threatened him, the Boss confessed, was 'them damn pictures'." [47]

NOTES

The author wishes to express his sincere gratitude to David Haroush, George Hazma, Victor Nahmiyas, Kriel Gardosh ("Dosh"), Yaacov Reinich, Rivka Yadlin, Dan Arazi of 2002 Films, Amikam Salant, Amira Margalith and particularly Sasha R. Weitman, for their kind assistance with the preparation of this article. Very special thanks are due to Esther Tal, for her wonderful devoted help.

1. Published by the Amon Carter Museum of Western Art, Fort Worth, 1975. The quotation is from p. vi.

2. While there appears to be ample study of caricatures and cartoons as forms of graphic art, the body of literature on the theory and function of this art is very small indeed. Some important recent studies are: Lawrence H. Streicher, "David Low and the Sociology of the Caricature," *Comparative Studies in Society and History*, vol. viii, 1965, pp. 1-23; and "On a Theory of Political Caricature," *Comparative Studies in Society and History*, vol. ix, 1967, pp. 427-445; W. A. Coupe, "Observations on a Theory of Political Caricature," *Comparative Studies in Society and History*, vol. ii, 1969, pp. 79-95; Kriel Gardosh ("Dosh"), "Political Caricature from Its Beginnings to Our Day," *Yearbook of the Association of Journalists*, 1964, Tel Aviv, pp. 111-128 (in Hebrew); and "Trends in the Political Cartoon," *Yearbook of the Association of Journalists*, 1976, Tel Aviv, pp. 393-399 (in Hebrew); Tsivya Ben-Shalom, "How Does the Caricature Influence?" *Yearbook of the Association of Journalists*, 1976, Tel Aviv, pp. 400-405 (in Hebrew); John Culhane, "The Cartoon Killers

Thrive Again," *New York Times* (Magazine) 9 November 1975. There are also some studies dealing with anti-Semitic cartoons.

3. Some particularly interesting recent examples are: W. A. Coupe, "The German Cartoon and the Revolution of 1848," *Comparative Studies in Society and History*, vol. ix, 1967, pp. 137-167; Victor Alba, "The Mexican Revolution and the Cartoon," *Comparative Studies in Society and History*, vol. ix, 1967, pp. 121-136; David Kunzle, "200 Years of the Great American Freedom to Complain," *Art in America*, March-April 1977, pp. 99-105 (dealing with an exhibition and book on the American presidency in political cartoons: 1776-1976); Y. Nir, *The Arab-Israeli Conflict in Soviet Caricatures, 1967-1973*, Tel Aviv, 1976; Y. Nir, "U.S. Involvement in the Middle East Conflict in Soviet Caricatures," *Journalism Quarterly*, vol. 54, 1977, pp. 607-701, and 726; A. Hill, "The Carter Campaign in Retrospect: Decoding the Cartoons," *Semiotica* 23 (1978): 307-331.

4. This concluding date does not signify any turning point in the Egyptian policy towards, or perception of, the U.S. The date was chosen arbitrarily in consideration of a technical deadline dictated by the Shiloah Center International Colloquium. *Al-Ahrām* has continued to publish daily cartoons by Salāḥ Jāhīn.

5. These were:
   (A) 1 May-7 August 1964, due to a trip Jāhīn made to the U.S.
   (B) 19 June-20 August and 21-28 August 1965, due to Jāhīn's illness.
   (C) 16 June-6 August 1967, unaccounted for.
   (D) 3 July-25 November 1971, due to Jāhīn's medical treatment in the U.S.S.R.
   (E) 6 October-1 November 1977, due probably to Jāhīn's trip abroad (to Europe?).

6. Part of this data is oral and was supplied by some persons who have met Jāhīn. The author wishes to apologize for any inaccuracies which have occurred in the biographical information.

7. See *al-Ahrām*, 14 July 1965, for information on a military song written by Jāhīn.

8. Until August 1965, Jāhīn's cartoons were not published on Fridays. Then from October of that year, Jāhīn published two cartoons every Friday, one usually devoted to social issues.

9. See *al-Ahrām*, 3 May 1964. From 1 May through 7 August *al-Ahrām* did not carry Jāhīn's daily cartoons.

10. These were published as of 8 August through 27 August (with one interruption on Friday, 21 August 1964. For their contents, see below p. 310. For an example, see fig. 6.

11. *Al-Ahrām*, 29 June 1971. His cartoons did not appear from 3 July through 25 November 1971.

12. For a full text of the memorandum, see *al-Anwār*, 12 January 1973. Among its other signatories were Tawfīq al-Ḥakīm, Louis 'Awad, Najīb Maḥfūz, Yūsuf Idrīs, and Lutfī al-Khūlī.

13. See *al-Jumhūriyya*, 12 November 1974 (text of the memorandum by the Journalists' Union); *Al-Ahrām*, 20, 27 November 1974 (text of the debate at the *Majlis*); *al-Balāgh*, 2 December 1974, pp. 16-17. One interesting reaction was a full page portrait of Salāḥ Jāhīn by "Laythī, a fellow cartoonist" published in *Rūz al-Yūsuf*, (11 November 1974, p. 11) with a short poem under it saying:

> "My beloved son Salāḥ Jāhīn
> Return my beloved and walk near the wall
> What do you care? This is neither our corpse
> nor our country.
> Your bereaved mother: Egypt."

14. The Shiloah Center Documentation System holds a 16 mm. copy of an interview by Victor Nahmiyas with Salāḥ Jāhīn, broadcast in the popular Israeli Television program "This Week—A Diary of Events," on Friday night, 16 January 1978. The interview is interesting in that it provides a good and rare insight into the making of Jāhīn's cartoons, and an ample taste of his sense of humor as well as his political sensitivity.

15. See Nir, *The Israeli-Arab Conflict*, p. 17 and p. 124, n. 11.

16. Wherever the major figure or symbol of the cartoon connotes the U.S., the latter was considered to play a dominant role in the "super sign." When the U.S. appears in the cartoon in a supporting or complementary role, the U.S. was considered to be a secondary sign. Where the U.S. is either merely mentioned in the text accompanying the cartoon, hinted at in the drawing itself, or appears as a background figure or symbol, its role in the cartoon was regarded as tertiary.

17. While some issues of *al-Ahrām* were not available (see above, p. 302.) there were certain periods and Fridays when the newspaper did not publish Jāhīn's cartoons. This figure can therefore be accepted as rather close to the number of Jāhīn's published cartoons for the period surveyed here, i.e. from 2 March 1962 until 20 March 1978.

18. In November 1969, 12 out of 30 cartoons (40%) contained a refer-

ence to the U.S., the second highest rate over the whole period surveyed (the highest rate being that of August 1964, i.e., after Jāhīn's trip to the U.S.).

19. Cf. the interesting article, using this kind of content analytic approach by Sasha R. Weitman, "National Flags," *Semiotics*, vol. viii, 1973, pp. 333 and 357.

20. Obviously, some cartoons contain more than one symbol while others contain none at all and the U.S. is merely mentioned in the *text* (caption or explanation) of the cartoon.

21. During the period covered by Jāhīn's U.S.-related cartoons, Kennedy's presidency lasted 21 months, Johnson's 58, Nixon's 69, Ford's 26, and Carter's 17.

22. See also *al-Ahrām*, 14 March 1970.

23. *Al-Ahrām*, 27 May 1972.

24. *Al-Ahrām*, 24 December 1972.

25. *Al-Ahrām*, 21 October 1969, 2 April 1970, 19 December 1972.

26. *Al-Ahrām*, 10 March 1970.

27. *Al-Ahrām*, 8 December 1971.

28. *Al-Ahrām*, 2 December 1970.

29. *Al-Ahrām*, 18 September 1970. He is also depicted twice as a magician (30 January 1969, 15 February 1970), once as an astronaut (22 February 1972), a woman (28 May 1972) and a question mark (8 November 1968). Cf. President Kennedy, depicted as a military man (25 October 1962), wolf (27 October 1962), and bullfighter (17 September 1962); and Johnson, as a cowboy (twice: 3 June 1965, 19 March 1968), cow (7 January 1968), camel (28 May 1968), knife thrower (9 February 1964), physician (4 September 1967), and Santa Claus (29 December 1964). It should be noted that neither Ford nor Carter have ever been depicted with an unusual body or attire.

30. *Al-Ahrām*, 13 December 1973.

31. See above, n. 22.

32. See *al-Ahrām*, 24 July 1973, where the U.S. is symbolized by a snake.

33. *Al-Ahrām*, 11 July 1974.

34. *Al-Ahrām*, 8 August 1964.

35. *Al-Ahrām*, 9 August 1964.

36. These are: a civil rights demonstration (*al-Ahrām*, 8 August 1964); Senator Goldwater's extremist views (8, 10, 16 August); excessive surplus of food: "the food the U.S. throws away in a day can suffice for the

whole of Finland for 20 days'' (11 August); the usage of names from the old world, the mixture of races like that in Noah's Ark, the richness of natural resources and the large quantities of food and clothes stored (12 August); the mixture of cultures, striptease (13 August); the degraded and oppressed state of the American Indian (18, 25 August); the problem of the blacks and racial attitudes (20, 21, 23 August); the Washington scene (23 August); the American auto industry (26 August); and the beatniks (27 August).

37. *Al-Ahrām*, 17 August 1964. He also mocks the fact that T.V. programs are interrupted to show commercials dealing with dogs, and that large sums of money are lavished on them.

38. *Al-Ahrām*, 19 August 1964.

39. *Al-Ahrām*, 24 August 1964. The only other "air letter" which does not refer to a domestic American theme deals critically with a U.A.R. Cultural Students' Association in the U.S., *Al-Ahrām*, 16 August 1964.

40. See p. 358. Cf. the cartoon on the "American Worm" in *al-Ahrām*, 11 July 1974 (described above, p. 310.)

41. For the sake of comparison it should be noted that the "Star of David" as a symbol representing Israel appears only eight times, the symbol of a soldier once.

42. Twice, however, on 28 July, and 12 November 1977 (before the Sādāt trip to Jerusalem!), Israel is represented by a completely new, and positive, symbol, that of a kibbutz member. In his interview with Mr. Nahmiyas, Jāhīn explicitly refers to this change and says that after the October 1973 war he felt the time had come for a change in attitude towards the Israelis. See fig. 28 where a clear distinction between a "bad" (*Jude*-type) and "good" (kibbutz-type) Israeli is made.

43. Streicher, "On a Theory of Political Caricature," p. 429.

44. Afaf Lutfi al-Sayyid Marsot, "The Cartoon in Egypt," *Comparative Studies in Society and History*, vol. 13, 1977, p. 14.

45. Lutfi al-Sayyid Marsot, "The Cartoon in Egypt," p. 15.

46. For an elaborate discussion of the *nukta*, see Lutfi al-Sayyid Marsot, "The Cartoon in Egypt," p. 6 ff.

47. This well-known story is quoted from "Editorial Cartoons: Capturing the Essence," *Time*, 3 February 1975.

Appendix:

Relative Frequency
of U.S.-related Cartoons

Year	All cartoons	Absolute frequency of U.S.-related cartoons	Relative frequency of U.S.-related cartoons
1962[1]	198	17	8.5
1963	156	10	6.4
1964[2]	192	18(35)[3]	9.7(18.2)[3]
1965[4]	173	17	9.8
1966[5]	163	17	11.6
1967	98	19	19.3
1968	340	59	17.3
1969	339	56	16.5
1970	336	96	28.5
1971[6]	203	34	16.7
1972	348	59	16.9
1973	283	65[7]	22.9
1974	322	50	15.5
1975	344	55	15.9
1976	320	12	3.7
1977[8]	300	27	9.0
1978[9]	77	14	18.1
Total	4,192	644	15.3

1. The count began on 2 March of that year, the date Jāhīn commenced his work with *al-Ahrām*. Until August 1965 his cartoons appeared daily (except Friday).
2. See above, p. 319, n. 5(A).
3. The figure of 18.2% U.S.-related cartoons for the year 1964 is accounted for by Jāhīn's visit to the U.S. that year and the 18 "air letter" cartoons that were published in its wake. If these are deducted from the 35 U.S.-related cartoons in 1964, the rate of U.S.-related cartoons (35−18=17) out of all cartoons (192−18=174) is 9.7%.
4. See above, p. 319, n. 5(B). In September of that year Jāhīn's cartoons were published only on Friday.
5. See above, p. 319, n. 5(C).
6. See above, p. 319, n. 5(D).
7. Of these, 8 out of 27 cartoons in November and 15 out of 31 in December dealt with the U.S. (29.6% and 48.3% respectively). Together these account for 39.6% of all cartoons published during these two months.
8. See above, p. 319, n. 5(E).
9. Up to 20 March 1978.

Nixon and the military men crack down on opponents of the American invasion of Cambodia.

Nixon: Eh ...Haven't you ever seen a person with a shirt and pants on?
(*Bantāgun*, i.e. Pentagon — a pun on *Bantalūn* = trousers, pants)

20 May 1970

Nixon's Inauguration

The Oath!

21 January 1973

324

Nixon expresses delight at his welcome by the Egyptian people and their smiles.

Why are you so surprised? Haven't you ever met a person with a heart of gold (who does not hold a grudge)?

14 June 1974

The American-Israeli riddle

I just want to know...who is whose tail?

5 November 1969

Up-to-date picture of the American eagle

The missiles . . . The missiles . . . The missiles.

14 October 1970

— "Eat to please thyself"

18 August 1964

Cartoon study of American intelligence problem

⑦

Since we didn't manage to carry out a coup ...we just robbed a bank and that's that.

8 May 1966

The Jordanian massacre

⑧

Don't look at me ...I'm not involved.

24 September 1970

American plans to fill the British vacuum in the Arab [Persian] Gulf

America: That's it, son. This vacuum must be filled.

22 January 1968

Nixon accused of illegal behavior

Everything I like is labeled either illegal . . .or immoral

328

20 May 1973

America officially pays its last respects to Luther King

He murders a man, and then attends his funeral. (*popular saying*)

9 April 1968

A cartoon study of the American-Arab problem

My policy is based on peace... Peace (on you) ..."hand over"!

26 January 1964

Fire and destruction all over America

American soldier: I kept repeating that I wouldn't go to Vietnam, I wouldn't go to Vietnam... Until Vietnam came to me...!

10 April 1968

A millionaire is appointed U.S. Secretary of Defense

That's all right... There is nothing better than frankness.

330   *o May 1973*

Attrition

Another two-three (holes) . . .and it will be marvelous!

10 November 1969

Masterpieces of modern art

"Israeli-American Relations" . . .As drawn by the members of the International Parliamentary Conference

6 February 1970

The "watchdog" of imperialist interests

The Middle East

Israel

Uncle Sam to the world: Pardon, what's funny?

13 June 1971

The hermaphrodite

Is the call for me as Nixon . . .or as Golda Meir?

20 October 1969

A cartoon study of Israel's aggression against Jordanian villages

Eshkol: Look, I'm a big boy now ...and I'm doing just what my Daddy does.

3 June 1965

A cartoon study of the world situation

No comments

25 January 1964

Rabin anticipates a sharp confrontation between America and Israel.

The sharp confrontation

19 March 1977

Begin attacks the American statement.

What to us? We want our land back that's all.

14 February 1978

More Phantoms to Israel

Oh little boy don't play with matches. Take bombers and play with them.

29 August 1969

The Golda Meir-Nixon talks

No comments.

26 September 1969

The Security Council today discusses Israel's crime.

Uncle Sam: Please hand me my veto ...I am going to the Security Council.

16 April 1973

America says: The [supply of] Phantoms to Israel is a pressure of sorts in order to have her contact Jarring.

Press harder ... I love this kind of pressure.

2 January 1972

Successful transplanting of a girl's heart into a man

No comment.

10 December 1967

Stories of the stupid and the foolish

I would like good relations between us two...and let the whole world fall apart.

12 November 1977

337

On diplomatic craftsmanship

(29)

Please design this plan so both the Egyptians and the Israelis like it.

1 February 1978

America proposes that every Arab state should solve its problems with Israel separately.

(30)

Uncle Sam: You can't swallow it in one go, so take (this knife) and cut one piece at a time.

6 December 1968

Kissinger and Peace

(Peace): I gave you the Nobel prize...what will you give me?

8 November 1973

Nixon on his way to Cairo

I say... Have you seen the dove of peace by any chance?

12 June 1974

Carter makes a stop in Egypt during his trip.

8 (Carter): Why haven't you landed in the Middle East yet?
— Believe me Mr. Carter its no use unless the Palestinians attain their own state.

4 January 1978

Joint planning

Point of resistance

11 March 1970

Nixon is re-elected

In a spirit of sportmanship — I congratulate you.

9 November 1972

Spotlight on Jordanian-American relations

Her looks and her morals don't matter... It's enough that she's your daughter!

24 March 1972

The Saudi authorities arrested several Egyptians.

Faysal — Our prisons are very nice . . .and ready to receive all Arab peoples . . .

2 June 1966

The Gulf states reaffirm the oil embargo against America.

So what . . . I couldn't care less!

28 December 1973

In anticipation of the Resolutions of the Arab oil ministers

(39)

You'll get your sentence commuted for good behavior.

16 March 1974

American requests the UN to stop terrorism

(40)

I order you to put an end to all terrorist activities or else...

2 November 1972

A cartoon study of the American-Israeli question

What's next!?

5 December 1967

On the quadrilateral conferences

This, ladies and gentlemen is the crux of the problem of peace in the Middle East . . . Would any one claim that the mule is inside the pitcher?

7 April 1969

344

I called for your help and it turns out that it's you who need help!

23 June 1973

17 September 1962

Carter at a press conference: No Palestinian state!

So what ...when Uncle Brezhnev wakes up he'll get me a homeland better than the West Bank.

30 December 1977

Diplomatic tension betrween America and Israel

No comment.

5 January 1975

The Implications of *Infitāḥ*
for U.S.-Egyptian Relations

John Waterbury

"Any falling out with the United States cannot be and never was regarded as a success, as something desirable. It could only be regarded as a failure of some sort. It has generally been a failure of judgement and understanding rather than the result of a concerted plan. No one rejoiced in our difficulties with the U.S.A. Reliance on the U.S.S.R. has not been a policy but rather a counter-policy. The problem is that the U.S. has failed to understand Egypt's obsession with independence and nationalism. It is new for us, dating only since 1954, and ended, whatever anyone says, in 1967. It is new, it is cherished, and no one can truly be Egyptian now who denies it. We cannot afford the luxury of internationalism for we have not yet lived out our nationalism. Nationalism is like bachelorhood—sooner or later it comes to an end, and one recognizes one's dependency, even one's subordination, but that moment has not yet come for Egypt, and as long as it hasn't, what are viewed as impingements on Egyptian independence will be fiercely resisted."[1]

The above declaration is not analytically neat but then neither is reality. It does reflect a combination of perceived and empiric truth that is at the heart of Egypto-American relations. It also reflects an affective disposition toward the great powers that I believe to be common to most of the Egyptian elite and perhaps even to the Egyptian masses. Close cooperation with the Soviet Union has been a matter of convenience or lack of alternative; cooperation with the West and the United States is a goal far more deeply rooted in Egypt's cultural aspirations and self-image. In this sense Egypt's proclaimed socialism and revolutionary values have weighed lightly in the determination of this disposition. Betrayal of socialist goals and ideals have moved and will move little more than the Egyptian left.[2]

By contrast, tampering with national sovereignty—however defined and however perceived—will move the entire nation. If such tampering seems the result of policies of one or another of the great powers, no Egyptian regime can politically afford to turn a blind eye in the name of cultural aspirations or affinity.

Thus Nasser's regime, despite a manifest desire to guide Egypt to its "rightful" place among Western nations, felt belittled, rebuked, and treated as less than sovereign by the Western great powers. In the series of unhappy confrontations with the West in the middle 1950s, Nasser rode a groundswell of Egyptian mass opinion that not only supported his positions but would have forced them upon him had he not adopted them voluntarily. The point that must be drawn from this somewhat obvious observation is that the obsession with national sovereignty and national image is of primary importance in the shaping of Egypt's foreign and domestic policies. It is also at once stimulus and pretext for policy changes in all domains. So powerful is its symbolism that when it is invoked to justify new policies, shifts methodically occur on all fronts and are not restricted only to that domain in which the initial change took place. With this general background in mind, we may turn to a particular instance of policy reorientation, Egypt's domestic and external "opening" or *infitāḥ*.

There are four relevant axes (at least) that intersect in Egyptian policy making. They are:

1. Policy toward and relations with the two superpowers
2. Policy toward Israel and, derivatively, relations with Arab allies and adversaries
3. Domestic politics and their organization, a sphere subject to policy planning in Egypt
4. Organization of the domestic economy, to which is linked the question of external financing.

Policy changes along any one axis will ineluctably entail changes along all the others, but, beginning with the Czechoslovakian arms deal of 1955, it has been axes 1 and 2 that have led consistently to changes in 3 and 4. One will note that this line of influence or cause and effect is the inverse of what one would expect to find in more developed societies, above all in those of the continental powers. This is but another way of calling attention to the "subordination" of Egyptian domestic policy, the very stuff of national independence, to the exigencies of maneuvering in the international arena.

It is, moreover, with respect to axes 1 and 2 that U.S.-Egyptian relations are implicitly defined, but it is in light of all four that they will be judged by Egyptians. Because of the intersection of these axes (from the Egyptian point of view) the *infitāḥ* and the turn to the West constitute a package deal. From the point of view of the policy maker in Washington it may be both convenient and desirable to compartmentalize relations, but as the Soviet Union has learned, such is an unrealistic expectation. The upshot is that a change in one's favor in Egypt's foreign policy will bring along with it major dividends in related spheres—military, economic, and political—but the inverse is equally true. A position of strength, such as that enjoyed by the U.S.S.R. from 1964 to 1970,[3] or of that of the U.S. since Nixon's state visit in June 1974, can unravel with astonishing speed.

The term "Egypt's turn to the West" does not fully convey the essence of the country's new course. What has happened since 1971 is an at first gradual (1971-October 1973), then an accelerated (November 1973 to the present) turn to the U.S. Once compensation for British and French properties seized as a result of the Suez War of 1956 had been settled, Egypt maintained correct, even cordial relations with Western European nations (except Germany) and Japan. In the last seven years Egypt had sought from these countries a greater flow of bilateral aid and freer access to their markets. The latter goal was partially achieved through a preferential trade agreement with the European Economic Community (E.E.C.) in 1977. On both counts, policy has been formulated with respect to axis 4, the domestic economy and external financing. No consistent approach has been elaborated with respect to the E.E.C. and Japanese role in the conflict with Israel, perhaps because no one can be sure, especially after the deaths of de Gaulle and Pompidou, of the amount of leverage these nations can or would exert in favor of the Arab cause. Indeed, it is within the framework of the Euro-Arab dialogue that, in desultory fashion, the Egyptians and other Arabs are seeking an answer to that question.

By contrast, a real falling out had occurred with the U.S., beginning with the Johnson administration in 1963, exacerbated by the suspension of the Food for Peace shipments in 1966, and culminating in the break in diplomatic relations following the June War of 1967. From then until Kissinger's first trip to Egypt in November 1973, U.S. interests were represented only by the Spanish Embassy, the American University, and various unofficial emissaries from Saudi Arabia, the Gulf, and Jordan. It is useful to recall that during these years of nearly total estrangement the only major Egyptian voice to urge a rapprochement with the U.S. was that of Muḥammad Ḥasanayn Haykal, and he was rebuked as a defeatist by both left and right. He has subsequently urged that the Soviet Union not be excluded from the search for a settlement in the Arab-Israeli dispute and that it continue to play a role in Egypt's economic development. That stance cost him more than verbal criticism, but what is significant is that the kind of balance between the superpowers in Egypt's foreign policy that he advocates has eluded the country two times over since 1967. The reasons why, several knowledgeable Egyptians are prepared to argue, go far beyond the whims of different heads of state and relate directly to the new international political order stemming from détente between the U.S. and the U.S.S.R.

This brings us to the crux of the matter, Egypt's *ouverture* or *infitāḥ*, which is commonly but inadequately rendered as the open-door policy. The turn to the U.S. is an absolutely essential facet of this policy. The first steps were taken in the light of axes 2 and 4, that is, the state of no war, no peace with Israel and the deterioration of the Egyptian economy. Then, even before the October War, a propitious climate for further steps settled in, as the implications of détente were weighed. This assessment shifted the focus of attention to axis 1 and, once decisions were made in that context, others quickly followed in the other three: war, the economic open door, and political liberalization. Before fleshing out this process, it should be noted that all of President Sādāt's policy "departures" have their antecedents in the waning years of the Nasserist era. What Sādāt has done with enthusiasm and good grace, Nasser may have felt compelled to do with distaste and foot dragging.

If *infitāḥ* is a departure from what went before, then what had been "closed"? Clearly it was Egypt's socialist experiment or "transformation to socialism." The major characteristics of this phase, lasting roughly from July 1961 to 1969, were as follows:

1. The public sector was to be the leading sector of the economy, and certain domains—banking, heavy industry, energy, foreign trade, and the like—were to be denied to private and foreign interests.
2. The roles of the public and cooperative sectors were to be reinforced in agriculture while accepting the preponderance of private interests.
3. The State's role in urban wholesale and retail trade was to be extended.
4. Centralized planning and the organization of the public sector according to sectoral specialization (that is, the establishment of the General Organization) were to displace market mechanisms for the mobilization of labor and other resources.
5. The state would monopolize upwards of 90 percent of all investment capital and control its allocation through the Ministry of Finance and sectorally specific, publicly owned banks.
6. The foreign exchange and import policies of the country would be under the comprehensive control of the State through the Central Bank and through the State monopoly of all foreign trade. Allocations of foreign exchange would be made in accordance with the Plan.
7. If not literally closed, the stock exchange would be allowed to atrophy. Foreign investment, moreover, would be accepted only under restrictive terms and was not seen as desirable in and of itself.
8. Severe restrictions would be placed on the emigration of workers and skilled personnel as well as upon the movement of private capital in and out of the country.

There are, of course, several other characteristics of the "closed" system beyond the purely economic. On the international level Egypt found itself heavily reliant upon the U.S.S.R. for military and economic support and for assured markets for Egyptian exports. Politically, the system was based on a single political organization, the Arab Socialist Union, in which broad functional or corporate interests were reflected (not really represented in any operational sense) to the exclusion of any class-based representation. The political arena was heavily policed by a myriad of special apparatuses linked to the presidency.

The economic system revealed its deficiencies by 1966, and Nasser found himself confronted with counselors who urged widely divergent courses of action upon him. One group argued that Egypt must intensify the socialist process domestically and rely more heavily upon the U.S.S.R. for external finance and project aid. Others countered that Egypt must obtain Western financing, technology, and, through access to Western markets, hard currency (if for no other reason than to pay for Egypt's growing food imports). The price would inevitably be compliance with International Monetary Fund (I.M.F.) standards of economic orthodoxy and U.S. political desiderata (including at that time winding down the Egyptian presence in the Yemen). Nasser never really chose, and it is indicative of the conundrum in which he found himself that when he brought 'Abd al-'Azīz Ḥijāzī into his cabinet in March 1968 as minister of finance, his only instructions to him were to find out what was really going on in the Egyptian economy. But short of choosing, Nasser revealed from what quarter the wind was blowing: legislation was prepared to make Port Said a free zone in 1966; a modest version of the own-exchange system was started in 1968; the private sector was encouraged to export to the ''agreement countries'' after 1967 in order to help service the debt. Politically, lip service was paid to revitalizing the Arab Socialist Union (A.S.U.) by free elections ''from top to bottom'' after student-worker riots in February 1968. Internationally, Egypt stayed out of the Yemen after 1967 and accepted hard currency transfusions pledged by Saudi Arabia, Kuwait, and Libya. The acceptance of the Rogers Plan and the implicit threat to the P.L.O. contained therein was a Nasserist initiative not very dissimilar to those of Sādāt in recent years. Weighing lesser evils, Nasser accepted some impingement upon his (or Egypt's) freedom of action within the regional Arab and the external finance spheres in order to safeguard some modicum of Egypt's capability to resist the direct assault on national sovereignty represented by Israel's occupation of Egyptian territory.

Nasser, it may be assumed, moved with great reluctance in these directions. Sādāt was far more at home with the new orientation and tried to push forward on all fronts. There was little hope of a direct breakthrough with the U.S. as long as the Congress and the president continued the massive arms flow to Israel. Rapprochement could come about along two avenues, a) the revival of the Rogers mission in the spring of 1971, and b) the reduction of the Soviet military presence to lessen the effectiveness of the Israeli lobby in its relations with the Congress and the White House. Both avenues proved to be closed. However, in this regard Sādāt tried to generate movement along all four axes: in February 1971 he announced his proposal for reopening the Suez Canal (another Egyptian foreign minister was taken by surprise), followed by Law 65 of 1971 to encourage foreign investment, and the proclamation of 1971 as the "decisive year" in the confrontation with Israel.[4]

Finally, in July 1972, some 25,000 Soviet military advisors were ordered home. All these initiatives produced virtually no change in the situation pertaining to any of the axes. What had gone wrong?

By the end of 1972 the culprit had been identified, and it was détente. It is hard to know if President Sādāt came to this conclusion alone or in counsel with others (Haykal? Ḥāfiz 'Ismā'īl? Maḥmūd Fawzī . . .?) but it was given formal airing in a document drafted by a joint committee of the People's Assembly and the A.S.U., issued on 4 August 1973, and known as the Dialogue Paper. The seminal passages are:

"The policy of global détente between the superpowers has led the U.S. to be more daring in its military, political, and economic support of Israel, and more open in its enmity toward the Arabs in its denial of the legitimate rights of the Palestinian people and the U.N. Charter. Its disregard for world public opinion is aimed at blocking all paths to a just, political settlement.

The policy of détente has weakened the U.N. in that many agreements and settlements have been reached outside its confines. In conformity with this trend. the U.S.A. has begun to endeavor to remove the Middle Eastern case from the U.N. framework in an effort to monopolize this arena for itself and to strengthen its grip on the Arab world.

The Middle East problem has become part of the strategy of the two superpowers. In light of this situation the Soviet Union, in accordance with the policy of global détente and (its) shared interests, is committed to prior review with the U.S. in several instances, for example in easing restrictions on the emigration of Soviet Jews.

Our reliance upon external forces, no matter how determined we are to nurture our relations with them, has become in the context of global détente, less effective and of reduced scope.'' (emphasis supplied)

In other words, the Nasserist formula of playing both sides to Egypt's best advantage was judged untenable. But where could Egypt go from there? Those surrounding Sādāt misread him, one is tempted to say "as usual," and drew conclusions almost directly opposite to those he eventually adumbrated himself. The Dialogue Paper, for instance, declared; "We must cherish and protect the friendship of our friends, especially that of the Soviet Union, by placing these friendships in their true and frank context.'' Further, the paper urged greater reliance upon Arab resources, both military and economic, the strengthening of the eastern front with Israel, diversification of sources of arms, more effective utilization of Third World arenas, such as the Non-Aligned which was to meet in Algiers in September 1973, and an economic open-door policy to attract Arab capital and western technology. The tone of the paper suggested a period of revitalization of the Egyptian economy and military, of steadfastness (*sumūd*) in the conflict with Israel, and continued estrangement from, if not confrontation with, the United States.

Gamāl al-'Utayfī, Deputy Speaker of the People's Assembly and frequent contributor to *al-Ahrām* and the now-defunct *al-Talī'a* on matters of national and foreign policy, produced several articles in the summer of 1973 which developed the basic points of the Dialogue Paper. His tone, however, was somewhat different. He notes[5] that in the official U.S.-Soviet Declaration of 29 May, 1972, following Nixon's visit to Moscow, both sides pledged not to maneuver for advantage at the other's expense. At the same time, al-'Utayfī pointed out, after Brezhnev's return visit, it became apparent that the two powers had not reached any detailed understanding on how to settle the Middle East conflict, other than endorsing U.N. Resolution 242 and calling for a "peaceful" solution.

But al-'Utayfī was relatively sanguine about Egypt's ability to maneuver in this arena. While acknowledging that the military equilibrium between the two superpowers would render disruptions of regional security anywhere in the world extremely difficult, he nonetheless saw factors at work in the opposite direction. He alluded to the growing power of the Afro-Asian Bloc, the Non-Aligned (prematurely citing the success of Allende's Chile), and "the strengthening of moral forces in the world." All these factors strengthened the hand of the developing nations in their dealings with the great powers. Moreover, the emerging world energy crisis, alluded to in Nixon's address to Congress on 3 May, 1973, gave the Arabs special leverage in their dealings with the industrialized West. In essence, al-'Utayfī suggested that Egypt could continue as in the past to use both superpowers to its advantage.

The domestic side of the coin, axes 3 and 4, had been relatively neglected in the Dialogue Paper, especially the implication of *infitāḥ*. In other articles al-'Utayfī took up this question in detail. For example, in "Are Foreign Investments Compatible with Socialism?" [6] he justified Egypt's new course by likening it to the experiences of other socialist countries, beginning with Lenin's New Economic Policy and continuing through the investment codes of Yugoslavia in 1966 and Rumania in 1972. If these countries could benefit from foreign investment, why not Egypt? The Egyptian left had an answer: that Egypt was dealing with foreign capital from a position of weakness, and that its leaders might lack the will to protect the socialist sector. By that time, however, 'Abd al-'Azīz Ḥijāzī had become Deputy Prime Minister and *infitāḥ* had become official policy.

The term was first given official blessing in Ḥijāzī's presentation of his government's program to the People's Assembly, 21 April 1973, and was subsequently amplified through interviews with relevent officials and the exegesis of various pundits. In an interview with Farūq Juwayda[7] Ḥijāzī's vision of the future was that of the wedding of Arab capital and Western technology, and it is to his credit that the first and only *major* project of this nature to date, the Suez-Mediterranean Pipeline (Sumed), was engineered by his government. At the same time, there was in his mind no special policy to be adopted toward the U.S., no special role to be reserved for that power in the context of *infitāḥ*. All he was prepared to advocate was greater equilibrium in Egypt's trade between socialist and capitalist countries:

> "We cannot deny the role played by the agreement countries in Egypt's economic growth, especially that of the Eastern Bloc countries which advanced us long-term cred-

it at a time when the West refused to advance us anything. No Egyptian can deny the results achieved as a
result of technical and economic cooperation with the
Eastern Bloc, led by the U.S.S.R. There are the giant
projects such as the High Dam and the Iron and Steel
Complex, etc., which are undoubtedly the foundation of
the Egyptian economy. However, our foreign trade in the
next phase must be redistributed. 50 percent of our
imports are from agreement countries while they take 70
percent of our exports. This has created a disequilibrium
in our foreign trade balance with other countries. This in
turn requires a broader *infitāḥ* to the world so that we can
put our foreign trade on a footing that achieves the greatest economies possible.''

   In sum, détente dictated new policies, but Egyptian policy makers
in 1973 saw these in terms of continued cooperation with the
U.S.S.R., increased solidarity with the Arabs with a view toward
confrontation with Israel and toward external finance, a search for
arms and markets in the European West, and continued alienation
from the U.S. Sādāt, we now know, had other scenarios in mind.
The conclusion he drew from détente was that 1) the post-1967
Arab-Israeli situation had been ''frozen'' in favor of Israel, and that
the U.S.S.R. would do nothing to unfreeze it, 2) that the U.S.
''holds all the cards'' in the dispute, and that only American action
could break the stalemate. But American action needed a catalyst,
hence the October War. Moreover, Sādāt could not really accept the
notion of *sumūd* as the economic situation worsened. There could
be little expectation of foreign investment, Arab or otherwise, as
long as war lay on the horizon. In one of those masterstrokes of
which he is occasionally capable, Sādāt went to war in order to
cooperate with the U.S. and to make his country safe for *infitāḥ*.[8]
Either or both required a settlement with Israel if they were to be
pursued to their logical conclusions.

   That spectacular initiative along axis 2 produced a major change
along axis 1 and derivative changes along 3 and 4. Sādāt was probably prepared to go farther and faster than circumstances then
allowed. Having ''blown up'' the military stalemate and provoked
the oil embargo, he may have expected the U.S. to resort immediately to unabashed twisting of the Israeli arm. Had not Eisenhower

ordered Israeli troops out of Sinai in 1956? One high-ranking Foreign Ministry official told reporters in November 1973 that he expected all Israeli troops to be out of the Sinai within six months and out of the other occupied territories not too long thereafter. Was Sādāt of like mind? Had he expected to be able to forget the U.S.S.R. as an arms supplier or source of economic aid in light of a speedy solution to the conflict at once acceptable to the Saudi Arabians and conducive to foreign and Arab investment? It is a fact that even before the October War, perhaps in the spring of 1973, he decided or was persuaded to scrap the project of integral union with militant Libya which would have entailed continued confrontation with practically everyone.

However slowly the situation evolved after the war, Sādāt had irrevocably cast in his lot with the U.S. It seems to the outside observer that many informed Americans have failed to realize the extent and quality of this change. Wise or foolhardy, it is a course from which Sādāt can back off with only the greatest difficulty. One need not go over the various stages in the deterioration of relations with the U.S.S.R. except to note that its implications are extremely serious for Egypt's military preparedness. In addition, in the last two or three years hardly a voice has been raised to praise or defend the contribution of the Soviet Union to Egypt's development. In sharp contrast has been the public treatment of U.S.-Egyptian relations. Lavish media coverage has been given to the visits of such luminaries as David Rockefeller, William Simon, Gerald Parsky, and the like (all of whom commented publicly and favorably on Egypt's turn away from socialism), and the flotillas of Congressmen, International Bank for Research and Development (I.B.R.D), U.S. Agency for International Development (U.S.A.I.D.) and I.M.F. teams that regularly sail for Cairo. Without doubt the apotheosis of this genre was President Nixon's state visit to Cairo in June 1974. At its conclusion, a joint declaration signed by both heads of state was issued which constituted a blueprint for diplomatic, economic, and even nuclear cooperation. The Declaration noted that an Egyptian-American working group had studied joint economic projects worth "more than $2 billion." *Al-Akhbār* seized this figure and gave it three-inch headline. All this coincided with the final passage of Law 43 (June 1974) for Foreign and Arab Investment and the Free Zones, the cornerstone of *infitāh*. From that point on, from both the popular and government perspectives, the fate of *infitāh* was indissolubly linked to the U.S., and great expectations of diplomatic and economic rescue were raised that have been only marginally eroded in the years since. In this sense there is a fundamental imbalance or lack of reciprocity in expectations between the two countries, with the U.S. looking for dividends in one among several regions in which it is active, while Egypt looks for nothing short of national salvation.

Without going into its chronology, what are the major facets of *infitāh*? Let us begin with the most contentious issues, some of which have been deliberately clouded to avoid charges of reversing the socialist experiment and undermining the public sector. The basic document defining policy in this respect remains the October Paper issued by President Sādāt in April 1974 as a sequel to, if not substitute for, the Charter of 1962. It reiterates the interpretation presented earlier in the Dialogue Paper:

> "We realize that the burden of progress and construction falls essentially upon the shoulders of the Egyptian people. But whatever the extent of the resources we are able to mobilize locally, we are still in dire need of foreign resources, and the circumstances of the world today permit us to have access to these resources in a way that strengthens our economy and promotes growth. It is on this basis that we call for the economic open door, and it is a call based on the one hand on Egypt's economic needs and, on the other, on available external financing."

The new stage following the October War is characterized by:

1. the need to achieve growth rates superior to those established up to now
2. the need to prepare Egypt for the year 2000
3. the initiation of the domestic and foreign open-door policy
4. comprehensive planning
5. support for the public sector
6. social development and the building of the individual
7. entering the age of science and technology
8. the advance of our civilization on the basis of science and faith
9. the establishment of an open society swept by the winds of freedom

10. a secure society in which each citizen is assured of his life and sustenance.

At the risk of perhaps gross and unfair simplification, it can be said that of these ten points, only the third has been granted any operational underpinning. The rest have remained slogans as frequently violated in practice as they are espoused in theory.

The economic open-door policy is structured by Law 43 of 1974 and its amendments contained in Law 32 of 1977. But that policy has gone far beyond these legislative acts to impinge directly upon the Egyptian public and private sectors. Schematically, the balance sheet to date is as follows:

A.   All projects, qualifying under Law 43 are automatically considered part of the private sector even if one of the partners is a public sector company. When Mamdūh Salīm replaced Ḥijāzī as prime minister in May 1975, he let it be known that the sole operative criterion for the acceptability of investments was whether or not they contributed to national production. Refusing to be the prisoner of socialist slogans, Salim in effect ended the principle of reserved sectors for public investment and activity. In the same year all the public General Organizations that supervised production sectors were abolished, and each enterprise was left to sink or swim as best it could. Regulations on profit-sharing and worker participation in management boards, it should be noted finally, do not apply to projects coming under Law 43.

B.   Public sector banks were converted from sectoral specialization to "full service" functions. Moreover Law 43 allowed for joint-venture banks with foreign partners as long as Egyptian interests—public or private—retained 51 percent of the shares. Such joint-venture banks would also be legally part of the private sector.

C.   While few practical steps have yet been taken, the principle of expanding the capital of public sector enterprises through stock issues available to the general public has been approved.

D.   Since 1974 there has been little pretense of subordinating foreign investments to the Plan (nor, until 1978, has there been a Plan). The guiding principle has been for Egypt to approve any relatively serious investment project whatever the sector of the economy.

E. Repatriation of profits has been a sensitive issue, and for the most part only projects with some prospects of self-sufficiency in foreign exchange have been approved. However, in housing and some activities coming under tourism laws (Wimpy's and the like) this principle has been disregarded. In general the Latin American experience of net capital drain after some years of foreign investment has not been discussed in Egypt.[9]

F. The entire question of exchange rates is linked both to investment legislation and Egypt's tractations with the I.M.F. Law 32 (1977) provides for the entry of capital and repatriation of earnings and royalties at the prevailing incentive rate for the Egyptian pound (LE). In addition, and in compliance with the I.M.F. stabilization plan, all imports, with the exception of 19 basic commodities (foodstuffs, fertilizers, and so on) are valued at the incentive rate and customs duties charged accordingly. This means an effective increase of nearly 80 percent in the value of imported goods and in the duties subsequently placed on them. Foreign investors are however exempted from such duties for upwards of five years.

G. Parallel to these measures have been others facilitating the reentry of the private sector in foreign trade. The most important legislation involves the "own-exchange" system whereby private importers need not account for their foreign exchange holdings, nor convert them through public sector banks in financing their imports. Moreover, imports valued at up to LE 10,000 in any one shipment may be brought in without an import permit. Finally, the private sector or joint ventures are now permitted to open shipping and trade agencies.

H. Again in view of recommendations of the U.S. Treasury, the I.B.R.D., the I.M.F., the Saudi Arabians and others, an assault upon the administered pricing system which has cost Egypt between LE 400 and LE 600 million in subsidies in recent years, is afoot. The social and political costs of eroding the subsidy policy are matters for wide-ranging debate. The goal is to reaffirm market forces in the allocation and utilization of resources.

I. The more efficient utilization of human resources is to be pursued through a) encouraging labor emigration (already about LE 300 million are remitted each year by those now abroad)

b) limiting university and professional school enrollments, and c) ending the practice of the State acting as the employer of last resort. No concrete steps have yet been taken toward b and c whose political and economic implications are as far-reaching as those of the abolition of subsidies.

One can tentatively conclude from the above that structures erected during the 1961-69 period are under heavy pressures. There are now mechanisms in place whereby the public sector, rather than strengthened, can be transferred in bits and pieces to private hands or allowed to languish, die, or be liquidated. The second coming of giant foreign banks into the Egyptian economy is a particularly sensitive issue for, even among advocates of *infitāḥ*, there is the fear that they will dominate their public sector partners. Indeed, Citibank refused to enter into a joint venture with a majority public sector partner, because general bank policy forbids such arrangements, and in the Egyptian case there were fears of "obstructionism" and "featherbedding." According to a 1977 report of the Central Bank, joint-venture and off-shore banks operating in Egypt held LE 26 million equivalent in deposits but had placed LE 160 million equivalent in parent banks in the U.S. and Europe. Instead of mobilizing capital for Egyptian purposes, Egyptian capital was or is mobilized for investment abroad.[10] These may or may not be desirable developments from the point of view of economic performance. They would pale in significance if there were at the same time investments under way likely to contribute substantially to Egyptian productivity. While we may concur with Zakī Shāfiʿī, former minister of Economy and Economic Cooperation[11], that Law 43 was given its first real chance only after the second disengagement agreement of September 1975, the balance sheet until now is not auspicious. Of the one hundred projects *in operation*, valued at LE 197 million, five projects in investment companies (LE 98 million), seventeen in banks (LE 40.2 million) and eleven in tourism (LE 28 million) account for 88 percent of the total value.[12] This distribution could change in the coming years, but nothing on the scale of Sumed (which does not come under Law 43) has yet been achieved.

Taken in its broadcast sense, success and failure of *infitāḥ* will be unevenly distributed across the Egyptian population. There is simply no question that if it is to work, the policy will require considerable belt tightening among the masses. The Nasserist policy of trying to achieve growth without curbing mass consumption, of delinking wages and productivity, of what one might call socialism without pain, or what the Egyptians *do* call "the gains of the revolution" (*makāsib al-thawra*), will have to give way. What will replace them is, implicitly, a neoclassic growth model whose Latin American variants have been critically described and analysed by Hirschman and Furtado among a host of others. The model is:

1. export (invisible and visible)-oriented to earn foreign exchange. Import substitution, unlike in the 1960-65 period, is not of prime concern;

2. premised on the tolerance of fairly high levels of domestic inflation in order to encourage private and public sector savings and investment;

3. designed to keep wages for the civil service and the bulk of the work force lagged behind the rate of inflation;

4. tolerant of middle class consumerism if not a direct incentive to it;

5. designed to promote market mechanisms to determine the price of labor and goods;

6. designed to promote labor migration to cushion the shock of inflation and underemployment;

7. conducive to an authoritarian political system necessary to cope with the inevitable disparities in the distribution of wealth. It is moot whether or not a "liberal" political system can contain the social pressures inherent in the model.

For many Egyptian policy planners the situation need be "contained" for only a relatively short period of time, for, they judge, Egypt's economic problems are essentially circumstantial and not structural. That, for instance, is the line adopted by Zakī Shāfiʿī (op. cit.) and was endorsed by an important I.B.R.D. report that was the baseline for the large aid program inaugurated in Egypt after 1974. The notion is that because of the dislocations caused by the war economy, as well as the effects of war losses, Egypt faces a peculiar balance of payments problem that could be remedied *within five years* by a) increased worker remittances, b) Suez Canal and Sumed revenues, c) oil revenues, d) tourism revenues, and e) technological transformation through the open door leading to increased exports. A combination of a settlement with Israel and voluminous transfusions of Arab capital are the *sine qua non* of surviving the transition period. One may and should question any or all of the assumptions contained in this view of the future, but the point is that once again all four of the original policy axes are seen to be inter-acting, and the U.S. is now actively involved along each one.[13]

Even if one assumes that the argument of circumstantial difficulties is basically correct, the challenges of the next few years are nonetheless awesome. Sādāt is undoubtedly acting in the light of them now. The riots of January 1977 revealed something of the limits of mass tolerance of inflation and austerity. Those strains will not go away, and the material privation of today can be assuaged only by offering concrete hope of gains in the future. Sādāt's trip to Jerusalem clearly symbolized such hopes.

The short term is likely to bring increasing real income disparities in Egypt and the reinforcement of economic interests that are becoming the visible symbols of the new wealth. Within the nonagricultural private sector, the resurgence of activity since 1973 has produced mixed results. A heterogenous but occasionally highly placed group of Egyptians has taken advantage of the liberalized import regime to enter into the trade agency and import sector. Their major instrument has been the own-exchange system. Imports through this instrumentality are now running at over LE 350 million per year (it is not clear if goods entering under the LE 10,000 ceiling are included). In addition, generous allowances are now granted Egyptians living abroad for bringing in "personal effects" much of which finds its way into the local market. There is heated debate as to the composition of such imports. The Ministry of Commerce insists that it consists mostly of essential goods (that is, foodstuffs, which however could include items such as Danish butter or instant coffee), and materiel, parts, and machinery that contribute directly to private sector production. Others feel that through fuzzy categorization it has been possible to mask the fact that by and large these imports consist of nonessential consumer items. Whatever the truth, no one can fail to have noticed the profusion of what *al-Ahrām al-Iqtisādī* has termed "provocative goods" in the streets of Cairo and Alexandria.[14]

In itself, this phenomenon, as well as substantial profits accruing to the importers, would not be matters for major concern. But it is going on at a time when the local private sector is under heavy pressure from three quarters. First is the potential competition from Law 43 projects which are allowed to operate for upwards of five years free from taxes and import duties. Second, and more important, is that elements within the private sector have been adversely affected by the shift to customs valuation of imports at the incentive rate. For those that rely on the importation of raw materials and intermediate goods in their production process, this has meant soaring costs and an inability to compete with goods imported through the own-exchange system. Finally, the suspension of trade agreements with the socialist countries in August 1977 has, temporarily at least, cut off this important export market upon which parts of the private sector had come to rely. Some believe that the neo-Wafd,[15] faithful to its past, will take up the cause of this part of the private sector and wage a campaign for increased protectionism and against foreign competition introduced through *infitāh*.

In the countryside, commercial farming interests have been growing since 1969. This can be seen in the marked expansion of fruit and vegetable acreage in recent years, many of the owners of which are city dwellers. Such produce falls outside the cooperative marketing system (that is, its prices and profits are not effectively controlled) and because of burgeoning urban demand the return on these investments is very high. Another important element of this interest group consists in the beef fatteners who supply the urban wholesale market. By exaggerating production costs, the fatteners are able to realize very high profits. These interests are well represented in the People's Assembly, and twice in the last five years they have been able to defeat legislation to tax orchards. At the same time they have attacked the cooperative marketing system and have successfully campaigned for the revaluation of the rental value of agricultural land (ca. 45 percent of Egypt's cultivated land is rented). In the same vein they have won the right to evict tenants for failure to pay rent and to convert cash-rent contracts into sharecropping contracts.

These segments of the Egyptian private sector, urban and rural, along with the host of middle men, fixers, and consultants, are in the best position to gain from *infitāh*. The return on their investments and activities outstrips the rate of inflation and allows them to plow back earnings into more fruit, vegetables, beef, poultry, etc., the acquisition of urban and rural real estate, consumer durables, and own-exchange imports. Under the general set of political and economic circumstances prevailing could one expect them to behave otherwise? Probably not, but they are earning, along with high-spending Arab and other foreign businessmen and investors, a bad name for *infitāh*. In the long run this trend will redound to the discredit of the U.S. seen as the great power patron of this policy.

The riots of January 1977 demonstrated the limits of Egypt's political liberalization. The press has been taken firmly in hand by the presidency, and the "opposition" elements in parliament, elected in November 1976, have limited their cautious attacks on the government in the face of a threat from below. By contrast, there are signs of small niches of autonomous political activity that have grown since 1974. Such activities may be filling the vacuum left by the moribund A.S.U. and the inability of the officially recognized parties to generate any broadly based support. In this vein one may note the consistent refusal of the courts to condemn those arrested as political accessories to the January riots despite the public pre-trial accusations of both the president and his prime minister. Likewise the open agitation of the Muslim Brethren on the one hand, and the neo-Wafd on the other indicate that some Egyptians will test the ground rules of the plural system. For the time being Sādāt, much like Ḥasan II through the Green March, has stolen the show from these actors by his second crossing, but, like the Green March, the immediate benefits may prove fleeting.

To summarize the character of political *infitāh*, it would seem that it is difficult to play the liberal game without abiding by the rules. That poses a major dilemma for the regime for its mainstay, the Misr Party, lacks credibility, and the regime has no other source of popular organizational support. Hence the regime cannot tolerate (for long) any others that do or might have such support. How to contain them without violating the liberal rules of the game is a question without an answer at present. The political vacuum remains, for the regime cannot fill it and cannot let anyone else try. Thus the armed forces, by the very nature of the situation, remain the final arbiters.

To conclude, let us return to the policy package outlined at the beginning. Along the first axis, the U.S. and its alleged appendages such as the I.B.R.D. and the I.M.F., are identified as closely with *infitāh* as was the U.S.S.R. with the socialist transformation. For *infitāḥ* to work there has to be a lasting settlement with Israel which in turn requires a form of U.S. involvement more favorable to the Arab cause (begging the question whether or not the Egyptian cause is distinct). This proposition can be *partially* inverted. To provoke such involvement required and requires policies such as those contained in *infitāḥ*. Whether or not political liberalization is a necessary part of the package is moot. There is little evidence, even under the Carter administration, that criteria of liberal democracy have any bearing on U.S. policy toward other nations. Nor is there good evidence that real liberalization has taken place in Egypt aside from the more discreet role assigned the police apparatuses. The new economic guidelines are more important, and in several respects Egypt has adopted formulae for the accumulation of capital more congenial to U.S. biases. But while accumulation is going on through new private interest groups, Egyptian migrants, and to a lesser extent through foreign and Arab investors, the use of their earnings has not often been in the best interests of growth. Finally, other than "quick kill" foreign capital, little long-term foreign investment has so far been forthcoming.

The peace agreement with Israel may be seen as an attempt to create the right atmosphere for substantial capital transfers to Egypt. Sādāt may have hoped that an Egypt triumphant in peace will be rewarded by the West for stabilizing a region crucial to the well-being of advanced economies.[16]

It might be, however, that the peace agreement will reduce Egypt's salience and hence the kind of aid support it might expect in the future from a fickle Congress. Moreover, in its desperation for peace, how long can Egypt jeopardize its ties to the oil-rich Arab states by supporting a deal that is unpalatable to Saudi Arabia, among others? If the peace agreement ultimately fails, then Sādāt or any successor would have to reconsider the entire policy package.

As we have suggested earlier, such a reversal would not be impossible if couched in terms of national sovereignty and dignity. The proper wording and empiric underpinning would not be hard to find. Even wealthy regional allies—Libya, Iraq, and perhaps Algeria—could be expected to support Egypt in a return to the orthodoxy of the 1960s, and the U.S.S.R. might well be tempted to gamble on Egypt once again despite its past losses. The process would be the more feasible for the fact that the strategically placed elites in Egypt, civilian and military, are fundamentally dependent upon or in control of the state apparatus, and while policies change the state and its personnel remain. It is, after all, those who implemented the Socialist Decrees of 1961 who are now in charge of the open-door policy. If major vested interests with strong lobbies and institutionalized support had emerged in Egypt as a result of *infitāḥ*, this judgement might well be unfounded, but the policies are too new to have fostered such groups yet. It would seem therefore that unless progress achieved along axis 2 is sustained, *infitāḥ* and U.S.-Egyptian relations will be subjected to potentially intolerable stress.

NOTES

1. Remarks of an Egyptian former foreign minister to the author, spring 1975.

2. Had ideological and programmatic socialism penetrated Egyptian society more deeply than it in fact has, this claim might be invalid.

3. The heyday of Soviet influence corresponds with Khruschev's visit to Egypt in May 1964 to inaugurate the Aswān High Dam, to Nasser's acceptance of the Rogers Plan in July 1970, but Egypt's "turn to the East" began well before. Whether or not the Gaza Raid of February 1955 was the real and sufficient cause for Egypt's seeking Soviet arms in the same year, the fact remains that the regime, invoking military preparedness and violation of national sovereignty, justified the Czech arms deal in those terms. Policy shifts, some designed and some imposed, then took place along a broad front. Military aid was followed by economic aid (Aswān High Dam and the Hilwān Iron and Steel Complex) paralleled by a major shift in Egypt's foreign trade toward the U.S.S.R. and East Europe. Domestically, great emphasis was placed on state-guided heavy industrialization, central planning, and after 1961, restricted private sector activity. The Charter of 1962 provided the umbrella of "scientific socialism" to protect the experiment.

4. It was to be the year of war or peace but no further stalemate. It aborted because 1) the U.S.S.R., according to the Egyptians, was preoccupied with the Indo-Pakistani conflict over Bangladesh, and 2) the U.S. was preoccupied with Vietnam and the reelection of Nixon.

5. In "Political Variables and Their Impact," *al-Talīʿa* 9, 10 (October 1973): 38-50.

6. *Al-Ahrām*, 16 August 1973.

7. *Al-Ahrām*, 19 August 1973.

8. Qadhāfī understood Sādāt's goal and consequently denounced him for having sold Egyptian blood cheaply in setting his sights on such limited objectives. Even in the euphoria following the October War, Egyptians quipped that the army had crossed the canal and stormed the Bar-Lev line in order to renew diplomatic relations with the U.S.

9. In the meetings of the 3rd Annual Conference of Egyptian Economists, this and other negative aspects of *infitāḥ* were given considerable attention, especially by Jalāl Amīn and 'Abd al-Khāliq Jawda: *al-Ahrām al-Iqtisādī*, 15 April 1978.

10. Rūz al-Yūssef, 17 October 1977.

11. *Al-Jumhūriyya*, 25 April 1976.

12. *Al-Ahrām al-Iqtisādī*, 15 October 1977.

13. This fact is explicitly recognized by the U.S. AID draft report on economic assistance to Egypt for financial year (F.Y.) 1979, prepared in compliance with section 9 of the International Security Assistance Act of August 1977. In several places it is affirmed that the primary goal of the program is "directed at the overriding objective of supporting the peace-making efforts and moderate policy orientation now being pursued by the Sādāt Government" (that is, axis 2), and "assumes that both adequate living standards and tangible economic progress are prerequisite to lasting peace in Egypt and the rest of the Middle East" (axis 4).

14. When *al-Ahrām al-Iqtisādī* ran a picture of the minister of commerce alongside that of Louis XVI (15 October 1977), the chief editor was ordered by the Director of *al-Ahrām* to cease his attacks on *infitāḥ*.

15. The neo-Wafd was authorized in February 1978 to reconstitute itself legally after twenty-five years of imposed inactivity.

16. Muḥammad Sayyid Aḥmad has made the intriguing argument that Sādāt's initiative was aimed at bringing Israeli interests in as underwriters of large capital investments, mobilizing international Jewish capital and contacts, for joint exploitation of Sinai resources, for example, or desalinization projects. Thus *infitāḥ* would be directly linked to normalization of relations with Israel. The mobilization of investments would constitute not so much an infusion of new blood for the Egyptian economy as a guaranty of Israel's future security. "La sécurité par le développement des liens économiques", *Le Monde Diplomatique* 25 (January 1978): 286.

Strategic and
Legal Aspects

Some Political and Strategic Implications of an American-Israeli Defense Treaty

Yair Evron

The objective of this paper is to discuss some of the political and strategic implications of an American-Israeli defense treaty (A.I.D.T.). I shall focus primarily on the implications for Israel, but shall refer from time to time to some of the possible implications for the U.S. I shall not discuss the feasibility of such a treaty from the American standpoint, as this requires an extensive study of the American mood and of positions taken by the political elite there. Moreover, it is difficult to assess the feasibility before the administration has formulated its position on that subject and before a serious public debate on the question has commenced. It is reasonable to assume, however, that the administration would eventually agree to the idea if it became convinced that an A.I.D.T. is a necessary condition for securing a settlement in the Middle East and especially that it will be a contributing factor to the evolvement of stability there.[1] If Israel were to insist on the A.I.D.T. as one of the main conditions for a settlement, this would be a major factor in formulating the administration's position. In addition, a serious public debate in the U.S. on the subject is necessary in order to assess the pros and cons of an A.I.D.T. from the point of view of American interests. A similar debate in Israel is essential to enable the government to receive inputs into its decision-making process.

It should be added, however, that an A.I.D.T. appears to be possible only within the framework of a general peace settlement, or at the very least a settlement that would relate to Israel's relations with Egypt and Jordan, that is, resolving the problems of the Sinai and the West Bank. It appears that the Israeli-Egyptian peace agreement and the Camp David agreements do not as yet constitute sufficient pre-conditions for the A.I.D.T. Indeed, the possibility of such a treaty was mentioned before Camp David, but apparently it was not a central theme in the discussions there. The Israeli delegation, for its part, did not raise that issue. It is conceivable, however, that when the ultimate future of the West Bank and the Gaza Strip are discussed, the A.I.D.T. might be raised once again as a subject for negotiations. Israel would then be in a strong position to demand extensive conditions which could be included in the security arrangements. These might very well include the A.I.D.T.

If a political settlement were to be achieved, what then would be the need for various security arrangements including the A.I.D.T.? The answer is that even then considerable potential for instability in the area would remain. In the first place, some Arab political elites would probably maintain their strong animosity toward Israel. Then, again, the Middle East is a complex multipolar system with several Arab states having active foreign policies, and competing intensely for hegemony in the Arab world. Thirdly, there are persistent conflicts in the periphery (in the Horn of Africa for example). Lastly, there is continued domestic instability in some Arab states. There is always the danger of a spillover from all these conflicts and instabilities into the Israeli-Arab relationship.

A very brief review of Israel's positions in regard to external formal alliances or guarantees is of interest. Within a few years after its establishment, Israel began to face the problem which almost every state (regardless of size) has faced at one or another stage of its historical development: the need to aggregate its power with those of other states, in order to deter or defeat enemies.

The traditional Zionist approach to the support of big powers had been an ambivalent one. The basic trend had been to seek support from big powers and this approach did not really change with the creation of the State of Israel. Indeed, already in 1951, David Ben Gurion began tentative negotiations about the possibility of a bilateral alliance with Britain.[2] At the same time, both in the pre-State period and after the establishment of the State there existed a strong undercurrent of "self-reliance" which opposed extensive support and rejected too strong a dependence on external powers.

These two trends coexisted not only in different political parties but in the attitude of many individual decision makers.[3] Until the

1967 War, however, the first trend was predominant. Wherever possible, the leading Israeli decision makers searched for either an alliance with, or guarantees by Britain, the U.S., NATO, France and again, NATO and the U.S. respectively.[4] In a sense, Israel preferred to have an "open system" in the Middle East, i.e., one in which the great powers would be involved, rather than a closed system. In the wake of the 1967 War and its aftermath, the Israeli position changed. The tremendous victory convinced the Israeli political elite and decision makers that it was probably preferable to have a "closed system" in the Middle East. Thus, so ran the ideal model of the time, if only the superpowers were to withdraw from the region, Israel could reach an agreement with the Arab states on her own terms. Short of such a withdrawal, Israel felt assured of her military superiority on the one hand, and of continued American transfers of arms on the other. Furthermore, it appeared that the "rules of the game" of superpower behavior in the region assured mutual deterrence against direct military intervention in the region. Thus, the whole issue of alliances and guarantees was abandoned. Eventually the idea was raised by some Americans whose motivation was very different. They proposed an American (separate or together with other powers) guarantee to Israel as an inducement to withdrawal from the territories. Needless to say, this approach only increased official Israeli lack of enthusiasm for the idea.

Following the 1973 War, it appears that a measure of fluidity has been reintroduced into Israeli thinking regarding the idea of guarantees or alliances. This change resulted from growing concern and uncertainty about the future development of the military balance between Israel and her Arab neighbors. To be sure, opposition to the idea remained strong and in any case the whole idea was seen as not very urgent. Indeed, it would seem that no serious, systematic thinking has really been devoted to this issue. All the more so, as it appeared clear that the U.S. would agree, if at all, only on condition that such an alliance be preceded by (or be part of) a comprehensive peace agreement, and this implied Israeli withdrawals from the territories. If anything, such a package is even more difficult for the current government to accept.

On the other hand, in the public debate in the U.S. there appeared another school of advocates for a defense treaty with Israel, whose motivation was different from that of their predecessors. Among them were pro-Israeli scholars who stressed the stabilizing potential of a defense treaty.[5]

As for the administration, some diplomatic "noises" came from time to time from that direction which indicated that a treaty was possible under certain conditions. Lately, the idea of an A.I.D.T. had been raised in a more definite way by administration officials whose main objective is probably to facilitate the peace negotiations. A limited and hesitant public debate in Israel has begun as a response.[6] The Memorandum on Agreement signed in March 1976 is a strong indication of the readiness of the administration to strengthen its *formal* commitment to Israel.

TYPES OF GUARANTEES

The theoretical possibilities are as follows:

(1) A.I.D.T.

(2) Two or three symmetrical defense treaties, i.e., A.I.D.T., Egypt-U.S.A., Jordan-U.S.A.

(3) A trilateral defense U.S.-Israel-Egypt treaty (which other Middle Eastern countries may join).

(4) A.I.D.T. on the one hand, and a Soviet defense treaty with one or more Arab countries on the other. (The possibility that Egypt would be the Arab party is, at present, and for the foreseeable future, extremely unlikely. On the other hand, Syria is a probable candidate for such a treaty if she feels that otherwise she may be left alone facing an American-backed Israel as well as other American-oriented Arab countries.)

(5) An American guarantee to Israel.

(6) An American guarantee of various security arrangements arrived at between Israel and Arab countries, primarily Egypt. It is probable that the main security arrangement would be the demilitarization of the Sinai (or most of it).[7]

(7) Joint American-Soviet guarantees for these security arrangements.

Some of these possibilities are mutually exclusive whereas others could be complementary and even derivative.

The main discussion will focus on the A.I.D.T. with some reference to other arrangements which might result from it. It should be stressed that the idea of an A.I.D.T. is different from that of a guarantee in several important ways. To begin with, a treaty connotes some measure of equality whereas a guarantee emphasizes dependency. Consequently, a treaty would be more acceptable to the Israeli public. Although the main element in the treaty would indeed be a guarantee of sorts, this distinction, nevertheless, has also considerable practical relevance. A treaty—if similar in structure to NATO, for example—would require the establishment of permanent mechanisms of political and strategic coordination.[8] Joint military exercises and joint military planning might also be possible. In the more extreme case American bases might be established and American forces be deployed in Israel as well. In contrast to a guarantee, a defense treaty theoretically imposes equal symmetrical obligations on both sides. In legal terms, there are several different types of American security commitments: Presidential Declarations, Congressional Resolutions, Executive Acts and Formal Treaties. The last requires full Senate approval by a two-thirds majority and is therefore the most binding.

SUPERPOWER GUARANTEES IN THE ARAB-ISRAELI REGION

The Tripartite Declaration of 1950 was the first formal U.S. undertaking, and was based on a joint resolution of the Congress. The U.S. took on the role of an "observer" in the Baghdad Pact. The Eisenhower Doctrine was endorsed by a Congressional Resolution. Thus, there were no formal defense treaties, in the full sense of the word, between the U.S. and powers in the Arab-Israeli region. Similarly, the Treaties of Friendship and Cooperation which the Soviet Union signed with Egypt and Iraq, although containing some elements of defense commitments, did not, nevertheless, amount to comprehensive defense treaties. Short of these, the superpowers maintained a posture of strong cooperation with and aid to regional powers which also allowed them a measure, rather limited though it was, of control over them. Elements of de facto defense agreements or of guarantees were, however, in evidence. First, there were the continued attempts to maintain deliveries of arms to allies and friends among the regional powers so that their military position would not be adversely affected or so that their relative military capability would be increased, and second, efforts to protect them in case a regional opponent in a regional war threatened to devastate them completely. An example of the first element was the airlift and sealift of the superpowers to Egypt, Syria and Israel during the 1973 War. Examples of the second were the Soviet intervention threats in 1956, 1967, the actual intervention in the War of Attrition, and the threats on the eve of the 1973 War.

These features of superpower-client relations form what might amount in some cases to a semi-alliance. At the same time a formal defense treaty is of a different nature. Its binding power on the parties, especially the big ones, is much greater than in the tacit informal arrangements existing at present. In the latter case there is always a considerable element of uncertainty as to the actions which might be taken by the parties; this uncertainty reduces the deterrence effect of the relationship and increases the anxieties of the regional party. The formal alliance relationship—specially in the case of the U.S.—is much less affected by changes in the American public's perceptions of the national interest. Hence, the element of uncertainty is reduced.

EFFECTS OF AN A.I.D.T.

An A.I.D.T. must be considered one security measure among several whose common objectives are the enhancement of Israel's security and increased stability in the Middle East. The two objectives are interrelated as it is contended here that once Israel withdraws from the territories conquered in 1967 and a comprehensive peace settlement has been signed, Israel would again become a status quo power and her security would be one important element in the stability of the region.

Continued Israeli occupation of the territories has long been seen in some quarters in Israel (and outside it) as constituting a major strategic asset for Israel. Such an asset—so the argument stands—should not be given up at all. Another school of thought holds that some parts of the territories, although important strategically, might be given up provided very extensive security arrangements were coupled with it, and under conditions of full peace.[9] This is not the place for a discussion of this enormous subject which in fact and very surprisingly has received only very scant serious treatment in the academic strategic literature, both in Israel and outside it.[10] In this context I would venture to state in an extremely condensed form only several of my basic assessments about this subject without substantiating them. First, security depends on a complex politico-strategic cum military set of factors. Politically, the occupation of the territories by Israel is counterproductive both because it increases Arab motivations for war, and because it critically strains Israeli-American relations. Both these developments have a far-reaching adverse strategic and military impact on Israel. Increased Arab motivation for war means not only the greater frequency of wars but also the greater mobilization of Arab resources for war. As all Arab-Israeli wars since 1956 have proved, the political fruits for the victorious side—Israel—are very limited, and sometimes war is even politically counterproductive. In more limited operational terms, a strong case could be made for the notion that the demilitarization of Sinai following an Israeli withdrawal would favor Israel, as compared with the present situation. As for the Golan Heights and the West Bank, demilitarization might not be preferable in military terms to the present situation, but would probably not pose a qualitatively greater security threat. Additional security arrangements, whose main objective would be to impose constraints on attempts to remilitarize the territories partly through limitations on the deployment of forces beyond demilitarized zones, would most probably limit any possible security threats. Once all these security arrangements come into being, the main elements operating against their violation would perforce be the Israeli deterrence capability on the one hand, and the changed political configuration in the Middle East on the other.

Deterrence against Arab Attacks

In this context, what might be the stabilizing consequences of the A.I.D.T.? It would in the first place decrease the likelihood of an Arab attack on Israel or of politico-military moves which might end up with a military operation against Israel. It should be noted in this context that the threat of superpower intervention has always played an important role in the calculations of regional leaders when contemplating military actions. Thus, for example, one of the main arguments voiced by the Egyptian leadership during the 1960s (before the 1967 War), explaining why Egypt was not initiating hostilities against Israel, was the possible intervention by the U.S. against an Arab attack.

In assessing the deterrent effect of an A.I.D.T. one has to consider the following elements: Under what contingencies would the A.I.D.T. have to be exercised, how credible is the U.S. as a formal ally, and lastly, what are the available and accessible American forces?

Broadly speaking, there are three types of possible Arab-initiated military operations. First, there is unlimited conventional war in which all the military capabilities of an Arab state, or a coalition of states, are committed in order to secure unlimited political objectives, i.e., the complete destruction of Israel or its total defeat followed by the imposition of impossible political conditions. A second possibility involves limited attacks on Israel in order to achieve limited military and political objectives. This type of war may be either mobile or static-attritionary in nature. The third can be termed subwar violence, consisting primarily of terroristic and guerilla attacks and sometimes small scale warfare along the borders (examples of the latter are the Syrian military operations on the Golan Heights in 1972 and the occasional Jordanian military operations along the Jordan river during the 1967-70 period).

The main threat to Israel arises from the first type of war. The probability in the forseeable future of an Arab victory in such a war is close to nil. However, the war could be rather costly and the political gains in most scenarios rather debatable. A war of attrition might under some conditions cause severe harm to Israel and could contribute to difficult economic situations and grave political losses. The third type of violence, although sometimes painful, by no means constitutes a serious threat to Israel.

Would an A.I.D.T. be an effective deterrent against subwar violence? That is unlikely. Terrorist groups would not be affected by it and small scale violence by regular forces would also not be seen as a cause justifying the involvement of a superpower. It appears therefore that this type of violence would have to be tackled by Israeli forces themselves or, better, in conjunction with Arab forces, should this be agreed upon and the political context allow it. The most likely area from which terrorist activities might ensue would probably be the West Bank. The most efficient way of handling potential attacks from the West Bank, following a peace settlement, would be through joint Israeli-Jordanian mechanisms of control and patrolling. An important motivation for Jordan's involvement in such mechanisms would be the shared interest with Israel in suppressing extremist Palestinian activity—which, in the first place, undermines Jordanian authority—and the possibility that if such activity got out of hand, a major crisis might result which would serve as a *casus belli* for Israel to reoccupy the West Bank.

The probability of war of the first two types following a settlement appears to be rather limited. In the first place, once Israel withdraws from the occupied territories, the motivations of the separate confrontation states to begin another war with Israel would decline. Then again, Israel is now considered to have a wide margin of military superiority over various combinations of Arab states. The demilitarization of the territories, especially in the Sinai, would make a major military operation against Israel even less attractive for the Arabs.[11] The A.I.D.T. therefore comes as a supplementary deterrent on top of all these arrangements. It is, however, important in two contingencies: if for any reason Arab decision makers miscalculated the ratio of military capabilities between their countries and Israel, or if a political crisis developed whose dynamics would force the hands of the Arab leaders and impel them to make mistaken escalatory decisions. In such cases, there is a possibility that a limited war would ensue. The A.I.D.T. would act as a further deterrent against such moves.

It should be added that the main Arab decision makers have shown that they behave rationally when choosing the means for the implementation of their objectives, even if the latter sometimes prove to be irresponsible or self-defeating. Arab decision makers may err in their means/ends calculations, but basically they apply rational criteria to the process of choosing them. If they decide to go to war (as in 1973) when they recognized their inferiority, it was because of a *rational* calculation of the political gains which could be derived from the use of force even in a situation of defeat. It is doubtful that such a situation could recur in the future after a peace treaty. Then, the political gains to be derived from a military operation ending in defeat would be extremely debatable. The various security arrangements mentioned, including the A.I.D.T. could therefore act as a set of serious constraints on Arab decision-making.

Another aspect of the deterrence problem is the credibility question. As already mentioned, the Arab decision makers have attached considerable importance to the American informal commitment to Israel. Indeed looking back at the performance of both superpowers in the Middle East in the 1950s and since then, they must come to the conclusion that the superpowers tend to intervene, or issue effective threats of intervention, when certain "red lines" are crossed. That was one of the chief lessons of all the Arab-Israel wars from 1956 on, of the 1970 Jordan civil war, etc. In all or most of these cases, the superpower whose ally's vital interests were threatened preferred to help the ally first through ordinary diplomatic means; then, whenever possible, to mobilize regional support—be it political or military—in order to rectify the situation; afterwards to issue threats of military intervention; and lastly, if all else failed, to actually intervene. In almost all cases, the threats were sufficient to eventually halt the violation of the "red lines."[12] America's commitment to the existence of Israel has been accepted as a basic feature of the Middle East situation. However, all these commitments apply to critical situations in the midst of war. The A.I.D.T. aims at reducing the likelihood of war breaking out in the first place, and doing so by involving the U.S. in the crisis before it escalates beyond control.

Here the credibility of American deterrent threats would increase if they resulted from a formal undertaking such as a defense treaty. The main reason for this is that if the U.S. refused to honor its obligations under the A.I.D.T., the credibility of its other formal security commitments elsewhere would be seriously affected. Another reason is that the very existence of the A.I.D.T. would affect American perceptions of the American "national interests" in such a way as to make the commitment appear to be part of the national interest.

In the post-Vietnam period, what is the overall credibility of the American commitments anywhere? There is no easy and simple answer to that question. On the one hand American readiness to become involved in regional wars has probably diminished. On the other hand, with the passing of time since the Vietnam experience, it might be argued that American readiness for such an exercise might reawaken. The U.S. has refused to abandon its world-wide role, but has tried to formulate it in a different way. The Nixon Doctrine was one attempt in that direction. The Carter administration in contrast to former administrations has put greater emphasis on the economic and social problems besetting the world and related to it, giving increased attention to the Less Developed Countries

(L.D.C.) problems. This appeared to indicate a shift from traditional "high politics" to other dimensions of international relations. However, side by side with this we witness other developments: American support for NATO and the insistence on the commitment to Western Europe has lately indeed been revitalized. Then again, the possible scarcity of resources rekindled new interest in the interface between the economic dimension and the "high politics" dimension. Nowhere is this more apparent than in the Middle East itself where the relationship between oil and strategic issues—and hence "high politics" considerations—is obvious.[13] Just to mention another major factor: whatever might be the grievances of L.D.C. against the "north," within the former there are many regional conflicts and the American role in many of them is central. Indeed, it would seem that in some areas the U.S. might find it increasingly necessary to reintroduce its power in order to stabilize regional situations or to compete with the Soviet Union.

Needless to say, this does not mean that we are witnessing a new era of the Cold War. On the contrary, competition for resources, the need for arms control agreements and the shared interest of the superpowers in curbing nuclear proliferation might in fact create grounds for increased American-Soviet cooperation in some areas of the world. However, it does mean that "high politics" will continue to play an important part in American foreign policy, unless the U.S. decides to completely opt out of an active role in many parts of the world and, in the process, endanger some of the most vital interests of her main allies, Western Europe and Japan. It also means that the U.S. will probably adopt a different approach (which it has in fact already done in some manner for quite some time more or less successfully), combining increased cooperation with the Soviet Union on some issues (for example arms control), while continuing severe competition with it in other areas. In addition, it means that the U.S. will continue to attach great importance to its strategic worldwide interests. The credibility of its commitments will be an important factor in this strategy. Furthermore, if the U.S. continues to consider nuclear proliferation as a major destabilizing and dangerous development, it would perforce have to continue to honor its defense treaties with potential nuclear powers even if for many other reasons it might prefer to opt out of them. For the abrogation of such treaties would increase the motivation among erstwhile allies to develop an independent nuclear capability.[14] In summary then, it is possible to argue that the U.S. will have to continue to honor its defense treaty obligations and signals to this effect will probably be issued. The Taiwan case will most probably remain an exception.

In the Middle East context it could be argued that, to the extent that the saliency of the Arab-Israel conflict diminished in regional politics, the credibility of the A.I.D.T. as a deterrent would increase. The potential military attack on Israel would then result from tensions arising from the complex relations in a multipolar system in which there is always a "floating" potential for conflict and escalation, more than from the traditional Arab-Israeli conflict. Under such circumstances, the U.S. would be less constrained in exercising its commitment as such an exercise would not automatically lead to a general alienation of the whole Arab world.

The credibility of the American undertaking is also connected with the overall relationship between Israel and the U.S. Various studies have indicated that the effectiveness of military alliances, both as a deterrent and, if deterrence fails, as military intervention, depends to a large extent on the general close relations between the parties to the alliance.[15] If the overall scope and intensity of the international interactions between the allies is high, there is a good likelihood that the alliance will be effective. Intensive relations demonstrate that the allies have strong shared and mutual interests, thus signaling to potential opponents the stakes that are involved for the senior ally in maintaining its interests in the junior ally. In that sense, the special relationship existing between Israel and the U.S. is a demonstration of the links existing between the two countries and can serve as a firm basis for the development of a credible formal relationship. Moreover, the very signing of the A.I.D.T. would, on its part, reemphasize this special relationship.

Another component in the equation of the credibility of the deterrence posture of the U.S. is related to the actual forces which the U.S. may be able to dispatch to the Middle East in times of crisis and war. One of the significant developments in the Middle East is the extensive increase in the conventional military capabilities of the regional powers. The size of forces available to the three Arab confrontation states—Egypt, Syria and Jordan—is itself amazing. To these one would have to add parts of the inventories of other Arab states in case they join in war. According to one estimate[16] the confrontation states alone have among them about 640,000 men in their standing armed forces, some 1,400 combat aircraft and close to 5,000 tanks. If one adds parts of the capabilities of Iraq and Saudi Arabia, the figures mount higher. Ostensibly, compared to such a concentration of military capabilities, the available American forces in the Mediterranean basin appear limited.[17] This, however, is a mistaken analysis. The Israeli military capability is so formidable that the need for massive American military involvement would probably not arise. Even if a change in the balance of conventional forces in the Middle East does develop, it will be an extremely gradual process and much uncertainty remains regarding its significance. In other words, if at any point in the future Israeli superiority were to diminish or even disappear, the process would be very slow and irregular. Moreover, it would not mean that the Arab forces would be able to crush Israel in a sudden surprise attack. What it would mean is that a war might drag on and on and would probably degenerate into a war of attrition, with the Israeli forces gradually losing ground to their opponents. Both sides would incur heavy losses and the Arabs would probably be divested of much of their capability in the process. In such circumstances an American intervention—even if limited—would be of decisive importance. Another important form of American support relates to a war in which Israel is superior but could nevertheless benefit from extensive aid through reconnaissance missions or even limited selected air strikes against important enemy targets. These operations would not involve major capabilities but could be of significant help to Israel.

Logistical Support

Equally important is the institutionalization of arms transfer to Israel in an extended war, as was already demonstrated during the 1973 war. In that war, the airlift (and eventual sealift) to Israel was decided upon largely as a result of the Soviet airlift to the Arab countries. In the future there might be other scenarios. One possibility is the accumulation of large stocks of arms in the Arab countries which would allow them to continue fighting without an airlift from the Soviet Union. It is not clear what the position taken by an American administration would be without an A.I.D.T., but with an

A.I.D.T. the supply of arms would be almost automatic. It should be emphasized, however, that such arrangements necessitate the creation of permanent mechanisms for strategic and operational planning which would operate on an ongoing basis and be involved in long-term planning. Combined American-Israeli exercises at least for logistical support are also required.[18]

Changes in American Force Deployment

Although as noted it is not very likely that actual American forces would be called upon to intervene in case of hostilities, nevertheless it is important to enhance the American "reach capability." This applies in the first place to the bodies that would provide the logistical support, then to selected units that might be called upon to intervene in a limited way, and lastly to the general capability of intervening en masse. The relevant measures would be: further increasing the refueling capability and the long-range mobility in general of the Military Airlift Command (steps in this direction are already being taken as a result of the experience of the 1973 War[19]); increasing American air capability in the Mediterranean basin; earmarking some U.S. forces deployed in Western Europe for contingency missions in the Middle East; similarly, earmarking either some units of the army Strategic Reserve or of the Marine Corps units deployed in the U.S. for contingency missions in the Middle East. To facilitate quick deployment of these units, stocks of armor, spare parts and ammunition could be placed permanently in Israel.

Deterrence against Soviet Direct Intervention or by Proxy

Another important function of the A.I.D.T. would be to strengthen U.S. deterrence of a possible Soviet intervention against Israel. The broad possibilities of such intervention are as follows:

(a) If an Arab state is on the verge of suffering a devastating defeat at the hands of Israel, the objective of the intervention would be to halt the Israeli military operations and/or to compel Israel to withdraw from the territories occupied.

(b) If a war of attrition develops and Israeli limited operations threaten a particular regime in the Arab state (for example, the Israeli deep penetration bombing in 1970), Soviet intervention might ensue.

(c) When a crisis situation develops and the Arab states summon Soviet troops as a deterrent against an Israeli attack, military clashes between Israel and Soviet troops might then develop.

(d) Air and sea clashes might develop between small Israeli and Soviet units as a result of a deliberate Soviet small-scale intervention in a regional war, or of miscalculation, for example, if Soviet naval units are deployed in Arab harbors.

The probability of deliberate Soviet massive intervention—in conjunction with Arab forces—in order to defeat Israel completely is extremely low. The Soviet threat to intervene in situations (a) and (b) is quite credible, but has lower credibility in situations (c) and (d). The threshhold for intervention by proxy (for example through Cubans) would be somewhat lower.

Generally speaking, it could be argued that the A.I.D.T. will diminish the threat of intervention in each one of these cases. The Soviet decision makers will have to take into consideration the fact that the U.S. is bound by its formal commitment to Israel and will have to intervene. The probability of such American intervention would be higher than at present for two major reasons: First, an A.I.D.T. should (and probably would) incorporate high level politico-strategic understanding and cooperation between the two parties. If a crisis and war situation were to develop, it would seem that Israel acted in consultation with the U.S. and hence, the U.S. would have apparently considered the possibility of escalation leading to possible Soviet intervention and nevertheless agreed to Israeli moves, thus having already taken the calculated risk of Soviet moves and being ready to confront them. Secondly, the A.I.D.T. being a formal guarantee, must be honored by the U.S., otherwise the credibility of its commitments in other parts of the world would be called into question.

The politico-strategic cooperation between the U.S. and Israel, entailed by the A.I.D.T. would diminish the likelihood of Soviet intervention, increase the deterrent effect against Arab attacks on Israel, and would also impose constraints on some military operations by Israel. The combined effect of all this is increased stability in the region. The third point is of particular interest. An Israeli option to preempt and launch first strikes in a situation of crisis might act as a deterrent against some Arab military moves. Thus, the A.I.D.T. might further encroach on Israeli freedom to take preemptive action in a serious situation, and hence adversely effect Israeli security. On the other hand, preemption might occur on the basis of Israeli misinterpretation of the nature of Arab military moves, for example, if the Arabs were not planning a war and conducted military exercises as part of a bargaining process. A partial solution to this problem may be found in a system which would link the demilitarization of the territories with a system of *casus belli*, and the A.I.D.T. Freedom for Israel to intervene militarily in the demilitarized zones in the event of an Arab state violating the demilitarization should be recognized and incorporated into the A.I.D.T. In other words, the A.I.D.T. should refer to a system of legitimate Israeli *casus belli*.

Institutionalizing the American-Israeli "Special Relationship"

The A.I.D.T. would institutionalize the existing special relationship. This relationship has developed gradually as a result of widespread strong sympathy and identification with Israel on the part of large sectors in the American public, to which were added over the years strategic and realpolitik considerations. Then, again, there existed a positive feedback system in which prior American commitment enhanced present and future ones. The special relationship has come under growing pressure since 1967. American interests in the Arab world clash to some extent with U.S.-Israel relations. This was caused by the increased saliency of the conflict in various Arab states resulting from continued Israeli occupation of the territories. There were, of course, factors which alleviated these strains but the latter became far more apparent since 1973 and up to the Camp David agreements. Soviet influence has receded; the current Israeli government is taking an unrealistic and dangerous course; and the influence of oil has increased. However, with Sādāt's visit to Jerusalem and the Israeli-Egyptian peace treaty the existing explosive situation has been defused. A comprehensive peace settlement would, of course, again strengthen the special relationship as it would remove the strains mentioned. However, even then, there is the danger that because of the increased influence of the Arab oil countries the special relationship might nevertheless be weakened. It is therefore important to institutionalize it. Such institutionalization would have its own impact on the American public and decision makers. It would have a positive impact, even if at any point in the foreseeable future American and Israeli interests were to clash strongly, a situation which indeed is less likely once a settlement has been achieved.

Thus the A.I.D.T. could also ensure continued large-scale financial and military support to Israel. Such an American undertaking must be an integral part of the A.I.D.T. Indeed, if the A.I.D.T. came into force, the U.S. would have an additional reason to continue its support. For without such support, Israel's deterrence posture would be weakened and thus one of the constraints on an Arab decision to go to war at any point in the future would weaken considerably. Then, the probability of an Arab attack would become greater and consequently the necessity of American involvement. In order to avoid this, the U.S. must necessarily prefer a strong Israel.

The U.S. would, of course, have some benefits from the A.I.D.T. in addition to securing a peace settlement. One possible development—to be discussed below—is the emergence of a stable and strong American-oriented bloc in the Middle East. Another is an additional hedge against nuclear proliferation in the Middle East. Finally, an A.I.D.T. would also ensure close cooperation with the strongest military power in the Middle East, Israel. In the conditions which would be obtained after a political settlement, and with the saliency of the Arab-Israel conflict reduced, such cooperation could have important strategic advantages in regional terms for the U.S.

SOME POLITICAL IMPLICATIONS

Any predictor about the future system of political and strategic relations in the Middle East is liable to be hazardous. At the same time, some tentative looking into the future might be helpful. The starting point would be an analysis of the structure of inter-Arab relations. Since the emergence of the modern state system in the Middle East following World War II, these relations have been characterized by very active foreign policies and continued competition among the leading Arab powers for positions of hegemony in the Arab world. One of the main features of their interactions was a high rate of formation of coalitions and alliances of different types and rapid shifting of members from one of these alliances to another. The fast changes in alliances created a high level of flexibility in the system. Coalitions (formal and informal) continued to be formed and dissolved, friendships of today very quickly turned into heated rivalries, and vice versa. No one state was allowed a position of predominance, and whenever one (or a coalition) tried to achieve such a position, a competing and counterbalancing one emerged. Thus, a sophisticated, intricate "balance of power" system operated in the region. Israel was also partly involved in it, through the de facto guarantees extended to Jordan and Lebanon against hostile Arab intervention in these countries.

An American-oriented Bloc

The Saudi-Egyptian semi-alliance that emerged in 1973, coupled with the increasing power of Saudi Arabia in international life, as well as President Sādāt's peace initiative and the prospect for an Israeli-Egyptian peace agreement created some interesting options for the future. One of them is the formation of a politically American-oriented bloc comprising some of the strongest regional powers in the Middle East and its periphery: Saudi Arabia, Egypt and tacitly (or perhaps eventually also explicitly) Israel as well. Other states such as Jordan would also join. The signing of the A.I.D.T. would promote such a development.

Another possible outcome is linked to the first in a different way, but might have some counterproductive implications for Israel. During his visit to Israel President Sādāt stated that he would accept any system of guarantees for Israel: American, joint superpower, four-power, or U.N. He did however add that Egypt would like a symmetrical system. It is not clear whether Egypt would really insist on such a symmetrical treatment. (Indeed, previously Sādāt had maintained that he would oppose the signing of a defense treaty with any superpower. He would be interested in guarantees only if Israel were to receive them.) Moreover, it is not clear whether the U.S. would have to comply with such demands if they were indeed made. A great deal depends on the process of negotiations with Israel. Israel is at present in a paradoxical situation. She has excellent cards: her occupation of the territories and military superiority. However, both these advantages are politically effective only for bargaining. Israel will eventually have to give up the territories although she can demand a very high price for them. Israel could also use her forces, but the political benefits from such are in most cases extremely limited or even counterproductive. Thus, her military power is effective for either real defensive war (even if used in an operationally offensive model), or as a threat in order to achieve political concessions. It could then be argued that provided Israel gives up the territories (and this, in fact, would not hamper her security and at least on one front would enhance it) she can demand many political and strategic considerations. One of them is an asymmetrical treaty with the U.S. However, if Israel fails, and a symmetrical system emerges, this would probably have the following consequences. In the first place, it would become much more of a real possibility that Israel would join the previously noted American-oriented bloc. Consequently, the danger of an Israeli-Egyptian military clash would further diminish because of the new political alignment. On the other hand, Israel would cease to be the preferred benefactor of high technology weapons in the Middle East. Also, the American guarantee for Israel, in the remote case of an Israeli-Egyptian clash, would become more equivocal.

A Flexible System

The continued shifting of coalitions in the Arab world and the subtle and intricate set of "rules of the game" operating in the Middle East up to the present have a certain potential for instability. On the other hand, it could be argued that with some important modifications and the enhancement of some features of this system, stability might in fact increase. As a first step, the modifications include the acceptance by the Arabs of Israel as a legitimate and full "member" of the Middle East flexible system. Until recently this seemed a remote possibility but it has become much more probable with Sādāt's new policy and the backing it received from several other Arab states. Another modification concerns the achievements of a more stable system of coalitions, thus reducing the instability resulting from the frequent coalitional changes. Another condition is that nuclear weapons should not be introduced into the area. Lastly, the superpowers should agree to reduce their direct political and military intervention. Such a system requires a high level of sophistication and subtlety on the part of regional decision makers. Obviously an A.I.D.T. would diminish the likelihood of such a development. However, as the emergence of such a flexible *and* stable system does not at present appear to be very probable, this particular cost does not seem to be very high.

Nuclear Proliferation

An A.I.D.T., the emergence of an American-oriented bloc, and a possible system of Soviet guarantees to some Middle Eastern countries, or defense treaties with them, would diminish the likelihood of nuclear proliferation in the Arab world. Since my assessment is that proliferation would constitute a major destabilizing development, it seems then, that the A.I.D.T. would have an additional stabilizing function.

However, the possibility exists that the A.I.D.T. would limit the Israel nuclear option but would leave open the possibility for nuclear proliferation in the Arab world. As things stand at present, the likelihood of proliferation in the Arab world via independent development is rather low. Even the Iraqi project will become significant in this respect only in the mid 1980s and is subject to some safeguards. Theoretically, however, other possibilities exist, such as the direct sale of bombs to rich Arab countries. If this were to happen, the A.I.D.T. system would have to be reviewed.

SOME FURTHER ASPECTS OF A.I.D.T.

It seems reasonable to assume that Israel would prefer to increase her own freedom of action within the framework of an A.I.D.T. system, while the U.S. would prefer to impose a greater measure of control. Similarly the U.S. would prefer to have less binding clauses on her own spectrum of decisions. This dilemma is well known and solutions would have to be worked out. Because of the probable American insistence on control, some limitations would no doubt be imposed on Israel's range of military options. As against this, it could be argued that the additional security gained through the A.I.D.T. would more than compensate for them. Moreover, Israel has in any case become so dependent on the U.S. that she cannot initiate major military operations without prior consultation with the U.S. Without consultations there are likely to be heavy political costs involved.

A different question applies to Soviet reactions. We have already mentioned the possibility of Soviet guarantees to some Arab countries as a possible (but not inevitable) consequence of an A.I.D.T.

If this were to happen, there is a possibility of development of a model of "partition" of the Middle East. I shall not go into this now, since it requires a separate discussion. A more immediate problem is how an A.I.D.T. would affect Israeli-Soviet relations. It could be argued that it would further strain them. It is reasonable, however, to contend that an A.I.D.T. would strengthen Israel's posture vis-à-vis the Soviet Union through the enhancement of Israeli security. This strong position would allow the development of political relations beyond the security dimension. The experience of Western European countries (although they have a different context of relations with the superpowers) is indicative. Once the military status quo in Europe had been assured through military stability dependent on American guarantees (although it requires permanent attention and handling), Western European powers were able to develop more relaxed relations with the Soviet Union.

Indeed, the A.I.D.T. must emphasize that its objectives lie within a regional context. It should serve as a deterrent against the Soviet Union as well, if it tried to attack Israel, but not a defense instrument within the American-Soviet context of relations.

Every major measure in foreign and defense policy has benefits and costs. In this paper the discussion focused primarily on some of the benefits that Israel could get from an A.I.D.T. The costs to Israel and the U.S. and some additional benefits to both countries have not been discussed at all or only briefly. A comprehensive balance sheet of benefits/costs has not been proposed here. In any case a policy decision on such matters is based on assessments which could not be validated scientifically. At the same time, it appears that an A.I.D.T. would constitute an important additional contribution to Israeli security.

NOTES

This paper is based on research conducted at the Center for Strategic Studies (CSS), Tel Aviv University. A more comprehensive study on the same subject is being published by the Center for Strategic Studies in its series of CSS papers.

1. Indeed, several newspaper reports at the time of writing suggested a growing administration interest in the idea of an A.I.D.T. According to one, the president has actually instructed various agencies to conduct

studies of the various implications of an A.I.D.T.; see *Yediot Ahronot*, 2 June 1978.

2. On this see Michael Bar-Zohar, *Ben-Gurion*, vol. 2 (in Hebrew) (Tel Aviv 1977) pp. 902-906. Bar-Zohar points out that the initial initiative for this was a British one. Ben-Gurion apparently already then preferred a treaty with the U.S. but became interested in the British possibility.

3. See, e.g.: *Divrey HaKnesset* (in Hebrew), vol. 18 (1 June 1955), pp. 1755-1759, 2102; vol. 37 (7 August 1963), p. 2629; vol. 61 (14 July 1971), p. 3279.

4. See Bar-Zohar, vol. 3, pp. 1316-21, 1347-48, 1352-53, 1362-63, 1400.

5. A useful survey of American attitudes towards the idea of an American guarantee to Israel or a defense treaty with her, is included in Mark A. Bruzonsky, *A United States Guarantee for Israel?* (Washington, D.C.: The Center for Strategic and International Studies, Georgetown University, 1976). One of the representatives of the first group is Senator Fulbright. His original proposal is included in Congressional Record, 24 August 1970, p. 29805. Richard Ullman represents the second group. See his "After Rabat: Middle East Risks and American Roles," *Foreign Affairs*, January 1975 and "Alliance with Israel?" *Foreign Policy*, Summer 1975. Alan Dowty in his *The Role of Great Power Guarantees in International Relations* (Jerusalem, 1974) discusses the problem on the background of an historical analysis of the efficacy and credibility of international guarantees in general. Michla Pomerance in her *American Guarantees to Israel and the Law of American Foreign Relations*, Jerusalem Papers on Peace Problems, The Leonard Davis Institute for International Relations (Jerusalem 1974) discusses the problem from an international legal point of view. Lastly, the famous Brookings Institution Report on the Middle East again raises the idea of a guarantee to Israel but leaves completely open the question of what kind it would be: a bilateral defense treaty, a unilateral American guarantee or joint guarantees by the two superpowers to Israel alone or to several Arab countries as well.

6. See, e.g., the article by Amnon Sela in *Davar*, 26 September 1977, and the articles by Shimon Peres, *Ma'ariv*, 5 May 1978 and Itzhak Rabin in *Yediot Ahronot*, 5 May 1978.

7. The Memorandum for Agreement is almost such a guarantee but it lacks the endorsement of the Congress.

8. Thus, e.g., two committees could be set up, one to deal with high level political coordination, the other with military affairs. Both might handle complaints about violations of demilitarized zones and other secu-

rity measures agreed upon between Israel and Arab states. The military committee might deal with military coordination, contingency plans and joint exercises.

9. This school now has the upper hand in Israel, as proved by the Camp David agreements and the Israeli-Egyptian peace agreement.

10. See, e.g., Dan Horowitz, *Israel's Concept of Defensible Borders,* Jerusalem Papers on Peace Problems, No. 16 (Jerusalem 1975); Steven Rosen, *Military Geography and the Military Balance in the Arab-Israeli Conflict,* Jerusalem Papers on Peace Problems, No. 21 (Jerusalem 1977); Yair Evron, *The Demilitarization of Sinai,* Jerusalem Papers on Peace Problems, No. 11 (Jerusalem 1975); and id., *The Role of Arms Control in the Middle East, Adelphi Papers,* No. 138 (International Institute of Strategic Studies [I.I.S.S.], London, 1977); Yigal Allon, "Israel: The Case for Defensible Borders," *Foreign Affairs,* 55, 1 (October 1976).

11. This analysis relates primarily to Sinai, where demilitarization would give Israel several clear advantages over the current situation in which Israeli forces are deployed in most of Sinai. For details, see Y. Evron, *The Demilitarization of the Sinai,* op. cit.

12. See, e.g., Yair Evron, "Great Powers Military Intervention in the Middle East," in M. Leitenberg (ed.), *Great Powers Intervention in the Middle East* (New York, Pergamon Press) to be published.

13. Africa also appears as such a region. Indeed, at the time of writing, it seems that the U.S. is searching for ways to halt Soviet intervention in African affairs.

14. The intended abrogation of the defense treaty with Taiwan does indeed add to the Taiwanese motivation to "go nuclear." It is however debatable whether Taiwan will go all the way in this direction. For one thing, Taiwan still considers the U.S. its main military ally and for good reason. For another, the development of a nuclear capability which could deter China is a major operation and appears to be beyond Taiwan's capability (unless the simplistic approach of General Gallois is accepted).

15. See for example Bruce M. Russet, *Power and Community in the World Politics* (San Francisco 1974), pp. 212-215.

16. See *The Military Balance 1977-1978* (I.I.S.S., London, 1977).

17. For detailed information about U.S. military installations in the Mediterranean area see *United States Military Installations and Objectives in the Mediterranean,* a report prepared for the Subcommittee on Europe and the Middle East of the Committee on International Relations (March 1977) pp. 8-47. For the composition and strength of the Sixth Fleet, see

the annual *The Military Balance* (I.I.S.S. London).

18. The Memorandum on Agreement specifies an American commitment to supply Israel in time of need. It therefore goes a long way towards what is required. As mentioned, it still lacks the power of a formal treaty.

19. See *United States Military Installations and Objectives in the Mediterranean,* op cit., p. 51.

International Guarantees and the
Middle East Conflict

Yoram Dinstein

The more complex international conflicts are, the greater the faith
among the uninitiated that somehow all the difficulties would disappear if only they were dealt with in treaty form. Laymen suffer
from the two common diseases of pactomania and resolutionitis:
they believe that pacts and resolutions per se can solve problems.
This is particularly true of the most important treaties of all,
namely, peace treaties. It takes international lawyers to remind the
non-professionals that all treaties, including peace treaties, are
merely pieces of paper. International lawyers are not impressed even
if a treaty is engraved on parchment. They know that most wars
begin between states that have already concluded peace treaties. The
trust in treaties usually grows in inverse ratio to the observer's prox-
imity to the treaty. The lawyer who handles it from up close per-
ceives that what counts in the final analysis is not form but
substance.

If this is true in general, it is true with a vengeance as regards
treaties of guarantee. First, a few words about terminology. What is
a guarantee? Essentially, it is "an assurance for the fulfillment of a
certain condition." [1] Such assurances may be expressed in a number
of ways. Thus, in a store one may encounter the sign "satisfaction
guaranteed or money back within seven days." In this context the
guarantee is simply a condition of sale. The guarantor is the vendor
who guarantees his own product or workmanship by a promise to
refund the purchase money if the buyer is not satisfied. What an
assurance of this kind actually guarantees is peace of mind. For our
part, we are interested more in another type of assurance: one that
guarantees not only peace of mind but also real peace.

In international affairs, when two states conclude an agreement, neither party is expected to issue a verbal guarantee that it is going to keep its word or deliver certain goods. That is simply taken for granted. At times, however, one of the parties may place in guarantee, as a surety bond, a certain territory or property. For example, Article 428 of the 1919 Peace Treaty of Versailles[2] provided that the German territory situated west of the Rhine (the Rhineland) would remain occupied for a period of fifteen years by the armies of the victorious Allied and Associated Powers, as a guarantee for the implementation of Germany's undertakings under the treaty. Again, this is not the type of guarantee which interests us in this paper (though Israel and Egypt could theoretically solve the problem of the Pithat Rafiah area in Northern Sinai by placing it in Israeli hands for a fixed term as a guarantee for Egypt's compliance with the peace treaty contemplated). What concerns us here is an international guarantee in the sense of a trilateral transaction,[3] whereby State A is obligated vis-à-vis State B to respond in a certain way to the conduct of State C (which is not necessarily a party to the arrangement). A guarantee in this sense may be economic in nature: State A is obligated vis-à-vis State B to respond in a certain way to the conduct of State C (which is not necessarily a party to the amount outstanding). But, although this is a common transaction among private persons, it is quite rare in interstate relations. The usual international guarantee is not economic but political and military in character. It relates to the sovereign existence of a state, to its territorial integrity or to specific boundaries. The meaning of the guarantee is that, should State B (say, Israel) be attacked by State C (e.g., Egypt), State A (for instance, the United States) would extend to it military aid with a view to repelling the aggressor.

The guarantee is ordinarily given by a Big Power (capable of marshaling the forces necessary)—or by a number of states—to a small state (which might not be able to stem the tide of an armed attack alone). It is generally issued as an integral part of an overall political settlement, of territorial modifications or of an arrangement of permanent neutrality.[4] The guarantee may be given *erga omnes* (against one and all) or be confined to an attack from a single specific source. If Israel is taken as an example, the United States may guarantee it against attack either from any source whatsoever or only from Egypt. Should an attack be launched against Israel by, say, Saudi Arabia (or entities which do not even amount to states—and do not represent Egypt), the guarantee will be triggered if it is the former type but not if it is the latter.

Although a guarantee may be issued in the form of a binding unilateral declaration,[5] or a decision of the Security Council, it is generally incorporated in a treaty between the guarantor and the guaranteed state. We must distinguish treaties of guarantee from two related though dissimilar categories of treaties, namely, mutual aid treaties and military alliances.

A mutual aid treaty is a bilateral or multilateral treaty in which the contracting parties proclaim that an armed attack against one of them will be regarded as an armed attack against the others, and undertake to aid one another in such circumstances. The watchword is, like that of Dumas' Three Musketeers, "all for one, one for all." An example of a bilateral mutual aid treaty is the agreement concluded between the United States and South Korea in 1953.[6] An illustration of a multilateral mutual aid treaty is that of the 1947 Rio de Janeiro Inter-American Treaty of Reciprocal Assistance, which establishes the basic principle as follows in Article 3 (1):

"The High Contracting Parties agree that an armed attack by any State against an American State shall be considered as an attack against all the American States and, consequently, each one of the said Contracting Parties undertakes to assist in meeting the attack in the exercise of the inherent right of individual or collective self-defense recognized by Article 51 of the Charter of the United Nations."[7]

The trouble with mutual aid treaties is that they do not always work. A state usually acts in conformity with its political interests at the time of action rather than in the past (when the treaty was concluded). Hence, a state may rush to help another even in the absence of a mutual aid treaty, and may fail to come to the succor of yet another with which it does have such a treaty. If the state refuses to act, it can be relied upon to find an escape clause in the text of the treaty. Even if the treaty is drafted in an unequivocal manner, and does not leave legal loopholes enabling a contracting party to decline aid altogether, it is incapable of resolving in advance practical questions—which in the reality of an armed attack assume crucial significance—such as the speed with which the military aid is to be offered, its dimensions and form. After all, aid can be sent instantaneously by airlift, but it can also be sent on camelback or by sailboat and arrive after the war is over. How many troops will be required to honor the commitment of assistance, several army corps or a corporal's squad? And, assuming that a figure is established, what should be the combat readiness and equipment of the soldiers? Is it necessary to send armored units and paratroopers or will second-echelon garrison troops suffice? The state sending the assistance and the one receiving it are likely to have conflicting viewpoints about what is required in the particular circumstances. Hence, a mutual aid treaty as such cannot give adequate assurance that sufficient aid will actually be rendered when called for.

Admittedly, contracting parties do not always seek ways to avoid implementing a mutual aid treaty. The classical case is that of the Agreement of Mutual Assistance concluded between Britain and Poland in 1939[8], the implementation of which turned the Nazi invasion of Poland into World War II. But one must pay attention to the relevant dates: the Agreement was done on 25 August, the Nazi invasion of Poland began on 1 September, and the British Declaration of Was was issued on 3 September. That is to say, it all happened within a span of ten days. The greater the lapse of time after the conclusion of the mutual aid treaty, the fewer the chances for its actual implementation. At any rate, the aid Britain extended to Poland was nominal and failed to save it. Ultimately, Polish soldiers fought for Britain instead of British soldiers fighting for Poland.

Another type of treaty is the military alliance, of which there are two varieties. At times, a military alliance is struck after hostilities have already begun. This is the case when two or more states fall victim (simultaneously or consecutively) to an armed attack by the same aggressor. It must be borne in mind that even when states find themselves cobelligerents against a common enemy, they are not always prepared to cooperate. If there is some historical enmity or contemporary political competition between them, each may choose to defend itself independently of the other. But often states under attack act on the basis of the principle that "the enemy of my enemy is my friend," and, even if peacetime relations between them have not been ideal, sign a military alliance. This is what happened, for instance, in the course of World War II, when Nazi Germany invaded the Soviet Union in June 1941. By July of the same year the U.S.S.R. and Britain (two countries which had not exactly been friendly up to that point) had made an Agreement for Joint Action in the War against Germany.[9] Later, in May 1942, they concluded a Treaty of Alliance in the War against Hitlerite Germany and Her Associates in Europe and of Collaboration and Mutual Assistance Thereafter.[10] It is noteworthy that the alliance was bilateral (i.e., it did not include other countries fighting against Germany like the United States), and it referred only to the war against Germany (thereby excluding Japan with which Britain, but not the U.S.S.R., was then at war).

The second kind of a military alliance is concluded in peacetime, in anticipation of war. It is designed to surmount a major obstacle encountered by mutual aid treaties, namely, that without prior coordination in peacetime between the armed forces of the different countries concerned, it is not easy for those armies to collaborate in the fight against an aggressor, even if the political decision is taken to activate the mutual aid treaty. A military alliance of this type is based on the idea of *si vis pacem, para bellum* (if you want peace, prepare for war), and it is not confined to an abstract commitment on mutual aid to be activated when hostilities erupt. The alliance goes beyond this potential obligation and sets in motion in peacetime actual preparations against the possibility of an armed attack, by creating a joint military command, establishing military bases, holding joint maneuvers, exchanging intelligence information, etc. Although within the framework of a military alliance, too, the political decision on whether or not to proceed to war in support of a state under attack is still theoretically at the discretion of each ally,[11] in fact the armed forces of the alliance may be so closely intertwined that an armed attack against one state is liable to draw all the allies into the vortex of war without giving any of them an opportunity to make a decision on whether it desires to go along.

It is not always possible to tell on the face of a given document if it is a mutual aid treaty or a military alliance, nor is the basic text always the determining factor. The basic text may be limited to enunciating the guiding principle of mutual aid and structuring central organs, whereas the details of military cooperation may be settled in supplementary agreements or in practice. An example is the 1949 North Atlantic Treaty,[12] which in Article 5[13] promulgates the principle of mutual aid in a formulation similar to that of Article 3

(1) of the Rio de Janeiro Inter-American Treaty. The North Atlantic Treaty further provides, in Article 3, that the parties "will maintain and develop their individual and collective capacity to resist armed attack"[14] and sets up central organs in Article 9.[15] These innocuous clauses have produced the North Atlantic Treaty Organization (NATO), which has evolved over the years (particularly in the aftermath of the Korean War) and emerged as a sophisticated military alliance with a joint military command, joint bases and so forth.

Mutual aid treaties and military alliances do not have to be aimed at every eventuality of armed attack against one of the contracting parties, but may be restricted to a specific case. A specific case which activates the commitment of the contracting parties to come to the assistance of the state under attack is called a *casus foederis*.[16] Sometimes the obligation of assistance is limited to an armed attack by a certain state (and no other), or to an armed attack, from whatever quarter, in a given region (and no other). Thus, in 1925, two mutual aid treaties were made in Locarno between France, on the one hand, and Poland and Czechoslovakia, on the other, in which the contracting parties undertook to extend immediate assistance to one another in case of an attack by Germany.[17] Under the aforementioned Article 5 of the North Atlantic Treaty, an armed attack against one of the contracting parties shall be considered an attack against them all only if it is carried out in Europe or North America, and not in other regions of the world.

A military alliance may be based on a Big Power (like the United States in NATO), whose military might constitutes the mainstay of the alliance, or on the joint strength of numerous small states, all of which contribute more or less equally to its vigor. But in all instances military alliances, like mutual aid treaties, are founded on the principle of reciprocity. A Big Power like the United State does not merely provide a nuclear umbrella for its allies: it also benefits from their active support (contribution of armed forces) and passive assistance (permission to use military bases).

A treaty of guarantee looks superficially like a mutual aid treaty, but there is a cardinal difference between them. In a mutual aid treaty (as in a military alliance) all contracting parties are duty bound to rush to each other's assistance in case of an armed attack against one of them. Conversely, in a treaty of guarantee only the guarantor state undertakes to help the guaranteed state in case of an armed attack and not vice versa. In other words, a treaty of guarantee is unidirectional in substance: the traffic of assistance goes only one way. True, in some instances the instrument is a complex treaty embodying mixed components of guarantee and mutual aid. An example is the 1925 Locarno Treaty of Mutual Guarantee,[18] concluded between Germany, Belgium, France, Britain and Italy. In Article 1,[19] the contracting parties collectively guaranteed the borders between Germany and Belgium as well as between Germany and France. From the viewpoint of France and Belgium (each being both a guaranteeing and a guaranteed state) it was in effect a mutual aid treaty; but from the standpoint of Britain and Italy it was a genuine treaty of guarantee. The term mutual guarantee appearing in the title of the Locarno Treaty actually combines two separate and independent concepts of guarantee and mutual aid.

The point is that if a treaty of guarantee were concluded between the United States and Israel, only the United States would have to come to the rescue of Israel should it be attacked. On the other hand, if the two countries were to enter upon a mutual aid treaty or a military alliance, Israel would also have to assist the United States should the latter be embroiled in war.

Insofar as Israel is concerned, the prospect of international guarantees raises three basic questions: What will the scope of the guarantees be, who will give them, and what will their outcome be?

As to their scope, the guarantees, if meaningful and not just lip service, will have to be military in nature. That is to say, they will have to assure Israel of Big Power military aid if it is subjected to an armed attack. By military aid we do not mean supplies or equipment alone, but genuine expeditionary forces. Needless to say, eliciting such a guarantee will not be a simple matter, and formulating watertight provisions is all but impossible. The quantitative and qualitative definition of acts amounting to an armed attack may also become a bone of contention. Will the guarantee cover small-scale incidents, including guerrilla raids? What about infringements of freedom of navigation on the high seas? How should violations of the status of demilitarized zones be regarded? These are all thorny problems, not lending themselves to simple solutions when war looms. Not every eventuality can be predicted when the guarantee is drafted, and in any case actual occurrences can be interpreted and evaluated in more than one way. From the lofty vantage point of a

Big Power, most border incidents in far-away countries are viewed with a certain degree of philosophical equanimity. What is trivial for a Big Power may nevertheless be considered a *casus belli* by Israel. Who will judge the propriety of activating the guarantee?

Secondly, should the guarantee be given to Israel by a single Big Power (namely, the United States) or by all (including, in particular, the U.S.S.R.)? It may seem that the greater the number of Big Powers appending their names to the guarantee, the better. But experience has demonstrated that this is an instance where more means less. Suppose that all the Big Powers were to guarantee Israel's borders and that Egypt attacked. What happens if the U.S.S.R. declines to render assistance to Israel? Can the United States intervene by itself? Many international lawyers are of the opinion that if the guarantee is collective, it implies a duty to act together or not at all, so that one Big Power—by dragging its feet—may thwart action by the rest.[20] Admittedly, the legal obstacle can be surmounted by adopting a formula whereby the guarantee is issued by the Big Powers "jointly and severally," so that they can act either in conjunction with one another or separately.[21] But the issue is not confined to a mere legalism. When a number of states are thrown together as guarantors, at the very least one expects them to consult each other and compare notes when the time for action arrives. Since inaction is always a temptation in such circumstances, and responsibility may be shared, Israel may find itself fighting alone and getting the run-around in its call for help.

Moreover, a treaty of guarantee—like a mutual aid treaty and a military alliance—may serve as an excuse for interference in the internal affairs of a contracting party to the instrument, particularly a guaranteed state. An illustration is the Turkish invasion of Cyprus, in 1974, designed to protect the Turkish minority in the island. Legally speaking, Turkey relied on two treaties concluded in Nicosia in 1960: (a) a Treaty of Guarantee of Cyprus, in which Greece, Turkey and Britain guaranteed the independence, territorial integrity and security of Cyprus;[22] (b) a Treaty of Alliance between Greece, Turkey and Cyprus, setting up a military alliance against aggression aimed at the independence and territorial integrity of Cyprus, in accordance with which Greek and Turkish soldiers were stationed in Cyprus in fixed numbers.[23] If a state (such as Israel) is apprehensive of another country (like the U.S.S.R.), it can only invite trouble by concluding a military alliance, a mutual aid treaty or a treaty of guarantee with that other state. Such a guarantee is apt to become, politically and legally, a Trojan Horse.

The primary question is the third one, relating to the outcome of the guarantee. Owing to its unidirectional nature, a guarantee is usually viewed by the guarantor as a burden weighing it down without any visible advantage. Initially, the Big Power will tend to bear and forbear, recalling the circumstances in which it undertook the guarantee and the reasons why. But before long it is going to feel like the wrestler in the Greek parable, who commenced by carrying a calf on his shoulder and in time found himself holding an ox.

In the absence of a joint command and interlinked forces, the problem of activating the guarantee—even in the clear-cut circumstances of an all-out invasion—may become all but insoluble. Israel can appeal to Washington for help. But only in Western movies does the U.S. cavalry rush to the rescue as soon as the bugle call is sounded. In real life all depends on the powers-that-be in Washington at the time. Plunging into war is no light matter. Nobody can tell now what priorities are going to merit the attention of the president and Congress at an indeterminate future date. Presumably, these will not be the same president and Congress who approved the guarantee when concluded. Their outlook may be different. And if they are not prepared to shed blood to save another country, they will find reasons—legal, ethical and political—to justify a decision not to budge. A guaranteed state is, therefore, in the position of a gambler, playing political roulette for high stakes, unable to tell in advance whether his chips are going to be cashed by the casino.

It is arguable, no doubt, that if an international guarantee per se cannot help Israel, it can do no damage either, and one should not disdain even slight contributions to the country's political and military position. But, psychologically, the quest for guarantees is dangerous. For one thing, the negotiation of a guarantee treaty is likely to eclipse the larger issue of a Middle East settlement, namely, Arab willingness to undertake to live in peace with Israel. The prospect of a guarantee treaty will create a counterproductive atmosphere in which pressure is going to be put on Israel to concede allegedly insignificant points to the Arabs in the light of an insurance policy, as it were, underwritten by the United States. Whenever the Arabs refuse to make a move forward, Israel will be assured that—by way of compensation—the ambit of the American guarantee is going to be expanded. Finally, Israel may find itself holding on to an empty bag of promises, promises. Consequently, if a treaty of guarantee must be concluded with the United States, it had better be negotiated separately and independently, preferably after the settlement with the Arabs has been elaborated to completion. It is essential that the terms of settlement stand on their own feet without leaning on any extrinsic guarantees. The efficacy of the settlement must be gauged on the assumption that no guarantees are necessary or forthcoming.

NOTES

1. *Webster's New Collegiate Dictionary* (Springfield: G. & C. Merriam Co., 1976), p. 509.

2. Versailles Peace Treaty with Germany, 1919, Fred L. Israel, *Major Peace Treaties of Modern History, 1648-1967* (New York: Chelsea House, 1967), vol. 2, pp. 1265, 1524.

3. See Lord McNair, *The Law of Treaties* (London: Oxford University Press, 1961), p. 240.

4. On permanent neutrality, see Yoram Dinstein, *The Internal Powers of the State* (Tel Aviv: Schocken, 1972), pp. 145-148. (Hebrew)

5. On binding unilateral declarations, see Yoram Dinstein, *International Treaties* (Tel Aviv: Schocken, 1974), pp. 14-17. (Hebrew)

6. United States–Republic of Korea, Washington Treaty, 1953, 48 *American Journal of International Law*, Supplement (1953): 147.

7. Rio de Janeiro Inter-American Treaty of Reciprocal Assistance, 1947, 43 *American Journal of International Law*, Supplement (1949): 53, 54.

8. Great Britain–Poland, Agreement of Mutual Assistance, 1939, 35 *American Journal of International Law*, Supplement (1941): 173.

9. Great Britain–U.S.S.R., Agreement for Joint Action in the War against Germany, 1941, 36 *American Journal of International Law*, Supplement (1942): 58.

10. Great Britain–U.S.S.R., Treaty of Alliance in the War against Hitlerite Germany and Her Associates in Europe and of Collaboration and Mutual Assistance Thereafter, 1942, 36 *American Journal of International Law*, Supplement (1942): 216.

11. See Sir W. Eric Beckett, *The North Atlantic Treaty, the Brussels Treaty and the Charter of the United Nations* (London: Stevens 1950), p. 28.

12. North Atlantic Treaty, 1949, 43 *American Journal of International Law*, Supplement (1949): 1959.

13. Ibid.

14. Ibid., 159.

15. Ibid., 161.

16. See L. Oppenheim, *International Law*, 8th ed. by H. Lauterpacht (London: Longmans, Green, 1955), vol. I, p. 963.

17. France–Poland and France–Czechoslovakia, Locarno Treaties, 1925, 20 *American Journal of International Law*, Supplement (1926): 32-33.

18. Locarno Treaty of Mutual Guarantee, 1925, 20 *American Journal of International Law*, Supplement (1926): 22.

19. Ibid., 23.

20. See McNair, p. 240.

21. See e.g., Article 1 of the Locarno Treaty of Mutual Guarantee, note 19 above.

22. Article 2 of Nicosia Treaty of Guarantee of Cyprus, 1960, 13 *International Legal Materials* (1974): 1259 *id*.

23. Nicosia Treaty of Alliance, 1960, 13 *International Legal Materials* (1974): 1254-1255.

Index

Index

List of Contributors
and Active Participants
in the Colloquium

List of Contributors

UZI B. ARAD
Department of Political Science and Center for Strategic Studies, Tel Aviv University.

YORAM DINSTEIN
Faculty of Law, Tel Aviv University.

YAIR EVRON
Department of Political Science and Center for Strategic Studies, Tel Aviv University.

GIDEON GERA
Shiloah Center for Middle Eastern and African Studies, Tel Aviv University.

GAD G. GILBAR
Department of Middle Eastern History, Haifa University.

ELIE KEDOURIE
School of Economics, University of London.

WILFRID KNAPP
St. Catherine College, Oxford.

BERNARD LEWIS
Institute of Advanced Studies and Near Eastern Studies, Princeton University.

ITAMAR RABINOVICH
Department of Middle Eastern and African History and Shiloah Center for Middle Eastern and African Studies, Tel Aviv University.

BERNARD REICH
Department of Political Science, George Washington University.

YAACOV RO'I
Department of History and the Russian and East European Research Center, Tel Aviv University.

RICHARD ROSECRANCE
Center for International Studies, Cornell University.

SHIMON SHAMIR
Department of Middle Eastern and African History and Shiloah Center for Middle Eastern and African Studies, Tel Aviv University.

HAIM SHAKED
Department of Middle Eastern and African History and Shiloah Center for Middle Eastern and African Studies, Tel Aviv University.

STEVEN L. SPIEGEL
Department of Political Science, University of California, Los Angeles.

UDO STEINBACH
Deutsches Orient-Institut, Hamburg.

JOHN WATERBURY
Woodrow Wilson School, Princeton University.

List of Active Participants
in the Colloquium

MOSHE ARENS
    The Knesset

GABRIEL BAER
    Hebrew University, Jerusalem

MOSHE BITAN
Paz Oil Company

DANIEL DISHON
    Tel Aviv University

TREVOR N. DUPUY
    Historical Evaluation and Research Organization, Dunn Loring,
    Virginia

ABBA EBAN
    The Knesset

ODED ERAN
    Tel Aviv University

JOSEF JOFFE
    Die Zeit, Hamburg

ELIYAHU KANOVSKY
    Bar Ilan University

STEVEN J. ROSEN
    Brandeis University

DAVID VITAL
    Tel Aviv University

AHARON YARIV
    Tel Aviv University